"...a superb contribution, not c  y but also to
our deeper appreciation of the   : in England
and Scotland."

                                                                    dern History

"...imaginative, ambitious and   n presents a
provocative theory analyzing l   constituted
power, influence and legitimacy in politics over two centuries."

– **David Gutzke**, *Reviews in History*

"Amusing and well-written."

– **Giles MacDonogh**, *Decanter*

The Politics of Wine in Britain

A New Cultural History

Charles Ludington
Teaching Assistant Professor, Department of History, North Carolina State University

First published 2013 by
PALGRAVE MACMILLAN

Palgrave Macmillan in the UK is an imprint of Macmillan Publishers Limited,
registered in England, company number 785998, of Houndmills, Basingstoke,
Hampshire RG21 6XS.

Palgrave Macmillan in the US is a division of St Martin's Press LLC,
175 Fifth Avenue, New York, NY 10010.

Palgrave Macmillan is the global academic imprint of the above companies
and has companies and representatives throughout the world.

Palgrave® and Macmillan® are registered trademarks in the United States,
the United Kingdom, Europe and other countries.

ISBN 978-1-349-31576-5   ISBN 978-0-230-30622-6 (eBook)
DOI 10.1057/9780230306226

ISBN 978–1–137–58387–1   Paperback

This book is printed on paper suitable for recycling and made from fully
managed and sustained forest sources. Logging, pulping and manufacturing
processes are expected to conform to the environmental regulations of the
country of origin.

A catalogue record for this book is available from the British Library.

A catalog record for this book is available from the Library of Congress.

Typeset by MPS Limited, Chennai, India.

Contents

List of Tables, Figures, and Graphs

Tables

Figures

Graphs

Preface: A Word or Two on Statistics, Measurements, and Spelling

This study relies upon official import statistics in order to discern a general picture of the taste for wine. Import figures are the most accurate way of inferring broad-based English or Scottish tastes for wine in any given period, but aggregate amounts do not account for individual preferences, for the differing qualities of the same type of wine, or for more general class, regional or other group-based tastes. In other words, a cross-section of aggregate imports reflects the relative popularity of different types of wine, and as such it gives a general outline of English and Scottish tastes.

That said, existing English, Scottish, and British import statistics are not unproblematic. For example, until 1675 London Customs returns did not always report the provenance of incoming wines, although a boat's port of embarkation was usually listed. From 1675 onwards, London port records are more detailed, although the ledgers of English and Welsh outports do not necessarily list the wine's provenance until 1697.[1] In that year, Charles Davenant became the Inspector General of Customs for the entire kingdom, and it was he who first compiled detailed English wine import statistics in a two-part report he submitted to the Parliament in 1713.[2] The first part of the report gave import statistics for London in the period 1675–96, and the second part gave import statistics for all of England and Wales in the period 1696–1712. Davenant's Toryism cannot be entirely overlooked when assessing the accuracy of his statistics, but unfortunately these cannot be verified, as some of the port ledgers he used are now partially illegible, and in some cases lost altogether. Compiling the information that does exist—which of course would not be definitive—would take a team of researchers even in the computer age, because for each port in which records do still exist, entries for wine are listed every day and are never totaled. However, random samplings of London wine imports from the years 1675 to 1696 are consistent with the overall percentages of wine recorded by Davenant during the same period, and therefore I rely upon his figures for this early period.[3]

Likewise, Davenant's statistics for all of England and Wales for the period 1697–1712 very nearly match those of later compilers such as Alexander Henderson and Cyrus Redding (who updated Henderson's statistics to 1850). Neither of these men used the original port books, but instead relied upon résumés of port records made by the Inspectorate of Customs, which may mean that Davenant's mistakes, if he made any, were simply repeated.[4] To overcome these possible inaccuracies I turned to the exhaustive 1897 Parliamentary Report on the history of customs tariffs, which gives a complete set of figures for English wine imports from 1697 to 1785.[5] These figures have the disadvantage of being listed in imperial gallons, which was neither the standard of measurement nor how wines were entered in the import ledgers until 1825. Instead, prior to 1825 wine imports were listed in terms of tuns, hogsheads, and gallons. My conversion of imperial gallons back to tuns, hogsheads, and (old) gallons (four-fifths of their respective imperial measures—see Table P.1), found that Davenant's figures for 1697 to 1712 were essentially in line with later attempts to quantify the wine trade. Hence, this study also relies upon Davenant's English and Welsh wine import statistics for the period 1697–1712.

Table P.1 Wine measurements

Tuns	Pipes/Butts	Hogsheads	Imp. gallons	Gallons	Quarts	Pints
1	2	4	210	252	1,008	2,016
	1	2	105	126	504	1,008
		1	52.5	63	252	504
			1	1.2	4.8	9.6
				1	4	8
					1	2
						1

For the period 1713–91 in England, I rely upon Elizabeth B. Schumpeter's statistics published in 1960, which are generally considered by economic historians to be the most accurate set of import and export statistics for England in the eighteenth century.[6] Schumpeter derived her figures on wine and other commodities from the *Ledgers of Imports and Exports of England and Wales, 1697–1780* and the *Reports on the State of Navigation, Commerce, and Revenues of Great Britain from 1772*. In the main, Schumpeter's figures for wine correspond to those of Henderson, Redding, and the Parliamentary Report of 1897. The slight discrepancies between all sets of figures can be ascribed to clerical mistakes in copying from the originals (mistakes that are then repeated down the line), the omission in some résumés of marginal wines such as Canary or Levantine, or the practice of carrying over entries from a previous year that were entered late.

For all-inclusive British wine import statistics from 1786 onward, I use the 1897 Parliamentary Report, but for Scottish statistics alone other sources are necessary. Unfortunately, wine import figures for all of Scotland were not compiled by the Customs Office until 1756, so that prior to that year I rely upon existing Leith port records, and from those figures I derived approximations of national totals based upon the estimate that Leith accounted for at least two-thirds and as much as three-quarters of the Scottish wine trade.[7] Beginning in 1756, the Customs Office listed wine imports for all of Scotland under the country from which the wines arrived.[8] Thus, in every year small amounts of wine are listed under imports from such places as Sweden or the various Caribbean or North American colonies, although in every instance the type of wine is also given, so that it is possible to draw a complete picture of Scottish wine imports from 1756 until 1815, which is when the records cease. As far as I know I am the first to have compiled these Scottish wine import totals from the original figures, thus any mistakes made in counting and deriving statistics are completely my own.

It should be made absolutely clear that all of these figures together provide an accurate measurement of *legal* trade, but by definition official import figures cannot account for smuggled wine, nor for fraudulently declared wine, such as when French wines were imported as "Spanish" or "Portuguese"—a frequent occurrence in England during the late Stuart era, and in Scotland for the first three-quarters of the eighteenth century. Thus, my method in using import figures from before 1787, when Pitt simplified and reduced the wine duties, is to compare the official figures with evidence of false declarations and smuggling, most of which is derived from government reports, private letters, and even popular literature. Broadly speaking, what I found is that prior to 1713 in England and 1780 in Scotland, the relative amount of French wine within the total amount of wine imported was never so low as official figures suggest, and the relative amounts of Portuguese and Spanish wine rarely so high. Perhaps more importantly, the actual total of all imported wines was somewhere between 25 percent and 100 percent greater than the recorded legal trade, with England usually closer to the former figure and Scotland closer to the latter. With these disparities in mind, I have not attempted to provide a precise revised figure for every year prior to Pitt's duty reforms, but I do provide a more accurate picture of the broad trends in the English, Scottish, and British wine trade.

It is also important to note that all measurements of wine quoted in this study are direct citations from the primary sources or conversions based on old-style (non-imperial) liquid measurements, which were used in the United Kingdom until 1825 and are still used in the United States today (see Table P.1). In this system, a gallon is 231 cubic inches or 128 (US) fluid ounces, tuns are 252 gallons, pipes are 126 gallons, and hogsheads are 63 gallons (see Table P.1). Where these amounts have been converted to bottles, 32 (US) ounce quart bottles are implied unless otherwise noted. Surprising as it is to many people, the quart bottle was the standard bottle size, and was slightly larger than a modern 75 centiliter wine bottle (see Chapter 10 for evidence of bottle sizes). Of course, all of these figures are necessarily approximations, as both casks and bottles were rarely the exact amounts stated.[9] However, except where the evidence tells specifically how many bottles were derived from a particular cask, it seems reasonable for the sake of consistency and the reader's understanding to standardize the amounts based upon perfect conditions. So, when a cellar or import record speaks of a hogshead of wine, that translates to 252 gallons or 1,008 bottles, although in reality the amount of wine was slightly more or less than that.

Likewise, unless otherwise stated all duty rates quoted are for tuns of wine arriving in the port of London in English ships and, from 1707 in British ships. Wines arriving in London in foreign ships paid roughly £3 more. Wines arriving in any of the "outports," (i.e. not London), which from 1707 included Scottish ports, paid up to £3 less, unless they arrived in foreign ships, in which case they paid roughly the same amount as British ships arriving in London. To be completely accurate, outport rates varied slightly from port to port, as certain ports had ancient privileges granting different rates, while other ports tacked on their own local imposts. Thus, it is for the sake of consistency and convenience for the reader that I use duty rates based on wine arriving in London in British ships.

Lastly, the capitalization of wine names is (and was) as inconsistent as the quality of early-modern wines themselves. Consequently, I have tried to be consistent without imposing a uniform rule for all wines that would needlessly capitalize some names and awkwardly put others in lower case. To wit, wines named after towns or regions are capitalized except where the name is (or was) commonly known, such as port, sherry, canary, palm, madeira, burgundy, and champagne. Rhenish wine, which was essentially synonymous with German wine, is therefore capitalized, while red wine from Bordeaux is referred to as claret. I have regularized the spellings to reflect modern usage, because English and Scottish spelling of wine names in the seventeenth and eighteenth centuries was erratic at best. However, in instances where the original spelling is particularly colorful or inconsistent within the same cellar record, I have retained the original spelling by placing it in quotations, in parentheses, or in a note.

Charles C. Ludington

Acknowledgments

The book began as a dissertation at Columbia University, where I had the privilege to be a graduate student at the turn of the new millennium, and where I was encouraged by my teachers to combine my fascination with British history and my historical interest in wine. If that did not sound like a particularly promising prospect at first, I was soon disabused of my concerns, as I discovered that there was indeed a wonderful history to be told about Britain and wine. In the process of researching and writing that history, I have incurred many debts.

At Columbia University, thanks are due to the history department for awarding me a President's Scholar Fellowship, and to the Research Council on Western Europe for awarding me with a dissertation travel grant. Special thanks go to Kirsten Olsen and Barbara Locurto in the Columbia history department for making my life easier, and to Bob Scott and Trevor Dawes for making Butler Library a splendid home away from home. Also in New York, I owe a particular debt to the Mrs Giles Whiting Foundation for selecting me as a fellow in 2000–1. In London, where the Whiting Foundation grant made research possible, I am deeply indebted to the staff and librarians at the British Library, the Public Record Office at Kew (now known as the National Archives), the Guildhall Library, and the Institute of Historical Research at the University of London. Particular thanks go to Joshua Lunn, Clive Jones, and Donald Munro. Thanks to John Roberts of John Roberts Wine Books Ltd, London, who kindly allowed me to examine some very rare documents in his possession. My thanks also go to the staff at the National Library of Scotland, the National Archives of Scotland, the Northumberland Record Office, the Durham Record Office, the Worcestershire Record Office, the Suffolk Record Office, the East Sussex Record Office, the Bibliothèque Municipale de Bordeaux, and the Instituto do Vinho do Porto. Olga Laçerda of the British Association in Oporto deserves special thanks for her warm welcome and for introducing me to many port producers. Among those producers, Dominic Symington of the Symington Family Estates, and Natasha Robertson Bridge of Taylor, Fladgate, and Yeatman, shared their time, energy, and wine with me, and gave me full access to company papers. In Bordeaux, Jean-Philippe Delmas and Prince Robert of Luxembourg, both of Chateau Haut Brion, must also be thanked for their time and generosity. Back in the United States, I am grateful to Maggie Powell at the Lewis Walpole Library of Yale University for awarding me with a fellowship, and to Joan Sussler and Anna Malicka for their invaluable research assistance. Likewise, thanks go to Robert Ritchie and Mary Robertson for their financial support and research help at the Huntington Library in San Marino, California. Here in the Research Triangle of North Carolina, the staff and librarians at the University of North Carolina at Chapel Hill, North Carolina State University, and Duke University have all been invaluable.

Parts of this book have already been already been published as articles in books or journals, and I would like to thank Boydell & Brewer, Berg Press, and the University of Chicago Press for their permission to use those materials here. For permission to use illustrations, I would like to thank the British Library, the Lewis Walpole Library of Yale University, the Bridgeman Art Library, the National Portrait Gallery (London), the British Museum, the 7th Marquess of Cholmondeley, Dr Johnson's House Trust, the Museu da Cidade Lisboa, and Domaine Clarence Dillon. Early versions of chapters were presented at various conferences in the United States, the United Kingdom, and Australia, and my thanks go to those who invited me to speak and to those who asked questions or commented upon my presentations. I am especially indebted to Lynn Martin, Adam Smyth, Brian Cowen, Deborah Harkness, Lara Kriegel, Allen Grieco, Phil Withington, and Tom Nichols for their constructive criticism.

Numerous other friends and scholars have contributed to this book with their generosity, support, humor, advice, patience, and help of all sorts. At Columbia, Simon Schama, Isser Woloch, Filip Vermeylen, and the late Wim Smit helped to get this project off the ground by discussing ideas at a very early stage. In London, Art Gresh, Jonathan and Anne Beswick, and most especially Dick Schumacher (and more recently Karin Thyselius Schumacher), provided a receptive audience, good company, and very often, good food and wine. At the Lewis Walpole Library, David Lemmings, Andrew Thompson, and Holger Hoock gave excellent commentary on some of my early ideas about the politics and culture of wine consumption, and the way these things were depicted visually. More recently, David Zonderman has read and commented upon nearly the entire manuscript, while Andreas Kraebber, Angela McShane, Linda Colley, Paul Cheney, Phil Stern, Everett Hutt, Jed Purdy, Brent Sirota, Tim Harris, Carl Wennerlind, and Matthew Booker have all read specific chapters and helped improve the final product with their insightful remarks. Doug Ellis, Julian Cochran, Hissan Waheed, and Herman Berkhoff provided much-needed technical help with graphs, charts, and images, Lloyd Kramer offered his exceedingly valuable thoughts upon the strengths and weaknesses of New Cultural History, and Jonathan Ocko has been a particularly supportive colleague during many trying semesters. For all of these friends and colleagues I am deeply grateful.

Of my many intellectual debts, however, two in particular must be singled out. David Armitage has read every chapter of this book with an eagle eye for detail. He has pushed, prodded, and cajoled me at appropriate times, always being honest with the quality of my efforts. Similarly, David Cannadine made timely remarks at each stage of research and writing, and has been accommodating with his time and energy on both sides of the Atlantic. I could not have been more fortunate than to have both of them as mentors and teachers, and now as colleagues and friends. Their influence upon this book has been profound, sometimes in obvious, other times in less obvious ways. Nevertheless, any mistakes made in this book are entirely my own.

My greatest debt, of course, is to my family. My parents, Jane and Townsend Ludington, have encouraged my interest in the past, in ideas, and in writing well for as long as I can remember. My in-laws, Eleanor Hutt and Peter Barton Hutt, have allowed me the opportunity to enjoy many of the wines about which I have written, albeit wines of a more recent vintage. My children, Liam, Jasper, and Nathan, have been burdened by this book as much as anyone. They have never known me not to be involved with it, and for each of them it has literally been a lifelong project. I hope they are both surprised and delighted to discover that this book is done, and that new projects await. But while the work has lasted, all three boys have helped to sustain me more than they will ever know, even if their father has, on occasion, been irritable or difficult to remove from his computer. Finally, my wife, Sarah Hutt Ludington, deserves the greatest thanks. She has lived with the ups and downs, ins and outs of this study for as long as I have, and as such it is as much hers as it is mine. As we have both discovered, when two people try to be demanding teachers and productive scholars, while raising three children together, life is not simple. But without Sarah's love, support, encouragement, and fierce editor's eye, this book would have been much less than it is. For that reason it is dedicated to her, with all my love.

Introduction

This is a book about politics, power, taste, and wine. In particular, it is a historical study of the way in which the taste for wine—by which I mean the type of wine and the way it was consumed—both reflected and constituted political power in England, Scotland, and ultimately Great Britain, between 1649 and 1862. These dates do not mark the absolute beginning and end of wine as a politicized and politicizing commodity, but they do demarcate an era in which the politics of wine was particularly intense. They also correspond, it should be stressed, to the time in which England (Wales inclusive) and Scotland went from being warring nations on the margins of European affairs to being a united if not entirely unified kingdom and the world's premier economic and imperial power. As such, a study of taste formation in this period provides a fascinating window into English, Scottish, and British state formation, identity creation, and cultural practices that had both a national and global impact. But most of all, the history of the taste for wine in this period reveals how political power was constructed and manipulated by the interrelated ideas and practices of class, masculinity, and national identity. In short, wine was integral to British political culture.

My starting premise is that wine, in both England and Scotland, was a symbol of political power and legitimacy because it had long represented the court, the aristocracy, and the Church. This symbolism became more acute when the authority of these institutions was challenged in the mid-seventeenth century, as supporters and detractors of the established order fought each other physically, verbally, and symbolically. And of all the symbols that were argued over and with, wine was perhaps the most potent and lasting. In fact, those who successfully challenged the old pillars of authority maintained the link between wine and political legitimacy when they themselves came to power. Thus wine and political legitimacy remained linked regardless of who was in power long after the authority of the court, the aristocracy, and the Church had begun to erode. Consequently, my primary argument is that throughout the period under study, the taste for wine was a blatant political statement because it structured social relationships. It follows from this argument that the strengthening of, or changes in, taste for wine—whether within or between England and Scotland—were politically significant and, therefore, warrant historical investigation. Indeed, the purpose of this study is to understand

1

what drove the major shifts in the taste for wine, and to discern their broader significance for politics and culture.

And this leads to my second argument. Simply put, the various tastes for wine in England, Scotland, and Great Britain during this period were not only political because they helped to order society, they were also created by politics, especially acts of the English, Scottish, and British Parliaments. This is not to deny the influence of tradition, geography, and concomitant consumer trends on the taste for wine; rather, it is to say that politics—by which I mean the acts, decisions, and affairs of the state—were the primary determinant of these tastes. Specifically, the politics of the period 1649 to 1714 gave rise to new political meanings for wine in general, to specific wines in particular, and to the ways in which wine was consumed. These politically constructed meanings were then used by competing groups to gain, maintain, or reject political power, and all subsequent politics surrounding wine were reactions to the meanings that had been set in motion during the Interregnum and late Stuart era. This study ends in 1860, precisely because the legislation passed at that time was an attempt to undo what the politics of wine of the previous two centuries had wrought.

As the previous paragraph implies, the meanings of different wines and consumption habits were malleable. However, unlike wine itself, they were not fluid; they could only be altered within a limited range of meanings from those they already possessed.[1] What did in fact change dramatically was the political landscape that the taste for wine both reflected and helped to instantiate. This meant, for instance, that the reputation of port (a wine from northern Portugal) as a manly wine might prove positive in the late eighteenth century but less so by the 1820s when the martial masculinity of the previous era was rejected in favor of greater "respectability" and decorum. So the idea of port as manly remained constant, but the social value of martial masculinity changed.

Admittedly, my argument that politics created the taste for wine is not new. Not only did Chancellor of the Exchequer William Gladstone and the majority of Parliament in 1860 think this was the case, but so too have the few historians, antiquarians, and wine writers who have explored the history of wine consumption in England and Scotland. For example, in English historiography responsibility for taste has been ascribed to the Tory/Whig political divide in general, and to the Methuen Treaty of 1703 in particular.[2] The party divide is well known, the treaty less so. In fact, what has come to be called *the* Methuen Treaty was the third of three treaties negotiated in 1703 by the English special envoy to Portugal, John Methuen. This latter treaty guaranteed that the duty on imported Portuguese wines would be at least one-third less than the amount of import duty on French wines, in return for which the Portuguese agreed to remove prohibitive tariffs on English cloth. According to those who see the Methuen Treaty as the key determinant of taste, Whigs drank port because of their hatred of the French and their support for the treaty, while Tories drank claret—red wine from Bordeaux—because of their admiration for France and the Bourbon monarchy, their support for the exiled house of Stuart, and their antipathy to the treaty that foisted Portuguese wine upon an unsuspecting English public. Consequently, Whig political dominance and the politically dictated lower cost of Portuguese wine insured that port was overwhelmingly the most popular wine in eighteenth-century England.

But there are two major problems with this story. First, Portuguese wine—most of which was port—surpassed French wine on the English market some years *prior* to the Methuen Treaty; and second, the greatest consumers of claret in early and mid-eighteenth-century England were *Whigs*. By overlooking these problems, historians and wine writers have failed to notice that the original claret versus port debate was about economic policy and popular English taste for wine, not the preferred wines of Whig or Tory aristocrats and gentlemen.[3] This misunderstanding seems to have developed in the late nineteenth and early twentieth century, a time in which the divided political allegiances of the British elite apparently could be discerned by their preference for fine, vintage port or top-growth claret.[4] But in the first half of the eighteenth century, while Whig leaders decried open trade with France, they saw nothing wrong with drinking claret themselves. The issue was not which wine they preferred, for that was French; rather, the issue was which country should supply the bulk of England's wine; or, put another way, which country should supply England's middle-ranking consumers.[5]

Within Scottish historiography, to the even smaller degree that wine has been dealt with, taste has been explained as a result of Jacobitism and widespread resistance to the Union of 1707.[6] Accordingly, Scottish wine drinkers preferred claret because it came from France. To Scottish Jacobites, who wanted to return the Stewart family to the throne of Scotland, France symbolized their aspirations; while for Scottish Hanoverians, French wine represented resistance to English domination within the newly created Kingdom of Great Britain.[7] However, as some authors have reluctantly acknowledged, and as this study conclusively shows, during the second half of the eighteenth century Scottish popular taste for wine switched from claret to port.[8] Clearly, this was a significant change, although no historian has addressed its probable meaning. To wit, if claret symbolized Scottish opposition to either the Hanoverians, the Union, or Anglicization, then surely when the majority of Scottish wine drinkers willingly began to drink more port than claret, it was an indication of the acceptance of some or, as I will argue, all of these things.

So, while others have asserted that English, Scottish, and British taste for wine were politically constructed and had political meanings, they have either failed to explain correctly how the taste was created, or what the political meanings of taste actually were. In some instances they have omitted explanation altogether. For example, just as no one has attempted to explicate the Scottish switch from claret to port, neither has anyone dared explain why heavy drinking and drunkenness was so fashionable among the English and Scottish elite in the late Georgian era other than to suggest that port was the culprit.[9] Likewise, the reason for the rise of sherry to primacy on the British market in the early Victorian era has yet to be investigated, much less explained. Yet surely this latter change was significant given that port had come to represent a particular idea of aggressively masculine, Anglo-British identity during the wars of the late eighteenth century. Indeed, sherry's ascendancy had everything to do with its reputation as a feminine—but not effeminizing—wine.

The preceding discussion of politically constructed taste leads to my third argument, which is that taste and the consumption habits it fosters are socially complex, complexly motivated, and never move in one direction. This is hardly a radical proposal. Yet there persists a school of thought among economists and historians alike that wittingly or otherwise follows Thorstein Veblen's emulation theory of consumption—that is, that people always try to keep up with the social strata just above them—thereby making the wealthiest consumers the heroes of a consumer-driven economy.[10] Yet, as the taste for wine in England and Scotland shows, taste does not always trickle down from the top. However, this does not mean that that taste marks fixed differences between social classes, an idea that is sometimes, and not entirely fairly, attributed to the sociologist Pierre Bourdieu. Bourdieu correctly argued that taste is a reflection and creator of class differences, yet he could not explain how or why taste changed over time, how a specific commodity might have different meanings in different societies, or how taste crossed class boundaries within a given society.[11] Consequently, I employ a more dialectical approach for understanding changes in, and meanings of, taste. For instance, because taste is a statement that helps to establish and naturalize the social order, taste is a battleground for those who want to maintain or change the social order. Members of the ruling elite must, on occasion, change their tastes to address and rebut the charges against them. But since such changes in taste are a compromise, or synthesis, the ruling elite does not give over entirely to its opponents. As Bourdieu notes, elite consumption habits must have something about them that gives the consumer social distinction, otherwise the elite are no different than those over whom they claim the right to rule. And this is where elite tastes, which might on the surface look the same as those of their social inferiors, are different. Consequently, elites emphasize the quality, rarity, and "authenticity" of the things they consume, while dismissing cost as irrelevant.

The aforementioned trends can be seen clearly in the taste for wine in Britain. For instance, in England, Parliamentary legislation beginning in the 1670s dramatically differentiated the price and availability of wines, and ensured that the elite and middle ranks had different taste because of cost. Meanwhile in Scotland, the higher tariffs brought about by the Union of 1707 had the unintended consequence of increasing smuggling and strengthening the idea that drinking French wine in Scotland was a form of resistance to Anglicization. However, after the failed Jacobite Rebellion of 1745–6, Scottish taste began slowly to mirror socially divided English taste; and during the final decades of the eighteenth century, the ruling elite throughout Britain began to drink more port than anything else, thereby mimicking middle-ranking English taste for wine, even though the port they drank was of a discernibly higher quality. In other words, the taste for wine, like the political legitimacy it represented, not only coalesced around English taste, but also trickled up, so to speak. What this transformation reveals is that political legitimacy was increasingly derived from the political views of the middle ranks, or what was called "public opinion."[12]

To assert that middle-ranking, and specifically male middle-ranking opinion, had become a critical component of political legitimacy by the middle decades of the eighteenth century is not, however, to revive the old Marxist (or simply materialist) belief that the events of seventeenth-, eighteenth-, or nineteenth-century England—chronological imprecision was always a problem in the argument—illustrated the triumph of the bourgeoisie over the aristocracy.[13] It is true that the wealth and political influence of merchants, professionals, and financiers grew in both absolute and relative terms during these centuries, as England became a more commercial society.[14] However, revisionist scholarship of the last generation has shown that the aristocratic order did not end entirely in 1649, 1688, or even 1832.[15] This realization has led to a new orthodoxy, which emphasizes the survival of the landed elite over and against the futile efforts of the bourgeoisie and bureaucratic state. But this interpretation, like the Marxist one before it, is overly reductionist.[16]

Fortunately, an understanding of the taste for wine helps us to revise both of these explanatory narratives. For instance, rather than the demise of the aristocracy, what one sees throughout the two centuries under study here is an aristocracy that frequently reinvented itself by accommodating the cultural, and only gradually the political, demands of the middle ranks.[17] Specifically, by the mid-eighteenth century the landed elite had to appeal to, and eventually appear as, the more prosperous members of the middle classes. This was done to maintain power, not to give it away or acknowledge defeat. Concomitantly, and very much a part of the same process, the taste for wine allows us to see how English middle-ranking men successfully defined commercial interests as the national interest by the turn of the eighteenth century, which in turn, gradually allowed them to claim that they, whose money came primarily from commerce, embodied the nation as whole.[18]

Of course, continuity and change are a constant in human history and are never mutually exclusive; however, from the mid-seventeenth century until the mid-nineteenth century, the continuity and change in the social positions and cultural practices of the elite and middle ranks in Britain was remarkably simultaneous. Indeed, it is the simultaneity of these trends that has caused so much confusion and dispute among historians about the structure of British society in the long eighteenth century. Was it an *Ancien Régime* society or the first modern society? Paradoxical as it seems, the answer is, both. The aristocracy managed to maintain its privileged position atop British society during the very same period that the middle classes gained political parity and cultural supremacy. Because the taste for wine both reflected and constructed cultural and political power, it allows us to see how this paradox of continuity and change unfolded.

Class: Definitions and problems

And that brings us to the problem of class. Studies such as this one, which seek both to reveal social divisions and use their existence as a way to understand the past, must define the various major social groups in the clearest possible terms. Inevitably, that means speaking of ideal types, which are just that, ideal, and never apply *in toto* to any actual individual or to a social group as a whole. But since historians are in the business of looking for both broad trends (the forest) as well as individual differences (the trees), we necessarily rely upon a certain amount of generalization whether our goal is to explain major currents in history or to provide the context in which individuals and institutions have operated. Here then, is my social terminology, some of which is obvious, some less so.

The aristocracy, or titled landowners, should be clear, as should the greater gentry, who were untitled but substantial landowners. I refer to both of these as the landed elite. I use the more general term "elite" to include the landed elite and the politically and culturally powerful figures who did not come from landed wealth, but who were wealthy and fashionable, who perhaps purchased or married into a landed estate, and who certainly accepted the aristocratic order and sought to be a part of it.

The middle stratum of British society is more difficult to define.[19] For purposes of expediency, this study uses the terms "middle classes," "middle ranks," and "middling sorts" to discuss those people in the seventeenth and eighteenth century who, while not major landowners, made and reinvested capital for the sake of future profit, which implicitly suggests people who were trying to improve their economic status. This group included a broad range of (mostly) men, from wealthy merchants at the top to successful artisans and shopkeepers, and rural leaseholders at the bottom. In between, there were manufacturers, bankers, and tradesmen, as well as men in the professions of medicine, the law, university teaching, civil service, and lower-ranking officers in the army or navy.

What united all of these people was freedom from domination by the aristocracy and/or an all-powerful employer whose decisions could deny them any chance at earning a livelihood.[20] In that sense, being "middling" in the seventeenth and eighteenth centuries was by definition masculine.[21] This is not to deny the existence of women in the middle ranks, it is only to say that women and "femininity" were not a significant aspect of middle-ranking identity until the early nineteenth century, precisely because that identity was linked to conceptions of independence and self-sufficiency—something which very few women obtained.[22]

To be sure, the term "middle classes" was used in the eighteenth century, although like "middle ranks" and "middling sort" it referred to a multitude of social ranks rather than a collective, self-conscious group.[23] However, by the early nineteenth century, and especially after 1832, the idea of the middle classes as one large, and largely united, "middle class" began to prevail. Moreover, compared to their forebears, the middle classes of the nineteenth century were dominated by financiers, professionals, and manufacturers, rather than merchants and successful tradesmen.[24] Perhaps more importantly, the middle classes of the nineteenth century were not only independent from the aristocracy, they were also broadly united as a group in their desire for greater political power.

Notably, however, I avoid the term "middle class" as a noun to describe a distinct group of people on the grounds that it is overly reductionist and, as Dror Warhman has pointed out, a conspicuous historical construction masquerading as an ineluctable historical force.[25] Instead, I use the term "middle class" as an adjective to describe the tastes and habits of the middling sorts. But this is not to agree entirely with Wahrman, for attempts to deny historical agency to the broadly defined middle classes have been as unsuccessful as attempts to portray the middle classes as united and acting solely in their class interests. My semantic distinctions are, therefore, an attempt to acknowledge the social and political complexity of those who stood between the aristocracy and wealthy gentry on the one hand, and the laboring classes on the other, without denying the broad, collective existence of the middle strata as a historical force that pushed Britain in a more commercial and democratic direction. Thus, when referring to the period after the end of the Napoleonic Wars (1815), I use the term "middle classes" or "bourgeoisie."

Likewise, I use the terms "laboring classes," "working classes," and "lower orders," when referring to the majority of English, Scottish, and British subjects who, whatever their many differences as individuals, had little to no discretionary income and certainly no capital to invest. Some artisans fell within the working classes, others among the middle ranks, but those who purchased wine on a routine basis were making a clear statement that they had some discretionary money and saw themselves (and wanted others to see them) as "middling." Wine drinking did not draw a clean economic division between classes because such a division was never clean. But wine drinking did draw a division between social representations, and this is precisely why wine provides a helpful demarcator between the middle and lower classes.

In analyzing these different social groups, I see class as both a linguistic construction and a social reality. This reality is proven by material differences that inflect worldviews, life opportunities, and personal health. Nevertheless, the precise contours of class as social reality are subjective since they rely upon the viewer, the time, and the place. More specifically, as David Cannadine has shown in his brilliant study of class in modern Britain, class is generally seen and discussed in one of three ways: as a complex and finely graded hierarchy; as a triadic division of upper, middle, and lower; and as a dichotomous split between the rich and the poor, the haves and the have-nots, the rulers and the people.[26] The first of these is probably the closest description of social reality in that there were (and are) many gradations of social difference, and any model that does not acknowledge as much is necessarily reductionist. However, the hierarchy model is not merely a description of society, it is also a politically potent model that has its roots in the Great Chain of Being, which articulated a divinely created and, therefore, static social order. Not only has this model historically been invoked to keep people "in their place," it has also been used to elide broad-based social divisions where they have existed (and still exist). In other words, stressing the infinite complexity of social divisions is the divide-and-conquer model of society, and not surprisingly it has been most wholeheartedly adopted by the ruling elite and those who, for whatever reason, find themselves on top.

Equally unsurprisingly, the triadic and dichotomous models are also deeply political. For instance, people who think of themselves in the middle of a social hierarchy, at least since the eighteenth century, have often preferred a triadic view of society. In this model, one most often finds the virtuous middle classes stuck between the idle aristocracy or filthy rich on the one hand, and the indolent poor on the other. Fighting on all fronts against various forms of sleaze and sloth while upholding God's and the marketplace's command to be honest and industrious, it is clear in this model who the heroes are, or at least should be.

The dichotomous model meanwhile has generally been favored by those who perceive themselves to be on the bottom of society, although when expedient it has been adopted by almost anyone who feels that his or her society is an oligarchy and he or she is not among the oligarchs. Conversely, the dichotomous model has also been invoked by the political and economic elite who see themselves as the rightful rulers of the ignorant and often unappreciative masses.

In other words, none of these models is an exact description of social reality, because all descriptions of social reality are inflected by the subjectivity of the viewer. Nevertheless, all three models contain a degree of truth, which can be shown by examining the material conditions, life patterns, and cultural practices of the groups described.

However, a book cannot simultaneously invoke three analytical models any more than an author can speak simultaneously in three voices. Yet one can write with all three models in mind and allow the evidence to speak for itself, and that is precisely what I have tried to do. For example, the taste for wine divided both English and Scottish—and later British—society into two broad groups: those who drank wine on a regular basis, and those who rarely ever drank wine except perhaps as medicine. In that sense, the taste for wine, some or none, reveals a clear dichotomy in British society between the "haves" and the "have-nots." But the taste for wine created a second dichotomy among wine drinkers, the "haves", based on the type or quality of the wine being consumed. This division was between those who generally purchased the most expensive wine, and those who usually drank the less expensive sort. Of course, there was a subtle hierarchy of taste among wine drinkers, but broadly speaking the division between wine drinkers helps us physically to recognize a triadic division of society: those who drank expensive wines, those who drank inexpensive wines, and those who drank almost no wine at all. And these categories, in the main, correspond to what I have defined as the elite, the middle classes, and the lower classes.

Methods and objectives: A new cultural history

And now we arrive at the book's subtitle. It follows from my belief that class is both a social reality and a linguistic construct, that this book endeavors to reconcile the materialist insights of social historians of the previous generation, and the dexterous decoding of language, cultural practices, and material objects that is the distinguishing feature of more recent cultural history. Methodologically, this book is indebted to both camps. As a social historian, I count—in this case mostly casks and bottles—I derive statistics, I compare them synchronically and diachronically, and I look for trends. I argue that these trends reveal the existence of structures such as class, gender, and national identity, and that these structures helped to organize and influence the behavior of people within them. But as a cultural historian, I reject the idea that structures are fixed and that numbers reveal the entire truth. Instead, there is symbolic meaning in language, cultural practice, and material objects—types of wine and wine drinking, for instance—far beyond what is readily observable or quantifiable, and these symbolic representations must be read and interpreted like texts in order to find that meaning. In this regard, quantitative analysis should be a valuable tool in the cultural historian's toolbox, precisely because it helps to reveal patterns and delimit possible interpretations of the meanings of things. To summarize, the "New Cultural History," which has been much theorized but rarely practiced on a grand scale during the past generation, acknowledges the deeply representational nature of culture without dismissing the social structures that are created by and help to create the physical and emotional realities that shape human lives.[27] This book is my attempt to write such a history.

That said, I emphatically reject the propensity of much cultural history to over-look the significance of politics. Like social history before it, cultural history has been engaged in the entirely laudable undertaking of moving the practice of his-tory far beyond the study of statesmen, statecraft, elections, political revolutions, and wars, and instead, trying to understand more about how ordinary people lived their lives, what they believed, how they behaved and why. In the process of discerning the meaning of cultural practices, cultural historians have been keen to point out how behavior, language, and material objects are all deeply political (i.e. they help to order social relationships). But in so doing, the acts, decisions, and affairs of the state—what we might call high politics—are often seen as mere representations of culture, while the consequences of high politics are often dis-missed, despite the fact that they help to construct the culture that they represent. In contrast, this study of the taste for wine uses a high political narrative (as it pertains to wine) in order to reunite politics with cultural history, and in so doing show that politics shape political power and cultural practices as much as they were, and are, shaped by them.

This book is also concerned with gender. In particular, this is a study of mascu-linity and the way that competing forms of masculinity are often manifestations of struggles for political power. In making this argument, I rely upon R.W. Connell's theoretical conception of hegemonic masculinity, which is the idea that at any given point in the history of a polity, there is a set of masculine norms that are most valued and as much as possible practiced by the politically domi-nant class, and that these norms help to maintain that class in power. However, hegemonic masculinity, in whatever form it takes, is always being contested by other forms of masculinity and is therefore rarely stable. Moreover, hegemonic masculinity is not always about physical strength, battlefield courage, practical competence, and independence from other men, although these are powerfully recurring themes. But where Connell overstates his case is in his assertion that hegemonic masculinity is synonymous with patriarchy.[28] In fact, this study of the taste for wine reveals that hegemonic masculinity is often just as concerned with establishing a pecking order among men as it is an attempt to uphold sexual domination over women. Hegemonic masculinity and patriarchy often overlap, but they are not the same thing.[29]

Lastly, while this book is principally an argument about taste, power, and British political culture, it is also intended to be a major contribution to the history of food and drink. This exciting, young field has been inspired by cultural history's interest in ritual and everyday objects, by concern about the environment and human health, by globalization, and by the "foodie" movement that both benefits from and rejects aspects of the increasingly homogenized world. Food and drink history, if you will pardon the dual metaphor, is mushrooming so quickly that it is difficult to keep up with the field. That is the good news. The less good news is that too much food and drink history is journalistic, or, if it has nice pictures, coffee-table history. In other words, much of it is fun without also being rigorous or terribly insightful. But it can and should be both of these things.

My vision of food and drink history is of a field of inquiry that seeks to answer difficult historical questions about the two things without which human beings cannot live. Food and drink history should, as much as possible, combine the approaches and insights of various sub-disciplines within the historical profession, while borrowing from the approaches and insights of other disciplines such as sociology, anthropology, psychology, economics, political science, law, biology, and medicine. Because of food and drink's centrality to our lives, perhaps no other aspect of human history offers the opportunity for such interdisciplinarity. Just as importantly, food and drink history needs to ask (and hopefully answer) difficult questions. It is not enough to assert that this plant, or that animal, or that type of food or drink that was derived from that plant or animal, helped to create the world as we know it. There are very few plants, animals, foods, and drinks about which that cannot be said; indeed, on an environmental level, perhaps none. Instead, we need to know how and why specific plants, animals, foods, and drinks became so important, how they helped structure society and were structured by it, what they signified, and what their relationship was to such things as government policy, cultural practices, wealth and poverty, social and gender relationships, the environment, and human health.

It should be abundantly clear by now that this study attempts to overcome the all-too-frequent compartmentalization of professional history. As I have just acknowledged, sub-disciplinary approaches to studying the human past are critical components of historical research; narrow digging can go deep, and it often draws attention to hitherto neglected sources and subjects. However, narrow digging, by its very nature, cannot reveal the complexity, the diversity, or anywhere near the totality of the evolving historical process. We historians need to rise above our narrow fields of interest whenever possible, to pollinate our work with the insights of other sub-fields and disciplines, and to write history that matters both to our colleagues and a broader audience. Whatever its imperfections, this book is my attempt to do just that.

Sources, chapter outline, and omissions

In writing the 12 chapters of this book I have drawn upon a shamelessly eclectic array of sources. I rely upon official import and export statistics from England, Scotland, Great Britain, France, and Portugal to form the skeleton of my narrative; but it is the other evidence—Parliamentary papers and reports, letters and diaries, cellar records and merchant ledgers, newspapers and journals, auctions records and advertisements, novels and memoirs, poems and ballads, print and paintings, and even a few wine-tasting notes—that fleshes out the story.

Part I shows how and why wines were politicized and given specific meanings in England and Scotland from the mid-seventeenth century to the end of Queen Anne's reign in 1714. Chapter 1 argues that the abolition of the monarchy in 1649 fastened the symbolic link between wine, the aristocracy, and the Royalist cause, despite the fact that Cromwell's court was no stranger to wine. The link between wine and Royalists became a more specific claret–Tory link by 1681. Chapter 2 explores three different types of fraud created by the various embargoes and tax increases against French wine in the period 1678–1702, and shows how by the end of that period both Portuguese and Spanish wines already surpassed French wine imports. Chapter 3 turns to Scotland and reveals how claret became a symbol of Scottish resistance to English political domination at the turn of the eighteenth century.

Part II focuses on claret and its alternatives. Chapter 4 examines the debates about wine in England from the Methuen Treaty with Portugal in 1703 until the rejection of the Commercial Treaty with France in 1713. At the latter date, claret was rejected as the tavern wine of England while port became linked to a Whig conception of English national identity that emphasized commercial wealth and bluff masculinity. Chapter 5 shows why the Whig ruling elite in England, despite promoting port as the drink for the middle ranks, drank large amounts of claret, and usually the most expensive sort. Chapter 6 returns to Scotland to uncover the mystery of how Scottish consumers, rich and poor alike, continued to drink vast amounts of claret long after the Treaty of Union should have made French wine prohibitively expensive for all but the very wealthy.

Part III shifts the focus to port, and shows how port became the dominant wine among all classes of drinkers during the second half of the eighteenth century in both England and Scotland. Chapter 7 reveals the symbolic connection between port and the English middle ranks, and Chapter 8 argues that it was precisely this connection, along with improvement in quality, that caused port to be embraced by the English elite in the second half of the eighteenth century. Chapter 9, meanwhile, explains why a majority of Scottish wine consumers began to drink more port than claret by at least 1780, and is intended as a major intervention in the ongoing debate about the Britishness of Scottish identity.

With English and Scottish taste for wine unified by the last decades of the eighteenth century, the chapters in Part IV examine Great Britain as a whole. In particular, Chapter 10 asserts and explains the extreme drunkenness of the elite and middle ranks in the period c. 1780–1820, while Chapter 11 shows how and why fashionable dissipation was rejected in the post-Napoleonic War era. Two results of this new sobriety and the values surrounding it were the rise of sherry and the increased importance of women wine consumers in shaping the British market. Chapter 12, the concluding chapter, unearths the now-forgotten nineteenth-century wine debate that occupied the minds of politicians, economists, wine merchants, and social reformers from the 1820s until 1860. In the latter year, Chancellor of the Exchequer William Gladstone, representing the reforming goals of the Liberal Party, tried to undo the politics of wine of the previous two centuries and return British taste to unfortified, French wine.

***

If it is clear what this book is about, it should also be stated at the outset what it is not about, or what it does not include. For instance, this book is not about the wine trade. Rather, it deals with the wine trade insofar as merchants entered the political arena with petitions, circumvented the law, shaped the law, put pressure on producers, solicited consumers, and in all these myriad ways helped to create taste. But the reader will not find any close analysis of how individual wine merchants ran their business on a day-to-day basis. Nor does this study illuminate the daily lives of grape growers or wine producers. Rather, growers and producers enter the story inasmuch as they responded to political actions or to the demands of consumers.

More controversially perhaps, this book focuses on the taste of elite and middling British men. Why? This is a study of how the taste for wine reflected and constituted political power, of how politics created the taste for wine, and of what wine tells us about political culture from the mid-seventeenth to the mid-nineteenth century. It is therefore a study of the political nation, and in the period under study, the English, Scottish, and British political nations were dominated by elite and middling men. Moreover, men are the focus of this study because, quite simply, they drank most of the wine. Indeed, until the middle of the nineteenth century, just before this study ends, women's taste for wine seems to have had very little impact upon British taste as a whole. That said, the concept of femininity plays a large role in the construction (and destruction) of political power in England and Scotland, but femininity was such a powerful idea among politically powerful or aspiring men precisely because it was necessary for the construction of masculine identities that helped to maintain or challenge political power.

Finally, although this is a book about the meaning of taste for wine in the past, it is also meant to speak to the present. Commodities have meanings and consumption remains a political act. I do not lament this fact. However, this book is written in the hope that we who live in the world of consumer capitalism might be less naïve about the widespread belief that there is no accounting for taste, or that we are all rational consumers freely constructing our identity in the marketplace. That, of course, is nonsense. We can account for taste, and when we do, what we find is that laws and market availability, class and gender, national identity and ethnicity, custom and geography, and price, dramatically circumscribe the choices we make. Within a limited range of choices, taste both reflects and creates our social relationships. Taste stratifies, solidifies, and undermines the social order all at once. Taste is political. Taste is power.

Part I
The Politicization of Wine

1

"A Health to our Distressed King!"

The Politics of Wine and Drinking in England, 1649–1681

King Charles I awoke at 5 a.m. on the morning of his execution and declared to his page, Sir Thomas Herbert, that today would be his second marriage, the first being to his beloved wife, Queen Henrietta Maria, and the second to Jesus Christ, whom Charles had every certainty he was about to meet. The king then famously put on two shirts; it was a bitter-cold January morning and he did not want to shiver lest people think he was scared to die. He then received the Blessed Sacrament from Bishop Juxon, and asserted that he would have no more food or drink that day; the nourishment of Christ was enough. But as the morning wore on Juxon implored the king to eat a piece of bread and drink a glass of wine, lest he should faint from hunger prior to his execution. Charles ate the bread and washed it down with a glass of claret while surrounded by guards at Whitehall, and that, not the Eucharist, was the last thing he had to eat and drink. By mid-afternoon he was dead, his head severed from his body for being "a Tyrant, Traitor, Murtherer, and a Public Enemy," according to the people who had tried and convicted him.[1] And who were they? They were less than one quarter of the members of the House of Commons who had been elected in 1641, who claimed that they—not the king, nor the aristocracy, nor even the other three-quarters of the members of the House of Commons whom they had evicted—represented "the People of England."

Much has been said by historians and others of Charles's demise and the rise to power of the Rump Parliament, which within days was to become the legislative branch of an English Republic that would eventually encompass Scotland and Ireland as well. But among all the commentary, the symbolic significance of many details has often been lost. For instance, it was no mere accident that the last bit of nourishment to cross Charles's living lips was bread and wine. Commodities have meaning and politics is theater, and no one better understood but was more confounded by these realities than Charles himself.[2] Indeed, his decision to eat bread and drink wine while waiting for the call to the scaffold—a symbol of his own Christ-like martyrdom—was no doubt intended to be seen by the regicide soldiers who were guarding him. Of course, it made no difference to the outcome of the day, and even to posterity Charles has not been entirely convincing as a martyr.[3] But the symbolism of Charles's last repast that did adhere whether it was the king's intention or not, was that wine was distinctly Royalist. That Charles drank claret and not some other wine was also prescient, because as a product of France, claret would soon become the most Royalist wine of all. In fact, the period from the Civil War to 1681 witnessed the intense politicization of wine and wine drinking in England, a politicization that was to last for the next two centuries, and, in a less direct form, beyond that.

***

Long before the English Civil War, wine had been affiliated with the Court, the Church, and those with political power. Wine in England had to be imported, especially after the Little Ice Age of the late-medieval period and the dissolution of the monasteries in the late 1530s put an end to almost all domestic production. The result was that wine was heavily taxed and primarily for the wealthy.[4] Kings, courtiers, aristocrats, high-ranking clerics, gentry, and affluent townspeople all consumed wine as a way to project or acquire status.[5] A comedy written in 1629 by John Grove, entitled *Wine, Beere, and Ale, together by the Eares*, reveals wine's place among the commonly consumed alcoholic beverages of the early seventeenth century.

Wine	I, generous Wine, am for the Court.
Beere	The Citie calls for Beere [i.e. ale infused with hops].
Ale	But Ale, bonny Ale, like a lord of the soyle,
	In the country shall domineere.
Chorus	Then let us be merry, wash sorrow away,
	Wine, Beere, and Ale shall be drunk to-day.[6]

Alas, the harmony of these three drinks and the three social groups they represented was not to last, because when the violent struggle broke out between the supporters and opponents of Charles I, wine was clearly on the side of the king and aristocracy, while beer and ale sided with the Parliamentarians. Of course, that does not mean that Royalists never drank beer or ale, or that Parliamentarians never drank wine. But there was enough truth, and more than enough perceived truth, in the social affiliations of these drinks that Royalists claimed wine as a symbol of their cause, while simultaneously linking beer and ale to the middle-ranking and laboring class Parliamentarians who wanted at first to circumscribe and, eventually, jettison the monarchy altogether.

Evidence for the political meaning of wine, beer, and ale during the Interregnum comes from literature and song, and mostly from the Royalist side. It was they, after all, who had the most to gain politically from exploiting the link between beverages and social class. For instance, Alexander Brome repeatedly used wine to symbolize the king's cause. His poem "The Royalist," written in 1646 and circulated clandestinely until 1661 when it was published, shows how toasting Charles I with wine was meant to console the king's supporters while he was in captivity.[7]

> Come, pass about the bowl to me,
>> A health to our distressed king!
> Though we're in hold, let cups go free,
>> Birds in a cage may freely sing.
> The ground does tipple healths apace
>> When storms do fall, and shall not we?
> A sorrow dares not show his face
>> When we are ships, and sack's the sea.

Just as toasting the king with wine (in this case "sack," i.e. sherry) was a Royalist act, so too was getting drunk from so much loyal drinking. As Brome continues,

> When we are larded well with drink,
>> Our heads shall turn as round as theirs;
> Our feet shall rise, our bodies sink
>> Clean down the wind, like Cavaliers.[8]

Thus for Brome and the choir to whom he was surreptitiously preaching, to be a Cavalier—as opposed to a "Roundhead"[9]—meant to "drink in defence of the king." In the process, toasting Charles I and his cause "represented an act of loyalty," and drinking, especially wine, was an act of symbolic resistance to the Parliamentary regime.[10] Indeed, the symbolism of toasting the Royalist cause in wine became even more potent after Charles I's execution in January 1649, when the king himself was only a memory and the return of the monarchy in the form of his son could only be hoped for. As the anonymous author of a broadsheet ballad from 1649 punned: "The Father of our Kingdom's dead, / His Royall Sun from England's fled, /.../ A Royall Health I then begun, / Unto the Rising of the Sun."[11]

"In this miserable condition," writes the leading scholar of seventeenth-century English political ballads, "the Cavaliers caroused and soused, drinking sorrows away in gallons of wine."[12] Critically, only wine would suffice for articulating Cavalier hopes and sorrows; spirituous liquors were still considered to be medicinal, not recreational, while beer's and ale's affiliations with the lower ranks made these drinks politically anathema to those who believed that only the aristocracy were politically legitimate. In fact, Royalists attacked the legitimacy of the Cromwellian regime by pointing out that Cromwell, a member of the Huntingdonshire minor gentry, had links to the brewing trade.[13]

"In Small Beer," a poem from 1653 by the Catholic Royalist Richard Flecknoe, emphasized the established political meanings of liquors by suggesting that the clergy should promote wine and discourage beer consumption:

> Let the Divines, if they would mend it, preach
> Gainst small beer only, and no Doctrine teach,
> But drinking *wine*; no other vice dispraise,
> But *Beer*, and we may hope for better days.[14]

Similarly, Brome made a distinction between the effects of drinking beer and ale, versus wine:

> Beer and Ale makes you prate
> Of the Kirk and State
> …
> But we while old sack does divinely inspire us
> Are active to do what our Ruler require us.[15]

The lyrics of "Canary's Coronation," a song from *Fancy's Festivals, a Masque*, are even more politically explicit. In this instance "Canary," the eponymously named sweet wine from the Canary Islands, is a metaphor for the exiled Charles II, while beer and ale represent the existing social (dis)order. As the lyrics exclaim:

> From Hopps and Grains let us purge our brains;
> They do smell of Anarchie.
> …
> Why should we droope or basely stoope
> To popular ale or beere?[16]

According to the self-affirming logic of the Royalists, because wine was the drink of the Court, the aristocracy, and the Church, wine was the drink of political legitimacy. Likewise, beer and ale were the drinks of those for whom God had never intended political power, and who had destroyed the order, beauty, and divinity of the Church of England. Consequently, the allegedly beer-drinking Parliamentarians were politically and religiously illegitimate. Moreover, Royalists claimed that their drinking made them honorable men, while Parliamentarians were dishonorable because they rejected the rules of behavior that governed male conviviality. To reject the rules of the group by drinking alone or refusing to drink at all was a direct affront to other men. It was, in fact, both dishonorable and womanly, for who but a false man would fail to uphold his own honor and that of his friends? Conversely, to subscribe to the rules that affected every man equally, showed respect for the members of the group and assured a man an honorable reputation.[17]

Wine under the Commonwealth and Protectorate

However much Royalists adhered to their rules, rituals, and symbolic commodities, the truth was that neither wine, nor beer, nor ale demarcated clear political or social divisions, largely because those divisions themselves were not ironclad. Beer and ale, for example, were ubiquitous beverages in England and Wales, consumed by all social ranks, genders and ages.[18] And while wine was relatively expensive and therefore consumed only by those who could afford it, this did not relegate wine to the aristocracy alone; the middle rank of consumers also drank wine. Moreover, some of the aristocracy were Parliamentarians, just as some of the middle ranks were Royalists. But whatever their social backgrounds, Parliamentarians were convinced that it was the Royalists, not they themselves, who were ungodly and effeminate. In their minds, loss of self-control was an affront to God and honorable manhood.[19] But Parliamentarians were certainly no strangers to drink. They may have been dominated by religious Puritans who wanted to "purify" the Church of England of its Papist vestiges, but they were not like the evangelical Protestants of the nineteenth and twentieth centuries who shunned all forms of alcohol.[20] In fact, while Cromwell's court was not as lavish as that of the Stuarts, scholars now know that it was not nearly so drab in dress and decorum as its puritanical reputation has suggested.[21] Instead, Cromwell and his courtiers dressed and behaved according to their audience. Sometimes that meant worsted, broadcloth, and beer, and at other times it meant velvet, lace, and wine.

Wine import statistics for England and Wales exist only in fragments for the Interregnum period, but these tell us that wine continued to arrive in England, and that the new government saw the advantages of a healthy wine trade. London Customs accounts from March 1, 1650 until August 26, 1650 show that the Commonwealth collected over £5,746 revenue on "sweet wines" (i.e. wines from Spain and the Canary Islands), and more than £5,414 on French and Rhenish wines.[22] Indeed, the financially indebted Commonwealth government was anxious to collect taxes on wines, and therefore did not want to stifle a trade that had already been diminished by the fighting of the 1640s, as well as the death or impoverishment of many prominent aristocrats.

In its attempt to increase government revenue from trade the Commonwealth Parliament passed the Navigation Act of 1651, which required all goods imported into England to arrive either in English ships, or ships belonging to the nation from whence the goods originated. This act was meant to unseat the Dutch as leaders of the carrying trade, which included the transport of wine. While a clause in the Navigation Act allowed the Dutch to bring Rhenish wines into England, despite their German origins, there was an immediate scarcity of Spanish and French wines on the English market as the old channels of trade were broken. Many English wine merchants petitioned the government to drop wine from the Navigation Act, but they were ignored. Nevertheless, the government granted permission for English wine merchants to import French and Spanish wine via Dutch ships if the merchants paid an extra £2 per tun duty upon arrival. This measure temporarily brought the Dutch back into the trade, but when the Dutch went to war with England in 1652 because of the overall effects of the Navigation Act, the wine trade, along with English trade in general, was further disrupted.[23]

The end of the First Anglo-Dutch War in 1654 brought about an immediate revival in the wine trade in the spring of that year, and the new Cromwellian government (i.e. the Protectorate) sought to regulate and raise revenue from it. In fact, and not for the last time, the Protectorate government did precisely the sort of thing for which Parliamentarians had condemned Charles I. First, they raised Customs duties by £9 per tun on all wines; second, they resurrected an act passed under King Henry VIII, which established the government's right to fix the prices of different wines. Not surprisingly, merchants complained that the fixed prices would ruin them because they had purchased much of their stock during the war when costs were high. Not wanting to kill a trade it was trying to tax, the government agreed to delay the implementation of fixed prices.

If all of this uncertainty in the wine trade was not already enough to dampen it, the English navy seized the island of Jamaica from Spain in 1655. This act of aggression prompted the Spanish temporarily to cut off all trade with England. Nevertheless, the popularity of canary and sack in England was so great that some of these wines still arrived, and it is possible that their scarcity made them even more sought after among the wealthy. When in the summer of 1657 it looked like the wine trade was picking up, the Protectorate government once again tried to set maximum prices on wines, and once again agreed to delay implementation. Finally, beginning in January 1658, it was decreed that no merchant could charge more than 1s. 6d. per quart for Spanish wines, 1s. for Rhenish wines, or 7d. for French wines.[24] Ironically, this economic favoritism toward French wines, which the Cromwellian regime clearly endorsed, would later produce a backlash from Cromwell's spiritual descendants, the Whigs.

Equally ironic, especially given the choices of subsequent rulers, is the fact that Cromwell's government did not impose a single embargo on wines from countries with which England was at war. Nor did they reject wines from any country on political grounds. In the first half of 1654, Cromwell's court purchased at least 135 tuns of wine, mostly French, but in 1655 Spanish wines seem to have been favored—perhaps these were seized in war—and Rhenish wines were esteemed by the court throughout Cromwell's reign.[25] Moreover, Cromwell revived many of the royal privileges that had been abolished by the earlier Commonwealth regime. For example, Eton College and King's College, Cambridge, each had their grant of Gascon wine (i.e. claret) restored, while Customs farmers were once again allowed to collect prisage on imported wine. Prisage gave them the right to claim wine, or a share of the tax on wine, that arrived in English ports.[26] Furthermore, Cromwell kept his navy happy, or at least sated, by ensuring that British naval vessels were supplied with wine, while ambassadors to his court—a hardship post given the Protectorate's pariah status within Europe—were allowed the ancient privilege of importing wine for their own use, duty free.[27]

***

Despite these measures by the Cromwellian government, the wine trade during the 1650s seems to have remained relatively small compared to previous decades, and Royalists took advantage of this situation to claim that the Cromwellian regime was against wine altogether. Obviously, they were not against wine, although as self-proclaimed godly Protestants they were certainly more moderate in their habits than the carousing Cavaliers, who took pride in their loyalty to the king and the drunkenness that expressed it. Indeed, defeated Cavaliers, both in England and in exile, portrayed Puritan moderation as abstemiousness and, therefore, immoderate and unnatural behavior. For instance, Abraham Cowley, the Royalist poet who accompanied Queen Henrietta Maria to France in 1644 and returned to England in 1654, published a book of poetry in 1656 that included his well-known *Anacreontics*, a series of cantos about love and wine. In one of these cantos, "Drinking," Cowley begins by waxing metaphysical about the aqueous nature of our planet.

> The thirsty earth soaks up the rain,
> And drinks and gapes for drink again;
> The plants suck in the earth, and are
> With constant drinking fresh and fair;
> The sea itself (which one would think
> Should have but little need of drink)
> Drinks twice ten thousand rivers up,
> So fill'd that they o'erflow the cup.

But after establishing that thirst is natural, Cowley quickly reveals his political message.

> Nothing in Nature's sober found,
> But an eternal health goes round.
> Fill up the bowl, then, fill it high,
> Fill all the glasses there—for why
> Should every creature drink but I?
> Why, man of morals, tell me why?[28]

If drinking is what nature does, those who drink act naturally, while those who do not are unnatural. By extension, drinkers believe in a natural form of government—divinely ordained monarchy—while non-drinkers practice an unnatural form of government—the Cromwellian Protectorate. Therefore, far from being the godly Christians that the Cromwellians claimed to be, they were blasphemers against God's natural order.

In 1656 Cowley's message had to be cryptic, but by the summer of 1659, after the death of Oliver Cromwell and the quick rejection of his son Richard by the army, Cowley's critique of the "men of morals" became increasingly mainstream. Maybe, as Royalists said, killing the king was unnatural and God was punishing the people of England by unleashing anarchy? The result of such queries and of the chaos in which England found itself in the winter of 1659–60, was that leaders of the army along with members of a self-convened Parliament called upon Charles II to return from his Continental exile. In a carefully orchestrated bit of timing, the new king arrived in London on his birthday, May 29, 1660, an event for which Cowley composed an "Ode upon his Majesty's Restoration and Return." Not surprisingly, the drink of once despondent Royalists was now used by Cowley to express their triumphant joy:

> With wine all rooms, with wine the conduits flow,
> And we, the priests of a poetic rage,

> Wonder that, in this golden age,
> The rivers, too, should not do so.[29]

In fact, great celebrations occurred throughout England and Wales, and wine was a major recreational and symbolic component. According to the Royalist polymath John Evelyn, who witnessed the seven-hour procession of the king's retinue as it came into London, public fountains ran with wine for the general enjoyment of the people.[30] As one balladeer exclaimed after the celebration, "Conduits did shine / with liquor divine, / the people did bear away hats full of wine."[31]

Along with the Restoration, heavy drinking triumphed over moderation, while Royalist wine won out over allegedly anarchic beer and ale.[32] However, just as loyal drunkenness had contributed to infighting among Charles's supporters in exile, triumphalist drunkenness back in England was unhelpful to a king who wanted to accommodate all his former enemies, excepting the most recalcitrant regicides.[33] As a result, Charles began the day after his return, May 30, with a *Proclamation against Vicious, Debauched, and Prophane Persons*, who "spend their time in Taverns, Tipling-Houses and Debauches, giving no other evidence of their affection to Us, but in Drinking Our Health, and Inveighing against all others who are not of their own dissolute temper."[34] Given the king's own fondness for debauchery and his undoubted appreciation for loyal supporters after a decade of uncertain exile, there is not a little irony in this proclamation. But Charles had enough political experience to know that there were limitations to the benefits of drunken admirers and belligerent sycophants, and some of his more perspicuous supporters agreed. For instance, Samuel Pepys, who had gone to the Netherlands to help retrieve the king, said that news of the proclamation "against drinking, swearing and debauchery," which he heard read aloud on June 4, "gives great satisfaction to all."[35]

While Charles II's proclamation was good politics, it apparently had little effect upon Royalist behavior. In August, he was forced to issue a new proclamation that called for the previous proclamation to be read every week from every pulpit in England and Wales, for six months running.[36] Pepys, who approved the initial proclamation, nevertheless revealed just how little effect it had upon Royalist behavior. On the night of Charles II's English coronation, April 23, 1661—he had been crowned king in Scotland back in 1651—Pepys and his evening companions "drank the King's health and nothing else, till one of the gentlemen fell down stark drunk and there lay speweing." Pepys himself continued drinking, although he had a rough night when the festivities finally ended:

> But no sooner a-bed with Mr Sheply but my head begun to turne and I to vomitt, and if ever I was foxed it was now—which I cannot say yet, because I fell asleep and slept till morning—only, when I waked I found myself wet with my spewing. Thus did the day end, with joy everywhere.[37]

Moralizing Christians, many of whom were former Parliamentarians, once again condemned such behavior as effeminate on the grounds that drunken men were not in control of themselves. Indeed, for moralists of all stripes Restoration libertines were the most effeminate of all because they combined frivolity with alcoholic excess and excessive interest in women.[38] The anonymous author of *Remarques on the Humours and Conversations of the Town* (1673) mocked gallants who "will admit of their society, if you can but Discourse tollerable of Good Wine, of dressing and the Mode of your habiliments ... and at the other divertissements of their lives, which are Women and Wine."[39] Clearly therefore, wine was not an uncontested signifier of political legitimacy, and never had been; wine talk and wine drinking could be overdone. But such criticism was more about style than substance, because wine continued to be politically legitimizing and, in the 1660s and 1670s, was a statement of allegiance to the Restoration political order.

The wine trade during the Restoration

One obvious consequence of heavy wine consumption during the Restoration era was that the wine trade began to gather wind and leave behind the doldrums of the preceding decade. It is also clear that the most popular (and least expensive) wine of the Restoration era was claret, because Bordeaux was the leading port of embarkation among ships bringing wine to England. Other ships brought French wine from La Rochelle and Rouen, Spanish wine from Cadiz, Malaga, and the Canary Islands, and various Mediterranean wines from Italy, Greece and the Levant.[40] When England was not at war with the Dutch—the Second Anglo-Dutch War lasted from March 1665 to July 1667—Rhenish wines from Germany arrived via Rotterdam and other Low Country ports.

Precisely this taste for wine—diversity with claret predominating—was found in Pepys's cellar on July 7, 1665:

> Up, and having set my neighbour Mr. Hudson, wine cooper, at work drawing out a tierce of wine for the sending of some of it to my wife— I abroad, only taking notice to what a condition it hath pleased God to bring me, that at this time I have two tierces of claret—two quarter-cask of canary, and a smaller vessel of sack—a vessel of tent, another of Malaga, and another of white wine, all in my wine-cellar together—which I believe none of my friends of my name now alive ever had of his own at one time.[41]

The predominance of French wine was even more pronounced at the pinnacle of English society, where aspirations to duplicate the court of Louis XIV meant that all things French were fashionable. For example, in October 1666, the wine cellar of Robert Spencer, 2nd Earl of Sunderland, contained one bottle of Languedoc wine, two pints of Spanish wine, 12 bottles of white wine [unspecified origin], 22 bottles of madeira, 36 bottles of champagne, 37 bottles of Rhenish wine, 38 bottles of Mountain,[42] 40 bottles of Côte-Rôtie,[43] 41 bottles of Cyprus wine, 84 bottles of burgundy, 149 bottles of Lord Galloway's wine,[44] and finally, 191 bottles of claret (along with 24 pints of bitter water, 43 bottles of strong beer,

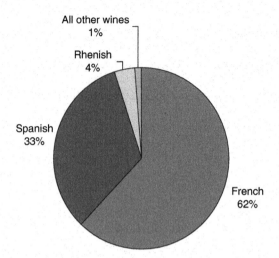

Graph 1.1   London wine imports, 1675
Source: *Journal of the House of Commons* (JHC), XVII, 363.

and a small amount of brandy).[45] In sum, over half of all Sunderland's identifiable wine was French, and among these, claret comprised at least a plurality.

Port of London figures for 1675, the first year for which complete London import figures exist, confirm the picture presented by Pepys's and Sunderland's cellars (see Graph 1.1). French wines accounted for 62 percent of all incoming wine, Spanish wines 33 percent, Rhenish wines 4 percent, and both Italian and Portuguese wines less than 1 percent.[46] Subsequent years show similar figures for the port of London: French wine, and especially claret, was the leading wine of Restoration England.

While Charles II and his courtiers were known to enjoy wine, what the king and his ministers appreciated as much as anything was the ability to tax wine, and therefore, to raise much-needed revenue. In fact, after consolidating all the duties on wine in 1660,[47] Parliament acceded on four separate occasions to Charles's demands to raise the duty on wine as a way to produce revenue for the royal government. Two of these duties were permanent, while two others expired after they had succeeded in raising the desired amount.[48] But money coming into the government's coffers through customs duties often meant money going out to another country to purchase the wine. On both of these grounds Charles encountered Parliamentary resistance. In fact, as one of Restoration England's most costly imports, wine was central to the vexing questions of how money should be raised and spent by the royal government, and which nations should be favored as trading partners or penalized as rivals. Consequently, wine was an instrument of both fiscal and foreign policy, and in these domains the Court and Parliament often clashed. In particular, the great foreign policy divide in Restoration England was whether the Netherlands or France posed the greatest threat to England. Generally speaking, supporters of the Court thought the Netherlands was the greater danger, while the so-called Country Bloc ascribed that role to France. But it was France, not the Netherlands, that produced England's favorite wine, while England was the primary source of imported cloth for France. And therein lay the problem.

The Anglo-French trade wars began when Louis XIV's finance minister, Jean Baptiste Colbert, increased the tariff on English cloth in 1654, 1660, 1664, and 1667, in an attempt to protect and strengthen the French cloth manufacturing industry. For much of that time, the English Parliament was preoccupied with its own economic and maritime policies meant to unseat the Dutch, but Colbert's actions did not go entirely unnoticed. For example, in 1663, a gentleman of the king's bedchamber named Samuel Fortrey tried to shift the English economic focus to France. His book, *England's Interest and Improvement; Consider'd in the Increase of Trade in this Kingdom*, asserted that trade with France "is at least sixteen hundred thousand pounds [£1,600,000] a year, clear lost to this kingdom." Chief among imports from France was wine, upon which Fortrey believed his countrymen spent some £600,000 per annum.[49] To combat this alleged "over-balance" of trade—which Fortrey did not substantiate with anything more than his own assertions[50]—he proposed sumptuary laws for the court (i.e. that courtiers should wear only English cloth), that all English land be enclosed (thereby privatizing all commonly held land), and that high import duties be placed on all finished goods from France that were "not to be again transported."[51] As the primary French import into England, wine was to be the principal victim of Fortrey's proposal and of his legacy, which, considering the book's republication in 1673, 1713, and 1744, was decidedly long.[52]

Fortrey's influence was also almost immediate, because after France joined the Netherlands in the Second Anglo-Dutch War in early 1666, Parliament outdid Fortrey's recommendation by imposing a complete embargo on French and Canary wines beginning in 1667. This embargo was meant to penalize the French and to keep as much gold and silver in England as possible, because both French and Canary wines had to be paid for with coin; they could not be bartered.[53] But whatever effects this embargo might have had on trade were quickly undone by the special licenses sold by the king to merchants in order to import these wines. In other words, Charles wanted to penalize the French for allying with the Dutch (although he had no qualms with the Spanish); but his government also needed more money to wage the war, and wine licenses (which formed part of the king's hereditary revenue) provided a crucial source of income.[54] When the conflict with the Netherlands and France ended in July 1667, the prohibition against French and Canary wines was immediately lifted;[55] but the economic war with France, which would have a major impact upon English taste, had only begun to run its course.

In the wake of the Second Anglo-Dutch War, which occurred simultaneously with an outbreak of the plague in London in 1665 and the Great Fire of London in 1666, the English wine trade was once again sluggish. Nevertheless, economic protectionists like Fortrey continued to call for high tariffs against French wines, while English clothiers continued to petition Parliament for help in lowering French tariffs on English cloth.[56] Moreover, a third Anglo-Dutch War (1672–4), in which the English were now allied with the French against the Dutch, actually led to a shift in public opinion against France, on the grounds that France posed a greater military and ideological threat than did the Netherlands.[57] In this context, a Parliamentary report in 1675 painted a bleak picture regarding England's trade deficit with France.[58] But despite the rising tide of Francophobia, from 1670 to 1678 Customs duty in England stood at £7 per tun on French wines, £8 per tun on Spanish wines, and £9 per tun on Rhenish wines. Sweet wines from the Levant were charged £12 per tun, and were supposed to be landed exclusively at the port of Southampton. However, merchants could simply pay a "Southampton Duty" and unload Levantine wines in other ports, which is what often occurred.[59] Furthermore, throughout Charles II's reign a government tribunal continued to set the maximum price on wines every year, and the price for French wines, like the duty upon them, was consistently lower than for all other wines.[60] For example, in 1674, at the height of protectionist complaints about a French "over balance" of trade, the maximum retail price on French wines was set at 12d. per quart, while Rhenish wines could be sold for as much as 1s. 4d. per quart. Meanwhile, southern European wines were sold by the pint and were more expensive. The maximum retail price for "Sacks and Malagaes" was 10d. per pint (1s. 8d. per quart), and for "Canary, Alecants and Muscadels" 1s. per pint (2s. per quart).[61]

Portuguese wines were so scarce at the time they were not even mentioned by the tribunal, but were simply lumped together with Spanish "Sacks and Malagaes." So it is odd that in 1677 a group of English merchants trading with Portugal had enough optimism to petition the House of Commons that "by an Act of Parl[iament]: the Custome of Portugal Wynes be reduced to be the same with French Wynes and no More."[62] Little could they have imagined that their hopes would soon be surpassed, and that the reigning tariff structure would be overturned within a generation, leaving Portuguese wines the least taxed, and French wines the most. Yet that is precisely what happened.

The Exclusion Crisis and the attack on claret

By 1678, a majority of the House of Commons wanted the king to declare openly that he was an enemy of France and an ally of the Netherlands. Charles was reluctant to do this, as he was secretly receiving a pension from Louis XIV, who was both a friend and cousin. But as Charles was pushed towards war, Parliament responded by raising money with a poll tax, and prohibiting all trade with France.[63] In the end, war never materialized, but the prohibition of trade with France was maintained by Parliament on the grounds that things like French claret and clothing had a particularly pernicious effect on the English treasury, character, and constitution.[64]

The anti-Court argument about the deleterious effects of French wine was part of the broader debate about the potentially corrupting influence of luxury goods that occupied many minds in the seventeenth and eighteenth centuries.[65] But the consumption of wine in general was so inveterately linked to the social order that no one who had pretensions to political legitimacy argued that wine *per se* undermined English masculinity and corroded morals. Broadly speaking, for those who could afford it wine was considered to be a necessity; although cost and availability could and did turn certain wines into a luxury.

The first sustained attempt by Parliament to make French wine a luxury occurred in 1678, at the outset of what is known as the Exclusion Crisis.[66] The cause of this crisis was James, duke of York's Catholic faith, and the question of whether his faith barred him from becoming king upon the death of his brother Charles II. The anti-Court, or Country bloc, which was also the most anti-French, coalesced around the idea that James should be excluded from the throne on the grounds that, as a Roman Catholic, he would necessarily be an anti-Protestant, authoritarian and pro-French king. Instead of James, the Country bloc proposed that the duke of Monmouth, the king's oldest bastard son, and a Protestant, should inherit the throne. The Country bloc was led by the 1st Earl of Shaftesbury, and was quickly given the pejorative name "Whiggamores" by their opponents, a name that referred to a group of zealous Scottish Presbyterians during the 1640s. Shortened to "Whigs," the name was meant to convey the idea that the Country bloc was fundamentally foreign, opposed to the Church of England, and without respect for the laws and customs of the kingdom. Conversely, the Court party, led by supporters of Charles II, coalesced around the idea that hereditary succession was both divinely ordained and politically necessary to keep religious fundamentalism and social chaos at bay. The Court party, which found much to admire in Louis XIVs government, were derisively called "Tories," an Irish word for outlaws, which was a clear attempt to suggest that they were fundamentally un-English, dangerously Papist, and without respect for the English constitution.

Having dissolved his long-sitting Parliament in early 1679, Charles II convened and dismissed three short Parliaments between 1679 and 1681, each of which was dominated by Whigs who called for James's exclusion from the throne. However, a tired voting public eventually came around to the idea that the Whigs were obstructionists who represented the real danger to the Church and State with their fantastical stories of "Popish Plots," and that James had the right to succeed his brother even if his Catholicism made him a less-than-ideal heir. After all, argued Tories, what need was there to worry? James was old, he had no sons, and his two daughters were both raised as good Anglican Protestants. And while the pro-Court Tories were victorious in their initial battle with the "Country" Whigs, the struggles between the two parties were hardly over. Indeed, the age of increasingly organized and disciplined political parties in England had just begun, and conflict between the Tories and the Whigs grew so intense during the reigns of William and Mary (1689–1702), and especially Queen Anne (1702–14), that the first age of party in Europe, if not the world, was also known under the punning sobriquet as the "rage of party."[67]

Given that wine was an outward symbol of the Court and Court interests, and that the soon-to-be Whigs had just imposed an embargo on French wines, it should come as no surprise that the politicization of drinks and drinking that occurred in the mid-seventeenth century returned with a vengeance. Tories drank the health of the king and the duke of York, while Whigs drank the health of the king and the duke of Monmouth.[68] Accusations of drunkenness that were hurled at Cavaliers in the 1640s and 1650s were now thrown at the Tories, who, just as before, responded that their drinking proclaimed their loyalty. Meanwhile, Tories asserted that Whigs were either "miserable Puritans who could not enjoy a drink, or the worst kind of drinkers: those who drink not to be merry, but to cause trouble."[69] The wine versus beer and ale theme also re-emerged, emphasizing the alleged social divisions between Tories and Whigs. More importantly in the long run, the second go-round of the drunkenness-versus-sobriety and wine-versus-beer debate sharpened one aspect of the old argument: if wine was a broad symbol of support for the king and court, French wine was the most symbolically potent of all. And because claret was England's most popular French wine, claret was a symbol of the Tories.

This claret–Tory link was clearly articulated in the midst of the Exclusion Crisis by the young, satirical poet John Oldham, in his poem "The Claret Drinker's Song; Or, the Good-Fellows Design" (1680). In this poem, Oldham defends the Tories against charges of involvement in a "Popish Plot" to kill the king, dismisses the significance of sumptuary laws that require English subjects to be buried in English wool, and attacks the Whigs for imposing an embargo against French wine:

> A friend and a Bottle is all my Design
> H'as no room for Treason that's top ful of Wine.
> I mind not the Members and makers of Laws,
> Let 'em Sit or Prorogue as his Majesty please;
> Let 'em Dam us to Woolen, I'll never repine,
> At my Usage when Dead, so Alive I have Wine.
> Yet oft in my Drink I can hardly forbear,
> To Curse 'em for making my Claret so dear.

Oldham rejects what he considers the petty concerns over foreign policy and religion, saying instead: "From whence Claret comes is the place that I mind,/ And when the Fleet's coming, I pray for Wind." Oldham's feigned indifference to political and religious matters was in fact Tory, because it was an implicit argument for the king's right to make decisions on behalf of the people as a whole. Whigs, argued Oldham, should just shut up and drink while leaving weighty matters of state and religion to the king. In other words, Oldham was reiterating the old Royalist trope that wine drinking proved loyalty to the crown and Church of England, while sobriety was itself a form of political and religious sedition.

> Then here's a good health to all that love Peace,
> Let Plotters be damn'd, and all Quarrels now cease;
> Let me but have Wine, and I care for no more,
> 'Tis a Treasure sufficient, there's none can be poor,
> That has Bacchus to's friend, for he laughs at all harm,
> Whilst with high-proofed Claret he does himself Arm.[70]

In Oldham's mind, and that of the Tories for whom he spoke, claret drinking was a metaphor for the social harmony created by Tory principles, while the embargo against claret symbolized both the tyranny of an overzealous Parliament and the threat of anarchy posed by those who plotted against the king and Church.

Similarly, a ballad published in 1681 under the title, "The Wine Cooper's Delight," attacked Whig political ideology and promoted Tory beliefs, using French wine as the central trope:

> The Delights of the Bottle are turn'd out of doors,
> By factious fanatical Sons of damn'd whores.
> French wines Prohibition meant no other thing,
> But to poyson the Subject, and beggar the K—.
> Good Nature's suggested with Dregs like to choak her,
> Of fulsom stum'd wine by the cursed Wine-Cooper.[71]

Having blamed the "factious fanatical Sons of damn'd whores" (i.e. Whigs) for prohibiting French wines, and thereby promoting adulteration, the ballad goes on to describe a tavern scene in which an anarchic mob of laborers ("Tinkers and Cobblers, the Broom-men and [chimney] Sweep") shouts down the king and asserts the nobility of its own members, all the while drinking a concocted invention of the "Plaguy Wine Cooper." Eventually, everyone but the wine cooper is drunk and sick and reeling on the floor. However, he too finally succumbs to his own toxic concoction, and falls down amidst the spew and excrement of his customers (see Figure 1.1).

The political allusions of this satirical song would have been clear to all but the most politically obtuse English listeners. Those who were against French wine were also unpatriotic for being against the monarchy; and those who were against the monarchy were doubly disqualified in that that they promoted an adulterated form of government *and* they came from the lower orders of society. In contrast, drunkenness from wine and especially from claret was a sign of loyalty, while those who approved of the embargo against French wines could not be drunk on wine at all. They could only be drunk on the chemical creation of a dishonest wine cooper. That the tavern keeper was a "wine cooper"—not a barrel maker, but a professional wine blender who prepared the wines for sale—was a strident Tory metaphor for the supposed impurity of Whig political ideology as well as a direct allusion to the 1st Earl of Shaftesbury, whose name, conveniently for Tory critics, was Anthony Ashley Cooper.

***

So, by 1681 claret reflected aristocratic wealth and belief in a strong monarchy, while intoxication from claret was a manifestation of loyalty to the king and his policies, the Church of England, and the naturalness of aristocratic rule. Moreover, drinking claret helped to construct Tory power by physically demonstrating wealth, loyalty, and the natural inclination of all God's creation to drink. Whig wine drinkers liked claret, but were fearful of trade with France, and they dismissed loyal drunkenness as immoral, effeminate, and childlike behavior.[72]

Figure 1.1   The Wine Cooper's Delight (1681)
Note: "Factious, fanatical Sons of damn'd whores."

After all, they argued, God condemned Noah's drunkenness and to lose control of oneself was what women and children did. But, as we shall see, these meanings of claret, drunkenness, and sobriety would change repeatedly in the next two centuries, and they were never fixed for long to one political party. What would not change, however, was the political nature of wine.

2

"What's become of rich Burdeaux claret, who knows?"

Fraud and Popular Taste in Revolutionary England, 1678–1702

The embargo on French wines that was passed by an angry Parliament in 1678 was repealed in 1685, but another embargo on French goods was imposed from 1689 to 1697, during the course of an actual war against France. Both of these embargoes, along with a series of tariff hikes meant to burden French wine, ultimately caused wines from Spain, and to a lesser degree Portugal, to replace claret as the Englishman's "common draught" by the turn of the eighteenth century. In other words, contrary to popular wine lore, claret's decline and port's rise on the English market occurred before, not because of, the so-called Methuen Treaty with Portugal in 1703. But if the popular turn away from claret and the rise of Iberian wines were the most noticeable result of the politics of wine in the two decades following the Exclusion Crisis, it should not blind us to an equally dramatic development, and that is the prevalence of fraud in many forms.

First, and most obviously, the embargoes and high tariffs on French wines caused innumerable fraudulent declarations of French wine. Second, because such fraudulent declarations were a standing joke among wine consumers, the embargoes and tariff hikes were themselves fraudulent, or at least partially so. And third, the Whig politicians and noblemen who advocated embargoes and Customs increases on French wine were—to their Tory critics—political frauds, because they themselves had no intention of forsaking French wine.

Wine fraud during the first embargo

Nominally, the embargo of 1678–85 against French wine was a success. However, a close look at the evidence shows it to have been a massive failure. According to London port records, fewer than four tuns of French wine were imported in 1679, fewer than two tuns in 1680, only 65 gallons in 1683—and these wines were taken as prizes of war. In 1681, 1682, 1684, and 1685, there were officially no French wine imports into London at all.[1] Meanwhile, Portuguese wines, having only recently been imported into England in any substantial quantities, went from their official pre-embargo average of under 200 tuns annually to nearly 14,000 tuns in 1682 and almost 17,000 tuns in 1683. In fact, official imports of Spanish, German, and Italian wines during the period 1679–85 also increased during the

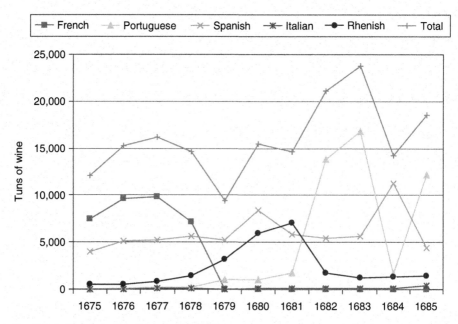

Graph 2.1   London wine imports, 1675–85
Source: JHC, XVII, 363.

French wine embargo, but no wines gained as much ground on the London market as did Portuguese (see Graph 2.1).

The extreme fluctuations in wine imports from year to year might, under unobstructed market conditions, reflect the fact that wine is an agricultural product and therefore subject to the caprice of weather and other natural factors that can determine the level of supply. But under the first embargo on French wines, the dramatic differences in imports from year to year raise suspicions about the veracity of the wines' supposed provenance. The low total amount of wine imports into London in 1679 indicates that the embargo against French wines had an immediate effect upon legal trade by cutting off the supply of Bordeaux wine, while the return to more normal overall import levels in subsequent years suggests that importers soon found sufficient compensatory sources for French wine in Portugal, Spain, and various German states. However, the abrupt shifts in annual totals for different countries of production are too great to be explained by the vicissitudes of weather or the whims of English taste. Moreover, mutually satisfactory trade connections between producers, importers, and retailers take time to establish and are broken only under extreme duress. They tend not to come and go overnight. Equally true, consumers who prefer one type of wine are reluctant to switch to another unless they have absolutely no choice. And yet, official London import figures for 1679–85 suggest that English taste for wine was as whimsical as English weather.

No doubt the embargo did cause some shift in English imports to Portuguese, Spanish, and German wines. However, what almost certainly explains the constant and dramatic changes in English import figures was that with the help of producers and brokers in France, English merchants circumvented the embargo by importing French wines through whatever channels were available. In some years that meant getting French wine via Portugal (1682, 1683, 1685), and other years Spain (1680, 1684) or the Netherlands (1680, 1681). In fact, members of Parliament were well aware that false declarations and smuggling were the true result of the prohibition against French wines.[2] However, when the third, Whig-dominated "Exclusion Parliament" met at Oxford and was abruptly dismissed by Charles in January 1681, it could only pass an angry resolution against false declarations rather than the requisite laws needed to enforce the prohibition against French wines.[3]

The surreptitious nature of wine fraud makes it difficult to prove, especially with the removal of some three hundred years from the time of the activity itself. However, what was once clandestine may be easily perceived by a comparison of export statistics from the city of Oporto in Portugal with contemporaneous London import figures for Portuguese wines. According to the former, during the supposed bumper years for Portuguese wine exports to London in 1682, 1683, and 1685—when the average annual amount was 14,272 tuns—the total number of tuns exported from Oporto to England averaged only 203 tuns per year.[4] While some of this disparity can be explained by the export of Portuguese wines from Lisbon, Viana and other Portuguese cities, Oporto was already the principal port of embarkation for Portuguese wines to England.[5] If, therefore, as the Tory economist Charles Davenant believed, London totals represented roughly three-quarters of all English wine imports, then the disparity between English imports and Oporto exports was even greater than the comparison indicates.[6] In other words, during the embargo, most of what passed for Portuguese wine in England was not Portuguese at all. A graphic comparison of London import and Oporto export figures in the peak years of "Portuguese" wine imports of the 1680s clearly illustrates the startling extent of wine fraud (see Graph 2.2).

While one cannot say for certain that the fraudulently declared wine was from France and not some other country, logic and Parliamentary outcry suggests that it was French. Therefore, it was probably claret. In reality then, the embargo against French wines was a spectacular failure for the Whig Parliament that imposed it. True, Charles II did not receive customs revenue from French wines (excepting the small amounts of prize wine). But because of so much fraudulently declared French wine, he fared even better.[7] After all, the Customs duty on French wines during the embargo stood at just over £7 per tun, while Portuguese and Spanish wine, whether alleged or real, paid roughly £8 per tun, and Rhenish wines more than £9 per tun. As Daniel Defoe would later observe, under these circumstances Charles II had no incentive to undo Parliament's punitive action because fraudulently declared French wine was paying more than it would have had there been no embargo.[8] Consequently, Charles was receiving more revenue than he would have without the embargo, and because of fraud, English wine drinkers were still drinking more claret than any other type of wine. In this situation, principled Whigs were no doubt unhappy, but by 1683 this increasingly small group of men

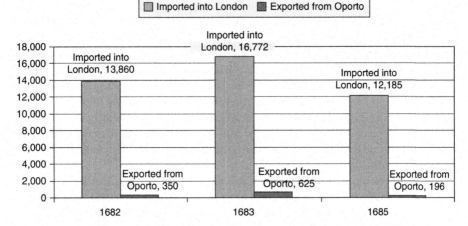

Graph 2.2 Tuns of Portuguese wine imported and exported, 1682, 1683, 1685
Source: London figures are from JHC, XVII, 363, and Oporto figures are from James Warre, *The Past, Present, and Probably the Future State of the Wine Trade* (London, 1823), appendix M; and Joseph James Forrester, *A Short Treatise on the Unequal and Disproportionate Imposts levied on Port-Wine, Shipped from Oporto to Great Britain* (London, 1850), table B.

was demoralized, without a sitting Parliament to voice their grievances, and in some cases, living on the run.[9]

Wine in the reign of James II: The apex of claret's popularity

When the Whig nemesis James II ascended the throne in 1685, the embargo against French goods was duly removed by a new Tory Parliament, thus furthering the affiliation between Tories and England's favorite French wine. However, the embargo was not ended in time to affect the importation of the 1685 vintage; nor did the repeal of the embargo prevent the Tory Parliament from placing additional duties on all wines, with more than £7 per tun being added to French wines, and £10 per tun added to all others. In fact, these new imposts were in line with Tory politics, as they were intended to provide additional revenue to the king. Moreover, these new tariffs continued to favor French wine, which bore the least amount of duty.[10] It is therefore no surprise that the taste for claret, officially absent during the embargo, "returned" with a vengeance in 1686. French wines averaged roughly 70 percent of total London wine imports during the four-year period, 1686–9 (see Graph 2.3).

The apparently sudden return to dominance of French wine in England's largest market confirms what the previous evidence for fraud suggests: despite the embargo, the vast majority of English wine drinkers had never stopped drinking claret, whatever their political sympathies. Indeed, during James II's reign the taste for claret was so strong among English consumers that French wines reached import levels they had not achieved since the Middle Ages (before the loss of Aquitaine in 1453) and were not to see again until the twentieth century.[11]

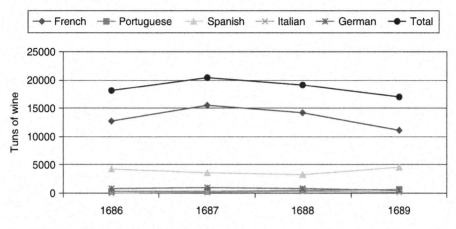

Graph 2.3 London wine imports, 1686–9
Source: JHC, XVII, 363.

Meanwhile, official imports of Portuguese wines dropped dramatically, contributing to the evidence that consumers had not actually been drinking much of them in the first place.

Wine in the reign of William III: The popular decline of claret

But, while claret remained the "common draught" or tavern wine of choice for Englishmen of all political stripes (although not necessarily of women[12]), and for both aristocrats and middling-sorts alike,[13] it did not remain so for long. And just as before, it was the rivalry with France that intervened, this time in the form of the "Glorious Revolution." Prince William of Orange, Stadtholder of Holland and son-in-law to James II, arrived in England with a multi-national army on November 5, 1688, and by mid-December, James II was in exile in France. Parliament offered the crown to William and his English wife Mary on February 13, 1689, and one month later James II landed in Ireland with French officers, arms. and money lent to him by Louis XIV.[14] William of Orange, now William III, received Parliamentary backing for the war with France he so ardently desired, and one immediate result was that a Parliament divided almost evenly between Tories and Whigs once again prohibited the importation of French goods.[15]

Officially, this new embargo was just as successful as the previous one; other than 770 tuns of French wine, which were imported in 1690 as a result of special import licenses granted to merchants who had already put down money, and another 15 tuns that arrived the following year (probably prize wine), no French wines were officially imported for the duration of the war, which lasted until 1697 (see Graph 2.4).[16]

There were some similarities between the effects of this embargo and the one that preceded it. In particular, official French wine imports dropped dramatically, while official Portuguese wine imports rose from minuscule amounts to relative

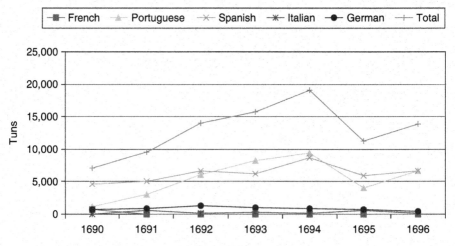

Graph 2.4 London wine imports, 1690–6
Source: JHC, XVII, 363.

parity with wines from Spain. But, whereas during the first embargo phenomenal quantities of French wine masqueraded as Spanish or Portuguese, during the second embargo the amount of fraud, while still frustrating to the government, was nevertheless diminished. How do we know this? First, the rise in the amount of Portuguese wines imported into England was matched by a similar increase in Oporto exports.[17] Second, and more generally, the annual amounts of wines arriving from different countries during the second embargo was relatively consistent compared to during the first embargo, suggesting that trade to England did not simply move to whatever country was willing and able to export French wine under false denomination (see Graph 2.5).[18]

If official statistics indicate a genuine decline in claret in the 1690s, statements made during and after the embargo suggest the same, and that port wine was the principal beneficiary of claret's decline. Writing in 1701, Thomas Cox claimed that "port-wines [came] into Esteem in England since the beginning of the late war."[19] In 1713, *The British Merchant*, admittedly a Whig journal, observed that the 1690–6 prohibition against French wines, and "more particularly the *high* Duties on those *taken by Prize*, put a check to the vast Importations" of French wine. The war and embargo lasted "so exceeding long," wrote the *British Merchant*, that "the Portugal Merchants soon enlarged their Trade, and filled the whole Nation with their Wines." Transforming national taste from claret to port was not without difficulties, however, as the Portuguese wines

being heavy and strong, did not at first please, and we hanker'd after the old claret of *Bourdeaux;* but in time the Quantities [of claret] wore off, and the Merchants found Ways and Means either to bring the *Portuguese* Wine to our Palates, or Custom brought our Palates to the Wine: So that we began to forget the *French* Wines, and like the others well enough.[20]

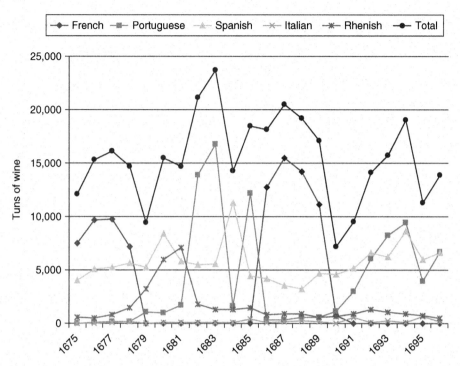

Graph 2.5 Embargoes compared: London wine imports, 1675–96
Source: JHC, XVII, 365.

For many consumers, being weaned from the red wine of Bordeaux was onerous in the extreme. Certainly this was the view of the claret-deprived Richard Ames, a self-described "student at Lincoln's Inn" in London.[21] Ames's first known humorous poem, *The Search after Claret* (1691), tells the tale of two boon companions who set out on a prototypical pub-crawl with the hope of finding "a bottle of good old dry orthodox claret."[22] Their thirsty perambulations take them from Whitechapel to Westminster, but to no avail. Ames's sarcastic tone is meant to suggest that some tavern owners still had claret, but if asked for by name they vigorously denied it, fearing they would have to account for it in the midst of the embargo. How one ordered this claret is not clear, but the customer probably had to be on very good terms with the tavern-keeper. However, the big lament of Ames's poem is that there was little claret to be found, and the humor of his poem comes from his dogged, but futile search.

While Ames could not find any claret, he must have found an audience for his poem because he continued the theme in five sequels published between 1691 and 1693.[23] These latter poems indicate that the situation for claret-lovers only got worse as the war and embargo went on. By 1693 Ames despaired: "But since Civil Wars have in Europe arose,/ What's become of Rich Burdeaux Claret who knows?"[24] And just as Ames lamented the dearth of claret, he was equally despairing that the wine being offered in its place was "port."

To be sure, seventeenth-century port was not the sweet and carefully aged wine it would become by the nineteenth century. Instead, it was usually a dry, table-wine, meant to be a substitute for inexpensive claret.[25] It varied greatly in style, but clearly Ames did not like it in any form. In one memorable scene from his poem the *Bacchanalian Sessions*, Ames once again tramps into a tavern with the hope of finding his favorite red wine, and addresses the young man who stands ready to take his order.

> Some Claret, Boy—Indeed, Sir, we have none.
> Claret, Sir—Lord, there's not a drop in town;
> But we've the best Red Port—What's that you call
> Red Port?—A wine, Sir, comes from Portugal,
> I'll fetch you a pint, Sir—Do make haste you slave.[26]

When the young man—known as a "drawer" because he drew the wine from the cask in the cellar—returns with a pint of port, Ames, like a good connoisseur, insists on examining the wine with his eyes and nose before tasting it and commenting. But when the verdict is delivered, it is unequivocal:

> Mark how it smells, methinks a real pain,
> Is by its odour thrown upon my brain.
> I've tasted it—'tis spiritless and flat,
> And has as many different tastes,
> As can be found in compound pastes,
> In lumber pye or soporifrous methidrate.[27]

When the chastened drawer then offers something else—Navarre, Barcelona, Syracuse, Calcavella, Galliac [sic][28] or Florence—the narrator interrupts:

> —Hold, you prating whelp, no more,
> Fetch us a pint of any sort,
> Navarre, Galicia, anything but Port.[29]

Certainly Ames used poetic license to voice his complaint, but he also may have been looking for claret in all the wrong places. Perhaps claret was hard to come by in taverns, but it was available somewhere in England, because claret fraud continued. For example, in 1689, with the new embargo about to take effect, Louis XIV's Intendant in Bordeaux asked for permission to send wine to England under the Spanish flag, and then reported that the dispatch of wines in Spanish casks was working well.[30] In his daily news summary, a *Brief Historical Relation of the State of Affairs*, Narcissus Luttrell noted in December 1691 that nine "English ships that went to Bourdeaux and took in wine ... after sailed to port O Porto, and then came home, pretending it to be port."[31] So common was this sort of activity that in 1696 the Commissioners of Customs reported to the Lords of the Treasury that the

> King looks upon it to be French wine, that comes from St. Sebastian [a Spanish port not far from Bordeaux], but directs two officers (such as the Commissioners of Customs shall approve) to be sent over to St. Sebastian to take knowledge of the wine there and its growth.[32]

The commissioners returned with proof that there was a regular trade between Bordeaux and San Sebastian, from whence claret was shipped to England. But short of prohibiting Spanish wine, there was little the English government could do to stop the illegal trade.

Between the wars: Popular taste for French wine does not return

In preparation for the Treaty of Ryswick, which ended the Nine Years' War in 1697, the embargo against French wines was dropped in time for the English to receive that year's vintage. However, unlike at the end of the previous embargo, official French wine imports did not return to their pre-embargo levels. In fact, during the six-year period 1697–1702, the average amounts of wine imported into all of England and Wales show that Spanish wines predominated, with Portuguese wines placed second, and French wines a distant third, on par with Italian wines (see Graph 2.6).

Of course, some of this Spanish and Portuguese wine was actually French, but it remains significant that French wine did not return to its customary position atop the English market. First and foremost, this was due to the fact that by the end of

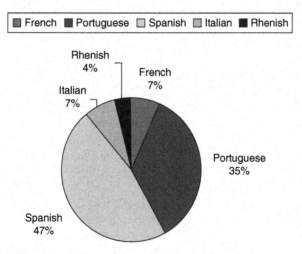

Graph 2.6 Percentage of English wine imports, 1697–1702
Source: JHC, XVII, 365.

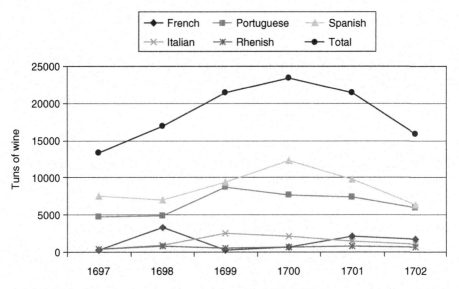

Graph 2.7 English wine imports between the wars, 1697–1702
Source: JHC, XVII, 365.

1697 French wine was fiscally disadvantaged. In 1692, during the middle of the embargo, a Whig Parliament added insult to economic injury by placing a "New Impost" of £8 on contraband French wine. Two years later a massive financial burden of £25 was tacked on to French wines, and in 1697 a "New Subsidy" was placed on all wines, bringing the total import duty on French wine to roughly £51 per tun, while Portuguese wines (including madeira) paid £21 per tun,[33] Spanish (including canary) and Italian wines £22, and Rhenish and Hungarian wines £25.[34] Therefore, even with relatively low transport costs, claret, when legally imported, was necessarily going to be among the most expensive wines on the English market. And while low cost could not guarantee a wine's popularity, high cost could certainly preclude it (see Graph 2.7).

   Indeed, there was a broad correlation between tariff rates and import levels in the period 1697–1702, just as there had been in previous decades. Spanish and Portuguese wines carried the least amount of duty and had lower transportation costs than Italian or Rhenish. They were also the most popular. However, wine import statistics from this period remain inexact because wine fraud did not cease with the end of war. In fact, the punitive tariff level on French wine perpetuated the incentive for a vibrant black market. For instance, in 1699 and 1700 there was an extraordinary increase of wine exported from Bordeaux to northern Spanish ports, especially San Sebastian. In 1700, Bordeaux exports to San Sebastian peaked at more than 4,500 tuns, despite the fact that the area around San Sebastian produced more than enough wine for its own inhabitants. Moreover, the wine from Bordeaux to San Sebastian was not carried in French coasting vessels; instead, it was transported in large Dutch, Flemish, Swedish, Norwegian, and English ships, indicating that San Sebastian was not to be the final port of call.[35] A letter written in June 1698 by the Intendant of Guyenne, Louis Bazin de Bezons, to the Contrôleur Général in Paris explains the reason for this peculiar situation.

> During the war [1689–97] you approved the use of Spanish casks for French wine to be sent to England: that plan worked. Wines entered successfully every year. The English were notified. They sent some commissioners to taste the Spanish wines in order to see if there were wines in Spain that resembled the ones that were carried to England. The commissioners gave the report that we desired: I have learned about the conduct that the negociants used towards to commissioners so that their report would be favorable [i.e. they were probably bribed] ... We have found ways to carry even greater quantities [of wine] since the peace [of Ryswick] because navigation is free from here to San Sebastian and is no longer interrupted by corsairs, [thus] we send many more ships to England with Spanish casks.[36]

In autumn 1699 nearly 60 English vessels in San Sebastian were loaded with Bordeaux wine in Spanish pipe barrels.[37] So alarming was the consequent increase in wines from Navarre that in January 1700 the Commissioners of Customs in London recommended that all such wines simply pay French duties.[38] This government action, along with the confiscation of 48 vessels arrived from San Sebastian—and the arrest and conviction of numerous sailors and merchants—greatly diminished this particular means of claret fraud.[39] But when the San Sebastian operation was effectively shut down in 1701, Bordeaux exports to Portugal rose sixfold within a year, from roughly 100 tuns to 620 tuns.[40] There can be little doubt that most of that wine was destined for England. In some instances, claret was not even sent to Portugal, but instead was put in Portuguese pipe barrels in Bordeaux and then shipped to England as if it were port. In fact, this practice was officially sanctioned by the Bordeaux municipal authorities, who in 1706 went so far as to form a commission to assist in the process.[41]

The false declaration of wine was so well known in England that the Irish-born playwright George Farquhar openly alluded to the practice in his play *The Constant Couple* (1699).[42] If the name of a character in the play, "Smuggler," revealed his profession to the audience, the familiar details of his illicit activities were what got the laugh:

> My ship the *Swan* is newly arrived from St. Sebastian laden with Portugal wines! [cries Smuggler in the opening scene, unaware that San Sebastian is in Spain not Portugal]. Now the impudent rogue of a Tide-waiter has the face to affirm 'tis French wines in Spanish casks, and has indicted me upon the Statute. O Conscience! Conscience! These tide-waiters and surveyors plague us more with their French wines than the war did with French privateers.[43]

***

Clearly fraud persisted after the second embargo was ended, but just as clearly, levels of fraud were nowhere near the levels of legal trade. How do we know this? Well, if one takes the amounts of wine shipped from Bordeaux to Spain and Portugal in the period October 1, 1698 to September 30, 1702—wine that presumably was destined for England—and subtracts that amount from the respective amounts of wine officially imported into England from Spain and Portugal during roughly the same four years (1699–1702), then adds those amounts to official French wine imports into England, one arrives at the following figures: Spanish wine accounted for 40 percent of the English imports, Portuguese wine for 36 percent, French wine for 13 percent, Italian wine for 9 percent and German wine for 3 percent.

This more accurate picture of English wine imports reinforces the conclusion that the 1690s witnessed a genuine shift in popular taste. The frequently interrupted supply and high tariffs that had been placed on French wines since 1679 caused them to lose their dominant position on the English market and to be replaced by wines from Spain and Portugal. Claret, the most popular French wine in Restoration England, had become hard to find and expensive when found. Under such conditions, it could no longer be the tavern wine or "common draught" of English wine drinkers.

Claret: Once again a Tory symbol

The decline in claret consumption in England contributed to strengthening the symbolic link between claret and the Tory party because it was Whigs who were always more enthusiastic to punish France by restricting the importation of French wine. For claret-loving Whigs like Richard Ames this was regrettable. In 1691 Ames wrote another wine-inspired poem, entitled *A Dialogue between Claret and Darby-Ale*, which was meant to attack the idea—promoted by fellow Whigs—that drinking claret was unpatriotic. In this poem, the anthropomorphised "Claret" proclaims himself to be "the most immortal liquor ... Sent down to be a Charm for mortal Cares, Son of the Sun, and brother to the stars."[44] In contrast, "Darby-Ale" is down to earth, unpretentious, and, as the reader is to understand, a bit dull perhaps, but solidly English. Darby-Ale attacks Claret for being haughty, impure and foreign, but it was on this last count that Claret threw down the gauntlet:

> You scoundrel Dog, am I not Naturaliz'd?
> The greatest part o' th' Nation own my Juice
> While they thy Justice Foggy-Ale refuse.[45]

Clearly, Ames was fighting an uphill battle against his fellow Whigs. He was trying to protect claret against the charges of being foreign, both in the sense that it was not English, and that it was unsuitable to English palates. Claret, claimed Ames, was not really French; after all, it had been "naturaliz'd" in England by its prolonged and widespread use. Furthermore, the English preferred French claret to their own domestically produced ale. This latter claim was no doubt true among a majority of the English aristocracy and middle ranks for whom ale was so common

as to be unremarked upon unless oddly good or bad, like tap water to later generations; however, it could not have been true for the laboring poor for whom cost
made wine unaffordable. But Ames was drawing a line between those who did and
did not have a political voice, and the former, said Ames, preferred claret to ale.

But an attempt to naturalize claret by a minor satirical poet was hardly enough
to undo what wars, party rivalries, embargoes, and competing economic policies
had wrought, because, however much Ames protested, claret as a symbol did not
transcend the party divide. It was Tory. After all, Tories were generally reluctant
participants in the Nine Years' War and unenthusiastic about the embargo on
French wines. In contrast, most Whigs embraced both the war and the embargo,
thereby pushing claret farther into the Tory camp and claiming Spanish wines as
their own. As Ames remarked in another poem in 1693:

> The Red Wines together march decently all,
> like a Call of New Serjeants which go by Whitehall.
> In Coats party-colour'd, so these by Extraction,
> Were half of them Spanish, and half the French Faction.[46]

Ames's precise oenological divisions may have been bent to the requirements
of rhyme, but his poem correctly reveals that port was not yet a symbol of Whig
sympathies. That affiliation did not begin until the Methuen Commercial Treaty of
1703 and, more so still, the rejection of a commercial treaty with France in 1713.
In the 1690s, red wine from Spain carried the Whig banner. Meanwhile, claret's
Tory links were strengthened as the war and embargo dragged on. This heightened
symbolism can be seen in Ned Ward's periodical, *The London Spy*, which was published between 1698 and 1700. Ward was a tavern-keeper, poet, and self-described
"tippling philosopher,"[47] whose monthly serial was a ribald satire on urban living,
supposedly written to inform his friends in the country about the "vanities and
vices of the town."[48] But in Ward's Tory view, London's most dangerous inhabitants were not the drunken blackguards who roamed the streets looking for fights,
but the self-righteous religious Non-Conformists who endangered the Church and
State, and would prohibit all earthly enjoyment in the name of King Jesus. In stark
contrast to these dour Dissenters—who were of course Whigs—Ward and his fellow Tory blades enjoyed the pleasures of this world, which wherever they went in
London included large amounts of symbolically charged claret.

What Whig policies wrought: Expensive claret and fraud

Despite claret's status as a symbol of Tory sympathies, not all Whig consumers
happily foreswore it. The claret-loving Ames died an early death in 1693, but his
conundrum continued on in the minds of Whigs for whom there was an irrec-
oncilable tension between a love of claret and hatred of the French.[49] As Ames
himself had written in one of his overtly Whig poems: "The FRENCH—Altho'
indeed no Terrour lye/ in the Word *French*, yet there's a strange,/ and almost

unaccountable Antipathy,/ Against 'em does in *English* Bosoms range."[50] In itself, this hatred had little impact upon English preference for claret. After all, one could hate the French but love French wine, as Ames himself did. But this hatred and fear of the French was precisely what drove Whig Parliamentarians to push for embargoes and punitive tariffs on French wines, and these were the political measures that led popular taste away from claret and toward more easily procurable and less-expensive Iberian alternatives. That said, Whig political leaders themselves had no intention of renouncing claret, for it was popular taste for wine that they wanted to change.

John Hervey, 1st Earl of Bristol

A stellar example of a claret-drinking Whig grandee was John Hervey, Baron Hervey and latterly 1st Earl of Bristol (1665–1751). Hervey had a cosmopolitan taste in wine; his cellar contained wines from Spain, the Canary Islands, Portugal, Madeira, Italy, and Germany. But above all, he enjoyed wine from France, and among French wines he preferred expensive claret. For instance during the 1689–96 embargo he managed to purchase claret, Hermitage (from the northern Rhone valley), and what he called "Hermitage claret,"[51] despite the fact that French wine imports were officially non-existent from 1692 to 1696. He also bought a suspicious amount of wine from Navarre and Galicia (i.e. northern Spain), and less suspiciously sack, canary, palm, and Rhenish wine.[52] Between the time the embargo was lifted in 1697 and the beginning of the next embargo against French goods in 1704, Hervey's choices were even more focused on France and especially Bordeaux. In 1699 he purchased the equivalent of 1,512 bottles of Navarre (probably claret via San Sebastian), 540 bottles of Languedoc wine, and 30 bottles of claret from St Laurent-en-Médoc. In 1700 and 1701 he bought small amounts of champagne and burgundy, and in 1702 he purchased still more burgundy and four hogsheads (roughly 1,008 bottles) of "Obrian Wine" (Chateau Haut Brion). With another embargo about to come into effect, Hervey purchased a hogshead (252 bottles) of "Margoose Clarett" (Chateau Margaux) in December, 1703.[53] In other words, by the time the embargo was in place, Hervey had hundreds of gallons of fancy French wine resting gently in his Suffolk cellar.

Clearly, for Whigs who could afford them, French wines knew no party limits, and to Tory writers like Charles Davenant this was outrageous hypocrisy. In his satirical commentary, *The True Picture of a Modern Whig* (1701),[54] Davenant asserted that Whig consumption of expensive French wine made them political frauds, or "Tom Doubles" as he called them. Davenant had a valid argument, but he was also missing or rejecting a distinction being made in the minds of Whig grandees. Men like Hervey saw nothing wrong with drinking luxury claret and other French wines if they could afford them; the issue for them was whether "good, old, dry, orthodox" claret—not Chateaux Haut Brion and Margaux—should be the tavern wine of England. Whig leaders believed it should not be, as this would mean sending large amounts of money to France. But if the English elite purchased

French wine, that would hardly be enough to constitute an imbalance of trade in favor of France. And it was this paternalistic, public-versus-private distinction that assuaged wealthy Whig consciences as they poured bottle after bottle of fancy French wine down their throats.

***

What, then, can be said about the politics of wine in late seventeenth-century England? Certainly, precise statements about import levels of different wines are difficult to make. However, we do know that the post-1678 era continued and strengthened the claret–Tory link, that a Whig–Spanish wine connection emerged, and that Portuguese wine finally entered the English market in a meaningful way. More broadly speaking, we can say that by the end of the seventeenth century—before the Methuen Commercial Treaty with Portugal—English *popular* taste had moved away from claret and toward Iberian wines. This movement was a reflection of the effectiveness of the second embargo, which, unlike the first, occurred during a time of genuine war, and at a time when the power of the English state to regulate and tax trade was growing at a phenomenal rate.[55]

But what is most striking about the politics of wine in late seventeenth-century England was that the entire era was marked by fraud—and fraud of many sorts. Most obviously, massive amounts of French wine imported into England, in some years probably a majority, was fraudulently declared. As a result, the embargoes against French wine were fraudulent because they did not prevent importation. Instead, they encouraged false declarations. Lastly, Whig politicians and supporters who favored embargoes and high tariffs on French wines were political frauds—or at least that is how their Tory critics saw them.

Perhaps in this latter instance the word fraud is too strong. More generously, we can say that Whig leaders drew a distinction between their own personal preferences and the national interest. Certainly, Whigs in the post-Exclusion Crisis era established the idea that importing large amounts of claret was bad for England as a whole, and it was this idea that guided Whigs in their economic and foreign policy debates with Tories in the years to come. But before exploring those debates we must turn our attention to Scotland, where wine was also politicized by the events of the late-seventeenth-century.

3

"The Cross ran with claret for the general benefit"

The Politics of Wine in Scotland, 1680s–1707

In England, wine became a highly politicized commodity as a result of the tumul-tuous events of the mid-seventeenth century; however, there is no evidence that the regicide, the British Civil Wars, or Cromwellian rule, had a similar effect in Scotland. Nevertheless, by the time of the Treaty of Union in 1707, which united Scotland and England into the Kingdom of Great Britain, wine in Scotland, claret specifically, was a politically charged commodity. The politicization of claret in Scotland occurred in the late 1690s and early 1700s as a result of the tensions between the Scottish and English Parliaments, and ultimately, the Treaty of Union between the two. In this environment, savvy, if not also unscrupulous Scottish politicians and merchants recognized that importing French wine was a way to assert Scottish parliamentary independence and make money at the expense of the English, since much of the wine would be re-exported south of the border. Thus, like the thistle that allegedly thwarted Norwegian invaders of Scotland in the Middle Ages by making them howl in pain and thereby awaken the sleeping clansmen, importing claret into Scotland at the turn of the eighteenth century was something that benefitted the Scots in large measure because it made the English squeal.[1]

"Lifeblood" of the Auld Alliance

By the turn of the eighteenth century, Scottish wine drinkers had relished claret for almost as long as English wine drinkers had. In Scotland, claret consumption began no later than the thirteenth century, when English and Gascon mer-chants found a ready market for wine north of the Cheviot Hills. In 1263, King Alexander III purchased 178 tuns of wine, most of it from Gascony, and therefore probably an early version of claret. Royal taste made claret a prestige drink for those who could afford it, and both the court and church helped to keep the wine trade active throughout the late Middle Ages.[2] Ultimately, Scottish fondness for claret was too great to be entrusted to foreign merchants alone, and by the fourteenth century the Scots themselves ventured south to Bordeaux to retrieve great quantities of wine.[3] After England lost Aquitaine in 1453, thereby ending the Hundred Years' War against France, Scottish merchants became even more involved in directly importing wines from Gascony.[4] From an economic stand-point if not from a cultural one as well, claret has aptly been called the "lifeblood of the Auld Alliance," which linked Scotland and France from 1295 to 1560.[5]

Interestingly, the gradual decline of Scottish–French political and economic relations during the late sixteenth and seventeenth centuries had little influence upon Scottish taste for wine. Between 1610 and 1620, approximately 250,000 gallons of French wine was landed annually in Leith, 50,000 gallons at Dundee, and 20,000 gallons at Aberdeen.[6]

From Restoration to Revolution

In Scotland, just as in England, the mid-seventeenth century wars had a dramatic impact. The millenarian joy inspired by Scottish Covenanter victories over the English in 1639 and 1640 was followed by civil strife in Scotland, frustration with the English Parliamentarians, humiliating defeats to the English army in 1650 and 1651, and loss of sovereignty to a pan-British and Irish government (in various forms) until 1660. The Restoration of the monarchy restored Scottish independence as well, but the Scots themselves remained bitterly divided in both religion and politics. The return of Charles II, therefore, provided a moment in which Scots could forget their differences and look forward to the future, if only with the help of wine.

> On 19th June [1660] commenced a period of thanksgiving through all the parishes of Lothian, for the restoration of the King. The Magistrates and Town Council of Edinburgh went to church in solemn procession. ... After service they went with a great number of citizens to the Cross, where a long board, covered with sweetmeats and wine, had been placed. ... Here the healths of the King and the Duke of York were drunk with the utmost enthusiasm, three hundred dozens [3,600] of glasses being cast away and broken on the occasion. At the same time, bells rang, drums beat, trumpets sounded, and the multitude and people cheered. The spouts of the Cross ran with claret for the general benefit.[7]

As we have seen, London witnessed similar scenes of joy and free-flowing wine upon the triumphant return of Charles II only a few weeks before; but even the carefully observant John Evelyn did not mention what type of wine the Londoners drank. To the Scottish observer, however, claret and wine were practi-cally synonymous.

Indeed, as it had been for centuries, claret was the common wine of seventeenth-century Scotland, and it was consumed in aristocratic castles, political clubs, urban howffs, and highland taverns.[8] In the period 1660–89, one in ten Scottish vessels was employed in trade with France, which was primarily concerned with "the young wine from the Gironde, shipped mainly from Bordeaux."[9] In 1681, a customs officer estimated Scottish annual wine imports at roughly 1,600 tuns, which amounted to more than 400,000 gallons.[10] Some 60–70 percent of that wine went to Leith, roughly 20 percent to Glasgow, while smaller ports such as Aberdeen, Ayr, Dundee and Inverness each received small amounts.[11] Leith Customs records for the period from the Restoration to the Union are incomplete; however, for those years in which records do exist, the evidence for claret's popularity is overwhelming. For example, during the fiscal year 1672–73, 96 percent of wine cargoes unloaded at Leith originated from Bordeaux.[12] Other years show a similar fondness for claret; in 1680–81, 94 percent of all wine unloaded at Leith came from Bordeaux.[13] Of the remaining wine that year, two deliveries contained unspecified French wine that arrived via Rotterdam and two cargoes were comprised of "sacke" from Cadiz.

Uninterrupted Leith customs records for the years 1682–6 provide a slightly longer-term view of Scottish wine imports in the Restoration era. During these four years, in which the pattern of trade was relatively consistent, Leith received between approximately 900 and 1,250 tuns of wine annually, nearly 85 percent of which was definitely French, and 80 percent of the wine-laden ships arriving into Leith came directly from Bordeaux.[14] The precise percentage of claret within the overall annual figures is impossible to deduce because some of the wine from Bordeaux could have been white, and French wines that came on ships arriving from Rouen, St Mâlo, La Rochelle, St Martin [de Ré], or via Rotterdam and Hamburg, might have been claret also. Given Scottish taste, much of it probably was.[15] But even without these exact figures it can be estimated that at least three-quarters of all wine arriving in Leith during the 1680s was claret.[16] The remaining wine landed at Leith during these years was invariably Spanish wine that came directly from Cadiz or via North Sea ports. Customs accounts for Leith in the politically troubled year of 1688–9 concur with this overall picture of Scottish taste for wine: of 103 entries for wine that year, 82 percent of the wine was French, every gallon of which came from Bordeaux.[17] The remaining 18 percent of wine was sack from Spain (see Graph 3.1).

Because Edinburgh was Scotland's largest entrepot and consumer of wines, and was representative of the overall Scottish wine imports the way London was for England, it is clear that in the 1680s Scottish and English taste for wine was remarkably similar.[18] London import figures for the four-year period 1686–9 (in which there was no embargo), show that almost three-quarters of all wine came from France, and most of this was claret. Most of the rest of London imports came from Spain (see Graph 3.2).[19]

Of course, the overall amount of wine imported into London was roughly seventeen times greater than the amount imported into Leith. But despite this difference in volume, on the eve of the Glorious Revolution, both Scottish and English consumption focused on claret.

Shards of evidence from private records in Scotland concur with customs accounts. Sir John Foulis of Ravelston (1638–1707), a barrister and diarist in Edinburgh, enjoyed claret, and was joined in his preference by his first wife, Margaret, who served claret to the "cummers" and "gossips" who attended her lying in (for her fourteenth child) on March 26, 1680.[20] The Foulises enjoyed claret, and John drank it almost daily, but their consumption level was not nearly so great as that of the 4th Duke and Duchess of Hamilton, who served "over five

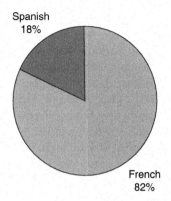

Graph 3.1 Scottish taste for wine, 1688–9
Source: NAS, E 72/15/42, Leith customs records, imported wine, 1688–1689.

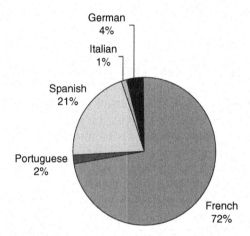

Graph 3.2 English taste for wine, 1686–9
Source: JHC, XVII, 363.

hundred bottles of claret, about two hundred bottles of canary, and several dozen of Rhenish and Madeira ... each year."[21] Grander still, on a scale of conviviality at least, was the hard-drinking household of Robert Dundas (d. 1726), who was both a Member of Parliament for Midlothian in the Scottish Parliament and later served as a judge of the court of Session, which gave him the title Lord Arniston. Dundas's household went through 16 hogsheads of claret a year at the turn of the eighteenth century, which was the equivalent of over 4,000 quart bottles.[22] Indeed, so dominant was claret in Scotland that it seems to have served as the reference point for all other wines. When Hugh Campbell wrote to William Douglas, the 3rd Duke of Hamilton, on July 22, 1673, informing him that he had sent three tuns of the "best Parisse wine," he explained that "it will not suffer to keep so long as Burdiox wine."[23]

A principal reason for the popularity of claret in a poor country such as Scotland was not only the weight of tradition, but also its relatively low cost compared to other wines—which was itself partially a result of tradition. Thus, while duty increases and embargoes on French wines helped to make claret expensive and scarce in late seventeenth-century England, in pre-Union Scotland there were intermittent attempts to hold the price of French wine down. To the Scottish government and many Scottish port cities, wine represented the single most valuable import for the revenue that it raised through tariffs. For example, in 1692, £37,000 (Scots[24]), which was over one-third of Edinburgh's revenue, came from the duty on wine landed at Leith.[25] Among these wines, French wines carried the lowest duty. The customs duty stood at £30 (Scots) per tun for all wines; however, the excise duty was £36 (Scots) per tun on French wines and £54 (Scots) on all other wines. Furthermore, burghs, or incorporated Scottish towns, frequently added their own imposts as a way to raise money, and these tended to favor French wine as well. For example, in 1689 Edinburgh was granted an impost of £30 Scots per tun on French and German wine, but £100 Scots per tun on Spanish wine.[26]

The Wine Act of 1703

As socially and fiscally privileged as claret was in Restoration Scotland, it was not immune to the effects of King William's war against Louis XIV. In early 1689 the Scottish Parliament, independent of the English Parliament, had voted to make William of Orange their king as well: King William II of Scotland (and III of England). As king, William brought his Scottish kingdom into the war against France that began in the spring of 1689, when James II and VII landed in Ireland in the hope of restoring himself to the thrones of England, Scotland, and Ireland. The French, who supported James, simultaneously placed an embargo on all Scottish, English, and Irish fish and woolen goods in 1689 and 1690 respectively. The response from William's multiple kingdoms was complicated: Ireland in 1690 was still at war and had no clear government; the English Parliament placed an embargo on French wines effective beginning in 1690; the Scottish Parliament considered an embargo on French wine, but was loathe to cut off such an important source of revenue. However, in 1695 the Scottish Parliament ended its fiscal favoritism for French wine by raising the customs duty to £48 (Scots) per tun, whereas other wines still paid only £30 (Scots).[27] This measure brought the total wine duties on all wines to £84 (Scots). As French wine was the most popular wine in Scotland, the net effect of the tariff hike was that the volume of official wine imports decreased by a third from their 1680s levels.[28]

The Nine Years' War ended in 1697, but by 1701 war between William's three kingdoms and France loomed on the horizon once again, this time over the issue of the succession to the Spanish throne. In response, the Scottish Parliament banned the importation of French wines altogether in January 1701, although the ban did not go into effect until 1702.[29] Officially the prohibition against French wines was effective, because Bordeaux export figures to Scotland declined dramatically from over 1,000 tuns per year in 1699, 1700, and 1701, to zero tuns in 1702 and 1703.[30] However, a clause in the prohibiting act suggests that Scottish smugglers had already found the loophole so ably exploited by their English equivalents. The Scottish ban stated: "In case French wine be imported under the name of red wine from St. Sebastian," no such wine could be landed until "the crew swear that the wine is not French."[31] How effective this measure proved is uncertain.

Upon the death of William and the succession of Queen Anne, a new Scottish Parliament was elected and convened in 1703. This Parliament immediately proved to be beyond the control of the Duke of Queensberry, the Queen's Commissioner in Scotland. Specifically, a majority in the new Scottish Parliament refused to vote for money with which to pay the Scottish civil list (i.e. run the government), until its grievances were met. In particular, "Country" party members of the Scottish Parliament led by Andrew Fletcher of Saltoun wanted to pass an Act of Security, which asserted that the Scottish Parliament had the right to decide on Queen Anne's successor in Scotland, and that Scotland and England would not have the same sovereign unless England granted the Scots freedom of trade with England and all its overseas colonies. Most importantly, the Act of Security demanded guarantees for the security of Scottish religion, sovereignty, and trade. Queensberry refused to touch this act, but did consent to a somewhat less pointed "Act anent [i.e. concerning] Peace and War."[32] This latter act gave the Scottish Parliament the right to declare war and make peace on its own, even if the two nations continued to share a sovereign after Anne's death.

Nevertheless, Country bloc and Jacobite members of the Scottish Parliament wanted the more aggressive Act of Security, and both continued to look for ways to put pressure on the English to stop meddling in Scottish affairs. Meanwhile, the pro-government faction within the Scottish Parliament was still desperate for money with which to pay the civil list, and it was at this point that wine became caught in the maelstrom of Anglo-Scottish politics.

Having voted in 1701 to prohibit the importation of French wine, the Scottish Parliament had pleased both the Crown and English Parliament; but this was not the goal of the Scottish embargo. Instead, the ban was imposed by an independent Scottish Parliament in retaliation for French embargoes on fish and woolen cloth that had not been removed at the cessation of the Nine Years' War in 1697. However, by 1703, some Scots realized that French wine importation was a double-edged sword that could be swung equally well in the direction of the French and English. Because the 1701 prohibition of French wine in Scotland had not convinced the French to drop their embargoes against Scottish goods, Queensberry and the government bloc in the Scottish Parliament proposed a repeal of the prohibition on French wines as a way to increase imports and raise money through customs revenue. In other words, the Crown's representatives in the Scottish Parliament took the ironic position of promoting trade with the enemy, while the Country bloc of the Scottish Parliament objected to the measure on precisely the same grounds. As Fletcher of Saltoun asked in a speech before Parliament on September 13: "are we become greater friends to France now in a time of open war, than we were before in time of peace?"[33] Fletcher's patriotic stance in this instance was disingenuous, or at least underhanded, as his real goal, and that of the Country bloc, was to stop any form of funding so that the government would be forced to address the Act of Security.

In the end, however, the Court bloc in Parliament was joined by some Jacobites and the representatives of the burghs, many of whom appreciated the money raised by local revenues on wine, and thereby overcame the objections of the Country bloc, and thus the Wine Act was passed. French wines could once again be landed in Scotland, although they could not be purchased directly in France. While Fletcher's argument had a certain nationalist appeal, and he was joined in a formal protest against the act by the claret-loving Duke of Hamilton and the Marquess of Montrose,[34] there were enough members of the Scottish Parliament, Jacobites in particular, who saw the Wine Act as a different form of patriotic gesture because it annoyed the English.[35] As Fletcher sarcastically stated: "To repeal such a law [that prohibits French wine] in time of war [with France], will sound admirably well in England and Holland: since 'tis no less than a direct breach of our alliance with those nations."[36] For many Scottish Parliamentarians, both pro and anti-government, that was precisely the point. In other words, for some of its supporters the Wine Act was about raising money for the government, no matter how dishonorable the method, while for others it was clearly a way for the Scottish to have their claret and simultaneously send a message to the English that Scottish foreign policy was not beholden to English interests. And no doubt there were some for whom both of these motives were valid.

Not surprisingly, Fletcher's predictions proved correct. The English Parliament was angered that the Scottish Parliament would trade with the enemy in a time of war. Moreover, it was well known by Scottish and English politicians and wine merchants that some French wine coming to Scotland would be smuggled across the border to the detriment of the English Customs revenue. Nevertheless, the Queen's government in London found itself in the awkward position of assenting to the Wine Act in the belief that it would raise the money that the Scottish civil government needed in order to function. It should also be noted that the passion on both sides of the Wine Act debate was at least partially bombastic, because a clause in the act continued to exempt the "peers and barons" of Scotland from paying Customs duty on wine for their own use, a privilege they had held since 1582.[37] In other words, whatever the outcome was to be for regular Scottish consumers, the landowners who dominated the Scottish Parliament would still be getting their claret at a cut rate.

***

Historians have long recognized that the Wine Act highlighted problems in Anglo-Scottish relations, and as such was one of the pieces of legislation that helped to precipitate the Union of 1707. More immediately, however, the Wine Act had the effect of increasing the amount of French wine that was landed in Scotland. Leith Customs records do not exist for the years leading up to the Wine Act; however, Bordeaux records from October 1, 1699 to September 30, 1707 reveal that after 1703

Table 3.1 Bordeaux wine exports to Scotland (in tuns), October 1, 1699–September 30, 1707

1699–1700	1,050	(No embargo)
1700–1701	1,036	"
1701–1702	0	(Embargo in effect)
1702–1703	61	"
1703–1704	257	(Wine Act legalizes indirect trade)
1704–1705	953	(Indirect trade continues)
1705–1706	853	"
1706–1707	1,028	(Union begins May 1, 1707)

Source: Huetz de Lemps, *Géographie du Commerce*, pp. 147–9.

there was an increase to pre-prohibition levels, despite the fact that the Wine Act only allowed for indirect trade with France (see Table 3.1). Perhaps most significant of all, however, was the long-term effect of the Wine Act, which has gone largely unrecognized by Scottish historians: claret became a commodity with which to defy the English.[38]

Wine and the Union of 1707

Just as English merchants and customs officials feared, some of the French wine that was landed in Scotland made its way across the border, either smuggled in directly or sold legally as Iberian wine. This system of "free" or "fair" trading, as it was known in Scotland, was annoying not only to English customs officers; it frustrated Leith administrators as well, because merchants who intended to send their wine to England refused to pay the Leith impost on the grounds that the wine was being re-exported. However, there was nothing other than the word of the merchant to guarantee that wine landed at Leith was actually going to England. In this circumstance, some Scottish merchants claimed they were sending the wine south of the border simply to avoid paying the local impost. As a result, tensions between Leith officials and merchants rode high until October 26, 1705 when the Leith Council ruled that

> it shall be lawfull to the merchant burgesses of Edinburgh … to send all sorts of wine from Leith to the south country … free of impost providing the said wines be carried straight from Leith Wynd up the same and down St. Mary's Wynd without stopping, or lodging in any other place except the waiter's lodge.[39]

The precise wording of this declaration reveals that a great deal of wine supposedly going from Leith to England had in fact already been re-landed just outside of Leith harbor, to be sold in Edinburgh. That said, some wine imported into Scotland was re-exported to England, but the quantity cannot be known. Certainly it was not enough to change the growing belief among Scots in England that the claret-deprived English drank inferior wine. Writing from London in 1705, William Clelland lamented in a letter to James Erskine, Lord Grange, that "All the wine here

is poison'd and all the women pox't at least I would fain fancie so whylst I have
no monie."[40] Clelland's self-mocking opinion aside, the Scottish wine trade with
England must have proved lucrative to some Scottish merchants—and no doubt to
some English as well—because when the terms of the Union were announced in the
winter of 1706–7, many merchants scrambled to increase their stocks of claret before
the customs duty was increased to the English level, as per the Treaty. Specifically,
Article VI of the Treaty of Union stipulated that all parts of Britain should be

> under the same prohibitions, restrictions and regulations of trade, and liable
> to the same Customs and duties on import and export; and that the duties and
> allowances in force in England when the Union commenced, should take place
> throughout the whole kingdom.[41]

Local governments could still apply their own imposts, but with the exception of
wine imported into London, which continued to be charged almost four pounds
more per tun than wine arriving any other port in England, Wales, and Scotland,
customs duties for wine were essentially the same throughout the new kingdom
of Great Britain.

With the implementation of Treaty on the horizon, savvy Scottish wine importers jumped at the opportunity to buy low and sell high; and not surprisingly,
English merchants protested. "Sir, I need to inform you," wrote a so-called Scots
factor in London, "that the extraordinary import of foreign goods into your
country, makes a great noise here [in England]."[42] The English Parliament—or
rather, as the author wrote, "The Wine Merchants, and other traders, who are
members of the House of Commons, together with the interest of others" outside
Parliament—

> exclaim mightily against the fraudulent practices now used to bring into this
> kingdom through Scotland, several commodities for easy duties, which pay
> much here; representing that fair traders will be ruined, and the government
> cheated thereby. ... [Others] who are for peace and ease to all concern'd in
> trafique are satisfy'd, that a general indemnity, or general indulgence, be granted
> for this once to all who have brought goods into Scotland on this occasion.

The conspicuous fact that the "letter" was published in London and not in
Edinburgh correctly suggests that it was an exposé of supposed Scottish stockpiling, the details of which were meant to anger *English* wine merchants.[43] So too was
the author's counterfeit conclusion:

> Whatever loss it may occasion to English men and forrigners [sic], it will be
> a sensible advantage to your merchants and traders, who by this means will
> have their rivals restricted, or brought under very unequal duties; and possible
> some artifices may be faln [sic] on, whereby goods of the forrigners [sic] may
> be disposed off by your merchants; which will be a further advantage to them,
> providing they can do it honestly.[44]

Obviously, the opportunity to exploit the uneven tariff levels that existed on the eve of the Union was not news to Scottish merchants; it was precisely the reason they were stockpiling so much French wine. In fact, Scottish importation of wines from France peaked in fiscal year 1706–07, at over 1,000 tuns. But honest artifices are hard to come by, and this is precisely what the author meant to reveal. The angry English wine merchants knew that contrary to the terms of the Scottish Wine Act, which officially allowed only for indirect trade with France, the Scots were importing large amounts of French wine directly from Bordeaux with the full intention of selling some of it to England once the Treaty of Union was implemented. In other words, by hoarding French wine before the Union went into effect on May 1, 1707, Scottish merchants were openly contravening a Scottish law to engage in claret arbitrage with the English.[45]

This activity aroused so much commotion in London that a bill was introduced in the English Parliament to prohibit the importation of wine from Scotland once the Union came into effect. In turn, the considerable number of Scots merchants who had invested in claret grew anxious. On April 22, 1707, Lord Grange wrote to his brother the Earl of Mar, who was busy smoothing out the terms of the Union in London: "People here [in Scotland] are in great uncertainty in that affair by the votes of the Commons, and no body knows whether to think they will allow the importation [of wine] or not." Nor was Grange only concerned with the plight of Scottish merchants; his brother's cellar in London was also at stake in the matter. "I wish you may write particularly about your wine, as soon as conveniency allows, that we may know what to do with it."[46]

Similarly, the Earl of Northesk was concerned for the Scottish merchants and their wine-laden ships, writing on May 26 that "tho they tootched Scotes ground, they won't be allowed to enter [England]." And he joined Grange in his personal concern for Mar's wine drinking in London: "you don't know how much you are oblidged [*sic*] this day to me, for I have been most of the afternoon with my Lord Grange and Davie Areskine [*sic*] tasting wine for you," to which he felt compelled to add, "I have no other apology for writing so confusedly to you."[47] The result of the men's afternoon exertions on behalf of Mar was not only minor intoxication, they also selected three tuns of claret, one pipe of canary, 16 gallons of brandy and a small amount of sherry.[48] However, Davie Erskine prevaricated on paying for the wines on account of "the English resolutions, which will have great influence upon the prices."[49] While Scottish merchants waited for the decision of the English Parliament regarding the legality of importing wine from Scotland, over 40 vessels loaded with French wine and brandy in Leith harbor were temporarily impounded by what were now British, and not Scottish, Customs officials.[50]

As it happened, the English Parliament found a ban on wines from Scotland too onerous and impolitic to implement. After all, England and Scotland had just become the new Kingdom of Great Britain, even though the first combined British Parliament would not sit until the autumn of 1707. Nevertheless, Scottish fears about their wine were not easily allayed. As Grange anxiously stated in a letter to his brother on June 10:

> I hope that after goods have been entered at the Customs House here as coming from such or such a port, that it will not be further enquired into at their being carry'd into England whether or no they really came from these ports: for the most part of our wine has com'd directly from Fr___ yet I believe it is entered as from Lisbonne, Holland or some such place, our own law not allowing trade with Fr___.[51]

By late June, however, Grange reported to Mar that "People here seem now to be pretty well satisfy'd as the wines and other prohibited goods." And with the issue settled, Erskine sent Mar's wine to London.[52]

***

Daniel Defoe, who resided in Edinburgh during the period of debate and implementation of the Treaty of Union, claimed that the furor over Scottish wine importation was overblown, and in fact that it was English, not Scottish merchants who had been importing large amounts of wine into Leith for the purpose of selling it in the south.[53] Despite these efforts, said Defoe,

> here in the *North,* where I assure you, Gentlemen, the good people drink very heartily; and where the Nobility and Gentry have laid in great stores of Clarret, some a Tun, some two, some three Tun of Clarret, and a proportion of Brandy ... there cannot be 800 Tun of Wine spared there to go for *England;* and a great deal of that is a small thin Sort of Wine, which will not suit the *English* market, or bear a price encouraging the export.[54]

The evidence bears Defoe out; Scottish imports of claret increased prior to the Union, but not enough to flood the English market (see Table 3.1) as the English Parliament feared.

How much claret was illegally imported is of course unknown, but certainly some was. For instance, a notice for an auction in the *London Gazette* in March 1708 was probably for smuggled claret that had been seized by Customs officials:

> On Friday the 19th March 1707 [1708 n.s.] will be exposed to sale at Lloyds coffee house, in Lombard Street about 30 hogsheads of Graus [Graves] claret and 40 punchions of Bordeaux Brandy, lately imported from Scotland.[55]

Whatever the exact story with this wine, Scottish merchants continued to supply English markets with claret long after the arbitrage scheme of 1707 had run its course. Writing to *The Times* in 1807, the much-traveled Scottish wine merchant William Ballantyne wrote:

> As late as 1770, when at York, Newcastle and Durham on the East; and Manchester on the West, I found all the five Northern [English] counties supplied from Edinburgh and Leith.[56]

At least officially, however, after 1707 all wine paid the same amount of import duty whether it arrived in Scotland or England.

What is more certain is that during the run-up to the implementation of the Treaty of Union, claret's symbolism in Scotland as a commodity with which to defy the English was solidified. From that position, claret was but one step away from representing Scottish national identity, even if that identity took many forms. Thus, by 1707 importing and drinking claret in defiance of English, and soon British laws, pleased the Scots on two grounds: they liked claret, and it irked the English.

Part II
Claret

4
"The interest of the nation lay against it so visibly"

Claret, Port, and English National Interest, 1702–1714

It seems a losing political argument to suggest that the fate of a nation rests upon the type of wine its subjects drink. And yet, that was precisely the claim of both Tories and Whigs in a debate that lasted throughout Queen Anne's reign and climaxed just before her demise. Tories argued that France produced the best and least expensive wines (so long as the tariffs were equal with other nations), and that all attempts to prohibit trade with France or discourage trade through high tariffs had only led to massive levels of fraud and smuggling. This deprived the English government of revenue and undermined the authority of the state by encouraging merchants and consumers to break the law. Moreover, maintaining prohibitive tariffs on French goods meant perpetual enmity with France, which meant more wars and high land taxes to pay for them.

The Tories had a point, but for Whigs these arguments were political folly. Whigs argued instead, that if free trade with France was allowed, the English liked French wine so much that they would sink their own economy and enrich the kingdom of France, which Whigs passionately believed posed an existential threat to England's mixed constitutional government. However, if the English purchased the bulk of their wine from Portugal—and there was no question among the elite and middling sorts that wine from *somewhere* was necessary—this was a way to guarantee the Portuguese market for English cloth, and stifle the power and wealth of mighty Bourbon France.

To be sure, this historically overlooked debate about wine during the reign of Queen Anne was part of a larger argument about political economy in general, and the wisdom of trade with France in particular. The latter debate came to a head in 1713 when Tories and Whigs argued over a Commercial Treaty with France that was proposed by Queen Anne's Tory ministry under the leadership of the Earl of Oxford and Viscount Bolingbroke. Despite Tory leadership in the House of Commons, 76 Tory MPs ultimately abandoned Oxford and Bolingbroke to vote against the bill to implement the Commercial Treaty, and all subsequent attempts to revive the issue failed.[1] Thus claret, England's erstwhile "common draught," was entrenched as a luxury good. Meanwhile, port, the red wine of Portugal that was offered by merchants as a substitute for inexpensive claret, became the tavern wine of England. Furthermore, as a result of arguments made by Whigs during the Commercial Treaty debate, port joined the Protestant Succession, the primacy of Parliament, and hatred of France as part of a triumphant idea of Englishness, and later Anglo-Britishness, that remained prevalent well into the nineteenth century.

There is, of course, a wonderful irony in the fact that "English" port came from a foreign and zealously Roman Catholic country. But just as French claret became "Scottish" because drinking it was seen to defy English laws imposed by the Union, port became "English" in Whig minds because it replaced claret as the common draught of English wine drinkers, and, therefore, denied money to France. And anything that hurt France was deemed by Whigs to be in England's national interest. Nevertheless, Whig leaders who clamored to maintain high tariffs on French wines and promoted port as the patriotic wine for the mass of English wine drinkers drew a distinction between the national interest and personal taste. Their own preference was for French wine, claret most of all.

The Methuen Treaty

The war that ended in 1713 with the triumph of Tory statecraft and Whig economics—and secured port's position atop the English market—began over the issue of the succession to the Spanish throne. When the inbred, impotent, and dolorous King Carlos II died in late 1700 he had no clear successor. Carlos had written in his will that the heir to the Spanish throne was Louis XIV's grandson, Philippe, Duke of Anjou. Louis happily concurred. This claim was based on the fact that Louis's deceased wife, and Philippe's grandmother, was Maria Theresa, Princess of Spain and half-sister to Carlos. The Castillian Spanish and Bavarians agreed to this succession; however, William III, who was king of England, Ireland, Scotland, and Stadtholder of most of the most powerful provinces in the Netherlands, joined forces with the Holy Roman Emperor (and most of his dominions), the Duke of Savoy and the Aragonese Spanish, to support the more tenuous claim to the Spanish throne of Archduke Charles of Austria. Thus, when Louis XIV added Portugal to his list of allies in late 1701, it was a severe blow to William III and his Grand Alliance against France. Without Portugal, the Grand Alliance had only a tenuous foothold on the Iberian Peninsula, and Aragon, the foothold, was hardly secure. Moreover, if Portugal remained allied to France, that increased the risk to English and Dutch ships as they sailed south to catch the Atlantic trade winds or attempted to enter the narrow mouth of the Mediterranean Sea.

As the mastermind of the struggle against a Bourbon universal monarchy, William believed it was imperative to win back the Portuguese. For this task he called upon John Methuen, the son of a Bradford-on-Avon clothier who had lived in Lisbon from 1691 to 1696 as a member of the English legation. However, just before his special envoy to Portugal departed, William famously died of complications stemming from a hunting accident; his horse, Sorrel, stepped in a molehill, tumbled, and tossed the king to the ground. Dead within a fortnight, William had nevertheless initiated one of his most lasting diplomatic policies. With cash in hand, Methuen, along with the Dutch ambassador and the dissident Almirante of Castile, succeeded in convincing King Pedro II of Portugal that his country's interests lay not with a mighty Bourbon empire, but rather with the Grand Alliance.[2] As a result, two political treaties were signed between England, Portugal, and the Netherlands in early 1703. The first asserted Archduke Charles's right to the Spanish throne, while the second fastened the military alliance between the three signatory nations. This is exactly what William III had wanted, and precisely what Queen Anne and her ministers got.

But after the two political treaties were ratified by their respective governments, the emboldened Methuen proposed a third treaty between England and Portugal uniquely, one that would cement the two nations' commercial relationship. Methuen the diplomat had been a successful woolen merchant, and with his own interests in mind he imagined in Portugal a new market for English cloth despite the fact that Portugal, like other European nations, jealously guarded its own small cloth industry against foreign competition. However, Portugal was geographically vulnerable and badly needed English assistance to keep the Spanish from taking over, as they had from 1580 to 1640. What Methuen needed, then, was to sweeten the deal just enough to convince the Portuguese to open up their domestic and colonial markets to English cloth.

Without receiving permission from Queen Anne or her ministers, Methuen took it upon himself to promise a favorable market advantage for Portuguese wines if the Portuguese would end their prohibitive tariffs on English cloth. Famously brief, the Anglo-Portuguese Commercial Treaty of 1703 stated:

> His Sacred Royal Majesty of Portugal promises, in his own Name, and in the Names of his Successors, that there shall be admitted at all times into Portugal, woolen cloths, and the other woolen manufactures of England, no otherwise than they used to be, before they were prohibited by Pragmatical Sanctions (i.e. sumptuary laws) … [for which in return] her sacred Royal Majesty of Great Britain be obliged in her own Name, and in the Name of her Successors, at all times to admit into England, Wines gathered from the Vineyards belonging to the Portugal Dominions, as that at no time … any more shall be demanded for such wines … than what shall, after deducting a third part of the Customs or Impost, be demanded from a like quantity of French Wine.[3]

In short, Portugal would remove all prohibitions on English cloth and England would impose at least one-third less duty on Portuguese wines than on French wines. That was the entire treaty. It said nothing about wines from Spain, the Holy Roman Empire, or anywhere else. Nor did it stipulate a maximum amount of duty the English could place on Portuguese wines. Nevertheless, by denying most-favored nation to status to French wines, the Methuen Treaty was setting in stone the very recent changes in English fiscal policy. It was therefore a risk for Methuen to offer these terms before consulting his government, but he felt assured that the Parliament elected in 1702, despite being predominantly Tory, would favor a treaty that opened a new market to England and hampered French wines during a time of war.

As it happened, Methuen gambled correctly. Tory opponents of the treaty could not afford to reject what Methuen and the Portuguese were offering lest they be accused of aiding and abetting the enemy. Consequently, in December 1703, Parliament ratified the Anglo-Portuguese trade agreement, which came to be known as *the* Methuen Treaty, although in truth it was one of three treaties negotiated by Methuen. The venerable historian G. M. Trevelyan called these treaties

> the most important group of diplomatic documents signed between the Grand Alliance in 1701 and the Peace of Utrecht. ... They remained the basis of England's power in southern Europe till the days of Nelson and Wellington, and affected her commercial policy down to the era of the Great Reform Bill [of 1832].[4]

And it was the third of these treaties that became an icon of Whig foreign policy, despite the fact that it was ratified by a majority-Tory Parliament. Even more ironically, and as we shall see, the iconic status of the so-called Methuen Treaty and of the port wine it promoted was far more a result of the arguments about the treaty in 1712–14 than of the initial treaty itself.[5]

The interest of the nation?

Having secured the Portuguese market with a commercial treaty in 1703, Parliament immediately asserted its right to raise duties on wines as a way to raise revenue for the war. In 1704 and 1705 respectively, the "One-third" and "Two-thirds Subsidy Acts" were passed, which raised the duties on all wines by more than £3.[6] These tariffs brought the duty on Portuguese wines to more than £25 per tun, on Spanish and Italian wines to over £26, on Rhenish wines to more than £30, and on French wines to nearly £55. While the Portuguese were dismayed to discover that the English would so readily exploit the open terms of the Methuen Treaty, they were pleased that Portuguese wines paid 54 percent less duty than French wines, which was far greater than the one-third difference necessitated by the treaty.[7] Furthermore, in late 1704 yet another embargo was placed on "all trade and commerce with France" and declared to be in force during the continuation of the war.[8] This new embargo was successful in reducing the already diminished legal importation of French wines, a trend that is revealed in the import figures during the years just prior to and during the new prohibition (See Graph 4.1).

Of course, some degree of fraud and smuggling continued, and this, said Tories, was emphatically not in the national interest. In fact, smuggling remained common enough that a House of Lords committee was established in 1704—the very first year of the embargo—to investigate the problem, if not also to embarrass the Whigs.[9] However, this came to naught. Moreover, new Parliaments in 1705 and 1708 were Whig-leaning, and thus showed little interest in undoing the prohibition. But when an overwhelmingly Tory Parliament was elected in 1710 on the promise that it would end the war, it wasted little time in seeking a complete repeal of the embargo against French goods. "It hath been by experience found

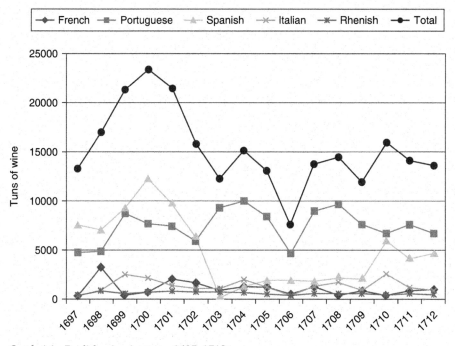

Graph 4.1 English wine imports, 1697–1712
Source: JHC, XVII, 365. Figures for 1697 are for the period October 1, 1696 until September 30, 1697, and figures for 1698 are for the period October 1, 1697 until December 25, 1698. All other figures are taken from Christmas to Christmas.

that the prohibition of French wines to be imported in to this Kingdom or Ireland, is injurious to your Majesty's revenue and many ways prejudicial to your subjects,"[10] stated the act that ended the embargo. Clearly, this act was in line with Tory politics, but to the extent that fraud, smuggling,[11] and adulteration actually occurred,[12] it was not merely party politics to assert that prohibiting French wines was a dubious tool of both fiscal and foreign policy.

Whether the embargo against French wines hurt the French economy more than the English (and after 1707, British) is debatable. However, Whigs remained convinced that as France posed a political and economic threat, an embargo against French wine was imperative for the survival of England. Gilbert Burnet, the Bishop of Salisbury and an outspoken Whig, wrote that the 1711 act to repeal the prohibition against French wine passed, although "not much to the honour of those who promoted it," inasmuch as "the interest of the nation lay against it so visibly, that nothing but the delicate palates of those who loved that liquor, could have carried such a motion through the two houses."[13] Similarly, in the Whig journal, *The Spectator*, Abraham Froth (i.e. Sir Richard Steele) wrote regarding the same act:

Verily, Mr. *Spectator,* we are much offended at the Act for Importing *French* Wines: A Bottle or two of good solid Edifying Port, at Honest *George's* made a

Night Cheerful, and threw off Reserve. But this plaguy *French* Claret, will not only cost us more Mony, but do us less good: Had we been aware of it before it had gone too far, I must tell you we would have petitioned to be heard on that subject.[14]

No one could deny that a bottle or two of port, a naturally strong wine and in some cases already fortified with a dash of brandy,[15] was better at "throwing off reserve" (i.e. getting one drunk) than a similar quantity of claret; but not all Whigs were swayed by this bacchic rationale. In fact, Steele was merely playing to the crowd. Two years later, when a commercial treaty with France was a topic of popular and Parliamentary discussion, Steele condemned the treaty on all but one ground, saying: "Things that are of absolute Necessity cannot be reckoned prejudicial to a Nation; but *France* produces nothing that is necessary, or even convenient, or but which we had better be without, except claret."[16]

In fact, leading Whigs like Steele were so torn by the prospect of readily available and inexpensive claret that in 1708, when they were in control of the newly combined British Parliament, a bill for the importation of French wines as an exception to the embargo on French goods was introduced by Tories and nearly passed a House of Commons vote.[17] And once the Tories succeeded in removing the embargo in 1711, there existed a very real possibility that they would carry things one step further by dropping the high tariffs on French wines and thereby break the Methuen Treaty with Portugal. The Whigs, who wanted to continue prosecuting the war so long as the Duke of Anjou remained on the Spanish throne, warned Queen Anne and her favorite minister Robert Harley not to be seduced by the prospect of French wines; or, in the words of one contemporary poem, "To send you the Wines the best that France affords, / To soften the Edge of your all conquering Sword."[18]

However, the Tory ministry under Harley and Henry St John was encouraged by the prospect of peace and good wine, and, just as the Whigs feared, they pushed for the end of the war and a treaty of trade and commerce with France. To most Whigs this was a perfidious act and another opportunity to decry the supposed foolishness of Tory policy that would sell English interests for the sake of French wine. As an anti-treaty ballad sarcastically cried:

> Here be de Portugueze, make Peace in good time,
> And here be de brave English a Toping French Wine.
> ...
> Here be de High Church [i.e. Tories] make Bonefire and Noise,
> And here be de Whig shake his head and be wise.
> Oh raree show, O pretty show, O fine Gallantie show![19]

The Commercial Treaty

Popular Whig propaganda did not succeed in perpetuating a war from which Anne's Tory ministry and most of the English political nation had grown tired; nor were the Whigs successful in keeping a commercial treaty off the agenda at Utrecht, the Dutch city where the various belligerent parties gathered in early 1712 to make peace. By the summer of 1712 the pace of negotiations picked up, and the British government was represented by Harley (now 1st Earl of Oxford) and St John (now 1st Viscount Bolingbroke). Over hysterical Whig cries of "No peace without Spain!" (i.e. without a non-Bourbon monarch on the Spanish throne), peace was signed in April 1713. But the treaty was not a simple one, and among the many complex strands of the agreement was a proposed British–French commercial arrangement. However, unlike the treaty to end the war, the Commercial Treaty required the approval of Parliament because it called for amending tariff rates—which was Parliament's jurisdiction—and from the start this was a hard sell. In particular, the Commercial Treaty entailed a mutual grant of most favored nation status and a removal by both kingdoms of tariffs and prohibitions directed at each other's manufactures since 1664.[20] Crucially, the French were allowed to maintain the tariff levels of 1699 on British woolen goods, although "commissaries" were to be established to settle the question of this and other excepted duties in the future.

In theory, therefore, implementation of the Commercial Treaty would mean that France would import large amounts of British hosiery, tin goods, leather, and most especially, woolen cloth, while British consumers would purchase large amounts of French silk, linens, ribbon and most especially, wine. But therein lay the rub; since the 1660s anti-French merchants and politicians in England had been promoting the idea that England always suffered an "over-balance" [i.e. deficit] of trade with France, and because the French insisted on maintaining a degree of protection for their own woolen industry, the English penchant for French wine would mean a one-way transfer of money that would make previous overbalances look piddling by comparison.[21] Moreover, it was quickly pointed out by the Portuguese ambassador in London that England (now Great Britain) still had a treaty with Portugal that guaranteed Portuguese wines a 33 percent fiscal advantage over wines from France. If this treaty were broken, there would be no guaranteed Portuguese market for British cloth.[22]

The debate begins in earnest

In preparation for the discussion surrounding the Commercial Treaty Bill, the Tory Parliament commissioned a report in July 1711 from the Inspector General of Customs, Charles Davenant, a Tory, although a moderate one. Davenant began his two-part report by attacking the idea that England had an unfavorable balance of trade with France. Instead, he concluded that an "over-balance" of trade with France, while rarely in fact the case, was not necessarily a bad thing for England. Many commodities had to be purchased abroad, and in some cases they were cheapest in France. Certainly this was true with wine, which was traditionally England's primary import from France in terms of both volume and cost. Therefore, argued Davenant, "unless Reasons of State intervene, the body of a Trading Nation collectively considered, is to look out where foreign goods are to be had at the lowest Prime Cost; which is not only National Gain, but profitable to the Merchant."[23] What was important was England's "Universal Trade; whereof nothing can be stronger than the mint accounts, Bullion being the true superlucration in Foreign Traffick, and Plenty of Bullion occasioning a great coinage."[24] On this account, Davenant claimed that England performed very well, especially from the Restoration up to 1688, since which time the wars with France had slowly drained England of coin.[25] In other words, it was Whig war, not Tory trade, that caused England's economic problems.

As for wine, Davenant's *Report* showed that it was France's chief natural product, and had been for many years England's chief import from that country, but that now "we are fall'n to deal with Spain, Portugal and Italy for that commodity which serves the *Middle Rank of Men*, (who must always be reckoned the greatest Consumptioners) as well as French Wine, and as to Brandies, that our own Home-made Spirits are come into their place."[26] Combined English and Welsh import figures from a subsequent report Davenant submitted to Parliament on May 21, 1713, illustrated his point. Officially at least, during the period December 1702 to December 1712, which corresponds very nearly to the period of fighting, Portuguese wines comprised 58 percent of the total, Spanish wines 22 percent, and Italian wines 9 percent, or together, 89 percent of all imports. French wines, meanwhile, accounted for only 7 percent of the total (Graph 4.2).[27]

In other words, from Davenant's perspective, lower tariffs on French wine would open the sluice gates and flood England with claret, but the result would be less expensive and superior wine for all English consumers, and "national gain," in that wealthy and populous France, as opposed to relatively poor Portugal, would constitute England's most important export market for woolen cloth and other British manufactures.[28] Moreover, Davenant believed that the benefits of

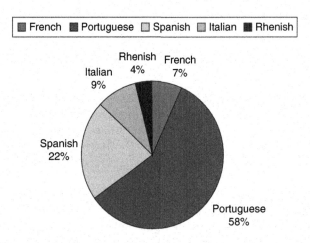

Graph 4.2   Percentage of English wine imports during the war, 1702–12
Source: JHC, XVII, 365.

Anglo-French trade extended well beyond the cheaper price of wine. Without free trade between the two nations, Davenant concluded,

> there can be no Sound and Compleat Peace, so that when ever the war deter-
> mines, their natural interest will incline 'em to listen to terms of a fair com-
> mercial treaty, such as ought to be between countries, who have no intentions
> to enter into a new war. ... A Free Trade with France can never be dangerous to
> England, and as to an Over-Ballance, that nation will have it, who has the most
> convenient ports, whose people are most industrious and best skill'd in the
> affairs of Traffick, and who most abound in the Natural or Artificial Products,
> necessary to the common uses and ornaments of life.[29]

As it happened, France's relative abundance of "Natural or Artificial Products," of which wine was the primary example, became the principal reason for fearful Whigs to fight against Davenant's recommendations for free trade with France. But at the time that Davenant submitted his initial report in December 1712, the debate was only beginning.

Davenant's economic views were forcefully stated, and he had greater access to import and export figures than his opponents. Nevertheless, he was fighting an uphill battle even as the actual fighting was grinding to a halt. The idea of free trade was not entirely new; it had been mooted by economic theorists in the 1690s. But by 1700 the prevalent school of political economy, among Tories and Whigs alike, believed that trade between nations was a contest over an allegedly fixed number of markets.[30] In this ideological environment, England's goal was to secure markets for its manufactured goods, as well as the products of its empire. If successful, the end result would be a favorable balance of trade.[31] Tories like Davenant believed that the best way to promote English manufacturing was to expand trade with nations like France that had a large market for English domestic goods and could provide England with things it desired but could not produce. For Davenant the Dutch were England's greatest economic rivals precisely because their manufacturing and trading strengths were identical to England's. And with a fixed number of markets only one of the two nations could win. Davenant bluntly stated the Tory perspective in the second vol-ume of his report, when he wrote that the Dutch were "beyond all disputes, are our most dangerous rivals in trade."[32] As always, free traders had their limits.

Whigs were just as adamant as Tories about the idea that England was a trading nation, and that the most important aspect of political economy was to find out-lets for British manufactures. However, Whigs firmly believed that France, not the Netherlands, posed the greatest economic and political threat. To purchase large amounts of French wine, as both the English and Scottish were wont to do, would mean a negative balance of trade because the French would not buy as much British cloth as the British would buy French wine. The logic of this argument was articulated by Daniel Defoe in the *Review* in 1708:

> if you lower the Duties, the Cheapness of the French Wine, and the Suitableness
> of it to the Gust and Inclination of the people is such, that we shall import

such Quantities, as will in a prodigious manner, over ballance our Export in Manufactures; and any Body may state the Consequence, *viz.* That the ballance must go from us in Money, which is manifestly to our Damage.

At present all our Wine Trade runs to our Advantage, Portugal and Spain take our Goods for their wine; and in that case no Import can hurt us, nothing can injure England in trade, that encreases the Consumption of the English Manufacture.[33]

In other words, Defoe believed that his fellow countrymen liked claret more than was healthy for the economic good of the nation. But as the War of the Spanish Succession dragged on, Defoe began to change his tune and his party allegiance. On May 16, 1713, with a vote on the Commercial Treaty Bill pending before Parliament, he argued on behalf of the Tory government:

That upon a Peace some of our high duties upon French goods, may be taken off without detriment to our trade, nay ought, for the advantage of Commerce, be taken off, is most certain. That all additional duties cannot be taken off, without ruining our trade in some of its capital articles, seems to me natural, and I cannot think any one will dispute it; a Treaty then, of Mediums and Proportions may most certainly bring this to a beneficial Period; Equalities always are the Foundation of Right; and Proportions, like weight for inches, among the horse-racers, bring every difference to an Agreement.[34]

Three days later in the *Review*, Defoe was even closer to the idea of open trade with France:

Now the French, it seems, do not demand to pay less than the Portuguese; I do not say it might have been better to have had a difference in favour of the Portugal Wine, but if you ask a freedom of trade into France, would you give nothing as an Equivalent? Can you expect the French to reduce all their duties, and you to keep all yours on?[35]

More passionate Tories and their wine-merchant allies who stood to gain from trade with France submitted their own published petition to Parliament in the form of five queries:

1. Whether the laws in force have effectually prevented the importation of Burgundy, Champagne, and Claret, for many years past, *sine custom*? [i.e. without paying Customs duties].
2. Whether such importation of French wines, together with what is legally brought hither from North Britain [i.e. Scotland], has either been prejudicial to the woollen manufacture, or totally ruin'd the Portugal trade, as some merchants did insinuate?
3. Whether Portugal has not annually found a vend for all the wine fit for exportation? And whether the vintners, excluding others, have not yearly been

induc'd, out of necessity or interest, to make use of cyder, malt-spirits, sweets, and other viler liquors, to lengthen out the common draught?

4. Since many people in Great Britain will not drink port, but rather find means to get in French wine, tho' paid for in specie, whether such practices, or the exchanging our tobacco, sugar, fish, etc., for French wine, will most conduce to the true interest of the kingdom and its plantations?

5. Why the British subjects should be under a necessity of drinking worse wine than the neighbouring nations, at four times the price?[36]

In what amounted to a very short petition, every major argument for open trade with France was clearly presented, and by the logic involved there was much to be gained and nothing to be lost but smuggling, fraud, adulteration, and uniquely high prices for French wine. In other words, ratifying the treaty was the best course for the nation because British subjects preferred French wines and were determined to get them at whatever economic or social cost.

The anti-Treaty argument

The problem, of course, was not only that Whigs disagreed with Tory logic, but that England's embargoes, wars, tariff increases, and treaties since 1678 had created a formidable group of merchants who traded to Portugal and other Southern European nations, and who stood to lose by increased trade with France.[37] These merchants published diverse petitions and pamphlets—in fact far more than their opponents—stating their own arguments against the treaty, which can be summarized as follows:

• if the duty on French wine is equalized, then the Methuen Treaty will be broken and the advantages of the Portuguese trade lost;

• the trade with Portugal, Spain, and Italy is beneficial to England because these countries purchase a variety of English goods, most especially woolen cloth, grain, dried fish, lead, leather, and tin, and the balance of trade with these nations is very much in England's favor;

• if England does not purchase wine from these countries, especially Portugal, then English ships will come home empty, which in turn will ruin the cod trade, because much Portuguese wine is re-exported to Newfoundland, where the wine is sold for cod, the dried variety of which is re-exported to Southern Europe;

• and finally, if three pence per quart difference in duty on wine is enough to secure the good will of the Portuguese, it is worth keeping, in order "that we will not lose the exportation of so noble a manufacture [as cloth] for such a trifle."[38]

In short, anti-treaty merchants, most of whom were Whig, responded by saying that they had the better balance-of-trade argument.[39]

Petitions by the Portugal merchants unabashedly claimed that they had the national interest in mind, while pro-treaty merchants were only looking out for their own selfish interests.[40] This assertion was based upon a fundamental agreement with their political opponents. To wit, despite many years of drinking Spanish, Italian, and most recently, Portuguese wines, the English still preferred wines from France. As one anti-treaty writer stated, French wines "being more agreeable to the generality of British Palates ... will be almost the only Wines in request, and become the Common Draught in every Tavern."[41] Consequently, admitting French wines upon an equal footing would mean the reduction and even bankruptcy of loyal merchants whose trade brought gold and silver to England. Furthermore, the French trade would drain England of specie because the English would buy far more wine from France than the French would buy cloth and other items from England. Once again, Burnet summarized the Whig view:

> but if the duties were, according to this treaty of commerce, to be made equal, then considering the difference of freight, which is more than double from Portugal, the French wines would be much cheaper; and the nation generally liking them better, by this means we should not only break our treaties with Portugal, but if we did not take off their wines, we must lose their trade, which was at present the most advantageous that we drove any where for, besides a great vent of manufactures, we brought over yearly great returns of gold from thence; four, five, six hundred thousand pounds a year.[42]

Despite these Whig arguments, and partly because of English consumer preference for French wine, the bill to ratify the commercial treaty sailed through the Tory-dominated House of Commons (by 146 to 12) on its first reading on May 28, 1713. In a panicky response, Whigs called upon the Huguenot refugee and successful financier Theodore Janssen to rebut Tory arguments. He dutifully asserted that free trade with France was guaranteed to create an "overbalance" in France's favor.[43] Proponents of the treaty referred to Davenant's *Report* to argue otherwise, and sought to expose Janssen's statistics as fraudulent, which they were.[44] But it was the Tories who continued to fight an uphill battle. As we recall, by the early 1670s the majority of the English political nation had come to believe that France posed a greater existential threat to England than did the Netherlands.[45] For these people, the idea of an overbalance with France was "true" simply because France was so obviously England's enemy. England's national interest was whatever was bad for France. This Francophobia found expression in innumerable pamphlets, broadsheets, sermons, and essays before, during, and after the Treaty of Utrecht negotiations and the Commercial Treaty debate, and was mockingly summarized by a Tory critic in a 1712 issue of the *Examiner*:

> This nation has been so long engaged in War with the French, that some of our unthinking Britons have contracted a kind of personal Malice against them; never considering, that if our Country be ruined, it is perfectly indifferent to us, whether it be done by the French, the Dutch, the Germans, the Turk, the Devil or the Pope. But they think perhaps it is impossible with regard

to the advantage of Britain, that the French should be too much crushed and confounded.[46]

Clearly, if one agreed with the Whigs that France was England's existential enemy, than Whig anti-treaty policy was in the national interest, and pro-treaty Tories were questionably loyal to their nation. In fact, one anti-treaty pamphleteer was more than willing to wonder out loud where Defoe's loyalty lay: "How much soever he would be thought a Patriot of England, he will hardly be able to persuade thinking Men that he is not a hired factor for France."[47] Another Whig propagandist responded with feigned disbelief to the pro-treaty argument that the duty on French wine should be lowered because the current duty encouraged fraud: "But sure this Reason can never weigh with any thing that has the Name of a Gentleman, and far less with a PATRIOT, when he sees 'tis against the true interest of this Country."[48] "Whimsical" Tories were not immune to this logic or politically protected from it, and ultimately this made for a powerful anti-Treaty brew.[49]

As May moved into June, the trickle of petitions to Parliament from English towns involved in the woolen trade became a flood. These petitions argued, as had the Portugal merchants, that trade with Portugal was beneficial to England, and if French wines were admitted at the same rate as Portuguese, Portugal would reimpose prohibitive tariffs on English woolens. Soon representatives from other manufacturing industries began to chime in as well. Silk weavers, distillers, linen weavers, and gold and silver thread makers all protested that trade with France would be their ruin and that of all England.[50]

Most of all, however, it was members of the woolen and silk trade who feared the results of the treaty. For those involved in the former trade, from landowners who grazed sheep, to carders, dyers, spinners, weavers, and cloth salesmen, the Portuguese market was in hand. Why risk losing it when it was not clear that the French would purchase so much English cloth, especially since the French insisted, at least for the moment, on maintaining the 1699 tariff level on English woolen goods? Similarly, for those involved in the silk industry, many of whom were French Huguenot exiles with no love for Louis XIV, the issue was even simpler: they could not compete with less-expensive silk from France. Burnet described the tense situation in June 1713 as follows:

> The traders in the City of London, and those in all other parts of England, were alarmed, with the great prejudice this would bring on the whole nation. The Turkey company, those that traded with Portugal and Italy, and all who were concerned in the woollen and silk manufactures, appeared before both Houses, and set forth the great mischief, that a Commerce with France, on the foot of the Treaty, would bring upon the whole nation; while none appeared on the other side, to answer their arguments, or to set forth the advantage of such a Commerce.[51]

Burnet, of course, was writing from a Whig point of view. Pro-treaty arguments *were* being made by Tories in Parliament and for public consumption in pamphlets and journals. Most notably, with the help of the Trade Commissioner Arthur Moore, the government gave Daniel Defoe full access to Customs accounts and made him editor of a new journal entitled *Mercator, or Commerce Retriev'd*, which began publication on March 26, 1713. *Mercator* stridently promoted the pro-treaty argument of the Queen's Tory ministers, and was an official government-sponsored version of the *Review*, which shut down on June 11, 1713, as a result of Defoe's new employment.[52]

But time was of the essence. On June 4 the Commerce Bill was read a second time and carried again, but by a diminished margin of 202 to 135.[53] Poor Tory management of Commons and the torrent of petitions had encouraged Whigs and unanchored many Tories. Fearing that the tide would turn entirely against them if they did not act quickly, the government put forth the bill for a third and final vote on June 18. On that day, 35 speeches were made—17 for the Commercial Treaty Bill and 18 against—in a debate that lasted from three in the afternoon to eleven at night. Support was voiced by Arthur Moore and other loyal Tories, while opposition came from English and Scottish Whigs, and disaffected ("Whimsical") Tories.[54] One of the latter was the formerly reliable Sir Thomas Hanmer, who announced that

> before he had fully examined the affair in question, he had given his vote for the bringing in the bill; but, that having afterwards maturely weighed and considered the allegations of the traders and manufacturers, in their several petitions and representations, he was convinced, that the passing of it, would be of great prejudice to the woollen and silk manufacturers of this kingdom, consequently increase the number of poor, and, in the end, affect the land.[55]

When after eight exhausting hours the bill for the Commercial Treaty was put to a third vote, it was rejected by 194 votes to 185.[56] Even Scottish MPs, who might have been expected to vote in favor of inexpensive claret, were deeply divided. In the final vote, 16 Scottish MPs voted with the Whigs and 16 with the Tories, while 13 were notably absent.[57]

Hanmer's speech has been credited by some historians as being the final straw against the pro-treaty argument,[58] while others argue that his influence has been exaggerated.[59] Paradoxically, both arguments are correct. After all, the Tory defection began right after the first vote on the Commerce Bill, and as such, Hanmer's speech marked a culmination of Tory rebellion rather than an epiphany for other party members. However, Hanmer's speech was momentous in that it articulated a convergence of the cloth manufacturing interest, which was largely Whig, with the landed interest, which was largely Tory, and at that point the Commercial Treaty bill was surely doomed.[60]

Oxford and Bolingbroke, however, continued to push the Commercial Treaty bill, despite now despising each other. Defoe was maintained on the government payroll at the *Mercator*, writing in support of the bill, and the battle for public opinion continued. Fearful that their victory was tenuous, anti-Treaty forces responded with more pamphlet literature and, significantly, in August 1713, a newspaper of their own: *The British Merchant; or, Commerce Preserv'd.*[61] Meanwhile, Bolingbroke invited French negotiators to London, while also suggesting a revision of the 1654 Anglo-Portuguese Treaty to the Portuguese ambassador in London, José Da Cunha Brochado. This treaty remained a source of tension for the Portuguese because of the powers it granted to the English factors in Lisbon and Oporto. But Brochado had got what he wanted with the rejection of the Commercial Treaty Bill and did not want to renegotiate anything. In fact, he did not have to. Instead, he offered to Britain the ultimate mercantilist prize: gold. Specifically, Brochado convinced his government to relax the restrictions on British trade in Brazil, and more importantly, on the export of Brazilian gold. With this offer, Bolingbroke was defeated.[62] The British would have Brazilian gold and the Portuguese market for their woolen goods, while the Portuguese would have Britain as a protector against Spanish aggression, and a steady market for their apparently unloved wines.[63]

The aftermath

Oxford's and Bolingbroke's hopes for inexpensive claret and peace with France through open trade had been dashed by members of their own party. In July 1714 Oxford was dismissed by the Queen, and in August Anne died, leaving Bolingbroke badly exposed to the incoming Hanoverians. Indeed, Bolingbroke was immediately dismissed from office by George I, and facing prosecution by the new Whig government, he fled to Paris, handing a massive propaganda coup to the Whigs in the process. Oxford meanwhile was called from retirement to face impeachment, and soon found himself in the Tower of London on charges of treason. The partisan strife was hardly over, but the creation of a Whig oligarchy had begun.[64]

The failure of the Tories to secure the Commercial Treaty with France has been lamented by economic liberals and claret connoisseurs alike as a great opportunity lost and a great mistake. Adam Smith famously decried the Methuen Treaty and the philosophy that maintained it in a memorable passage from *The Wealth of Nations* (1776):

> The Portuguese, it is said, are better customers for our manufactures than the French, and should therefore be encouraged in preference to them. As they give us their custom, it is pretended we should give them ours. The sneaking arts of underling traders are thus erected into political maxims for the conduct of a great empire; for it is the most underling tradesmen only who make it a rule to employ chiefly their own customers. A great trader always purchases his goods where they are cheapest and best, without regard to any little interest of this kind.[65]

No doubt there is some wisdom in Smith's critique, but it is not clear that France in all her protectionist glory actually wanted the Commercial Treaty with Great Britain either.[66] If Britain was slow to embrace the supposed virtues of free trade, France was also, and neither country was eager to test these radical ideas with its greatest rival.[67]

Port: Symbol of English national interest

Lost or not, the opportunity at Utrecht was not seized. The previously tenuous Methuen Treaty became the bedrock of Anglo-Portuguese relations and of the port wine industry, which operated with the knowledge that port would not be threatened by lower-priced wines from France. Moreover, in the process of rejecting French trade, Whig propagandists drew a link between port and English national interest by conflating the interests of English merchants with the interests of the nation as a whole.[68] This connection between "England" and its merchants is seen in an allegorical essay written by Joseph Addison at the height of the Commercial Treaty debate, in which Addison cleverly pits "Goodman Fact," plaintiff, against "Count Tariff," defendant.[69] Goodman Fact, much like his contemporary John Bull, was

> a plain spoken person, and a man of very few words. ... Tropes and figures are his aversion. He affirms every thing roundly, without art, rhetorick, or circumlocution. He is a declared enemy to all kinds of ceremony and complaisance. He flatters no body.[70]

If any reader did not get the point that Fact was a solid Protestant (Low Church) Englishman and a Whig, Addison continued:

> He appeared in a suit of *English* broad-cloth, very plain, but rich. Every thing he wore was substantial, honest, home-spun ware. His cane indeed came from the East-Indies, and two or three little superfluities from Turkey, and other parts. It is said that he encouraged himself with a bottle of neat *Port,* before he appeared at the tryal.

Just as Goodman Fact embodied the Whig idea of a true Englishman—a prosperous merchant, bluff in his countenance, and spare in his words—Count Tariff represented the equivalent Whig stereotype of a Frenchman (and Tory): aristocratic, pretentious, and effeminate. To wit, Tariff

> was dressed in a fine brocade waistcoat, curiously embroidered with Flower-de-luces [*fleur-de-lis*, a symbol of the French monarchy]. He wore also a broad-brimmed hat, a shoulder knot, and a pair of silver-clocked stockings. He abounded in empty phrases, superficial flourishes, violent assertions and feeble proofs.[71]

Tory broadsheet propagandists responded to the charges of disloyalty and effeminacy by resurrecting seventeenth-century arguments against Parliamentarians and Whigs. For instance, a broadsheet ballad entitled *The Jovial Drinker* spoke of "Fools, who exclaim against Wine", "brave Cavalier[s]", and "noble wine that's a friend of the Crown." Indeed, the lyrics were probably simply recycled from a ballad written in the 1640s or 1650s, or in response to the embargo on French wine

Figure 4.1 The Jovial Drinker (c. 1713)
This was tired Tory propaganda by the time the print first appeared.

in 1678. The accompanying engraving, however, is unmistakably from the period of the Commercial Treaty negotiations.[72] But just like the lyrics, it is full of tired, seventeenth-century tropes and allusions (see Figure 4.1).

In the foreground of the print, a well-dressed and armed—and therefore aristocratic—man stumbles drunkenly over the crest of the hill. In his right arm he cradles a wicker-covered bottle of claret (as identified in the ballad), and in his right hand he holds a full glass of wine. He is the epitome of a noble gallant, with his highly decorated coat, waistcoat, and cravat worn in the fashionable steinkirk style. The feathered brim of his hat also suggests his wealth, good taste, and Tory politics. He is the eponymous "Jovial Drinker," and just the sort of aristocratic blade whose praises the ballad sings.[73]

But the force of the print, if it had any, lay in the details. In the lower-left corner of the engraving four men sit around a table in different stages of insobriety; two are toasting, one is drinking, and one is vomiting (unable to plot against the king indeed!). In case the viewer is still lost, the men sit outside a solid-stone tavern in the countryside, revealing their landed status. Attached to the tavern is a semi-ruined courtyard, out of which two oak saplings grow. The oak had been a symbol of Royalism ever since Charles II escaped from the Battle of Worcester in 1651 by hiding in a hollowed-out oak tree. Meanwhile, in the lower-right corner of the engraving a plainly dressed man emerges from a town; he is a tradesman or professional, and no doubt a man of Whig sympathies. His hat, unlike the Jovial Drinker's, has a lone feather in it, which was a poor man's version of the feathered brim. Just as importantly, this middle-ranking urban dweller is vomiting; we might guess as a result of drinking too much beer. But the really crucial detail is that unlike the aristocratic men who are man enough to walk, talk, sit, and vomit on their own, the pathetic Whig has to be held up by a woman! As funny as this might have been to an aged Tory audience, the glory days of brave Cavaliers were long gone.

In a more up-to-date rebuttal of Whig accusations against Tory wine policy, Daniel Defoe argued that drinking port was synonymous with promoting Dutch commercial interests. He alluded in a December 1713 edition of the *Mercator* to one Herr Coopmanschap, the "Dutch agent to Sir Poll, chairman of a certain club who meet behind the Exchange to drink Neat *Port*, and give up the English trade."[74] However, like a great deal of Tory political philosophy by 1713, this one had also run its course; the old Royalist bogeyman, the Dutch, no longer heated the blood of most Englishmen the way the French did. After all, the Dutch had been allies in the two recent wars against France, and in matters of trade and commerce the English had largely surpassed them. In 1713 a jingoistic Englishman might dislike the Dutch, but he no longer feared them. The French alone had the privilege of being both feared and hated, a sentiment in which many Hanoverian Tories evidently partook.

Here then was the Tory government's problem: while they argued that open trade with France was in the economic interest of the nation, they defined both the nation and its interests in anachronistic terms. Since 1688, if not even since the early 1670s, "reason of state, or the 'national interest,' had superseded the ruler's honour as the dominant consideration in the conduct of foreign policy."[75] In other words, loyalty to the king and the financial interest of his government was no longer so important as loyalty to a broader idea of England as a mixed constitutional and mercantile state.[76] Certainly the Netherlands continued to be a trade and manufacturing rival to England in the early eighteenth century, but they had far too much in common with England to be the sort of threat posed by France, where the king was mighty, the aristocrats were impotent, and Parliament (or its Estates General equivalent) was dormant to the point of non-existence. The Francophobic Whigs, therefore, had a better economic argument precisely because it fit into the newly dominant narrative about the nature and purpose of foreign policy: *it should promote the national interest.* And what was good for France was clearly not in England's national interest.

As a result of the Whig victory in rejecting the Commercial Treaty with France, and thereby maintaining the Methuen Treaty, port was further anglicized, while claret was rendered suspect. As Don Felix says to his prospective father-in-law, Don Pedro, in Susannah Centlivre's allegorical play, *The Wonder: A Woman Keeps a Secret* (1714): "I have been drinking right French Claret, Sir. But I love my own Country for all that." "Ay, ay," responds Don Pedro, "who doubts it, Sir?"[77] Centlivre's point was that Don Felix's loyalty to his country was doubtful, and so too was the loyalty of those who promoted the Commercial Treaty.

In another play by Centlivre, *A Gotham Election*, written in 1715, she again uses the politicization of wine to satirize the Tories. Friendly, an agent for the Tory grandee Sir Roger Trusty, is trying to ascertain the political leanings of Score-Double, an Innkeeper in Gotham, who is fully aware of the political meanings of wine: "What do you please to drink, Sir?" asks Score-Double, a bit nervously.

Friendly:	Why, bring us the best your house affords.
Score-Double:	The best my house affords, ha, ha, ha, that is as you think it, Sir;—now most of our Gentry, for the last *vour* Years, d'ye mind, will touch nothing but *French* Claret—there are some that like your *Port* wines, but very few, and those of the poorer *Zort* too, as my barboard can witness.
Friendly:	Come, bring such as you like yourself.
Score-Double:	Why then, Master, we'll have a bottle of white lisbon.[78]

This was a clever evasion by Score-Double, because port and claret were the political give-aways. White Lisbon was of course from Portugal, but it had not been foisted upon the English public as a substitute for claret. Therefore, as a political symbol, it was neutral.[79]

We do not know what wine Centlivre preferred or if she drank wine at all; but we do know that she had a strong Whig bias in her plays and was an intimate of known Whigs such as Sir Richard Steele and George Farquhar.[80] Her own sentiments regarding the Commercial Treaty with France seem to have been summed up in another scene from *A Gotham Election*. In this scene, Tickup, a candidate for Gotham, is at a local tavern with Mallett, the son of Gotham's mayor, when the former commands a bottle of "French Red" from the drawer (i.e. barkeeper) at a local tavern. The drawer arrives with the bottle, they drink to Score-Double's health, and then Tickup asks: "Well, how do you like the Wine? I think 'tis pretty good." To which Mallett replies, "I think so too, Sir;—but second Thoughts is best."[81] That was the punch line, and a direct allusion to Parliament's ultimate rejection of the Commercial Treaty.

***

Despite having become a symbol of the Whig party, the merchant classes, and a certain type of middle-ranking English masculinity, not all Whigs preferred port to claret. Nor did all Tories prefer claret to port. As Centlivre wrote in 1714, most of the Gotham gentry drank claret, while only the poorer sort drank port. We know already from the example of John Hervey—who became 1st Earl of Bristol after the arrival of the Hanoverians in 1714—that Whig gentlemen could, in their own cellars, be indifferent to the popular politics of wine for which they were largely responsible. In fact, throughout the War of the Spanish Succession Hervey continued to drink claret, and the most expensive claret at that. Between 1702 and 1713, he purchased the equivalent of approximately 3,338 bottles of claret, four-fifths of which was Chateau Haut Brion and Chateau Margaux.[82] Claret was by far the most prevalent wine in his Suffolk cellar. In contrast, Hervey made only a small purchase of "Portugal wine" in 1710, and another hogshead of "Red-Port wine" in 1711. This amounted to roughly 504 bottles of Portuguese wine, a small fraction of his French wine purchases during the same period.

Similarly, John Churchill, 1st Duke of Marlborough, who began the War of the Spanish Succession as a suspected Tory Jacobite and ended it as a Whig hero, preferred French wine whatever his politics, although his preference seems to have been for champagne. Surviving letters and receipts from wine merchants show that from the outset of the war until the Treaty of Utrecht, the Captain General known throughout Europe for humbling France's once mighty army enjoyed "vin d'Ay," "vin de Sillery" and "vin d'Aville" (i.e. d'Hautevillers), all of them types of champagne. But Marlborough also enjoyed large amounts of burgundy, Hermitage and Haut Brion.[83] There is no evidence, however, of port among his wartime purchases.

Hervey's and Marlborough's taste in wine are outstanding examples of the way that for those who could afford them, fancy French wines transcended party politics. A letter cum advertisement from the wine merchant Charles Fary to Richard Steele in *The Englishman*—a successor to *The Guardian* and *The Spectator*—shows precisely how Whig gentlemen contemplated the potential effects of the Commercial Treaty upon their favorite French wines.

> But you are so warm in this latter Character, [i.e. being an "Englishman"] that I fear you will have an Aversion to my Liquor because is it *French* ... Thou jolly son of Nestor, be convinced that there is neither High nor Low, Whigg or Tory, against good Liquor. If the Bill of Commerce should pass, it will be all our Comfort; if it should not pass, we shall be able to pay for it, be it ever so dear.[84]

Well-heeled Whig wine lovers continued to revile Louis XIV's France. And just as surely, they still loved French wine. They believed that national interest and personal taste were entirely distinct. But as Fary readily acknowledged, they could afford to think that, come what may at Utrecht. We know, of course, that the Commercial Treaty was ultimately rejected, and therefore, that claret and other French wines remained prohibitively expensive for most English consumers. This situation, said wealthy Whigs (and even some Tories), was good for England, and it helped to make port a decidedly Whiggish wine. But the affiliation between Whigs and port had more to do with what Whig political leaders considered best for the nation—and what consumers could afford—than what Whig leaders actually preferred to drink. As for what wines people actually consumed in England, claret was the wine for the rich and fashionable, while port was a wine for the middling sorts.

5

"A good and most particular taste"

Luxury Claret, Politeness, and Political Power in England, c. 1700–1740

Political authority needs many props, and in early eighteenth-century England luxury claret was among them. As in the seventeenth century, wine represented the court, the church, the landed classes, and the ruling elite more generally. In short, wine was still affiliated with all the pillars of political power, and since the Restoration era, claret had been the most politically potent of all wines. As we have seen, between the Exclusion Crisis and the end of Queen Anne's reign, claret had become a well-established symbol of Tory interests and Whig fears. Nevertheless, the most prominent claret drinkers of the early eighteenth century were politically powerful Whigs.

To understand this apparent conundrum, it is first necessary to establish the difference between types of claret available on the English market in 1700. To wit, the claret consumed by prominent Whigs was not the same as that which had been consumed in the seventeenth century and before. The traditional claret that dominated the English market during the Restoration was generically named, haphazardly made, light in color and body, and probably very little changed since the High Middle Ages. However, the claret that became popular among the English elite in the eighteenth century was carefully produced, discernibly superior in quality and expensive both because of high import tariffs in England and high production costs in France.[1] By necessity, the consumers of this new type of claret were wealthy. And because it is consumers who ultimately give a commodity its various meanings, this new, "luxury" claret was neither Tory nor Whig (nor even Jacobite). Instead, it was "polite," and in early eighteenth-century England, leading Whigs were the most polite people of all.

The rise of luxury claret on the English market and its consumption by Whig elites both reflected polite culture and the post-1688 political order, and helped to constitute Whig political power by confirming the aesthetic and, therefore, moral credentials of the Whig elite.[2] Legitimizing the new elite was necessary because many of the new leaders, especially among the Whigs, came from commercial or gentry backgrounds; their legitimacy did not spring from the deep well of aristocratic inheritance. In this context, aesthetic appreciation, or taste, served as a new foundation for political power.[3] In other words, to legitimize one's position of authority, one had to be able to appreciate the finer things in life, and one of the many finer things available on the English market in the early eighteenth century was luxury claret. When combined with the fact that wine in general remained a symbol of political authority, luxury claret was an especially potent signifier.

So traditional claret was Tory, but luxury claret was polite, and politeness was power. This equation is critical to understanding and explaining why leading Whigs could drink so much luxury claret even if they rejected traditional claret for the nation as a whole. Did this make the Whig elite hypocritical, as their Tory critics charged? Certainly it did if one judges them by the standards of the Old Whigs who pushed for the Exclusion Crisis and a radical justification for the events of 1688–9.[4] But during Queen Anne's reign the majority of Whigs were not radicals; instead, they were increasingly the party of the establishment, and after 1714 they *were* the establishment.[5] Nothing better symbolizes this transition from outsiders to insiders than the elite Whig penchant for a polite wine from France.

Haut Brion and the origins of luxury claret

The dramatic arrival of luxury claret on the English market occurred during the reign of Queen Anne (1702–14); however, as with most historical phenomena, this one had antecedents. In fact, a limited number of London-based wine drinkers had enjoyed luxury claret as early as 1660. This was largely due to the production and marketing efforts of one man, Arnaud de Pontac, *Premier Président* of the *Parlement* of Bordeaux and a major Bordelais land owner.[6] Pontac keenly perceived that the re-establishment of the Stuart court—and Restoration court culture more generally—would increase the demand for luxury goods in London, and this inspired him to launch the prototype of top-growth claret on the English market. In fact, the first record of the wine called "Haut Brion" comes from King Charles II's cellar-book within a month of the king's return from Continental exile. In June 1660, the royal cellar master purchased 169 bottles of "Hobriono" for just over £180, and another 60 bottles of generic "Graves" wine for slightly more than £32, from the wine merchant Joseph Batailhe.[7] Both of these wines were sold to the king in bottles, remarkable for the time and no doubt an indication of high quality, but the Haut Brion cost more than £1 per bottle, while the generic "Graves" wine cost less than half that amount.

However, it was not only cost that separated Haut Brion from other clarets; it was also the taste. On April 10, 1663, Samuel Pepys wrote in his diary that he left the Exchange with his friends Sir John Cutler, an alderman, and John Grant, a draper, and went on to the nearby Royal Oak Tavern on Lombard Street where they met their friend Alexander Brome, the Royalist poet. There, Pepys writes, they "drank a sort of French wine called Ho Bryan, that hath a good and most particular taste that I never met with."[8] This quote from Pepys's diary was long thought by historians and oenophiles to be the first mention of Haut Brion in any language, but in fact, that distinction goes to Charles II's cellar book. And while previous historians are correct to stress that Haut Brion was produced for the London, not the Paris market, they have been wrong to imagine that Pontac was first popularized by successful professionals like Pepys and his friends.[9] Instead, Haut Brion was first fashionable at the Restoration court. Pepys, however, did provide the first tasting note for Haut Brion, and like many people since, he was impressed.

Clearly, Pontac's new production techniques and marketing strategy had worked. Prior to the creation of Haut Brion, claret in England was usually generically named, although it was sometimes referred to by the sub-region of origin (i.e. "Graves," "Médoc," "Gascon," or "High Country"). It is impossible to know exactly what this traditional claret looked and tasted like, but given the way it was produced, transported, and stored, it was very probably an uncomplicated, light red wine made from both red and white grapes, and rosé in color.[10] It was best when young and still fresh, and it was consumed straight from the cask, having been bottled only for transport from cask to table. Most claret arrived in England in the late autumn and early winter, and sometimes again in the spring after the mid-winter sea had calmed. If not consumed by the end of the summer, wine that was not carefully tended in its casks would begin to oxidize, acetify (i.e. to become vinegar), or possibly to re-ferment as cellars became warmer. These problems were "rectified" using countless different methods, almost all of which entailed some combination of cider, herbs, and native English berries, not to mention a host of less salubrious ingredients.[11]

Simple as it may seem to improve and "brand" a product, what Pontac did was extraordinary for his times. Out of the anonymity of traditional claret he carefully produced and named a wine that came from a small, circumscribed area of land in order to enhance its value on the palates and in the minds of English customers.[12] Nor was that all. Immediately following the Great Fire of 1666, Pontac sent his son François-Auguste to London to open a tavern from which the latter could sell his father's wine directly. "Pontack's Head," so named because of the portrait of Pontac *père* that hung above the entrance, was first on Lombard Street, then on Abchurch Lane in the City (near the Monument).[13] It quickly became London's finest tavern,[14] and the meeting place of the cognoscenti: John Dryden, John Locke, Christopher Wren, Jonathan Swift, Daniel Defoe, and the French exile Charles de Saint-Evremond all ate there, and it was the location of Royal Society dinners until 1746.[15] More importantly for the history of wine, it was there that many consumers first encountered luxury claret.

The bold marketing move by the Pontac family had an effect because Haut Brion soon became known by name and esteemed by the metropolitan cognoscenti. In 1677, John Locke, who was living in exile in France at the time, was inspired to discover empirically what made Mr Pontac's wine so especially good. On Friday, May 14 he rode on horseback just beyond the old Bordeaux city walls to the gravelly hillock known as Haut Brion, and there he made the following observations:

> The vine de Pontac, so much esteemed in England, grows on a rising open to the west, in a white sand mixed with a little gravel, which one would think would bear nothing; but there is such a particularity in the soil, that at Mr. Pontac's, near Bourdeaux the merchants assured me that the wine growing in the very next vineyards, where there was only a ditch between, and the soil, to appearance, perfectly the same, was by no means so good.[16]

Locke did not know exactly why the soil at Haut Brion was so particular, but he did notice the importance of a rising slope and a sun-exposed vineyard. He learned that pigeon and hen dung in the vineyard improved the yield of the vines without hurting the quality of the wine, "but horse dung, or that of any beast, they say, spoils the goodness of their wine." And he was told that the "older the vineyard, the fewer the grapes, but the better the wine."[17]

But *terroir* and vineyard tending alone cannot explain the increased quality of Haut Brion, because wine had been produced on the estate for decades, if not even centuries, yet there is no prior evidence to suggest that it had always been so distinctive.[18] Perhaps the Pontacs severely limited their crop of grapes, rejected unripe or moldy grapes, and allowed for a long, slow fermentation before putting the wine in new oak barrels. We do not know. However, we do know that they carefully "racked" their wines. That is, they drew off the wine from its "lees" (the sediment formed by crushed grapes and stems during fermentation), which entails the labor-intensive practice of siphoning the wine from one barrel to another at periodic intervals. This helps to clarify and aerate the wine.

After racking the wines, they ullaged or "topped-up" the barrels and continued to do so at regular intervals. In other words, they used wine from one barrel to replace the space occupied by the lees after the wine was racked, and they replenished the barrels that had lost wine through evaporation and absorption by the staves. Keeping the barrel topped up to the bung hole, which in the seventeenth century was left open until the final fermentation occurred, was necessary to prevent the wine from turning to vinegar (a process that occurs naturally when enough oxygen is available for the omnipresent *acetobacter* to multiply).

Moreover, evidence of ullaging from Haut Brion reveals the hierarchy of family wines. The Pontacs used wine from their estate at Pez to top up the more valuable barrels of Haut Brion. Finally, the Pontacs retained lesser wines for their own private consumption rather than attempt to sell all of their produce at the risk of lessening their reputation for quality.[19] Each of these practices was known in the seventeenth century, but none of them was standard, and perhaps the Pontacs' success was due to the incorporation of them all (see Figure 5.1).

Whatever the Pontacs did to make their wines superior, the response in England among the rich and fashionable was overwhelming. Locke wrote:

> A tun of the best wine at Bordeaux, which is that of Médoc or Pontac, is worth ... 80 or 100 crowns [i.e. £22 10s. or £25]. For this the English may thank their own folly, for, whereas some years since the same wine was sold for 50 or 60 crowns per tun, the fashionable sending over of orders to have the best wine sent them at any rate, they have, by striving who should get it, brought it to that price.[20]

In a similar vein, the polymath and diarist John Evelyn recorded on July 13, 1683:

> I had this day much discourse with Monsieur Pontaque, son to the famous and wise Prime President of Bourdeaux: This gent. was owner of that excellent Vignoble of Pontaque and Obrien, whence the choicest of our Burdeaux-Wines come.[21]

Figure 5.1   Chateau at Haut Brion, Pessac, Bordeaux, Gironde
Note: This was "Mr. Pontac's, near Bourdeaux," where John Locke went in 1677 to discover why the wine it produced was so good.

The difference, if any, between Pontac and Haut Brion wines remains unclear; but whatever the confusion over names, Arnaud de Pontac's experiment of making a discernibly better wine was clearly a success.[22]

Luxury claret: A failed experiment?

The Pontac family had created a type of wine that caught the attention of elite English consumers, but the family's good fortune was not to last. Arnaud died in 1682, and the Haut Brion estate was dragged into court and divided. Debts accumulated and the vineyard was badly managed. Adding insult to injury, the "Little Ice Age" made a deadly thrust in the early 1690s, reducing Bordeaux grape harvests to minuscule amounts. Most importantly of all, in 1689 the English Parliament placed another embargo on all French goods, and as a result François-August Pontac returned home to France. Pontack's Head was carried on in the family name, by a man who called himself "Pontack," but whoever he was, he would have had a difficult time procuring wines from Haut Brion.[23] What wines were made at Haut Brion during the 1690s were sold off to the French navy and Bordeaux tavern keepers.[24]

While French sailors and the *menu peuple* of Bordeaux were getting a treat that would never again be repeated, wealthy English consumers missed their Haut Brion. According to Richard Ames, in 1691 the cellar at Pontack's Head was devoid of the famous house wine:

> At Puntack's the famous French Ord'nary, where
> Luxurious Eating is never thought dear,
> We expected to meet with a glass of that same
> Wine, which carries the Master's own Name;
> But his Vaults could not lend us a drop of that Tipple,
> So we wish[ed] him well—for a crooked disciple.[25]

The trustworthiness of doggerel aside, it is clear that the 1690s were bad years for Bordeaux producers and English claret consumers alike. Nor did the end of the war bring much relief. By the time the English embargo was rescinded in 1696, the duty on French wines stood at roughly £47 per tun, and the so-called New Subsidy of 1697 added £4 to the cost of all wines. The result was that by 1698, the first full year of peace, French wines paid approximately £51 per tun, while Portuguese and Spanish wines paid slightly more than £21 and £22 per tun respectively.[26] Most English wine drinkers who did not have access to smuggled or fraudulently declared claret could not keep up with the increased cost of their favorite wine and changed their consumption habits accordingly. However, well-to-do consumers who remembered the taste of Haut Brion were willing to pay almost any price to have it back in their cellars and on their tables. Moreover, a handful of wealthy producers in Bordeaux were inspired by the memory of Haut Brion's earlier success. With the embargo over and peace declared, they envisaged a return to England.[27]

The triumph of "New French Claret": A paradox of war

And return to England they did. The revived wine trade between Bordeaux and England was small, even when accounting for fraud, but focusing on its size obscures the fact that England was the one and only market for luxury claret. Even another war with France that began in 1702. and another embargo against French goods that began in 1704, could not keep these luxury clarets out of England. Bordeaux export figures during the war and embargo indicate that there was no direct trade to England.[28] However, English import figures for French wine tell a different story: throughout the war and embargo they registered an annual average of over 800 tuns of French wine.[29] In other words, every year, despite the war and embargo, England continued to receive all of the luxury claret that a few wealthy Bordeaux vineyard owners could produce (Graph 5.1).

Proof that the English were purchasing luxury clarets during the War of the Spanish Succession and that these wines were intended for no other customers comes from the *London Gazette*, the official voice of the English government. While most of the information in the *Gazette* consisted of foreign news and royal

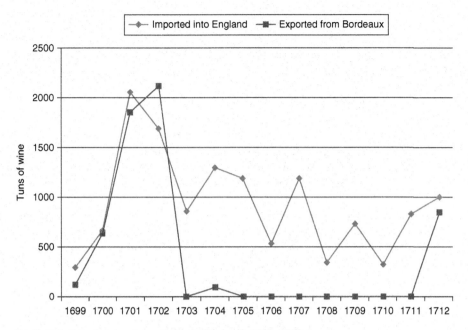

Graph 5.1   French wine imported into England, 1699–1712
Source: French wine imported into England, JHC, XVII, 365; wine exported from Bordeaux to England, Huetz de Lemps, *Géographie du Commerce*, pp. 147–50.

proclamations, its contents gradually expanded to contain a variety of official information and government notices, including the auction of foreign ships and their cargo taken as prizes of war and condemned for public sale by the Court of Exchequer.[30] Consequently, the "advertisements" for wine in the *Gazette* were in fact notices of wines to be sold at government-sponsored auctions, often held at coffee houses in the City of London.

Early in the war, seized claret was auctioned at £8, £40, and £60 per tun, indicating clear qualitative differences between the wines.[31] Nevertheless, all the wines being sold were called "claret": there were no estate names or descriptive terms to distinguish between them. Cost was the only difference.[32] However, in 1704 the most expensive claret began to be referred to as "New French Claret."[33] It is not stated in the notices what made these clarets "new," although the careful use of the word by the auctioneer to describe the wine for sale was not merely an indication of age, as almost all claret—indeed, almost all wine—was new in that it was less than a year old when it was sold. Instead, the word "new" was meant to describe a *new type* of claret.[34] In short, the nomenclature of luxury claret was very slowly beginning to catch up to its distinctive qualities, and in May 1705 "choice new red Obrian and Pontack prize wines ... to be had at Lloyd's" were once again being referred to by vineyard name.[35] One month later a wine called "Margaux" appeared in two different auctions, although typically the Court of Exchequer scribe found the French difficult and spelled it "Margoose."[36]

These announcements for Haut Brion, Pontac, and Margaux, which were now owned by the maritally related Pontac and d'Aulède families, add to the mystery of where Pontac wine came from, if not from the vineyards at Haut Brion. But amidst our confusion over names a truly startling point can be lost. In a period of six weeks in 1705, in the middle of a war in which England and France were the primary antagonists, 718 hogsheads and 9 tierces of Haut Brion, Pontac, and Margaux arrived in England for sale. This represents an enormous amount of luxury claret to have been captured in three successive shiploads, especially since these wines were produced by two allied families. And as records from the *London Gazette* show, the same thing happened year after year during the war. One must ask, as the wine writer Hugh Johnson does: "What prudent proprietor would have loaded it all in three ships at the same time?"[37] It seems that the Pontacs and the d'Aulèdes were making "a calculated assault once more on the London market: their only serious market, war or no war."[38] And because the English privateer who seized the wines upon the high seas received a large proportion of the auction price, while the government and the coffee-house owner each received a cut, it is entirely likely that the privateer was under contract to the château owners. In other words, the wines were not really being "seized" at all; rather, the seizures were carefully planned. As Johnson says, "the simplest explanation is that a private arrangement brought the auction price, less some fairly hefty commissions, back to Bordeaux."[39]

Whatever the clandestine arrangements made in advance—and one pines for a letter revealing the details—what is clear is that the Pontacs and d'Aulèdes were making enough money to inspire others to follow suit. An announcement in the *Gazette* on May 22, 1707 reads: "Under the Gate-way, at Brewer's Key next the Tower, in a cellar … is to be sold an entire parcel of New French Prize Clarets, upon the gross lees, and lately landed, being of the growths of Lafitt, Margouze and Latour."[40] In other words, by 1707 at the latest, all four of the original "first growth" wines of Bordeaux were known in England by name.[41]

If any more proof is needed to show that English consumers desired all the best clarets, and that to satisfy such a demand was precisely the goal of the producers themselves, it is found in the *London Gazette* on May 26, 1707, a mere four days after the previously mentioned sale of Margaux, Latour, and Lafite. "For sale at Lloyd's Coffee-House," reads the advertisement, "200 hogsheads of new French Obrian Clarets, taken and condemned as Prize out of the ship Liberty, lying at Wiggin's Key."[42] In other words, in one week in May 1707, perhaps the entire production of Bordeaux's four most prized vineyards was announced for sale to wealthy English consumers. And given that a hogshead of "New French Claret" cost between £40 and £60 during the war—between three and four times as much as ordinary claret, Spanish wine, or port—the consumers had to be wealthy.

The wine of the British court

Indeed, just as in 1660, the clientele for "New French Clarets" began with the monarch. The wine order book for Queen Anne's royal household reveals that the

Queen, her husband Prince George of Denmark, and their guests, were devotees of luxury claret. In 1702, the first year of Anne's reign, her wine steward purchased 111 hogsheads, or nearly 28,000 bottles of Haut Brion and Margaux. This trend continued; throughout her reign Queen Anne's butler purchased roughly 40 hogsheads (10,080 bottles) of Haut Brion, Pontac, and Margaux per year, not to mention unnamed "strong, deep French claret," "vin de Graves," champagne, Meursault, red burgundy, Hermitage, and other wines from France, as well as Rhenish wine from Germany, Mountain Malaga, sherry, and Galicia from Spain, palm and canary from the Canary Islands, red Florence (Chianti) from Italy, and white Lisbon, Calcavella, and madeira from Portugal. In December 1703, the Queen even showed her support for the Methuen Treaty by buying eight pipes of red port and two pipes of white port.[43] But overwhelmingly, the wine of choice for Queen Anne's court was luxury claret.

The arrival of the German Hanover dynasty in 1714 did not change the royal household's penchant for fine red wine from Bordeaux. In fact, among royal wine purchases, there was little to betray George I's Teutonic origins. Between 1720 and 1727, three-quarters of the 763 hogsheads of wine delivered to the royal household by Mr Cockburn, their primary supplier, was Lafite, Latour, Pontac, and other luxury clarets. Meanwhile, Mr Towers supplied the family with small amounts of Rhenish and Moselle wine.[44] When George II arrived from Hanover in 1727, he brought with him a more developed taste for his native wines, but claret still predominated.[45] For instance, in 1734 the royal household spent the extravagant sum of £10,308 on wine, roughly two-thirds of which was for luxury claret.[46]

Clearly, queens and kings, Stuart and Hanoverian, saw nothing wrong with drinking French wines even if France was the avowed enemy. And just as clearly, luxury claret was their favorite French wine. Individual exceptions aside, luxury claret was the preferred wine of most English political leaders during the early eighteenth century, a preference that can be seen in John Gay's first published poem, "Wine" (1708). The poem is set in the Devil Tavern in Temple Bar, London, where the narrator has gathered with his friends:

> The stair's ascent now gain'd, our guide unbars
> The door of spacious room, and creaking chairs
> (To ear offensive) round the table sets.
> We sit; when thus his florid speech begins:
> "Name, Sirs! the wine that most invites your taste;
> Champaign, or Burgundy, or Florence pure,
> Or Hock antique, or Lisbon new or old,
> Bourdeaux, or neat French white, or Alicant."
> For Bourdeaux we with voice unanimous
> Declare, (such sympathy's in boon compeers.)[47]

So claret it was, and unanimously so. From here, the "sanguine frothy juice" is brought in and the toasts proceed from "glorious Anna" and the "Royal Dane" (i.e. Queen Anne and Prince George of Denmark), to Marlborough, Devonshire, Godolphin, Sunderland, Halifax, and "all the worthies of the British realm." It is no coincidence that everyone mentioned as a "worthy" was pro-war, and either avowedly Whig or, like Marlborough and Godolphin, increasingly Whig in his politics.[48] Literary critics argue over whether Gay was being ironic or genuine in his praise of Whigs, but in either case these critics have overlooked the meanings of claret.[49] If Gay's praise was ironic, he was using claret to highlight the hypocrisy of preferring French wine in a time of war with France (and when French wines were officially being embargoed). If he was being genuine, he was using the most fashionable wine to praise Whig worthies and thereby seek a patron for his poetic efforts. Whatever the case, Whig leaders seem to have outdone their Tory rivals in the consumption of luxury claret and other French wines. After all, with a few notable exceptions, Whigs were the most fashionable people in early eighteenth-century England, and luxury claret was the most fashionable wine.

John Hervey, First Earl of Bristol

As we have seen, John Hervey, Whig MP for Bury St Edmunds, purchased slightly more than one hogshead (over 252 quart bottles) of luxury claret per year during the War of the Spanish Succession.[50] That trend continued long after the war ended and Hervey was made 1st Earl of Bristol by the new king. In fact, during the 40-year period from 1702 to 1742, Hervey made—or at least entered into his expense book—125 purchases of wine, of which French wine accounted for at least 57 percent of the his expenditures.[51] Haut Brion, Pontac, Lafite, Latour, and most of all Margaux, or what he sometimes modishly called "Chateau Margaux,"[52] accounted for half of his outlay on French wines, or 28 percent of his total wine expenditures.[53] As for his other French wine purchases, they were sometimes as expensive as luxury claret (champagne was even more expensive), but in no instance were they so popular (see Graph 5.2).[54]

Charles Spencer, 3rd Earl of Sunderland

Hervey's wine purchases represent one of the most complete early modern English records of individual taste over time, but other, less complete records indicate that his penchant for luxury claret was typical of his political and social milieu. For example, when Charles Spencer, 3rd Earl of Sunderland—son-in-law to the 1st Duke of Marlborough, First Lord of the Treasury and passionate Whig—died suddenly in 1722 in the wake of the South Sea Bubble collapse for which he was blamed, he left behind an impressively diverse and well-stocked wine cellar. French wines were his favorite, comprising 11 out of 28 entries for different wines (including bottled and casked wines).[55] Among bottled wines, and therefore probably his finest wines, the most numerous was Lafite, with Latour following slightly behind. Interestingly, there was only one listing for Portuguese wine, a hogshead of white port.[56]

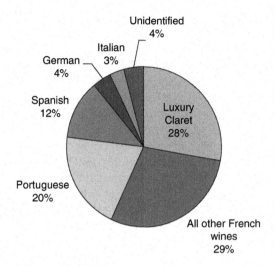

Graph 5.2   John Hervey's wine expenditures, 1702–42
Source: Suffolk Record Office, Bury St Edmunds, 941/46/13/14, "Expense Book of John Hervey, 1st Earl of Bristol."

Sir Robert Walpole

British monarchs and leading Whig aristocrats loved luxury claret, but perhaps no one was as devoted to it as the man who succeeded Sunderland as First Lord of the Treasury, Sir Robert Walpole (1676–1745). Walpole was the son of a prosperous country gentleman, Colonel Robert Walpole, whose modest political and financial success had enabled his son to go to Eton and then Cambridge. At these institutions, young Robert saw that there was a larger, more powerful, and elegant world outside of the family home in rural Norfolk, and it was this world upon which Walpole set his sights. In the end, he exceeded even his own lofty expectations, becoming the most powerful Whig leader of the eighteenth century, the first de facto Prime Minister of Great Britain, and a man of considerable fashion. According to Walpole's biographer Sir John Plumb, "in the brilliance of his taste and the grandeur of his opulence, he outshone the aristocratic world in which his talents had won for him and his family a distinguished and enduring place."[57] So, while Walpole's father the country squire drank mostly red port, such a wine would not do for the son who razed his family's modest ancestral home and built a palatial pile, the humbly named Houghton Hall (Figure 5.2). With political power and a palace of his own, the younger Walpole needed a wine to match his elevated station in life. That wine was luxury claret.[58]

At the height of his power in 1733, Walpole spent over £1,150 on wine, a sum that amounted to more than the annual income of a prosperous country gentleman like his father.[59] Of this amount, luxury claret accounted for 35 percent of the volume and 44 percent of the value. Specifically, Walpole purchased seven hogsheads of Margaux, three of Lafite, one of Haut Brion, and 36 bottles of unnamed "New French Claret."[60] Taken together, Walpole's purchases of luxury

Figure 5.2 Houghton Hall, Houghton, King's Lynn, Norfolk (built and furnished between 1722 and 1735)
Note: A mere "hall," Walpole's pile was meant to impress.

claret in 1733 amounted to approximately 234 bottles per month, or nearly eight bottles per day, more in volume and far more in value than any other type of wine in his cellar (Graph 5.3). To be sure, Walpole also bought large amounts of fashionable burgundy and champagne, which were slightly more expensive than luxury claret owing to their high transport costs. More noticeably, he purchased vast quantities of inexpensive white Lisbon and red port. These Portuguese wines seem to have been his workaday wines, or the wines for his "public tables," where he entertained dozens, sometimes hundreds of City merchants and professionals, and prosperous country squires, who formed the core of the Whig party.[61]

However, when Walpole meant to impress the elite among whom he had placed himself, his wine of choice was luxury claret. In a letter to Frederick, Prince of Wales, written in July 1731, John, Baron Hervey (second son of the 1st Earl of Bristol), described one of Walpole's semi-annual "Norfolk Congresses," which were gatherings of Walpole's cronies at Houghton, as being

> a little snug party of thirty odd, up to chin in beef, venison, geese, turkeys, etc.; and generally over the chin in claret, strong beer and punch. We had Lords spiritual and temporal, besides commoners, parsons and freeholders innumerable.[62]

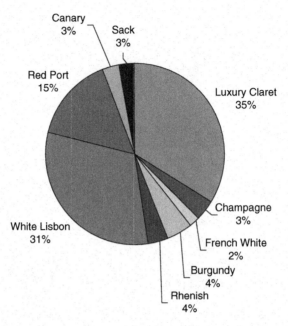

Graph 5.3 Sir Robert Walpole's Wine Purchases, 1733 (by volume)
Source: CUL, CH (H) "Vouchers, 1657–1745."

The claret in question was Haut Brion, and since Walpole's "Norfolk Congresses" were meant to pay thanks, intimidate, and impress with their material surroundings, so too was the wine he served there (Figure 5.3).

Politeness and the taste for luxury claret

But what, other than the apparent quality of the wine, made luxury claret such a compelling indicator of Walpole's status as one of the most powerful and fashionable men in England? Indeed, what does luxury claret's success on the English market in the early eighteenth century tell us about the society for which it was created? The answer, in short, is politeness. "Politeness" as a model of behavior was a major aspect of early eighteenth-century English urban culture, especially in London.[63] From its origins in the courts of Renaissance Italy, politeness spread to the court of Louis XIV in France, and then to England, where it moved beyond the court and into the town. There, in its new urban setting, it was transformed into a broad concept used to describe and prescribe the conduct and manners of the social elite, and an aesthetic standard for numerous types of human behaviors and artifacts.[64] Of course, politeness was always contested by allegedly impolite forms of behavior, and rarely did the English elite as a whole achieve the lofty standards of politeness that were proposed; the calls for polite behavior would not have been so strident and numerous were the model more consistently upheld.[65] Nevertheless, politeness was the hegemonic ideal of elite male behavior from

Figure 5.3 The Marble Parlour, Houghton Hall
Note: "A little snug party of thirty odd ... generally over the chin in claret."

roughly 1690 to 1760, precisely the period in which luxury claret arrived on the English market to stay.

Not surprisingly, given the deep divisions within England in 1689, politeness was a contested ground between Tories and Whigs, and it was the latter who claimed the prize. Post-1689, or "modern," Whigs embraced the newly combined aristocratic–mercantile elite and the commercial economy for which it stood. They explicitly rejected the backward-looking aristocratic culture of the Tories, and also the civic humanism of the Old Whigs, who were suspicious of trade and condemned luxury on the grounds that it softened and corrupted the ruling elite.[66] The triumphant Whig vision of politeness was anti-court and anti-French, gentlemanly not aristocratic, discursive not codified, and urban not rural— although a neo-classical pile in manicured parkland was certainly polite.[67] Broadly speaking, politeness was "situated wherever gentlemanly (and lady-like) society existed (the club, the drawing room, the coffeehouse, among others)," and "its characteristic activity was conversation, the substance of which was worldly, urbane things."[68]

Indeed, "things" were very important for polite behavior, and all of these things came at a price. Clothing, furniture, cutlery, chinaware, lacquered snuff boxes, silver candlesticks, lead crystal vessels of all sorts, paintings, music, and literature, were all important to the performance of politeness. And men were just as involved as women in thinking about and purchasing items that helped to fashion their identities.[69] So politeness was judged by one's behavior, but also by whether one owned the right items, whether they were sufficiently genteel in design, and whether one was capable of talking about them, appreciating their beauty, and using them in the "correct" way.[70] After all, the successful display of politeness was proof of one's good taste, and taste was a sign of virtue.[71] This virtue was what gave the post-1688 elite the right to rule and simultaneously denied that right to those who had money but poor taste, or more often, those who did not have the means to purchase the objects that would signal whatever taste they had. This idea of taste was not entirely new in the 1690s, but it acquired prominence in England in the late seventeenth century, and quickly became a justification for political power.[72]

Indeed, according to the leading historian of politeness, this behavioral ideal reached maturity in England between 1700 and 1715.[73] It is no coincidence that this was precisely the period in which luxury claret became firmly established as a symbol of allegedly superior taste of those who consumed it. Certainly other wines had the potential to be polite; wine was a key motif in classical civilization, which was itself a model for polite culture.[74] Furthermore, because wine in England was imported, consuming wine, like going on the Grand Tour, was an inherently cosmopolitan act and therefore a sign of one's politeness. Lastly, all wines could be part of polite display—chilled in a large silver wine cooler, served from a crystal decanter, poured into crystal glasses, and consumed while sitting around a mahogany table. But inasmuch as luxury claret was the preferred wine among England's most polite people, it was the most polite of all wines.

The politeness of luxury claret may also be measured by its importance in promoting conversation, and while this is difficult to measure, it is telling that wine features prominently in a number of so-called Conversation Pieces, a genre of painting that was immensely popular in early and mid-eighteenth-century England. Conversation Pieces typically depicted gentlemen or ladies, and sometimes both together, engaged in decorous conversation inside their well-appointed homes, or in manicured parks outside their homes. These paintings emphasized the social nature of polite society, and provide visual evidence of specific polite behaviors, such as appreciating wine.[75] For instance, a painting by Benjamin Ferrers painted c. 1720 depicts "Sir Thomas Sebright, Sir John Bland and Two Friends" sitting around a cloth-covered table smoking pipes and drinking wine (Figure 5.4). The men are clearly relaxed—three of them have removed their wigs—and a servant arrives through a door with a ceramic pitcher, probably wine directly from the cask, to join the pitcher already on the table. The central figure, Bland, holds a crystal decanter full of wine in his right hand, while pointing to the wine with his left hand, as if about to comment upon it.

Similarly, in what is technically a double-portrait by Sir Godfrey Kneller executed c. 1721, two members of the Whig Kit-Cat Club, the Duke of Newcastle and the Earl of Lincoln, are shown seated around a cloth-covered table (Figure 5.5). A heavy

Figure 5.4 Sir Thomas Sebright, Sir John Bland, and Two Friends (1723), by Benjamin Ferrers
Note: Polite gentlemen learning to talk about wine.

curtain hangs behind them, while a small window opens onto a clipped view of the sky and a country house. Newcastle returns the viewer's gaze, while holding a fluted wine glass in his right hand, and an onion-shaped, wicker-covered bottle in his left. He is about to pour the wine into his own glass. Lincoln looks directly at his friend, and holds an identical glass in his right hand. His glass, however, is full with red wine. His friend has already served him, and now one imagines, it is time for these two polite gentlemen to taste the wine and discuss it.

If the point of these paintings was to depict people in the midst of polite conversation, an even more successful effort comes from the Scottish artist Gawen Hamilton (1697–1737), who painted "The Brothers Clarke of Swakeleys and Friends," c. 1730–5 (Figure 5.6). In this painting, four bewigged and well-dressed men sit around a table while two similarly clad men stand on the far side of the table. Two busy servants occupy the left of the canvas, while a hunting dog lies somewhat uncomfortably in the lower right corner.[76] With their embroidered jackets, long perukes, Persian rug, gild-framed paintings, silver coffee service, crystal glasses, and large wine cooler, there is no mistaking the politeness of these men. But ultimately, the viewer is to understand that these gentlemen are not just drinking wine, they are also discussing their wine. Witness one of the two

Figure 5.5   Thomas Pelham-Holles, 1st Duke of Newcastle-under-Lyne; Henry Clinton, 7th Earl of Lincoln (c. 1721), by Godfrey Kneller
Note: Aristocrats, especially Whigs, were deeply invested in politeness.

standing gentleman pointing to his wine while clearly speaking to another fellow who is examining a piece of paper, which seems to refer to the wine that the men are enjoying. In other words, Hamilton is attempting to convey the fact that these men do not just drink wine; instead, they discuss and think wine.

Thinking wine is precisely what William Hogarth depicts in his painting of "Mr. Woodbridge and Captain Holland,"[77] which was also completed around 1730 (Figure 5.7). This conversation piece shows two men, a successful lawyer and a naval officer respectively, sitting around an ornately carved wooden table in the middle of what must be Woodbridge's office. In the background is a marble-mantled fireplace, shelves lined with law books, and a paneled wall upon which hangs a landscape painting. A servant or clerk walks through the door with a note in his hand. On the table are a book, a scroll, and a bottle of wine in a wicker-covered bottle. Both men wear perukes, jackets, silk stockings, and buckled shoes. They are not aristocrats, but they are both wealthy. Holland holds an empty glass in his right hand and casually points to Woodbridge with his left. Woodbridge, meanwhile, holds a walking stick in his left hand, while his right hand is raised, eye-height, and in it he holds a full

Figure 5.6   The Brothers Clarke of Swakeleys and Friends (c. 1730–5), by Gawen Hamilton
Note: Drinking, talking and thinking about wine among the gentry.

***

glass. He is looking intently at the glass and its contents. By painting the gesture of contemplation, Hogarth's painting is the most successful of all in capturing the connection between politeness and wine appreciation.[78]

***

Of course, we can never know if the wine depicted in any of these paintings was luxury claret, but that is beside the point. What matters is what the sitters wanted to convey, and what the viewers believed. The point of each painting was to use wine to convey the sitters' politeness, and the types of men in these conversation pieces were precisely the type who formed the market for luxury claret—aristocrats, wealthy gentry, and successful professionals. These men not only had the money for polite performance, they also enough money to record that performance on canvas, which in turn helped to reinforce and publicize their polite taste. Wine was a prop in their polite performance, and because luxury claret was the most popular wine among polite men, a knowing eighteenth-century viewer might guess that luxury claret was the wine in the glass. More certainly, the men in the paintings were all engaged in thinking about or discussing their wines. What could be more polite than thinking and talking about an imported product that was both expensive and distinct, that differed subtly from year to year and from vineyard to vineyard,

Figure 5.7   Mr. Woodbridge and Captain Holland (c. 1730), by William Hogarth
Note: A brilliant painter captures the moment of wine contemplation.

and that changed over time (and often for the better) while simply resting in one's cellar? And what polite person would not want to talk about that?

The emergence of the wine connoisseur

In fact, it is possible to trace the increasing sophistication in the language used to talk about luxury claret during the early eighteenth century, as well as a desire to think about and discuss the particularities of wine in general in the early eighteenth century. As we have seen, the advertisements for claret in the *London Gazette* began by using only price to distinguish between the different qualities of generically named claret. But soon the most expensive claret became "New French Claret," and this was quickly followed by specific estate names such as Haut Brion, Margaux, Lafite, and Latour.[79] By 1711, even these names began to be elaborated upon, so that the top wines were now referred to as coming from "the best growths," and being "deep, bright, fresh, neat" in taste and color.[80] These descriptions of wine pale in comparison to the purple prose of twenty-first century wine-writing; however, they mark the beginning of a trend toward more florid description. The price of claret was no longer sufficient to distinguish luxury claret from the traditional sort; the new consumer, a self-fashioned connoisseur, wanted more information, more to talk about. And increasingly those selling the wine were providing it.

James Brydges, 1st Duke of Chandos

The ability and desire to discourse upon wine was not new in 1700. As we have seen, Samuel Pepys commented upon the superiority of Haut Brion in 1663; Restoration rakes talked endlessly about wine (and women); and examples of the taste for wine in England being used as a subtle and more elusive measure for virtue exist as far back as the turn of the seventeenth century. But as scholars such as Keith Thomas and Terry Eagleton point out, it was not until the late seventeenth and early eighteenth century that the political use of taste really took hold.[81] And along with the politics of taste came more descriptive language about wine. This emerging polite language about wine is perhaps best illustrated by the cellar notes of James Brydges (Figure 5.8), a contemporary and acquaintance of Hervey, Spencer, and Walpole, whose cellars we have examined already.

Brydges was a Tory MP for Hereford from 1698 to 1714, although his politics became increasingly Whig as the War of the Spanish Succession wore on.[82] In fact, by 1714, when he became Baron Chandos and Earl of Carnarvon, he was a fully committed Hanoverian who generally supported the Whig government. Having amassed a great fortune during the war as Paymaster General to Her Majesty's Forces Abroad, Brydges became an avid collector of art and a patron of many artists.[83] He inherited a Jacobean mansion called Cannons at Edgeware, north of London, but as Walpole was to do, he razed the old building and built a palace in which to house his many collections. But Cannons was not for art and books alone; it also had an impressive wine cellar, which contained everything from Spanish Alicante to Greek Zante, and a great deal of luxury claret in between.[84]

From 1706 to 1711, Brydges ordered Pontac, Margaux, and Haut Brion, as well as champagne, Cahors, red and white Hermitage, and Capbreton wine, mostly through merchants in Holland who had negotiated wartime passports with the French.[85] When he was made Earl of Carnarvon in 1714, he celebrated by ordering six hogsheads of luxury claret, two of burgundy and two of champagne from his friend, the Irish economic writer Richard Cantillon in Bordeaux, as well as six hogsheads of "the best Bordeaux" and one of white Langon from Thomas Walsh, another Irish merchant in Bordeaux.[86]

But Brydges was not simply a fashionable aristocrat with a well-stocked cellar, he was also an epicure who thought about and remarked upon the qualities of the wine he drank, compared them with other wines, and aged them to see if they would improve in his cellar. This self-conscious awareness of his own preferences and the taste of his own wines made him a polite connoisseur. Brydges's wines were not just "good," "bad" or even "most particular." Instead, they had multiple dimensions: color, aroma, body, and a lifespan. Thus Rancio from Navarre was a "noble strong bodied wine," which he had aged in the cellar some twenty years until "it is grown to be strong racy wine, the sweetness all gone."

In 1719, the year he became 1st Duke of Chandos, he decided to age his Haut Brion in the belief that it would improve. The red Syracuse, he said, "does not fill the mouth as much as Monte Pulciano, and has a better body and tast [sic] than Syracuse Sarragosa." A wine called "Kill Priest" from the Dauphiné in France, was "tho' light in the mouth, the strongest French wine I ever tast'd." Champagne he considered

Figure 5.8 James Brydges, 1st Duke of Chandos (c. 1720s), by Michael Dahl
Note: A connoisseur of the arts in general, Brydges's wine-tasting notes were more descriptive than those of his peers or contemporaries.

a "ticklish purchase," and some he bought was "thick and ropy." His Rhenish wine had extraordinary cask age, originating as it did from vintages in 1666, 1684, and 1696. And his dry Mountain Malaga, supplied by the Tatems of Winchester, "when very old and perfect is mighty good to drink a glass of with fruit."

Brydges asked Mr Taunton, his merchant in Southampton, to be on the look-out for ships arriving from the West Indies, that they might have some well-traveled madeira on board. He purchased Margaux from Mr Taunton, but then complained that it was "not clear," as though mixed with port and tasting like Cahors. Another claret from Mr Taunton had a strong, fiery taste, and Brydges surmised that "the correspondents abroad had tampered with it" by adding brandy.[87]

Amidst all these different wines, the overwhelming favorite in Brydges's immense wine cellar was luxury claret. Not only was luxury claret the wine most frequently found there, it was also the most fashionable wine among his many dinner guests. When a party of six was due to dine at Cannons, as often happened, two to three dozen bottles of claret were automatically called for.[88] Of course, not all of the bottles were necessarily consumed at one sitting, but drinking vast quantities of wine was not incompatible with polite behavior. Politeness, especially among men alone, was not divorced from the idea of honorable drinking that required every man to keep up with the group. Moreover, so long as one talked about and drank fine wines, any resulting drunkenness could be excused as an excess of good taste. In that way, polite gentlemen could draw a distinction, false though it may have been, between their own drunkenness and the drunkenness of those who could not afford, or did not how to be polite.

***

Luxury claret was made for the Restoration court, but quickly became a wine of polite gentlemen. It was precisely what the post-Revolution political and social order demanded. After all, in an environment where aristocratic lineage no longer provided the ultimate rationale for political rule, having good taste became the foundation of political legitimacy for an aristocratic order that combined both old and new families. Thus, the gentility that legitimized political authority was not only materialized, it was aestheticized. As the 3rd Earl of Shaftesbury argued in 1711, to love and admire beauty is "advantageous to social affection, and highly assistant to virtue, which is itself no other than the love of order and beauty in society."[89] Following this argument, aesthetic taste correlated with moral and political judgment; or, the better taste a man had, the more legitimate was his moral and political authority.[90] Drinking luxury claret may have made Whig leaders hypocrites, but this was the paradox posed by the luxury debate more generally. Luxuries corrupted the political body, but "opulent display was an essential ingredient of aristocratic rule."[91] As Whigs like Walpole understood, taste was political, and polite taste was power.

6

"Firm and erect the Caledonian stood"

Scotland and Claret, 1707–c. 1770

While popular taste in England took an abrupt turn from French wine to Portuguese during the late Stuart and early Hanoverian era—and luxury claret became the fashionable wine for the English elite—the same was not true in Scotland. In North Britain, as Scotland was sometimes called in the wake of the Union, traditionally made claret (i.e. not the luxury sort) was the predominant wine in aristocratic homes *and* rustic taverns, from the Highlands to the Lowlands, throughout much of the eighteenth century. This point, seemingly unremarkable given the very real differences in the cultural practices of the two Stuart kingdoms that were united in 1707, is significant for the fact that one of the principal features of the Act of Union was the equalization of duties at the English level for almost all goods, including wine. What allowed the Scots to continue drinking claret was high levels of fraud and smuggling, as well as fraud and smuggling at high levels.

Although claret began the eighteenth century in Scotland as a commodity with which to defy English domination, it quickly grew to represent a Scottish identity that, whatever else it was, was not English. In other words, there was a wide range of Scottish identities in the eighteenth century, and consequently, many arguments about the meaning of the Scottish past and the best course for Scotland's future. But Scottish Hanoverians and Jacobites, Unionists and anti-Unionists, Tories and Whigs, Presbyterians, Episcopalians, and Catholics, could all agree that, as odd as it might sound, a red wine from southwestern France represented something far more than a familiar taste: it represented a proud and manly Scotland.

From the Highlands to the Lowlands

Evidence for the preponderance of claret in Scotland after the Union of 1707 is overwhelming, and that evidence is not limited to the aristocratic homes that once lined Edinburgh's Canongate. Quite the contrary; excepting the poor and indigent for whom wine had always been a rarity, claret was a national Scottish drink for much of the eighteenth century. Writing from Inverness in 1716, a year after the first major Jacobite rebellion, the future Lord Advocate of Scotland, Duncan Forbes, wrote to a friend in Edinburgh:

> For my own part I am almost wearied of this wicked world; one wish, and but one I had when I left you concerning myself, that I might enjoy eight days free of company and Claret. How I have succeeded, you may guess by this, that though today it be just a month since I saw you, I have not yet buckled a shoe, that is, I have not been for one day out of my boots.[1]

At that time Forbes was a prominent Highland lawyer and a staunch Whig who had opposed the Jacobite rebellion in 1715, despite the fact that it was led by his friend and fellow claret lover, the Earl of Mar. As it happened, the two men could agree on wine but not on politics.

A decade later, and somewhat farther down the social scale, the evidence for large amounts of claret in Scotland is still overwhelming. For instance, in 1725, the English officer Edward Burt ventured north to assist General George Wade in his massive road-building project to "open up" the Highlands to British government control. Burt kept an epistolary journal of his travels and, imagining himself something of an epicure, made frequent observations on Scottish food and drink. He enjoyed regaling his friends in London with hyperbolic tales of Scottish incivility and the severity of the Highland landscape, but for this reason his testimonies to the ubiquity of claret are all the more revealing. On his first night north of the Tweed, Burt was disgusted by the potted pigeons simmering in rancid butter that were presented to him by the innkeeper at Kelso, so he made do with a crust of bread and a "Pint of good Claret."[2] In Edinburgh he was again nauseated, this time by the cook, who was "too filthy an Object to be described." First impressions aside, Burt "supped very plentifully, and drank good French Claret" and all was merry until ten o'clock when he was again revolted by the sight of Edinburgh citizens jettisoning their ordure onto the streets from high above in their multi-storied "landings."[3]

When Burt finally arrived at Inverness, where he was stationed, he found that northern Scotland, filthy as the rest, was not without its creature comforts. "We have one great advantage, that makes amends for many inconveniences," wrote Burt, "that is, the wholesome and agreeable drink—I mean French claret, which is to be met with almost everywhere in Public Houses of any note, except in the heart of the Highlands, and sometimes even there."[4] Burt acknowledged that since the time he and other English soldiers had arrived in Inverness the price of claret had increased from 16d. per bottle to 2s., although "there be no more Duty paid upon it now than there was before, which, indeed, was often none at all."[5] Obviously, local merchants were aware that the claret-deprived English officers were an easy market and raised their prices. But to English officers stationed in the Highlands, claret was still cheaper and more readily available than back home, and that, thought Burt, was to be enjoyed.

Other evidence for the preponderance of claret throughout Scotland abounds. An inventory of the 3rd Earl of Leven's wine cellar at Balgonie Castle, Fife, in

1726, listed 156 chopin bottles (roughly one quart each) and 140 mutchkin bottles (roughly one pint each) of claret; another 13 chopin bottles of "old claret"; 30 chopin bottles and 10 mutchkins of sherry; 24 chopin bottles and 11 mutchkins of white wine; 5 chopin bottles and 9 mutchkins of sweet wine; 2 chopins of Lisbon; 7 mutchkins of Orange wine;[6] 6 chopins of "Aquavitae from Dalquees" [Dalkey?].[7] In other words, nearly three-quarters of all the bottles in Leven's cellar contained claret.

Moving to the less rarified environment of Edinburgh taverns, or howffs, we see from the vernacular poetry of the early eighteenth century that red wine from Bordeaux was the urban bards elixir of choice. William Hamilton of Gilbertfield (1665–1751) even dismissed Scottish whisky for the enlivening virtues of claret:

> The dull-draff drink maks me sae dowff
> A' I can do's but bark and yowff;
> Yet set me in a claret howff
> Wi folk that's chancy,
> My muse may len' me then a gowff
> To clear my fancy.[8]

Allan Ramsay (c. 1685–1758), whose life and work did so much to inspire Robert Burns, was even more effusive about the transcendent qualities of red Bordeaux:

> Gude claret best keeps out the cauld,
> And drives away the winter soon;
> It maks a man baith gash and bauld
> And heaves his saul beyond the moon.[9]

Smuggling and fraud

Many historians and wine writers have explained the abundance of claret in eighteenth-century Scotland, especially when compared to its paucity in England, by claiming that Scottish Customs duties on wine remained lower than English duties even after the Union.[10] This is false. After the Union wine duties in Scotland were the same as in any English outport, and thus roughly four pounds per tun fewer than in London. Consequently, evidence for the continued preponderance of claret in Scotland has caused confusion. Indeed, Scottish import records for the first half of the eighteenth century cannot explain the abundance of claret because officially very little French wine arrived on Scottish shores. Yet no one at the time was fooled by what was officially recorded.[11] Claret continued to be the common wine of Scotland long after the Union for the same reason that it was still readily available in towns and villages along the south and east coasts of England.[12] Smuggling and fraud, especially the latter, kept the cities, towns, and villages from Dumfries to Orkney well stocked with red wine from Bordeaux.

***

From the very outset of the Union, standardization of Customs duties throughout Britain proved exceedingly difficult. In Scotland prior to the Union, as in England and Ireland until the reign of Charles II, Customs collection was farmed. Thus, the Scottish government itself had very little experience in actually gathering the duty on wine.[13] In the spring of 1707 measures were taken to help the Scots conform to both the method of collection and the level of Customs duty taken in England. *The Book of Rates*, copies of the Acts of Parliament relating to the Revenues of England, standing orders, rules, instructions, and five English customs officers were all sent north; but by July 1707 it was clear that the terms of the Union could not easily be implemented.[14] A letter from the Commissioners of Customs in Edinburgh to the Treasury in London outlined the problems at hand:

> We find all the people and officers here at a loss concerning the computations after the English method, and therefore we shall put such South Britains [sic] as are here amongst them, and place the most expert in the ports of greatest business: and all of them shall be attended with plain and full instructions, that so the Comptroller-General and Collectors may agree in their articles, which will prevent the ruin of poor Collectors and their securities, and prove wholesome to the Revenue. We then resolved, that whoever is admitted into the Establishment shall first obtain a certificate that he is affectionate to Her Majesty's Government, Queen Anne; that he is clear of tax-men or late farmers; that he is of sober life and conversation and is not concerned in trade (a thing not hitherto regarded in these parts) nor in the keeping of a public house, or anything else that may divert them from Her Majesty's service.[15]

Nor, it seems, were confusion and divided loyalties among Scottish Customs officers the only problems. In many cases officers did not have the will or manpower to find and arrest the flow of smuggled goods. The consequence of this was "easy to discern," wrote the Scottish Commissioners: "goods, Custom free, will by one serpentine stratagem or other, be diffused not only into all parts of the six northern counties [of England] but perhaps to London itself."[16]

Despite the apparent goodwill of the Scottish Commissioners and their English assistants, smuggling continued to flourish. In fact, smuggling was

> the great growth industry of Scotland during the decades after 1707. This reflected not only a desire to make quick profits but also widespread popular opposition to the new customs and tax regime which had followed in the wake of the Union.[17]

As for illegally importing French wine, "serpentine stratagems" were legion. The most direct way to circumvent the law was to "run" the wine past Customs officers. Elaborate sail signals could be used to notify smugglers on shore that the boat full of French wine was arriving, which would trigger a signal to proceed into port if the "coast was clear"; cargo could be unloaded at night, often in a discreet cove or inlet; a ship full of wine could hover off shore and be unloaded slowly by smaller vessels that did not attract the attention of the tide waiters. Ships loaded with cargo were even purposely wrecked at a predetermined spot on the coast.[18] When apprehended, ship captains pretended that they were bound for another country but had been driven ashore. In the case of Scottish smugglers, the "other country" usually meant Norway (then a part of the Danish kingdom) or a port in the Baltic.[19] "You are to proceed without loss of time to St. Martins [St Martin de Ré]," wrote John Steuart of Inverness to Alexander Todd, master of the "Catherine" of Leith in 1726,

> and you are there to address yourself to Mr. Alex. Gordon, Mercht. there, and deliver him the letter herewith given you, who will furnish you in what quantity of salt your ship can taken in, and ye liquor which Mr. Robert Gordon of Bourdeaux is to ship for our accot. which will be about 12 tunns. And sd. Mr. Gordon is to provide you in foreign clearances. Yule endeavour to gett as much as possible, and notice that when, Please God, you return, in case you meet or is taken up by any Coustome House yachtes, to declare yourself bound for Riga in ye Baltick, and be shure you be well furnished with Clearances accordingly. If you gett safe to the firth yule endeavour to calle off Causea [Covesea in Morayshire] where orders will attend you. We beg your utmost care and Dilligence.[20]

There were other methods for running-in wine and other goods as well, all of them risky. Entire cargoes could be lost without compensation; fines for smuggling were stiff; and punishment, sometimes severe, was exacted on those who had no well-placed connections.

However, a majority of French wine coming into Scotland was imported in a less risky way: fraud. There were many, sometimes ingenious, ways of doing this. A general survey of the ports in Scotland, compiled in 1724 for the Lords Commissioners of the Treasury, and specifically for the claret-loving Sir Robert Walpole, stated that the "usual practice at Leith and other ports in Scotland" was to allow "French wines to be entered as from Bilbao and pay dutys under this denomination of Spanish wine." This was certainly a familiar practice to English Customs Commissioners, but the authors of the report stated that it is "at present almost unavoidable, the endeavours of the Commissioners to make the merchants pay up the French dutys for all they import having hither to proved ineffectual."[21] It was difficult enough for Customs officers to prove the provenance of any wine, and in Scotland it could be even more difficult to find a judge who did not sympathize with the "fair traders."[22]

According to the 1724 report, another slightly more elaborate ruse used by merchants involved condemned French wine that had gone bad. The oxidized or acetified wine was auctioned off at a low price and put on a coasting boat with a pass for Newcastle or another port in England, where it was to be made into brandy or vinegar. Once offshore, however, the boat full of bad wine would meet a ship carrying good French wine, exchange cargoes, and then proceed to port where the good wine was landed by virtue of the permit for bad wine. The bad wine itself was then sent to London, where it was declared a loss and then sold to brandy distillers, vinegar makers or unscrupulous vintners who would use it for blending. Of course, a similar transaction could also be done with good wine that was declared to have gone bad for the sake of a low auction price. In this instance, there would be no need for an exchange at sea; only the cooperation of the Customs House taster and the auctioneer was needed.

On other occasions French wine was landed and paid duty as Spanish wine, and was then reloaded for export to North Sea, Baltic and even Southern European ports (a situation so obviously unlikely that the authors of the report were startled by the audacity of the smugglers). The importer would then get the drawback (a partial Customs duty refund) on the wines for re-export; however, as the Customs officers knew, this process was "only pretended and for no other reason but to reland [the wine in Britain] and defraud the crown of dutys." The report went on to say that Glasgow and the southwest of Scotland were supplied with French wine from the Isle of Man, where the wines were landed unmolested before being run into Scotland. Ironically, however, smuggling in Edinburgh could be even easier. Wine was landed directly to the east and west of Leith harbor, "at which places no officers have been stationed."[23]

The report, which was submitted to Sir Robert Walpole as a follow-up to his attempts in 1722–3 to reorganize the Customs throughout Britain, blamed the extent of smuggling and fraud in Scotland on the incompetence or corruption of Scottish Customs officers. For example, according to the report, at Stranraer, James Gordon, Land and Tide Surveyor, "is old and infirm and not sufficiently active for his station." At Dumfries, John Muir, Boatman, "is unable to row and unskilfull in the managment of a boat." At Inverness, John Haldane, Tide Surveyor, "is not only negligent but was accused before us on oath of suffering foods to be run, of which we believe him guilty." At Dundee, Gilbert Smith, Tidewaiter, "is negligent and not capable of doing service to the Revenue." At Kirkaldy, John Anderson, Landwaiter, "is negligent and ignorant in his business, incapable of improvement and aged sixty two years." At Leith, John Colquitt, Collector, "neglected to cause the officers to take the proper oaths enjoyn'd by law, did not acquaint the Commissioners of the practice of exporting wine for the drawback, which has been often done there for the sake of relanding it, suffer'd traders and their agents to enter dispatches in his coast books, which are kept in great disorder."[24] Moreover, most Customs officers in Scotland had failed to take either the oath of office or the oath to the Government, or both.[25] The entire situation was complicated by the fact that the government itself had failed to standardize Scottish port fees, which led to disparities from one port to the next, and merchant weariness. The result was that "the merchants complain and are in many places uneasey under the burthen [of port fees] thereof."[26]

Never once do the authors of the 1724 report ask why such strong demand for French wine existed in the first place. Furthermore, smuggling and fraud were hardly Scottish issues alone. Similar surveys submitted to Walpole by the Commissioners of Customs in 1733 show that these activities were common in parts of England as well.[27] In fact, it was smuggling and fraud throughout Britain, along with notorious adulteration practices, that encouraged Walpole to attempt to place an excise tax on wine and tobacco in 1733.[28] But Walpole's move was blocked by Parliament, and controlling illegal trade remained one of the great challenges of the eighteenth-century British state.[29] Nevertheless, what made wine fraud and smuggling in Scotland so extraordinary was the involvement of so many state authorities in the illicit activities. In one incident in 1716, Archibald Dunbar, Provost of Elgin, was unfortunate enough to have his claret shipment seized by a tide surveyor at Inverness. Dunbar used his position to steal the wine back, and when Alexander Erskine, Collector of the Customs at Inverness, protested to him directly, Dunbar was unrepentant. Erskine tried to take the matter to a higher authority but the whole affair was dismissed upon the intervention of Charles Eyre, Solicitor to H.M. Customs, who was himself "a great lover of claret, and probably not averse to accepting cheap contraband wine when it came his way."[30]

Captain Burt told of a similar incident that occurred when a "considerable Quantity of Wine and Brandy was run, and lodged in a House on the north Side of the Murray [*sic*] Firth" at Inverness.[31] When the Customs officer, a sergeant and 12 soldiers arrived to arrest the smuggler and seize the liquor, the smuggler was able to extricate himself by threatening to expose the officer for his own connivance in a much larger cargo of smuggled goods. The red-faced officer was forced to feign incompetence in front of the sergeant and the soldiers by saying that he had forgotten the arrest warrant. He called off the operation and simply paid the sergeant and the soldiers to return to Inverness.[32] Presumably, the smuggler was not bothered again.

"It was notorious that the Scottish customs were honoured more in the breach than in the observance," says the historian Rosalind Mitchison. "All officers belonged to some great man's kin or following and could not easily be sacked."[33] Walpole's attempts to reform Customs collection in Scotland led to the abolition of a separate Board of Customs Commissioners for Scotland and the creation of a board for the United Kingdom as a whole, but, as J. H. Plumb remarks, this had no impact: "smuggling, frauds, evasions, loss of revenue remained—but the [Customs] jobs were now in the right hands."[34] That is, they were in the hands of the pro-government Campbells, who fleeced the government nonetheless.

Lastly, English officials like Captain Burt who were sent to Scotland to enforce the laws of Great Britain, were not entirely reliable when it came to claret smuggling. Writing from Inverness in the mid-1720s, Burt readily acknowledged his own ambivalence:

> I wish the Reformation [of smuggling] could be made for the Good of the Country (for the Evil is universal); but I cannot say I should even be contented it should extend to the Claret, till my time comes to return to England and humble Port, of which, if I were but only inclined to taste, there is not one Glass to be obtained for Love of Money, either here or in any other Part of Scotland that has fallen within my Knowledge: but this does not at all excite

my Regret. You will say I have been giving you a pretty Picture of Patriotism in miniature, or as it relates to myself.[35]

***

If smuggling claret was common, fraudulent declarations were even more so. As John Clerk of Penicuik, Writer to the Signet and former Union Commissioner, wrote in 1730:

> This trade in French wines and brandies [is] founded on notorious perjury for it is well known that since the Union, when high duties in these liquors took place, the wines have been entered on the oaths of the importers as Spanish wines and have all payed the Spanish duties, and the Brandies were run without any duty at all.[36]

That this was true is revealed by the surviving Quarterly Customs Accounts for Leith, which begin in 1742, although by that time the so-called Spanish wines were more often entered as "Portuguese."[37]

At first glance the Leith Customs Accounts for wine are carefully kept records of goods imported into the Scottish capital. For example, during the first quarter on record—October 1 to December 31, 1742—31 cargoes of wine were landed at Leith, of which 25 contained Portuguese wine amounting to 81 tuns and 23 gallons, and six contained French wine amounting to 8 tuns and 1 hogshead.[38] In subsequent quarters the number and size of wine cargoes varied but Portuguese wine invariably dominated over French, while occasional cargoes of madeira (listed separately, although technically a Portuguese wine), Levantine, German, Spanish, and Corsican wine arrived as well. In other words, except for the smaller volume, Leith Quarterly Customs Accounts in the 1740s suggest that Scottish wine imports mirrored those of Britain as a whole.

However, a more critical examination of the Quarterly Customs Accounts reveals how little they can be trusted. For example, in the first quarter of 1745, there were 19 wine cargoes landed at Leith, of which 17 were listed as Portuguese, one French and one Rhenish.[39] At face value then, this quarter was dominated by Portuguese wine imports even more than usual. And yet, of the Portuguese wine cargoes, six arrived via Norway in hogshead casks (i.e. Bordeaux casks), and another six arrived directly from Portugal but also in hogsheads, despite the fact that Portuguese producers shipped their wines in pipes, which were twice as large as hogsheads. Claiming to carry wine via Norway, usually Bergen or Christiansand, was essentially a form of state-sanctioned deception used by merchants to import French wine.[40] Fake Norwegian documentation of the cargo made the declaration look more genuine because it was supposedly stamped with the authority of another country's Customs officers, thus absolving Scottish Customs officers from any involvement should the wine declaration be proven false. This practice also made the fraud more difficult to prosecute, although the use of French casks for Portuguese wine was no less conspicuous for all that.

More brazen importers did not bother to go via Norway, but simply stated that their French wine was Portuguese or Spanish despite the use of French casks. For example, in one instance in April 1722, John Steuart dispatched the "Margaret" of Inverness to Rotterdam, where it was to pick up "Lisbon salt and about ten tuns of french wine" from Bordeaux, along with two casks of white wine and 100 flasks of burgundy. More importantly, he asked his Scottish contacts in Rotterdam, the factors Alexander Andrew and Alexander Carstairs, to make up invoices and bills of lading for the salt and wine as from Lisbon, "since the ship is to report here as from Lisbon, and the wine to be entered as Portugal wine."[41] In other cases still, what arrived as Iberian wine was actually French wine that had been transferred from French casks to Portuguese pipes and Spanish butts in Guernsey, Jersey, Rotterdam, or again Norway, where various types of Iberian casks were readily available. Applying this evidence to the Quarterly Customs Accounts reveals a very different picture of the early and mid-eighteenth-century Scottish wine trade. Whereas the official figures show only one cargo of French wine landed at Leith from January 1 until March 31, 1745, there were at least 13 cargoes of French wine, and instead of 17 cargoes of Portuguese wine, there were probably only five.

Such obvious fraud could not have been committed without the knowledge and involvement of Scottish Customs officers, and this state of affairs in the Scottish capital seems to have been mimicked in the provinces. Surviving wine bills of Laurence Oliphant, Laird of Gask (1691–1767), confirm that in the 1740s claret was still readily available in Perth, for example. Oliphant ordered his claret from Perth merchants since at least the 1720s,[42] and this did not change during the Jacobite Rebellion in 1745–6, in which Oliphant fought alongside Bonnie Prince Charlie and was appointed Treasurer of the Jacobite government in Scotland. On December 20, 1745 Oliphant held a dinner in celebration of "His Royal Highness the Prince's Birthday," which happened to be the very day that Prince Charlie crossed back into Scotland on his fateful retreat from Derby. The news, if it had already arrived, did not dampen the celebration because the claret flowed freely.

The bill from Ann Hickson, a tavern-keeper in Perth, included 29 bottles of claret, nine bottles of lisbon, three bottles of Preignac, two bottles of arrack, one bottle of rum, 44 bottles of beer, and only one broken glass. That, however, was just for dinner (a mid-afternoon meal at the time). The evening supper was some-what less revelrous, but again the claret flowed far more than any other wine: 11 bottles were served, along with one bottle of lisbon, one bottle of negus,[43] and three bottles of beer.[44]

When the Prince's army won a battle against the British army at Falkirk on January 17, 1746, there was more claret-based celebration in Perth.[45] Moreover, the Prince himself, already an established bon-vivant, seems to have preferred claret to all other wines, or at least that was true during his sojourn to Britain.[46]

But for all its optimistic celebrating, or perhaps because of it, the Jacobite cause was dealt a mortal blow at Culloden and its infamous aftermath. For Scottish merchants, Customs officers, and customers involved in illicit claret trade this was not the end itself, but the beginning of the end. Prior to the '45, the Hanoverian state rarely enforced laws in Scotland for fear of civil unrest—as had occurred in

Glasgow and Edinburgh during the 1720s and 1730s. But the Jacobite army's drive to Derby had put too much fear in the hearts of the Hanoverians for them to allow the Scottish to play by their own rules. It was not by coincidence that in 1745, while the Jacobites were in control of much of Scotland, the British Parliament increased the duty on French wines by £8 (Sterling) and on all other wines by £4. As before, revenue from wine imports was needed to pay for maintaining a loyal British army. But progress in collecting the new rates remained slow, and while direct smuggling of wine began to decline after 1745, it by no means ended.[47] In a letter to Thomas Barry at Guernsey written in 1768, the wine merchant Alexander Oliphant of Ayr showed that some things remained the same:

> Please ship on board [Captain McGown's] vessel for our account 10 tuns of claret, the best you can afford at about 700 livres per tun and one tun of good malaga white wine. You'll please get the claret rack'd into Spanish casks—one half in pipes and the other in hogsheads[48] and clear it out and ship under the denomination of Spanish Galicia; we must request you'll keep this to yourself, you need not even let the captain into the secret.[49]

***

Ultimately, it is impossible to say just how much fraud and smuggling of claret occurred in Scotland in the first half of the eighteenth century, but there are ways to estimate. For example, we can compare Bordeaux export records to Leith import records on the eve of the 1745 rebellion. In the early 1740s, Bordeaux statistics reveal an annual average of roughly 1,975 tuns of wine sent to Scotland, while Leith imports—which accounted for two-thirds of all Scottish wine imports—indicate that approximately 36 tuns of French wine (of any sort) were annually imported into Scotland.[50] These approximations suggest that the actual amount of claret coming into Scotland was a mindboggling 55 times greater than official imports. And while wine smuggling and fraud seem to have slowed in the wake of Jacobite defeat in 1746, they remained widespread practices in Scotland until the 1780s.

The meaning of claret in eighteenth-century Scotland

But why for much of the eighteenth century did people in Scotland go to such lengths to get their claret? The most obvious answer to this question is that the Scottish smuggled or falsely declared French wine because they wanted to avoid paying the high duty. As the historian T. M. Devine explains:

> Scotland had been accustomed to low taxes and relaxed methods of gathering revenue before the Union, so that the new impositions after 1707 were bitterly resented both on economic grounds and because they were seen as an attempt by London to force Scotland to contribute to the English National Debt, which had swollen hugely to finance the Spanish Succession War.[51]

From the Treaty of Union in 1707 until 1745 the cost of legally importing a tun of French wine in a British outport such as Leith was around £51, while duty on a tun of Portuguese wine amounted to only £19, Spanish wine to £20, and Rhenish wine to £27. In 1745 and again in 1763 the duties were increased, in both cases to help allay the cost of war. These increases brought the total duty in British outports to roughly £67 per tun for French wine, £30 per tun for Portuguese wine, £31 per tun for Spanish wine, and £35 per tun for Rhenish wine. In other words, the import duty on French wines was nearly twice as high as on wine from any other country. Clearly, then, there was an economic incentive for Scottish merchants to circumvent the law in order to provide their customers with claret. Yet understanding the economic incentive for illegally importing claret does not explain the consistently high demand for claret, because these same incentives existed in England where the amount of claret smuggling was markedly lower. Why, then, was there so much demand in Scotland?

One reason for Scottish demand for claret above all other wines was that Scottish consumers had been enjoying red wine from Bordeaux since at the late Middle Ages so that by the eighteenth century the taste for claret was deeply ingrained. It was therefore logical, so long as the demand for claret continued, that merchants would do their best to supply it at the lowest possible cost. And so long as merchants were successful in supplying inexpensive claret, whatever their methods, there was little incentive for claret-loving Scots to seek a substitute. Moreover, wine-drinking Scots were aware of one possible alternative to cheap claret; after all, they had the example of England to show them. If not claret, then "humble port," as Burt called it. And if not real port, then some adulterated version of it. In 1733, Walpole himself wrote of wine in England, that by "far the greatest part of what is sold in publick houses is nothing but a poisonous composition of unknown materials."[52] Admittedly, Walpole wrote with an eye on promoting his Excise Bill, but evidence suggests he was not entirely exaggerating.[53]

Another reason for Scottish demand for claret, at least among the elite, was exposure to luxury claret and the spread of "polite" behavior. At the outset of the Union, luxury claret was still rare in Scotland. Daniel Defoe declared that Scottish stockpiling of claret in 1707 would have little impact in England because the Scots drank a small, thin type of claret as opposed to the stronger, fuller-bodied type of claret that was preferred in England. Likewise, when Lord Mar had claret sent to him in London from Edinburgh in 1707, he suddenly found the wine disappointing.[54] Perhaps this allotment was particularly bad, but most likely Mar's palate had changed while in the metropolis. As the chief Scottish representative during the implementation of the Treaty of Union, Mar circulated among the English political elite who would have exposed him to luxury claret. Consequently, traditionally made claret would no longer suffice, especially if Mar were expected to entertain guests. Back in Scotland, Mar's correspondent Davie Erskine offered to send some different claret from his own wine merchant, a fellow named Gordon in Leith. But Erskine understood that there were limits to how much he could help Mar in his new environment. The replacement claret, wrote Erskine, "will serve for Alloa [Mar's home in Scotland], but not for London."[55]

Similarly, household accounts of Lady Grisell Baillie of Mellerstain reveal that from 1693 to 1718, the Baillie family spent between £5 and £25 (Sterling) for a hogshead of claret while residing at Mellerstain, their residence in the Scottish Borders. However, in London, where they spent half of their time after the Union of 1707, they spent between £27 and £47 for a hogshead of claret. Smuggling and fraud in Scotland may have accounted for some of the price discrepancy between Mellerstain and London, but so did the quality of the wine. In London, for instance, the Baillies purchased a "Hogshead Pontack wine bought at Bourdaux by my Lord Stairs," which cost them more than £34.[56]

The taste for luxury claret that elite Scots acquired in London was gradually brought back north, and no doubt abetted by the spread of "politeness" in Scotland.[57] The effects of this demand for luxury claret can be seen in the letter book of Bailie John Steuart of Inverness who in 1718 wrote to his agent in Bordeaux, the Jacobite Robert Gordon, entreating him to "Ship good Strong wine for us, Since Small doe not doe with us."[58] Again in 1722 Steuart made a similar request to John Gordon in Rotterdam, who had previously sent Steuart a shipment of wines that was "generally very small." A disappointed Steuart wanted, instead, a tun of "good strong wine, I mean Claret drawen off the Gross lead [i.e. lees, one hopes]."[59] Steuart must have got what he wanted because by the early 1730s he was assuring a potential customer, Robert Bigar of Edinburgh, that the claret he offered for sale was "a fine cullerd deep good wine."[60] Where it came from in Bordeaux is unclear, but by 1730, if not earlier, elite Scottish merchants and consumers, especially in and around Edinburgh, were well aware of Haut Brion, Lafite, Margaux, and Latour.[61]

However, luxury claret and its polite consumers represented only a tiny minority of Scottish wine and wine drinkers as a whole. The vast majority of claret in Scotland in the early and mid-eighteenth century continued to be the traditional, inexpensively produced variety whose price was kept low through smuggling and fraud.[62] The paramount reasons for the popularity of this type of claret in Scotland were because it was inexpensive and because the very act of consuming fraudulently declared or smuggled claret was a form of political and cultural resistance to the Union. In other words, smuggling and fraud—"fair trading," as the Scottish called it—was not merely an economic decision, it was also a way to preserve a Scottish cultural identity that, whatever the specifics, was opposed to English domination. Claret was a particularly compelling symbol in this regard because it was from France, which was not only Scotland's erstwhile ally, but also England's greatest enemy.

The link between claret and Scottish patriotism was most famously manifested in various forms of Jacobite behavior, which as scholars have shown were just as likely to be displays of anti-Englishness as they were signs of genuine allegiance to the House of Stewart.[63] In the many Jacobite clubs in Scotland, a vast amount of claret was used to toast "The Confusion of the Union," "The Cassin' o the Wanchancie Covenant,"[64] and, most famously of all, "The King o'er the water." While giving this last toast, two Jacobite gentlemen would raise their glasses of claret over a jug of water, thereby giving a literal meaning to their otherwise illegal toast to the exiled Stewart king who lived across the sea.[65]

But the crushing defeat of Bonnie Prince Charlie in 1746 and the British government's measures to eradicate the Highland culture that fed Jacobite support, meant that Jacobitism as a political force began to die out quickly in Scotland after the rebellion ended. Conversely, the Anglicization of Scotland began to accelerate in this very same period. This latter process did not entail an immediate or complete transformation of Scotland, nor did it entail Anglicization in all domains of Scottish life. Indeed, historians of eighteenth-century Scotland continue to debate the aspects, time-frame, causes, and degree to which Anglicization occurred; but all agree that British laws and English culture had a profound impact upon Scotland in the century after the Union.[66] What the evidence from wine drinking tells us about this debate is that English elite taste began to penetrate into Scotland in the early eighteenth century, which can be seen with the arrival of luxury claret. But broad-based Anglicization of Scottish taste was a gradual process that reflected the popular acceptance of the British state only after 1746, and picked up momentum as the century wore on. Specifically in terms of wine, this meant a move from traditional claret to port.

How quickly the shift from claret to port occurred and among what social groups it was most pronounced is difficult to ascertain because mid-eighteenth-century Scottish wine import figures are patchy, and where they exist it should by now be clear that they are less than fully reliable. But after 1746, and even more so after the Seven Years' War against France (1756–63), there seems to have been a genuine decline in Scottish claret consumption. Wine import figures for all of Scotland, which were first compiled in 1755, suggest that French wine imports were hurt by the Seven Years' War. Officially, French wines comprised only 7 percent of all wine imported into Scotland during the Seven Years' War, while, Portuguese wine comprised 61 percent, Spanish wine 27 percent and Madeira wine 4 percent. German and Ottoman wines made up the difference (Graph 6.1).[67]

While these figures are highly suspect because of the vast amount of fraud and smuggling that still occurred, Bordeaux export figures confirm a decrease in wines sent to Scotland during the Seven Years' War.[68] Cellar records also suggest a decline in the popularity of claret in Scotland after 1745. Families like the Baillies of Mellerstain appear to have been consuming more port than claret as early as 1749, when an inventory of the family cellar at Mellerstain in Berwickshire recorded a mere 26 bottles of claret, along with 65 bottles of port, 43 bottles of sherry, 33 bottles of Orange wine [probably Châteauneuf-du-Pape], 25 bottles of canary, 24 bottles of madeira, 15 bottles of white wine, and 4 bottles of Frontiniac.[69]

After the Seven Years' War ended in 1763, Scottish import figures for French wine actually rose above pre-war levels, and in the period 1764–77 French wine imports in Scotland averaged just over 10 percent of total imports. But it is unclear how to assess these statistics. Were Scots actually drinking more claret than before, or were import figures more accurate? Given the broad trend, the latter seems more likely. In other words, in the aftermath of the 1745–6 Jacobite Rebellion, the British state in the form of Customs officers was increasingly successful at enforcing the legal duty on incoming French wines. Therefore, what looks like a statistical increase in Scottish claret consumption is probably an indication of an overall decrease in

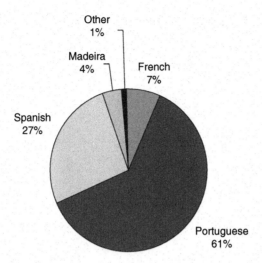

Graph 6.1 Scottish wine imports during the Seven Years' War, 1755–62*
Source: NA, Customs 14.
Note: * The Seven Years' War is usually dated 1756–1763, although the first major battle occurred at Fort Duquesne (later Pittsburgh) in North America in 1755. Scottish imports records for 1763 were destroyed in a Customs House fire.

claret consumption because of the greater ability of the British state to enforce its laws, which suggests not only greater power of the center over the peripheries, but the increasing acceptance of the British state by the people of Scotland.

***

As the amount of illegally imported claret in Scotland was declining and port importation increasing, the symbolism of claret in early and mid-eighteenth-century Scotland was crystallized for posterity. Sometime around 1760, John Home (1722–1808), a Scottish poet, dramatist, and erstwhile Presbyterian minister, wrote the following epigram:

> Firm and erect the Caledonian stood
> Old was his mutton and his claret good.
> Let them drink port, the English statesman cried.
> He drank the poison and his spirit died.[70]

The overtly masculine, indeed phallic, imagery of Home's epigram is clear: once-manly Scotland had been emasculated by the intrusive "English" state. Home was a proud Scot who was born in Leith and spent most of his life in Edinburgh; however, he was also a Whig, a tutor to George III, and an occasional resident of London. He fought on the Hanoverian side in the '45 and in his politics and prose was a fervent Scottish *and* British patriot (Figure 6.1).[71] In short, Jacobitism had

Figure 6.1   Rev. John Home (c. 1790s), by Sir Henry Raeburn
Note: Proud Scot, patriotic Briton, committed claret drinker.

nothing to do with his claret consumption. Nor is Jacobitism an adequate explanation of the Scottish zeal for claret during the early and mid-eighteenth century.
The symbolism of claret was far more expansive than that. Certainly claret represented resistance to the Union and historic ties to France, but ultimately it stood
for an idea of both the Scottish past and future in which Scottish identity was not
entirely crushed by the juggernaut of the Anglicizing British state.[72] Nostalgia for
that past and hopes for that future were hardly Jacobite alone; these emotions
affected all quarters of Scotland and the Scottish populace, and continued long
after the death of the Jacobite cause. Some Scots wanted full independence, but
most, like Home, wanted a distinct but equal Scotland inside the Kingdom of
Great Britain.[73] Within that wide range of Scottish identities and aspirations there
was much to argue about, but what could be agreed upon—from the Union until
1745, and for some decades after—was that drinking claret, especially illegally
imported claret, was a decidedly Scottish thing to do.

Part III
Port

7

"Port is all I pretend to"

Port and the English Middle Ranks, 1714–1760s

If a new commodity does not obviously solve a problem or make an aspect of life manifestly easier through its use, its popularity will depend upon a complex conjunction of events and trends with which the commodity intersects as it comes upon the market. Happily for early eighteenth-century producers, shippers and vendors of port wine, such a conjunction occurred. As we have seen, port began its life as the favored child of the Whig party and was nurtured into adolescence by a treaty that kept its cost lower than that of French wine. But fiscal favoritism could not guarantee that port would remain popular. After all, the Methuen Treaty said nothing about Spanish, German, or Italian wines, nor did it stipulate which wine or wines from Portugal were to be imported into England, and Portugal produced many different types of wine. Thus, the story of port's rise to pre-eminence on the English market is far from straightforward. Despite its favored fiscal position and reputation as a patriotic wine among Whig consumers, port's capture of the English market was neither uninterrupted nor inevitable. But ultimately, along with its reputation as a patriotic wine, cost, availability, and strength made port not simply the most common English tavern wine, but a symbol of middle-ranking Englishmen, precisely the group for whom port was originally intended.

Port and the "Middle Ranks of Men"

There can be no doubt that during the first half of the eighteenth century, the English middle ranks relished port above all other wines. In 1718, members of the Ironmongers' Company of London (a powerful City Livery Company) celebrated the Lord Mayor's Day with 150 bottles of red port, 96 bottles of white port, 36 bottles of Canary, and 18 bottles of Rhenish wine. In other words more than four-fifths of the wine they consumed that day was port, both red and white. Four years later the Ironmongers' Lord Mayor's Day festivities show similar wine choices, while at their Quarterday Dinner in 1725, red port constituted fully 84 percent of the wine consumed.[1] Members of the Barber-Surgeons Company—who by the eighteenth century were mostly licensed medical doctors and not barbers—exhibited a similar predilection for red port, on which they spent nearly three-quarters of their wine budget between the years 1720 and 1739. Their next favorite wines were white port and canary, each of which constituted 8 percent of their overall expenditures on wine, while claret accounted for less than 0.5 percent of their outlay.[2] Because cost was not directly proportional to volume, and red port was usually the least expensive wine on the English market, it constituted more than three-quarters of the Barber-Surgeons' total wine consumption.

As with merchants and medical doctors, lawyers and clerics enjoyed their port too. For example, in October 1751, Slingsby Bethell, Esq., paid the merchant Thomas Gordon for wine sent to the Old Bailey, which included 105 bottles of port, 84 bottles of sherry, 17 bottles of claret, ten bottles of old hock, and three bottles of Mountain. Notably, the small amount of claret cost nearly half as much as the much larger order of port.[3] What was true for London was also true for the provinces; the records of James Pardoe, a Worcester wine merchant in the 1740s, show that he sold mostly red port, along with lesser amounts of white port, white Lisbon, canary, Mountain, Rhenish, sherry, and unspecified white wine. Pardoe's most faithful customer was the Reverend Doctor Foley, who purchased 6 gallons of red port every three to four weeks, along with an occasional gallon of Mountain or canary. Pardoe also sold inexpensive white wine to Isaac Maddox, the Bishop of Worcester, and the same wine to Dean Stillingfleet (a son of the famous Latitudinarian bishop). Certainly these two men could have purchased fancier wine, but it is likely that they bought most of their wine from a more upscale merchant. Pardoe did not import his wines directly; instead he purchased his wines from those who had. Therefore, Pardoe was what might be termed a "second-tier wine merchant"; he sold mostly port, and his clientele was distinctly "middling," extending even to the lower end of that nebulous category. For example, a Mr Hadley, to whom Pardoe sold both red and white port, was a blacksmith.[4]

Successful artisans and shopkeepers were generally on the lower end of the wine-drinking middling ranks, and so too, in most instances, were university students (who had more earning potential than money). Certainly James Woodforde, the sixth child of a Somerset vicar, was hardly wealthy when he went up to New College, Oxford in 1759. Woodforde arrived in Oxford on October 2, and four days later made the following entry in his diary: "Geree, Peckham [fellow students] and myself had a hogshead of port from Mr. Cropp of Southampton."[5] Presumably they had shared the cost of the cask and now possessed the equivalent of 250 to 300 bottles with which to begin their studies. Two days later, Woodforde got around to purchasing 50 pens and some ink, but the celebratory spirit of his student days, as well as his preferred spirit with which to celebrate, was firmly established. The entry, "Had a bottle of my [port] wine," appears almost daily in his diary. Nor was Woodforde's penchant for port fed only by his own supply. For instance, on Christmas Day, 1759, he recorded that the "Bursars give us Scholars 8 Bottles of Port Wine to drink at dinner time."[6] When Woodforde's personal supply of port ran out, he did not suffer the usual fate of cash-strapped university students and cadge or go without. Instead, he bought more, as on July 26, 1761, when he alone purchased a half-hogshead of port, which rendered "12 dozen and six bottles."[7] From those early days in Oxford until his graduation in 1763 the port (and sometimes beer) continued to flow. Claret and other wines were nowhere in sight.

Another example of port's predominance among the middle ranks in eighteenth-century England can be seen in the tavern trade. Taverns, which specialized in wine and food, were in theory open to all members of society, although the working poor and indigent found little they could afford and rarely entered; their drinking domain was the ale-house or dram shop.[8] As the Spanish visitor to England, Don Manuel Gonzales observed in 1731, "taverns are very numerous yet alehouses are much more so, being visited by the inferior tradesmen, mechanics, journeymen, porters, coachmen, carmen, servants and others whose pockets will not reach a glass of wine."[9] At the other end of the economic spectrum, the most fashionable members of society continued to frequent taverns during the early and mid-eighteenth-century. They had not yet segregated themselves into purpose-built clubs; this was mostly an early nineteenth-century phenomenon. In fact, many private clubs began in taverns, where rooms could be rented out for the evening.[10] That said, eighteenth-century taverns were predominantly the enclave of the middling-sorts, which corresponded to the lower economic end of English wine consumers.[11]

Taverns could also be visited by foreigners who were interested in English society but who did not have the necessary entrée into its highest levels. One such visitor was the Swiss diarist César de Saussure, who traveled throughout southern England in the 1720s. De Saussure's remarks upon England are far more pedestrian than those of his *philosophe* contemporaries such as Montesquieu and Voltaire, but as such they contain detailed observations upon the minutiae of English life.[12] For example, de Saussure was impressed by the range of countries from which the English imported their wine, although he noticed that "More wine from Oporto, in Portugal, is drunk than any other." He speculated that this might be because of the

> cheapness (though it costs two shillings the bottle), or because it suits English palates. I myself think this wine heavy, hard, and coarse.

Interestingly, he also remarked that

> The French wines that are drunk are called claret, and come from Bordeaux. These wines after the sea journey are excellent, some of them costing up to five shillings a bottle when sold in taverns. This exorbitant price is owing to the great weight of the casks and also to the heavy duties on French goods.[13]

In fact, Bordeaux casks, or hogsheads, were not especially heavy, but the tariff on French wines was.

Notwithstanding de Saussure's description of port—with which many Englishmen concurred—his observation regarding its popularity in taverns helps to explain why port constituted the dominant wine in England.[14] After all, no matter how they are defined by historians, there were far more members of the middle ranks than of the claret-drinking elite.[15] And it was the middle-ranks (especially the men among them) who frequented taverns, and of course, drank so much port. In fact, from 1714 until 1750, Portuguese wines (not including madeira) rose from 46 to more than 70 percent of all wines imported into England.[16] And among Portuguese wine exports to England, port's share of the total rose in a similarly dramatic fashion; by 1750, no less than three-quarters of all Portuguese wine shipped to England was shipped from the city of Oporto.[17]

The preceding paragraph intentionally raises the question of women's taste, and in particular of just how much of the port imported into England was consumed by women. On the evidence, it seems that when Charles Davenant wrote in 1711 that Portuguese, Spanish, and Italian wines served the "Middle Ranks of Men" (who formed the largest group of wine consumers), he chose his words carefully. However, this does not mean that middle-ranking women never drank port, or other wines, although they were more likely to do so at home than in the tavern. For instance, Sarah Byng Osborn, the only surviving daughter of Admiral Sir George Byng and sister of the famously ill-fated Admiral John Byng, was a port drinker. Osborn was widowed at an early age, but her son, who inherited the family property in Bedfordshire, took great care of his mother. She was therefore comfortably well-off, but not wealthy, a condition that is confirmed in her letters and which influenced her self-perception and personal choices right down to her taste for wine. In 1738 she wrote from London to her son in Bedfordshire, describing the arrival of the "a hogshead of two-year old port," which she had purchased for herself and her own mother, with whom she lived. She wrote:

> If it should answer, and they generally have good wine at Southampton [from where she purchased it]—I will have a larger stock, for port is all I pretend to, and therefore would if possible have it in perfection.[18]

Obviously, all that Osborn pretended to was more than satisfactory for many English wine drinkers, male or female. In fact, some preferred port to all other wines, even if their finances allowed them a choice. Richard Bentley (1662–1742), the noted Homeric scholar and Master of Trinity College, Cambridge, summarized his own sentiments saying that claret "would be port if it could."[19] So renowned was Bentley's predilection for port that the poet Alexander Pope, who disagreed profoundly with Bentley's Whig politics and defense of the "Ancients" against the "Moderns," turned Bentley's taste against him for being uncouth. Thus Bentley, who died in 1742 while Pope was writing Book IV of *The Dunciad*, received the following elegy in Pope's famous poem:

> As many quit the streams that murm'ring fall
> To lull the sons of Marg'ret and Clare Hall,
> Where Bentley late tempestuous wont to sport
> In troubled waters, but now sleeps in port.[20]

Pope, a Tory, could not abide Bentley, and therefore used the middling connotations of port to ridicule the dead professor as a philistine. But Pope himself liked port, or at least he once did. In 1725, while completing his translation of Homer's *Odyssey*, he wrote to his friend Humphrey Wanley in search of a "Douzaine of quartes of goode and wholesome Port wine, such as yee drinke at the Genoa Arms."[21] In other words the taste for port, like the taste for luxury claret, could easily transcend political and cultural arguments, but port's social connotations made it ripe for exploitation.

Port and the claret-drinking elite

Port—and especially red port—was the preferred wine of English middling men, but how high up the social ladder did port consumption go? This question can be answered by briefly examining some of the account books and cellar records that we have previously scrutinized for evidence of luxury claret. For example, John Hervey, Baron Hervey and 1st Earl of Bristol, did not purchase any "Portugal wine" until 1710, despite having begun his meticulously kept expense book in 1689. This wine may have been port, although it is impossible to know. In that same year he bought a hogshead of "red moncon," most likely a wine from Monção on the Minho river in northern Portugal, which was usually shipped to England from Viana do Castelo.[22] Finally, in December 1711 Hervey purchased a hogshead of wine that he called by name "Red-Port."[23] He did not buy port again until January 1714, after which time some quantity of port, usually a pipe (approximately 504 bottles), was an annual expense among his purchases.[24] Nevertheless, the total amount of port in Hervey's cellar at any one time was relatively insignificant.

If we compare Hervey's wine purchases from 1720 to 1739 to the wine purchases of the Barber-Surgeons' Company of London in the same years, we see that while the latter regaled themselves in almost nothing but red port, the former spent only 11 percent of his budget on port of any color, and nearly 50 percent on luxury claret.[25] This suggests either that Hervey enjoyed a small amount of port, that some of his guests did, or most likely, that he gave port to his servants as a form of payment, a frequent practice in eighteenth-century England.

When he died in 1722, the 3rd Earl of Sunderland's cellar contained no red port, although it did contain a hogshead of white port.[26] As we recall, this was promptly claimed by his widowed wife Judith.[27] The 1st Duke of Marlborough's wine purchases show no port until 1722,[28] which was also the year of his death, although presumably nothing to do with it. Likewise, James Brydges, 1st Duke of Chandos, consumed very little port. Records indicate that the immensely wealthy Brydges purchased port for his cellar at Cannons for the first time in 1722, when he bought two pipes for £65.[29] According to his expense accounts, he did not purchase port again until 1732, a lapse which suggests his first experience was off-putting. Indeed, Brydges' cellar notes indicate that port was often a murky wine, an opinion with which the poet Matthew Prior clearly agreed. In a poem written in 1718, Prior rhymed, if somewhat poorly: "Else (dismal thought) our war-like men/ Might drink thick Port for fine Champagne." Prior, an avid Tory whose taste may have been politically influenced, would not let it go at that, and in the same lengthy poem struck another blow against the middling sorts' favorite wine: "And in a Cottage, or a Court,/ Drink fine Champaigne, or muddl'd Port."[30] But Brydges, who leaned with the political wind, spoke as a connoisseur and not a partisan consumer. He drank many different types of wine, and by the 1730s, like Hervey, he made regular, if small purchases of port. It is impossible to know for certain, but as in other aristocratic households at the time, this wine was probably meant for the servants and not for the guests.

The Walpoles: Squire and Prime Minister

Perhaps the best way to understand port's role in both reflecting middle-ranking taste and demarcating middle-ranking status in England is to compare the wine consumption habits of Colonel Robert Walpole (1650–1700), to those of his son, Sir Robert Walpole (1676–1745), Britain's first prime minister.[31] In the words of the historian Sir John Plumb, the contrast in wine preference and consumption habits between the father, a country squire, and the son, a great statesman, "illuminates the class structure of the Augustan age."[32] Robert Walpole the father, spent most of his life at Houghton, the family seat in Norfolk, where his activities revolved around the farm, and in the country pleasures of riding and hunting. He was a Colonel in the Norfolk militia and a well-read man who instituted Flemish farming methods (growing root-crops and clover) on his land long before the so-called agricultural revolution of the eighteenth century made this a common practice in England. He frequently rode to the port town of King's Lynn, to local fairs, and to the Norwich assizes, but he only journeyed to London for the first time in 1678, by which time he was in his late twenties. This trip was followed by occasional visits to the capital with his wife, but it was not until 1689, when he became a Member of Parliament for Castle Rising, that he was ever gone from Houghton for long periods of time. Once in Parliament, he used his influence to enlarge his landholdings and secure his parliamentary seat for his family for generations to come. Politically, he was a Whig, and when he died in 1700, at the early age of 50, "his life could be taken as typical of the most enterprising and effective of his class—the country gentleman."[33]

As for the wine Colonel Walpole drank, there is little evidence until the late 1690s, when he was at the peak of his power. In October 1698, he purchased 38 gallons of red port in cask from his cousin Charles Turner, a wine merchant in King's Lynn.[34] This was soon followed by half a hogshead of the same, and next April by a full hogshead of red port and half a hogshead of unspecified "white wine." Later in 1699 he bought a hogshead of red port and another of white port. Lastly, in August 1700, he purchased 13 gallons of "sherry."[35] When Colonel Walpole died in October 1700, he left a balance for wine with Charles Turner of £156. 13s. 0d, which was paid in full by his dutiful son, Sir Robert, in September of the following year.[36] Colonel Walpole was a rustic, although not uncultured country gentleman, and his taste for wine was true to type.[37] He drank mostly port, which was at that time still a rustic wine. Indeed, one sees in Colonel Walpole similarities with Addison's fictitious Goodman Fact. Both were middle-ranking men with only a few superfluities, and significantly, both drank port.

In contrast to his father, Sir Robert preferred claret to all other wines and used Haut Brion, Lafite, and Margaux to gain his place among the most fashionable people in England. But what is surprising about the younger Walpole's wine purchases, especially when compared to those of his Whig contemporaries like Hervey, Spencer, and Brydges, is the large amount of wine from Portugal. For example, in 1732 and 1733, Walpole purchased approximately 5,184 bottles of white Lisbon, and 2,520 bottles of red port, for a monthly average of 216 bottles of the former and 105 bottles of the latter. In fact, he received ten to 20 dozen bottles of these wines at his various residences approximately every fortnight, the white Lisbon costing him 2s. per bottle, and the red port 1s. 8d. This raises the question of why a man who spent so much time, money, and effort manifesting his superior taste through the consumption of luxury claret and myriad other endeavors would purchase so much inexpensive Portuguese wine.

One of Walpole's great strengths as a politician was his ability to embody simultaneously the values of urbane aristocrats, new-money merchants, prosperous gentry, successful professionals, and comfortable tradesmen, and to appeal to people within these groups. This characteristic was manifested in his taste for wine, which ranged from luxury claret, champagne, and burgundy at the top, to white Lisbon and red port at the bottom. For example, the numerous hogsheads of Haut Brion were always sent to Houghton, where he went to thank, impress, and win over his political allies. Similarly, Château Margaux, Lafite, and champagne were sent to Hampton Court Palace, although so too were lesser amounts of white Lisbon and red port. His houses in St James's Square and Chelsea received wines of all types, while interestingly, the lodge at Richmond Park, where he often went on weekends with his mistress Molly Skerritt, received very little wine at all.

As Walpole's own penchant for claret was famous, it seems that vast amounts of the white Lisbon and red port were for his household staff, and perhaps more importantly, for his frequent "public tables" wherein he entertained the middling lawyers, merchants and tradesmen who formed the core of the Whig party.[38] So, while luxury claret constituted a of plurality of Walpole's purchases, and was clearly meant to impress his vast coterie of friends and acquaintances, the amount of Portuguese wines suggests that they were the workhorse wines of his continuous entertaining, and the wines with which Walpole the political chameleon could suddenly be, like his father, a rustic country squire (Figure 7.1).[39]

***

In the early eighteenth century some port was "good and wholesome," and some of it, probably much more of it, "heavy, hard and coarse." But given all of the wines on the English market, including other Portuguese wines that paid the same duty, why was port in particular so popular among the middle ranks? We already know that by the first decade of the eighteenth century many consumers thought of port as the proper wine for English patriots. This association was crucial to the

Figure 7.1   Sir Robert Walpole as Master of the King's Staghounds in Windsor Forest (n.d.), by John Wootton
Note: Port-drinking squire *and* claret-drinking gentleman.

long-term success of port in England in part because the triumphant eighteenth-century Whig definition of Englishness resided within a conception of middle-ranking men, and it was middle-ranking men who constituted the bulk of English wine drinkers. Thus, the middling sorts drank port because they believed it was patriotic to do so; but they also drank port because it was what they, as middle-ranking men, could afford.

The price of port

The Methuen Treaty of 1703 guaranteed that the tariff on Portuguese wines was at least one-third less than the tariff on French wines, but until William Pitt's tariff reductions in 1786, the British government favored Portuguese wines over wines from all other countries, and far exceeded the required one-third differential in duty with French wines. Moreover, in 1745, 1763, 1778, 1779, 1780, and 1782 (all of them war years), the British government increased the duties on imported wine, so that by 1783 the duty on Portuguese wines stood at almost £46 per tun, or 84 percent over its 1714 level.[40] As much of an increase as that was, the duty on other wines was even greater. French wines paid £96 per tun, Rhenish and Hungarian wines paid £51, and Spanish and Italian wines paid nearly £47. But critically, despite the myriad tariff increases, Portuguese wine remained the least-taxed wine on the English market.

Of course, more important to English consumers than the level of Customs duty upon entry was the retail price of wine. But generally speaking, there was a correlation between tariff levels and retail cost.[41] Thus, in the early and mid-eighteenth-century Portuguese wines (excepting madeira) were almost invariably the least expensive wines on the English market, and red port, with relatively low production and transport costs, was generally the least expensive Portuguese wine. For example, toward the end of the War of the Spanish Succession, when John Hervey was paying from £25 to £40 for a hogshead of claret, the same amount of port cost him only £16. Similarly, in 1726, de Saussure recorded tavern prices of 5s. for a bottle of claret and only 2s. for a bottle of port. In the early 1730s Robert Walpole paid 5s. per bottle of champagne, 4s. per bottle of claret and burgundy, 3s. per bottle of sack, 2s. 6d. per bottle of French white wine, 2s. per bottle of white Lisbon,[42] and lastly, 1s. 8d. per bottle of red port.[43] In slight contradiction to this trend, wine prices quoted in the December 1731 issue of *Gentleman's Magazine* listed red port as more expensive than white Lisbon, French white wine, and almost all Spanish wines. The red port being advertised may have been of particularly good quality; nevertheless, it was less expensive than the white port, red Lisbon, old canary, Florence (Chianti), and of course, claret.[44] This, however, was a rare instance of red port not occupying the lowest rung on the consumer price ladder. For instance, the contract price of provisions served to Augusta Dowager Princess of Wales (mother of George III) in 1750 found champagne at the top (4s. 6d. per bottle) and red port at the bottom (2s. per bottle).[45]

In 1714 during the final phase of the Commercial Treaty debate, a Whig pamphleteer asked Arthur Moore, the Tory trade commissioner,

> if it is to be imagin'd, that any Body that can afford to drink Wine, will not sooner be at the extraordinary Expence of three half Pence for a bottle of French Wine, than confine themselves to drink Portugal Wine, for the sake of saving three half Pence, especially when French wine is so much more coveted than the other?[46]

If in fact French wine had only been three halfpence cheaper, than the question would have been a valid one. But as we have seen, the difference in price between a standard quart bottle of claret and port was closer to three shillings. This was not an insignificant amount to most English wine consumers—the group identified by Davenant as the "Middle Rank of Men." In short, cost mattered.

Foreign policy and the availability of wines

While British fiscal policy helped to determine the cost of wines, the related domain of foreign policy helped to determine different wines' availability and reputation. In this regard, Portuguese and Spanish wines should have been almost equally popular in Britain, as the duty on them was almost the same. However, Great Britain and Portugal remained steadfast allies during the early eighteenth century, while Great Britain and Spain had a strained relationship. One result was that from the end of the War of the Spanish Succession in 1714 to the 1740s Portuguese wines rose from 46 percent to over 70 percent of total wine imports into England, and most of this wine was red port. Having been hurt by the war, Spanish wines on the English market also rose in the two decades that followed, accounting for almost 40 percent of all wine imports by 1730.[47] However, another war between Britain and Spain began in 1739, the War of Jenkins' Ear, and legal trade between the two kingdoms ceased altogether from 1741 until 1748. The embargo was never strongly enforced, but the volume of legal wine imports into Britain declined noticeably, with Spanish wine imports hurt most of all. One clear result was that, more than ever before, port dominated the English market (Graph 7.1).

And how do we know that most of this Portuguese wine in England was port? The obvious answer is that the evidence we have already examined draws explicit distinctions between types of Portuguese wine, and by far the most common reference is to "port." But statistical evidence can help us here too, because export figures from the city of Oporto, from whence port wine was shipped, very nearly match up with English import figures for all Portuguese wines. The discrepancy between the figures is easily attributed to the fact that small amounts of other Portuguese wines were imported into England, and a small percentage of port exports went to nations besides England. Scotland, for example, received some port, as did Ireland, while a tiny amount of port went to nations along the North Sea and Baltic. But as late as 1850, the United Kingdom still constituted 90 percent of the market for exported port, and given its population and wealth, most of that wine went to England (Graph 7.2).[48]

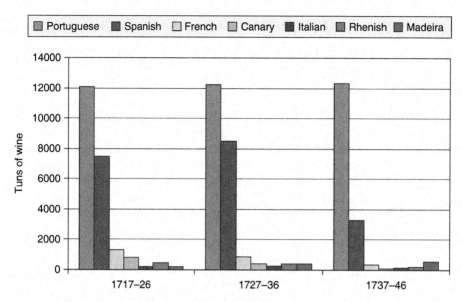

Graph 7.1 Wine imports in early Georgian England
Source: Schumpeter, *English Overseas Trade Statistics*, Table 16.

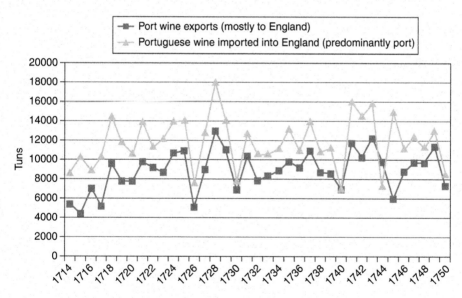

Graph 7.2 The dominance of port among Portuguese wines in England, 1714–50
Source: Port wine exports: Forrester, *A short treatise on the unequal and disproportionate imposts levied on port-wine, shipped from Oporto to Great Britain* (London, 1850), Table B, pp. 19–20; for Portuguese wine imported into England: Schumpeter, *English Overseas Trade Statistics*, Table 16.

Domestic policy and the taste for strong drinks

Patriotism, low cost, and easy availability were compelling reasons for middle-ranking English consumers to purchase port, but so too was the taste and effect of the wine itself. As we recall, in the early years of the century it was generally acknowledged that English wine drinkers preferred the taste of French wine to Portuguese. Yet there was something about the taste of port that appealed to an increasing number of consumers in England: high alcohol content. As early as 1698, an anonymous author proved prophetic in his satire upon the dishonest practices of English vintners and tavern keepers, when he wrote that between French and Portuguese wines the "Ports will carry the day, they have body, that is strength, and that now a days pleases, for our people love to have their heads and stomachs hot, as soon and as cheap as they can."[49] This argument was mostly absent from the debates surrounding the Treaty of Commerce with France in 1712–14, when it was almost universally agreed that English preference was for French wine and claret in particular. However, there were suggestions that because of their strength Portuguese wines would not disappear from the English market entirely. For instance, one pro-treaty pamphleteer argued that open trade with France would not effect the importation of Portuguese wines because "Portugal hath annually found a Vend for all their Wine that is fit for exportation," and would continue to do so as the English "have Occasion for more than that Country doth produce."[50] Another proponent of the treaty was more explicit, stating that Portuguese wines "always have been and always will be necessary to mix with such Wines of the growth of France as are too thin and meagre of themselves," and that "some stomachs require them, and some persons will always, for their strength, prefer them."[51] As it happened, this estimation was far too modest.

What was a presentiment in 1713 became within a few decades an empirically provable fact. When Daniel Defoe put his hired pen to work on behalf of the English distillers in 1726, he observed:

> There has been for some years, and still continues among us, a national gust or inclination to drinking stronger and higher pric'd liquors than formerly; I do not say we drink more, or to excess, that is subject of another nature, and however true, is not to my present purpose. But the stream of the nation's palate runs, I say, for stronger and dearer liquors.[52]

In other words, since people wanted stronger drinks, why not give them what they want?

> The Lady's and Gentlemen of Quality and Distinction, not content with the usual, and as I have said above, most wholesome dram, call'd right French brandy, now treat with Ratafia and Citron, at a Guinea a bottle.
>
> The Punch Drinkers of Quality (if any such there be) not contented with the best French Brandy in their Bowls, must have Arrack at 16s. to 18s. per gallon.

The Wine Drinkers of the better sort, not content with the Portugal and Barcelona wines, must have High Country Margeau, O Brian and Hermitage Clarets, at 5s. to 6s. per bottle.

The common draft of Red wine of Oporto and Viana [do Castelo], tho all stronger than the French wines formerly drank, is not now strong enough for the Citizens; but they must be made up (so the Wine-Brewers call it) with Lisbons, with Alicants, and Bene-Carloes: and the Oporto and Lisbon whites, tho very strong, are turn'd out of Doors, for the yet stronger Mountain Malaga.[53]

Defoe went on to say that "our common drinkers of Ale or Beer" have moved from porter's ale, to stout, and now to the "strongest North-Country Burton, and Tamworth's Pale Ale, Dorchester and Newbury Beers and the like." Lastly, the poor, "following this unhappy Humour of the Rich ... are fallen into the old Dram-drinking way," which they had given up for beer and ale.[54]

In fact, Defoe's observations were only partially true: French brandy was not out of fashion with the affluent; the "Oporto and Lisbon whites" had not been ousted by "Mountain Malaga"; and since acquiring the dram drinking habit in the 1690s, the poor had never forsaken it. What Defoe was observing was an expansion of consumer choices and not a simple replacement of one drink by another. Nevertheless, he correctly identified both the direction in which the nation's palate was running and the reason for this trend, which was the widespread consumption of ardent spirits, brandy and gin in particular. As a man of Tory sentiments in 1726, Defoe blamed this habit squarely on the Dutch:

In the course of the Dutch Wars, it had been observed, That the captains and the Hollanders Men of War, when they were to engage with our Ships, usually set a Hogshead of Brandy abroach, afore the mast; and bid the men drink lustick, then they might fight lustick: and our poor seamen felt the force of the brandy, sometime to their cost.[55]

A fashion that may have been abetted by Dutch naval prowess in the 1660s was most definitely continued by the arrival of a Dutch king in England in 1688. In 1689, two million gallons of brandy were imported from France, mostly from the regions around Bordeaux and Cognac. But, as with French wine, a heavy duty was soon imposed upon brandy, which gave English distillers (and brandy smugglers) a tremendous boost. English gin, a variation of Dutch *geneva* (also known in England as "Hollands"), was actually promoted by an act of parliament in 1694 that removed the requirement for a distilling and retail license, and set the excise duty on domestic gin at 2d. per gallon. The impetus for the new law came from the fact that the English landowners, who dominated Parliament, had a consistent annual surplus of grain which they were determined to sell lest the price of their land decline due to over-supply. The consequence of the new law was an explosion in the number of distilleries and dram shops in England, but most especially in London itself. By 1725 there were said to be 6,187 premises selling spirits in London (not including the City and Southwark), while one in four houses in St Giles and Westminster was said to be a dram shop.[56]

The amount of gin officially produced in England and Wales rose from 527,000 gallons in 1684, to 1,223,000 in 1700, and to 2,483,000 in 1720.[57] These figures continued to rise until 1751, when effective government legislation combined with harvest shortages finally to put an end to the "Gin Mania" that had ravaged so many lives.[58] The craze for "Mother Gin" (like a mother, it "comforted" its consumers) was especially damaging among the poor; however, it was not only they who drank strong spirits. Wealthier consumers continued to drink large amounts of French brandy and Dutch geneva, as well as rum from the West Indies, arrack from the Levant (for punch), and whiskey from Ireland. Scottish whisky would not become popular in England until the nineteenth century.[59]

The effect of increased spirit consumption upon the taste for wine—and on alcoholic drinks more generally—was manifest. English consumers wanted stronger drinks, and among wines, port fit the bill. The German historian Johann von Archenholz made this connection in 1789 when he wrote about what he called the "common people" he observed in English taverns: "It is their attachment to strong liquors that makes them so very fond of Port wine ... in London they like everything that is powerful and heavy."[60] The wine critic and antiquarian André Simon drew out the connection even more by highlighting the fact that port itself was a hybrid:

> The consumption of gin and other spirits [in the eighteenth century] increased to such an extent that it practically killed the taste for beverage wines, whilst the taste for ardent spirits created an unparalleled demand for a new type of wine, a blend of wine and spirit, which became under the name of 'port' the national wine of England.[61]

Demand meets production technology in the Douro: A happy convergence

Port's strength fit the changing taste of English consumers at a time when they desired stronger liquors, but this was not simply the result of producers responding to English demand. It was also a fortuitous consequence of English taste meeting the realities of Douro valley wine production. Early versions of port wine were naturally strong in alcohol because the Douro valley is extremely hot in the summer, and as a result the ripened grapes contain high amounts of natural grape sugar. Generally speaking, the greater the amount of sugar in the grapes, the higher amount of alcohol in the wine, because it is the reaction of yeast upon sugar that creates alcohol (and carbon dioxide). Thus, sweet grapes that are crushed and then fermented out to dryness (i.e. the majority of grape sugars are converted) create wines that are high in alcohol. This fermentation process has limits, however, as most yeasts cannot survive when alcohol levels reach 16 to 18 percent of total volume. In other words, there is a built-in cut-off for the fermentation process. If, however, there is still a large amount of residual sugar in the must (the macerated grape juice) when the fermentation stops, or is cut off, then the resulting wine will be sweet or "rich," as it was usually called in the eighteenth century. In most cases, however, the wine, if not checked by a temperature that is either too hot or too cold, ferments itself out to dryness before the alcohol level shuts down the fermentation process. Apparently, this was the case with a great deal of port wine in the eighteenth century, which was often dry, although there would have been years when the wine was relatively sweet, and by the mid-eighteenth century it is clear that sweet port was the more desired of the two results. But whether dry or sweet (or somewhere in between), unfortified wine from the Douro valley was relatively strong, probably around 14 to 17 percent alcohol,[62] and it was this strength that made port wines more appealing to some English consumers than the "thinner" red wines from the Minho region, which were shipped via Viana do Castelo.[63]

That said, the high heat of the Douro can be problematic during wine-making because external heat, and the heat of the grapes themselves, if too high, will cause a rapid, sometimes even violent, fermentation. This leads to a strong but "cooked" wine that is both tannic and tasting of raisins. Even more serious for the wine-maker, fermentation can become so rapid and hot (above 113° F/45° C) that it gets "stuck"—meaning literally that the yeasts cook themselves to death—leaving a tannic yet low-alcohol wine that has almost no fruit flavor and is susceptible to spoilage, because alcohol itself is one of wine's chief preservatives.[64] At the other end of the temperature spectrum, must that is too cool (below 50° F/10° C) will stop fermenting, although it will restart once it warms back up if it has not been stabilized with additional alcohol or sulphur dioxide.[65] Overly cool fermentation was not a great concern for seventeenth- and eighteenth-century port wine producers, although far to the north, in the Champagne region of France, cool fermentation was the bane of local wine producers because if fermentation recommenced in warmer weather, sealed containers would burst under the pressure of the carbon dioxide. As with port, it took many decades of experimentation with champagne, and stronger glass bottles, before the region's disadvantage became an advantage.

Clearly, the natural obstacles to making an export-quality wine in the Douro valley in the early eighteenth century were formidable, and early versions of port fit the description of wines that had a hot fermentation; de Saussure's "heavy, hard and coarse" could not have been more precise.[66] There were other problems faced by the Portuguese wine producers as well: rudimentary wine-making equipment and scant capital to invest in anything better; lack of wine-making knowledge; peasant conservatism against new techniques that might improve quality; disasters caused by vine diseases, floods, and hailstorms; and perhaps most of all, the incredible backbreaking work of growing vines and gathering grapes on the steep, schistous hillsides above the Douro river.

These were all problems to be overcome if high-quality wine was to be created, and some producers were more successful than others. Nevertheless, under normal climatic conditions, most early versions of port would have been high in alcohol, tannic, dark in color, and astringent. The wine antiquarian William

Younger states candidly that eighteenth-century port "was wine that would satisfy a cold and carnivorous English squire ... it was badly made and was a coarse drink whose only merit lay in its power to produce stupefaction."[67] Younger fell a bit too hard for the uncouth Squire Western image of the English squirearchy, and he did not appreciate the variability of port, but overall his description was probably more right than wrong.

Port was thus a naturally strong wine, but the hand of man often made it more so. To wit, Portuguese wine-makers and English factors in Oporto—who during the eighteenth century were generally wine buyers, blenders and exporters—laced their port with brandy. It is possible that this was done from the outset of the port trade, as adding brandy was well known to help stabilize wine, but it was not uniformly practiced in the eighteenth century.[68] An apocryphal story, which has long circulated within the port trade, asserts that as early as 1678 two Liverpool wine merchants discovered the abbot of Lamego monastery adding brandy to arrest fermentation and thus produce a strong, sweet wine.[69] More reliably, a Portuguese wine-making manual published in 1720, *A Agricultura das Vinhas*, recommended adding approximately three gallons of brandy to each pipe (126 gallons) during fermentation to increase the strength of the wine and improve its quality.[70] This amount of brandy was not nearly enough to stop the fermentation altogether, although depending on the timing, even a small addition of brandy would have slowed down the process, which was probably its purpose. But timing was critical, and most wine-makers could only guess when the appropriate moment had arrived. In some cases, the addition of brandy "only postponed the end of fermentation and virtually guaranteed a murky and unstable wine."[71]

However, since stabilizing the wine was the purpose of adding brandy, producers and shippers continued to experiment with adding it at different times and in different amounts. In 1724 the English Consul at Lisbon, Thomas Burnett, wrote that white ports were "all mixt and strengthened with Brandys," but that this was not the case with the red ports.[72] In 1734 the Northampton vintner Thomas Pratt complained to his supplier in London, Henry Hitchcock, that port wines of all types "taste too much of brandy."[73] Hitchcock was in a particularly good position to address this perceived problem, as it was his brother John who blended and shipped the wine from Oporto. As the century progressed ever more brandy was added.[74] By 1795, a self-interested salesman, John Wright, M.D., asserted "that no Port wine merchant will venture to aver, that he ever exported from Oporto, or imported into Britain for sale, three pipes of red wine, that had not been completed or mixed in his cellars, or strengthened with brandy."[75] Wright, of course, offered "pure" port at his premises in Clare-Market, central London—and at an excellent price.

Some consumers complained, but brandy was added to port not only to slow down or halt the fermentation process, but for two other reasons as well. First, it was meant to preserve the wine during transport. At almost every stage—before shipping down the Douro, upon arrival in Oporto, before the sea voyage to England and in England itself—a small amount of brandy was added to each pipe of wine in the hopes that this would prevent what was often an unstable and roughly transported wine from spoiling. At the time it was not known why this often worked, but the added alcohol helped to protect the wine against oxidation and the growth of acetobacter—the bacteria that turn wine into vinegar. Second, brandy was no doubt used to disguise the quality of wine whose flaws were often manifold.[76] Richard Ames's scathing review of port in the early 1690s certainly used poetic license ("And has as many different tastes/ As can be found in Compound pastes"[77]), but he may not have been exaggerating overmuch.

While fortification is the essence of modern port, which receives roughly 20 gallons of brandy per pipe, it should be clear that port's development into one of the world's finest wines was a long, slow process that required not only the demands and capital of a wealthy foreign market, but years of experimentation and hard-won knowledge, as well as sound barrel and bottle ageing.[78] But for much of the eighteenth century, these conditions had not yet been met, and the results were often disappointing to English merchants who had to sell the wines. A 1754 letter from the English factors in Oporto to the Portuguese wine brokers complains that the

> grower, at the time of vintage, is in the habit of checking the fermentation of the wines too soon, by putting brandy into them whilst fermenting—a practice which must be considered as diabolical; for after this, the wines will not remain quiet, but are continually tending to ferment, and become ropy or acid.[79]

Similarly, John Croft in his 1787 *Treatise on the Wines of Portugal* writes that

> sometimes Must, or new wine just pressed, or Brandy is thrown in, to render it stouter and check the fermentation, which makes it less wholesome, and it is, by the by, the great inherent mischief, as it were, in most of these sorts of wines, the Portugal ones in particular.[80]

Croft was not against fortifying port wine, but believed it should be done only after fermentation was complete. Significantly, he also advocated the use of French brandy, which he acknowledged was illegal in Portugal, so that "Port wines must ever partake of the same strong gross spirit, which is inflammable, and more like what we call spirits of wine than brandy."[81]

Variations in the taste of port

What we can say for certain is that there were many tastes to eighteenth-century port. Given the hot Douro climate, a wide range of wine-making technology and know-how among the Portuguese farmers and producers, different theories about when and how much brandy to add to the wine, varying degrees of integrity among the English factors in Oporto and vintners in England, along with inconsistent shipping and storing conditions, it could not have been otherwise. The wine historian A. D. Francis says with characteristic understatement, "Port-wine evidently varied much in character in the eighteenth century and it is hard to get a true account of it."[82] It is tempting to project the taste of modern port backward into the eighteenth century and say that sweetness must have been one of port's greatest appeals in a society where sugar consumption was sky-rocketing among all classes.[83] In fact, as we shall see in the next chapter, by the 1750s English factors, and therefore English consumers, did frequently desire a type of port that in description sounds very much like modern vintage port. However, there is no evidence from the eighteenth century that this ideal was agreed upon by all or frequently achieved. Certainly some port was sweet, but some was quite dry, strength varied, and while most port was red, it could also be white, purple, rosé, or even brown (when madeirized). In short, in the eighteenth century port was a common name for a variety of wines that came from northern Portugal.

The variability of port can be gleaned from descriptions of port throughout the eighteenth century. In 1724, the physician Peter Shaw described "Red Port of a moderate age" as "astringent," adding that it was "good in diarrhoeas, seminal weaknesses, gleets, etc."[84] Three years later an anonymous "Physician in the Country," who suggested the superiority of English soldiers and sailors over the French was due to the consumption of beer and not wine, described port and other Iberian wines as strong and "half fermented," which is the "reason for their luscious sweet taste."[85] A similar description of port as a sweet wine is contained in the response of the Douro wine brokers to the English factors in Oporto in 1754,[86] but neither Boswell nor Johnson, who drank a fair amount of port both together and apart, mention anything about port but its formidable strength. In an oft-quoted diary entry from 1763, Boswell wrote:

> A bottle of thick English port is a very heavy and very inflammatory dose. I felt it last time that I drank it for several days, and this morning it was boiling in my veins.[87]

Pierre-Jean Grosley, a Frenchman who visited London in 1765, said that port leaves "no taste in the mouth," and "acts upon the stomach only by its weight."[88] In 1775, Edward Barry said only that port was getting stronger by the year.[89] John Byng's descriptions of the port he drank in taverns throughout England and Wales in the 1780s and 1790s never mentioned sweetness or strength (perhaps he took that for granted), but were generally limited to "good," "bad," "decent," "likeable," "sad stuff," "very good," and "undrinkable," although on one occasion he did describe port as "puckering."[90] And Croft writes all within the same treatise that port had "superior mellowness and body," that it was "astringent and bracing" and—bizarrely for a man who had been a member of the English Factory at Oporto and at the time of writing was a wine merchant in York—that "it is entirely owing to the quantity of brandy thrown in at first that [port] will keep so long at any rate, which is a strong argument against the flavour and delicacy of Port wines in general."[91]

William Younger dismisses the whole question of port's taste altogether, saying that port was popular for its strength alone. "There is no doubt at all," says Younger, that Georgian era wine drinkers "drank for effect and not for taste." They drank port with fervor, says Younger, because "their diet was highly carnivorous. The heavy groundwork of meat called out for a deluge of strong wine and the call was abundantly answered. Add to this a loyalty to intoxication and the reasoning is completed."[92] Whether meat is washed down better with port, claret, brandy, beer, milk, water or any other beverage seems to be a matter of personal taste, although anthropologists have shown that personal taste is itself determined by the meanings of a specific drink within a given society.[93] Thus, it is not really personal taste at all. Instead, port was popular with many English wine drinkers because they wanted and were expected to use it to wash down the vast quantities of meat they consumed, not because it was or is particularly efficacious in dissolving the polypeptide chains commonly referred to as proteins. Similarly, the sheer variety of port increased its popularity among the middle ranks of consumers because port offered choices to a group who were themselves diverse, even if bound by broadly similar consumption habits.

But while the middle ranks drank port, elite English consumers continued to prefer the most expensive French wines, which were less strong in alcohol than port, and allegedly like the elite themselves, neither rough nor coarse. In some instances, affluent consumers did not even buy their French wines from merchants in England, but dealt directly with wine merchants based in France. By purchasing wines in this manner, they cut out one stage in the sales process, and thus one more chance that their wines could be misrepresented, mishandled, or adulterated. For example, during the 1730s, 1740s and 1750s, the Duke of Newcastle, a two-time prime minister, bought champagne from Louis and Gaspard Mollien of Calais, burgundy from Guillaume Joseph Harley of Liège and Mozell Disque of Calais, and claret from Theodore Hay of Boulogne-sur-Mer.[94] These merchants were also brokers, so that they purchased their wines directly from the producers. Consequently, they could give excellent advice about the wines they sold. For example, in 1754, Hay counseled Newcastle's purchasing agent, Richard Turner, against buying the most expensive 1752 clarets (at £30 per hogshead) but instead to buy a slightly less expensive claret, which he described as "smooth and mellow." Similarly, he recommended the 1753 rather than the 1752 burgundies, although not until they had spent a year in cask and "thrown their fire"; the "creaming" champagne was, he believed, the "best vintage produced ... and may be drunk now."[95]

***

While the relative merits of French wines were being discussed by fine wine merchants and polite members of English society, there is no evidence that early and mid-eighteenth-century port yet inspired this type of talk. The tradition of clubbable English gentlemen waxing nostalgic over various "ancient" port vintages did not emerge until the early nineteenth century. Nevertheless, port, a new wine in the late seventeenth century when it was first introduced to the English market, slowly improved in quality and by the middle decades of the eighteenth century was an established institution of middle-ranking Englishmen.

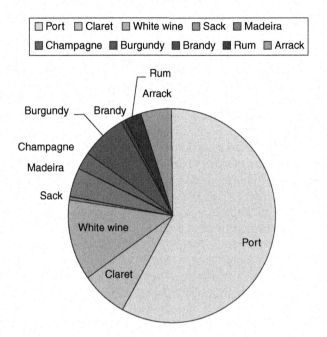

Graph 7.3 Dodsley's "Gentleman's Wine and Spirit Cellar", 1760s
Source: *The Cellar-Book: or, the Butler's Assistant, in keeping a Regular Account of his Liquors* (printed for J. Dodsley in Pall Mall, 1766).

For example, in 1766 the prominent London printer and bookseller, James Dodsley, thought it worth his while financially to publish *The Cellar-Book: or, the Butler's Assistant, in keeping a Regular Account of his Liquors*. This was the first commercially available cellar-record book in England, and it evinces what Hugh Johnson calls the "democratization of the wine cellar in England—that is, from the aristocracy to the middle classes."[96] Indeed, Dodsley's *Cellar-Book* was meant for the middle ranks. The elite, after all, would not have needed such a book; their own butlers had been trained in how to keep a cellar record. Instead, *The Cellar-Book* was meant to be both prescriptive and descriptive of an aspiring gentleman's taste for wine, and in the introduction to the book Dodsley included a sample page intended to instruct the butler or "common servant" on how to use the book, and what the hypothetical "gentleman's cellar" should contain (in bottles). To wit: 400 port, 48 claret, 85 white-wine [unspecified], four sack, 29 madeira, 19 champagne, 48 burgundy, 235 ale, 60 cider, four brandy. 18 rum, and 34 arrack.[97] In other words, a middle-ranking Englishman with a modest wine cellar could expect to drink almost twice as much port as all other wines combined (Graph 7.3).[98]

Port's status as the preferred wine of English middle-ranking men in the early and mid-eighteenth century is indisputable. So much was this the case that port became a symbol of middle-ranking, urban Englishmen, just as claret was a symbol of the polite, landed elite. These social and geographic distinctions can be seen in two anonymously engraved cartoons from 1772 sold by Matthew Darly, the leading London print publisher of the era (Figures 7.2 and 7.3). In one print

ROAST BEEF & PORT. or
Bully Bramble Esq Justice of Peace in Wasp Town.
Pub by M Darly acor to act April 1st 1772 Strand

Figure 7.2   Roast Beef and Port (1772), by Matthew Darly

142

V. 2

VENISON & CLARET. or
Sr. Humpy. Haunch Bart. of Glutton Hall.
Pub. by Darly Strand April 1st 1772 according to Act.

Figure 7.3   *Venison and Claret* (1772), by Matthew Darly

entitled "Roast Beef and Port," the engraver depicts "Bully Bramble Esq., Justice of the Peace in Wasp Town." A dour-faced and portly Mr Bramble walks with a cane, while resting his unoccupied hand on his ample stomach, between the buttons of his long but unembroidered waistcoat, whose pockets look heavy with coins. He wears a neck-length wig without ribbons, and a black tricorn hat. In contrast, the other print is entitled "Venison and Claret," and depicts "Sir Humphrey Haunch, Baronet of Glutton Hall." With a more pronounced belly than Bramble, Sir Humphrey smiles, while resting one hand on his stomach, and the other in a waist pocket. His waistcoat is embroidered, his wig beribboned, and, as a nobleman, he carries a sword.

According to these droll caricatures, port was the wine of the middling sort, those who made their money in urban trade; claret was the wine of the elite, or those who made their money from landownership. Of course, polite merchants drank claret at least some of the time, and the landowning elite were familiar with port, and certainly served it to their servants and humbler guests. But broadly speaking, port and luxury claret highlighted a division in society between mercantile wealth and landed wealth, and between the well-off and the very well-to-do. As Susannah Centlivre joked back in 1714, claret was the wine for the wealthy gentry, while port was the wine of the "poorer" sort.[99] Thus, port's real symbolic strength in the eighteenth century did not lie in its Whiggishness. Born as a symbol of the opposition Whigs, port became a symbol of another opposition group: the English middle ranks.

8

"Claret is the liquor for boys; port for men"

How Port Became the "Englishman's Wine", 1750s–c. 1790s

In May of 1762 the cellar master to King George III of Great Britain and Ireland purchased red port for the first time. Insignificant as this purchase may seem, it marked a change for the royal household, because port was almost impossible to find, and scarce when found, in the cellars of either of the young king's Hanoverian predecessors. Nor was this change minor. By June 1762 (i.e. one month later) port surpassed luxury claret, if only slightly, as the most common wine within the royal cellars. For the rest of the decade these two wines, which dominated the royal household accounts, were purchased and consumed in almost equal amounts.[1]

To be sure, the court of George III was *not* the ultimate arbiter of fashion and good taste in mid-eighteenth-century England, and much of the port in his cellar may have gone to household staff. Nevertheless, this move toward port reflected and may have helped to create the beginning of a broader trend among the English elite. For example, George Spencer, 4th Duke of Marlborough, embraced port with a passion. An account of wine delivered to Marlborough's three homes in the period from January 1763 to December 1767 reveals a breathtaking amount of wine, almost half of which was port. Langley Park, the duke's hunting lodge in Buckinghamshire, received 3,636 bottles of wine, 43 percent of which were red port. Marlborough House, the duke's palatial London residence, received 7,728 bottles of wine, 47 percent of which were red port. Finally, Blenheim Palace, the Duke's magnificent pile in Oxfordshire, received the most wine of all, 9,108 bottles in five years, 53 percent of which was port.[2] No other wine came close in any of Marlborough's cellars. Even claret, still the preferred wine of the English elite, hovered around 10 percent of the total in all three homes.

As Lord Chamberlain in 1762, and therefore head of the royal household, Marlborough may have been responsible for the rise of port in the royal cellars. After all, George III himself was moderate drinker, enjoying claret and hock (Rhenish wine) at his own table, but without a strong opinion for what others should drink. He may have been happy to follow the advice of his good friend Marlborough, who clearly had a penchant for port. But regardless of who was responsible, both the royal household and Marlborough were going against the grain of their own social class by embracing an established symbol of the English middle ranks at a time when luxury claret was still the preferred wine of most aristocrats. Yet, two decades later, a fondness for port among the aristocracy and other English elites was unexceptional. Indeed, by the last decades of the eighteenth century, port was no longer a wine for the middle ranks alone; it was also the preferred wine of the most politically and socially powerful men in England.

***

Port's ascent up the English social ladder was the result of the complex interplay between Portuguese government intervention in the production of port, the shifting symbolic needs of elite English consumers, and technological innovation. In particular, the second of these three factors caused port to become the dominant wine among all classes of English wine drinkers even prior to the outbreak of the French Revolution. Beginning in the 1760s the English elite slowly began to turn away from claret and other French wines precisely because the politeness for which they stood was losing its appeal as an ideal model of behavior. To middle-ranking critics of the elite, politeness was essentially insincere and effeminate, and thus antithetical to true English masculinity, which was straightforward and manly, and to be found in the behavior of the port-drinking middle ranks. As these beliefs began to take hold, the English elite turned to port for the "manly" connotations they sought and needed to maintain their political dominance.

The result of this elite shift in taste was that by the 1780s port could legitimately be called the "Englishman's wine."[3] To be sure, port was not consumed in any significant amount by the so-called lower orders. Nor is there much evidence of middling and elite women drinking port except in small amounts and usually at dinner parties prior to withdrawing for tea and conversation. Meanwhile, the men stayed at the table and drank port to the point that conversation became difficult. But among English wine drinkers, the vast majority of whom were middling and elite men, port (in all its variations) transcended party, class, age, and regional divides.

Crisis on the Douro: How port got better

Despite its ultimate success on the English market during the eighteenth century, port's climb up the English social ladder was hardly inevitable. In fact, the port wine industry almost collapsed in the 1750s. This near disaster for producers, brokers, shippers, and merchants occurred because the success of the port wine industry contained the seeds of its own demise. English consumption of port soared from 5,861 tuns per annum in 1713 to more than 12,000 tuns per year in the 1720s, and demand continued to grow.[4] However, the high level of demand for port on the English market could not be met every year owing to the natural variations in production. Moreover, the steep, rocky hillsides that would one day constitute Portugal's most famous demarcated wine region were only beginning to be laboriously converted from scrub forests to vineyards. Too much demand and too little supply, said the eighteenth-century wine merchant John Croft, "induced the English factors and Wine coopers to try the expedient of adulterating, and teaching the Portugueze to sophisticate the wines ... which was done principally with the juice of the elder-berry."[5]

Croft was not alone in his analysis. There is a host of evidence that adulteration had become a regular means of stretching the wines of the Douro to meet English demand. Nor was this practice only undertaken in Portugal; "wine brewers" in England were equally guilty. Instruction books for vintners on how to rectify "pricked" (i.e. spoiled) wine had long been available in England and throughout Europe.[6] However, as the English government steadily increased the tariff on all wines in the late seventeenth century, a new sort of instruction manual emerged. These were guidebooks for how to increase the quantity of imported wine by adding English ingredients, or indeed, how to make "foreign" wine from English ingredients alone.[7] As a fortified wine that was not always well made in Portugal, port was particularly susceptible to adulteration and imitation. Croft identified one such culprit as "Raisin Wine ... generally made of the very worst sort of raisins that come from Smyrna compounded with British spirits, extracted from malt."[8]

The increase in adulterated wines was such a concern for honest members of the wine trade that it became a problem for the British government as well. In 1733 Walpole proposed to transfer the duties on wine from Customs to the Excise because he was aware that there was far more wine being sold in England and Scotland than had been officially imported. This disparity was a result of fraud, smuggling, and adulteration.[9] As one defender of the government's proposal wrote:

> A second kind of Fraud [false declaration being the first] is known to the whole Town; and it is by a Composition that is made of several Ingredients, the Juice of Elder Grains, Wild Mulberries, and Cyder, which sell to the Vintners at a third or fourth Part cheaper than Wine sells at; and they, in their Retail, sell it mix'd with Wine, for real Wine, as many People complain they do, and especially the Wine Merchants.[10]

The purpose of transferring the duty from Customs to the Excise was that Excisemen would have the right to inspect vintners' cellars, and thereby ferret out the falsely declared, the smuggled, and the faked. Consequently, the bill had few defenders in the wine trade. Tobacco merchants, whose regulation Walpole also wanted to move from Customs to the Excise, took a similar view. These powerful interest groups cried out that their liberties would be violated by snooping Excisemen, and they rallied the Tories in Parliament to their cause. When some "Country" Whigs voted with them, the Excise Bill was defeated.[11]

But for English wine merchants the defeat of Walpole's Excise Bill was a pyrrhic victory. The flood of stretched, adulterated, and locally concocted "port" in England began to diminish the reputation of the genuine article. Not surprisingly, this was followed by a gradual decrease in demand, which became a precipitous drop by 1750. Average annual Portuguese wine imports into England between 1750 and 1756 reveal a 23 percent decline compared to the average annual amount imported in the 1740s. Oporto wine export figures for the same years reveal almost exactly the same percentage decline.[12]

As it happened, not all of port's competition came from English counterfeiters, for some of it also came from within Portugal.[13] In a declining market English wine shippers in Oporto were in a powerful position; they could pick and choose the wines they wanted from the Douro, and to keep costs down they could supplement their stocks with cheaper wines from adjacent wine-growing regions. The result was that the Douro farmers had to offer their wines at a lower price in order to stay competitive with producers from neighboring regions. By 1754 the cost of a pipe of port in the wine country had fallen from £5 to £8 (in the 1740s) to roughly £2 to £3.[14] During this same period, port exports to England and English imports of Portuguese wine both declined steadily (Graph 8.1).

With fewer orders from England, plenty of wine in stock, and an ability to get cheaper wine from adjacent regions, the English factors in Oporto were in no rush to buy Douro wines they could not sell. Instead, they sent an accusatory circular to the Douro wine brokers, who acted as agents for the English factors as well as salesmen for the Portuguese growers. The missive and its response, both from September 1754, have often been mentioned in histories of the port wine trade, principally because the crisis they precipitated resulted in the creation of the state-run company that controlled and dominated the port wine industry for decades to come.[15] However, the letters have not been examined by historians for what they reveal about the problems faced by various groups within the nascent port wine industry and the changing nature of port wine itself.

In brief, the factors told the brokers that the state of the trade was deplorable and getting worse. They said that the reputation of port wines, once held in great esteem in England, had fallen below that of all other kinds of wine.[16] Proof of their assertion lay in the fact that although the population of England was increasing

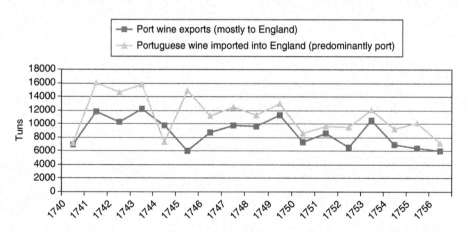

Graph 8.1 Port before Pombal: Crisis on the Douro, 1740–56
Source: Port wine exports: Joseph James Forrester, *A Short Treatise on the Unequal and Disproportionate Imposts levied on Port-Wine, shipped from Oporto to Great Britain* (London, 1850), Table B, pp. 19–20; Portuguese wine imported into England: Schumpeter, *English Overseas Trade Statistics*, Table 16.

the demand for port was diminishing, and, they claimed, would soon disappear altogether. Obviously, the end of demand would be calamitous to everyone in the port trade, and therefore all should "unite in applying such a timely and effectual remedy as will remove the universal opinion in England, that Oporto wines are injurious to health—an opinion so strong in the minds of many, that some even account them poisonous."[17]

According to the factors, the problems lay squarely on the shoulders of producers, who were cutting corners in production to save money and increase their profits. Such behavior, said the factors, resulted in poor-quality wines, which did not keep well.[18] Moreover, the factors accused the growers of adding brandy during fermentation. The resulting wine, claimed the factors, was subject to secondary fermentation and unpleasant tastes. The remedy was not to stop fortifying the wines, said the factors. Rather, it was to add brandy only after the fermentation was complete, and to use only high-quality brandy.[19] The factors concluded that if their instructions for improving the wines were adhered to, then the trade in England would revive, but that they would not purchase any wines where their "recommendations are not attended to."[20]

To this missive the brokers responded immediately, defensively, and furiously. Unlike the English factors in Oporto who usually traded in a variety of goods other than wine, such as English cloth and dried codfish from the North Atlantic, along with salt, dried fruit, and olive oil from Portugal, the brokers were not general traders. Their livelihood, and those of the growers they represented, depended almost entirely upon the sale of Douro wines. Therefore, what was an economic downturn for the factors was an impending disaster for the growers and brokers. In responding to the factors, the brokers acknowledged that a crisis was at hand, but placed the blame squarely on the "English Factory alone ... by their endeavouring to secure themselves increasing profit, and not leaving any advantage to the cultivator."[21] In particular, argued the brokers, it was the instructions that the factors had given the growers that were responsible for the decline of port's once exalted reputation among English consumers.

Specifically, the factors had encouraged the use of brandy to check fermentation (and thereby retain grape sugar), and elderberry to darken the wine, so that the resulting wine

> should burn in the stomach; that, thrown in the fire, it should flash like gunpowder; that its colour should be deep as ink; that its sweetness should be like the sugar of Brazil, and its aromatic flavour as the spices of India. ... It was by these DIABOLICAL INSTRUCTIONS of the Factory, that the wine growers were compelled to load their wines with elderberry, brandy, and sweets, or run the risk of not selling their wines except for common use.[22]

The most obvious proof of their argument, stressed the brokers, was that the wine growers would not willingly incur the additional expense of fortifying and adulterating their wines if they had not been instructed to do so and did not think such actions would increase the sale price. Furthermore, the brokers asserted that the English factors could not deny that they too fortified and adulterated their wines because they, the brokers, handled many of the factor's orders for brandy, elderberries, sweetened wines, and sour wines, which they would blend together to make various styles of port for the English market.[23]

The brokers were confident that if English wine merchants and consumers had this information, they would know whom to blame for the low quality of the wine and the subsequent fermentations. They would then demand from the factors only unadulterated Douro wines, and factors in turn would purchase only this type of wine from the growers. The brokers then concluded with a threat of their own. "If this is not to be," they averred, "as the Douro subsisted forty years ago without an English Factory, and as the Brokers then lived without their commissions, so now we will return to our lands, and you, Gentlemen to Britain."[24]

Along with fierce accusations and mutual blame, there are several historical ironies within these two antagonistic letters. The most significant of these is that adding brandy during fermentation and blending wines from various vineyards and vintages are essential practices in the production of most modern port wines. However, in 1754 these practices were not fully mastered, and to the degree that they were understood, the English factors wanted to be in control. What is also clear from these letters is that the demand for good Douro wines had outrun supply; and factors, brokers, and growers, all looking to make a profit, had rushed in to fill the gap by making wines they called "port." And because there was no regulation of the industry, no one was actually breaking the law. In other words, what happened to port was a classic economic scenario. Increased demand led to increased production, much in the form of inferior, adulterated, or non-genuine wines. This, in turn, led to a decline in overall quality and eventually decreased demand. The decreased demand meant a decline in prices, and while everyone involved in the industry was in economic trouble, the growers were in the most tenuous position of all: having staked their livelihood on the sale of their wines, they could not simply take a loss and rely on their other commercial ventures to keep them economically afloat.

To those interested in the evolution of port, it should also be clear that as early as the 1750s English factors and consumers had an ideal type of port in mind (and occasionally in cask), which according to the description of the brokers, looked, smelled, and tasted very much like modern vintage port: dark, strong, aromatic, spicy, and sweet. A wine fitting that description could be produced in optimal years when the grapes had a long, warm growing season, and when the fermentation was relatively cool and protracted. In this instance, brandy added after the fermentation had stopped would have helped to ensure that a secondary fermentation did not take place during transport or warm weather, and that the wines were protected against spoilage.

But to insure a well-balanced, strong, sweet wine would also have taken the knowledge of a skilled winemaker, and most port was made by Portuguese farmers (with the advice of brokers), who did not always have the technological means or knowledge to produce the type of wine described in the brokers' letter. Moreover, climatic conditions were not always optimal; in many years the wine would have fermented itself out to dryness at a rapid rate, leading to a strong, coarse wine. Thus, the problem for growers and shippers (who blended the wines to suit the tastes of their customers) was how to meet the demands of English consumers for this highly desired type of port when conditions were not optimal. Furthermore, this was not the only type of port that shippers and consumers demanded. In fact, until the practices of fortification and blending were better understood, meeting the vast array of consumer demands was always going to be difficult. The result was experimentation, adulteration, blending, and, in almost all instances, more brandy.

Pombal and the Douro Company

The result of this crisis on the Douro has been amply discussed by historians of the wine trade, and need only be summarized here.[25] In 1755, the Portuguese brokers took their complaints to earthquake-ravaged Lisbon, where they were warmly received by the prime minister, Sebastião José de Carvalho e Melo, the future Marquês de Pombal (a title he received in 1770). Pombal was in need of money to rebuild the Portuguese capital, and he had long regarded the English dominance of the port wine trade with envy and suspicion. The crisis on the Douro played right into his hands. Having gleaned much about commerce and trade while living in London as the Portuguese ambassador to the court of St James (1738–43), Pombal planned a series of state-run companies that would restructure Portuguese finances entirely, and one of these companies was to control the port wine trade. When the English factors got wind of the plans they too sent a representative to Lisbon. According to Croft, who was now writing about events in his own lifetime, Pombal not only dismissed English complaints out of hand, but berated the factors "for treating Portugal as scurvily and insignificantly as if it was the most petty Republic imaginable, and not a Kingdom that had an indispensable right to make its own domestic laws (Figure 8.1)."[26]

On September 10, 1756, the *Companhia Geral da Agricultura dos Vinhos do Alto Douro*[27] (hereafter, the Douro Company) was established by royal decree. According to the founding charter, the Douro Company was to maintain the quality, price, and reputation of port wine, demarcating a growing zone and delimited areas within the zone according to their quality; by establishing fixed prices for the different quality Douro wines; by prohibiting the blending of demarcated wines with wines from outside the zone; by limiting the production and sale of each grower; by limiting the use of manure within the better-quality zones; and by prohibiting the growth of elder trees within the entire demarcated zone—this last order being enforced upon the pain of transportation to Brazil. The Douro Company, acting as traders, had the right of first refusal on all wines and held a monopoly on trade to Brazil, the city of Oporto, and to all nations except Great Britain and Ireland.[28] These laws were to be enforced by a complex hierarchy of officials, ranging from a single president at the head to multiple deputies, judges, clerks, commissioners, bailiffs, and wine tasters.

The English factors were left with the right to export wines to Britain and Ireland, but these wines could only be wines from the Douro that had been passed by the Douro Company as "Factory" wines (i.e. wines from the best demarcated vineyards) and approved for export in Oporto by an official taster. Significantly for the English factors, Britain and Ireland were the only sizable markets for port other than Portugal and its colonies, although the English were never heavily involved in Portuguese imperial trade. In other words, but for their ability to drive down the price of wine from the producer, very little had been taken away from the English. Nevertheless, the factors were irate. They protested vociferously against these impositions on what had been essentially their monopoly, but Pombal had no sympathy and turned them out. Meanwhile, the British prime minister, William Pitt the Elder, wanted to stay on good terms with Portugal during the Seven Years' War (1756–63), and therefore turned a deaf ear to the factors' entreaties for diplomatic pressure.

Despite English complaints, which persisted into the mid-nineteenth century,[29] there can be little doubt that the Douro Company, at least initially, had a beneficial effect on the quality of port shipped to Britain, and on the quality of port wine more generally (Graph 8.2).[30]

The most convincing argument for the beneficial effects of the state-controlled Douro Company upon the port trade is the immediate increase of port exports, which suggests an increased demand. From an average of roughly 7,500 tuns in the crisis years of 1750–6, annual port wine exports (over 80 percent of which were to England), climbed to more than 9,000 tuns per year during the 1760s, and to almost 11,500 tuns during the 1770s.[31] That constituted a 53 percent increase even prior to the more dramatic take-off that began in 1786 after Pitt's tariff reductions. Likewise, English import figures show an annual average of approximately 9,000 tuns of Portuguese wine in the early 1750s, increasing to over 11,500 tuns in the 1770s.[32] The disparity in export and import figures in the early 1750s, and convergence in the 1770s, were due to two principal factors. First, the earthquake of 1755 destroyed many Lisbon area vineyards, meaning that port wine increased its already dominant share of Portuguese wines exported to England.[33] Second, some of what was initially imported and sold as "port" in England was Portuguese wine from outside the Douro river valley, and thus was not accounted for among official port exports. Of course, that was precisely the type of fraud that Pombal's Douro Company was intended to prevent.

So, port improved in quality from 1756 onwards because of careful regulation of production and declaration, but this alone does not explain the increasing popularity of port among English wine consumers. Nor, as one wine trade historian proposed, does the final Gin Act of 1751 or the temporary prohibition of gin distillation in England during the harvest shortages of 1757, 1759, and 1760.[34] These events may have been contributing factors to port's popularity in England, but the time gap between gin's rapid decline (1751) and the beginning of port's resurgence on the English market (1757) is too far apart to suggest that port was a replacement for gin among English consumers. More convincingly still, the bulk of English gin drinkers in the first half of the eighteenth century came from the urban (and mostly London) poor.[35] When they were forced by price and availability to stop drinking so much gin, they did not suddenly have the money to drink

Figure 8.1   *Sebastião José de Carvalho e Melo, Marquês de Pombal* (c. 1769), attributed to Joana de Salitre
Note: Bane of British port shippers, saviour of their industry.

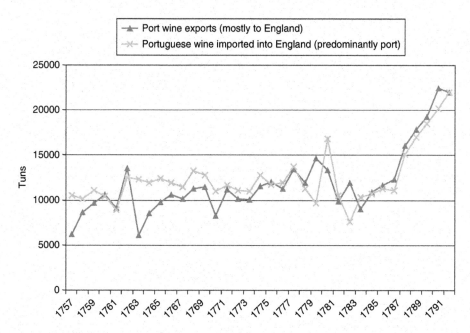

Graph 8.2 Port: The Englishman's wine, 1757–91
Source: Port wine exports: Forrester, *A Short Treatise on the Unequal and Disproportionate Imposts Levied on Port-Wine*, Table B, pp. 19–20; for Portuguese wine imported into England: Schumpeter, *English Overseas Trade Statistics*, Tables 16 and 17.

wine instead. Rather, the reasons for port's increased dominance of the English market during the second half of the eighteenth century was because port got better, and because elite men joined the middling sorts in their fondness for port.

The political need for port

Why would the elite men begin to drink a wine that they had formerly considered uncouth and the province of the middling sorts? Certainly, the improved quality mattered for the aesthetically judgmental elite, but by itself better quality cannot explain why port became increasingly fashionable among the elite. Improved quality of a commodity never guarantees increased sales. There has to be greater demand as well, and for that to occur, and be sustained, there must be an incentive to consume over and above the desire simply to try a product because it has, according to others or to its own advertising, improved in quality. Happily for port producers and shippers, just such an incentive emerged in England during the Seven Years' War.

An effeminate elite?

As early as the 1730s, social and political critics among England's swelling middle ranks began to appropriate the late seventeenth-century Country and Whig critique of luxury and effeminacy, and turn it against the Whig oligarchy led by none other than the claret-loving Sir Robert Walpole. "Effeminacy," in this context, denoted a "degenerate moral, political and social state that opposed and subverted the vaunted 'manly' characteristics—courage, aggression, martial valour, strength—that constituted patriotic virtue."[36] Admiral Vernon's resounding victory over the Spanish at Porto Bello in 1739 was seen as a vindication of the sort of aggressive and martial masculinity that the anti-war Walpole was said to shun in favor of trade, luxury, and politeness.[37] In the immediate aftermath of the Jacobite rising of 1745–6, the novelist Eliza Haywood censured the gentlemen officers in the British army for their supposed effeminacy,[38] despite the fact that they proved particularly brutal in their victory over the hapless Highland clansmen.

During the initial years of the Seven Years' War the trickle of such class- and gender-based criticism became a torrent.[39] With the calamitous losses to the French in the Ohio river valley, first by the famous patriotic Briton from Virginia, George Washington (whose plantation was named in honor of the British hero Admiral Vernon), and later by General Edward Braddock (whose bloodied sash Washington kept as a memento), the lack of manly virility among the British officer class (which corresponded to the landed classes) came under sweeping attack.[40] Criticism of the officer class grew worse still with the failure of Admiral Byng to relieve the British garrison at Minorca in May 1756. Anti-Byng rioters across England made clear their perception that the loss of Minorca to the French had everything to do with the effeminacy of the elite, a claim that was affirmed by Byng's own aristocratic parentage.[41] Effigies of Byng were carefully dressed in lace and other sartorial symbols of a courtier.[42]

Numerous historians have demonstrated how a "virulent strand of anti-aristo-cratic sentiment" entered political discourse during these crisis years.[43] This senti-ment was caused by anger at government policy abroad, as well as the supposedly "inexorable and, some feared, irreversible slide into 'effeminacy'" of the political and cultural elite.[44] The Reverend John Brown of Newcastle summarized much of middle-ranking opinion on the matter in 1757 when he stated that the "internal strength of a Nation will always depend chiefly on the Manners and Principles of its leading Members." The problem, to critics like Brown, was obvious: the current "luxurious and effeminate Manners in the higher Ranks, together with a general defect of Principle ... operate powerfully, and fatally," in the conduct of national affairs.[45] Britain, according to Brown, had become a nation wherein courage, prin-ciple, sacrifice, and liberty were forsaken for vanity, frivolity, selfishness, and the underlying element of all corruption, luxury.

And if luxury corrupted, French luxuries corrupted most of all because, accord-ing to this English masculinist rhetoric, France was the embodiment of an effemi-nate nation. A print entitled *The Imports of Great Britain from France*, published in May 1757—two months after Admiral Byng was executed for failing "to do his utmost"—highlights and links the cultural and material causes of Britain's alleged descent into effeminacy. Ironically, the print was engraved by Philippe Boitard, a French immigrant in London who either had cause to dislike his former homeland, or who knew all too well the prejudices of his hosts. In Boitard's print we see hordes of French cooks, dancers, priests, tradesmen, and coquettes disembarking in the port of London, having safely passed England's national defenses, symbolized by the Tower of London in the background. Stevedores have already unloaded the ship of its corrupting cargo, which lies on the dock, ready to contaminate England. Among the products listed and depicted are cheese, muffs, ribbons, cambrics, gloves, perfume, and, most prominent of all in the foreground, large casks of clearly labeled champagne, burgundy, and claret (Figure 8.2).[46]

The message of the print was simple: the consumption habits of the Francophile elite made them effeminate (like the French), and perhaps the most important of these habits, in that it was physically ingested, was the consumption of expensive French wines. For people who accepted this jingoistic and gendered critique of the English elite, the "politeness" of luxury claret—or any other commodity for that matter—was no longer a positive attribute, because politeness was frivolous and effeminizing, and not, as by design, a sign of one's superior aesthetic sensibility. Indeed, it was precisely during the Seven Years' War (1756–63) that politeness as a model of gentlemanly began to be rejected on the grounds that it was incompatible with the supposedly masculine national character of England.[47]

Of course, the rejection of polite behavior and its attendant commodities happened gradually, but the ultimate effect on the reputations of different wines was dramatic. Take, for example, Samuel Johnson's declaration on wines at a London dinner party hosted by Sir Joshua Reynolds on April 7, 1779. Johnson, who was almost completely abstemious at the time, harangued his fellow diners with his great contempt for claret, which all the others were drinking at that moment. Having made his point, he was persuaded by his companions to drink a glass, "that he might judge," writes Boswell, "not from recollection, which might be dim, but from experience." Johnson complied, then quickly ejaculated: "Poor stuff! No, Sir, claret is the liquor for boys; port for men; but he who aspires to be a hero (smiling,) must drink brandy."[48] Johnson went on to say that few men were heroic enough to withstand the power of brandy, implying that drinking port was proof enough of one's manliness, while claret drinkers were clearly not real men at all (Figure 8.3).

The masculinity of port, along with the improved quality, helped to make it attractive to the English elite. We have seen already how in the 1760s the 4th Duke of Marlborough purchased and served far more port than claret. Of course, one man's preference does not make a trend, but records from Christie's auction house, which begin in 1766, confirm port's ascent up the social ladder. The first listing of port in a Christie's sale comes from among the goods of "Mr. Wilson, an Innkeeper and Farmer" at Petersfield, Hampshire, in 1768. Similarly, a 1769 auction of the property of "Captain Fletcher from the West Indies," contained red port, along with tent, Calcavella, "old" madeira, "fine" madeira, and "old" hock. An innkeeper and a naval captain are precisely the type of middle-ranking Englishmen one would expect to see drink port in the eighteenth century. However, by the 1770s, port began to appear in more prestigious Christie's auctions. For example, in 1772 the Earl of Granard's auctioned wines included a pipe of port along with bottled port, claret, champagne, and white burgundy, and a

Figure 8.2 *The Imports of Great Britain from France* (1757), by Louis Philippe Boitard
Note: Effeminacy by the boatload, and the reason for Britain's decline.

Figure 8.3   A Literary Party at Sir Joshua Reynolds's (1781), by James Doyle
Note: "Poor stuff! No, Sir, claret is the liquor for boys; port for men."

hogshead of madeira. In 1778, the sale of the Earl of Kerry's wines included undisclosed amounts of "fine old port," claret "fine flavour," champagne, burgundy, Rhenish, red Cape, white Cape, Rivesaltes, and cherry brandy. [49]

In other words, by the 1770s port was not just a supplementary wine for the aristocracy, to be given to servants and laborers as a form of payment. It was an increasingly esteemed wine in elite wine cellars. Port's new status among the elite enabled Sir Edward Barry, Fellow of the Royal College of Physicians and of the Royal Society, to assert in 1775 that "Port wines are now universally preferred to the French claret."[50] Whether Barry meant to include women in this claim is uncertain, but it may have been true nonetheless. For instance, in 1777, Isabella Widdrington of Hauxley, Northumberland, a spinster, wrote to her sister Mrs Mills, who lived near Durham, asking her to relay an order to Mrs Mills's husband, a wine merchant. The order consisted of two gallons of brandy, 12 dozen pint bottles of the "best Frontignac,"[51] and a hogshead of port.[52]

Of course, port was not "universally preferred," as no wine can ever be the favorite of every single consumer in a large and economically diverse market such as England. Moreover, Christie's records and private cellar records from the 1770s reveal that most aristocratic wine drinkers still preferred expensive French wines to port, but significantly, the relative amount of port in their cellars was rising. Therefore, what Barry's statement reveals is an awareness that port was eagerly consumed by the wealthiest and most fashionable consumers and not just by the middle ranks. For example, receipts from the London tavern keeper Luke Reilly in 1777 show that the very fashionable Richard Brinsley Sheridan—having just struck gold with *The School for Scandal*—drank two to three bottles of wine per visit, and that wine was usually port, and less often madeira, Mountain, claret, or even "heroic" brandy.[53] By 1780 Sheridan would leave the theater and become a radical Whig politician, where his great nemesis was William Pitt the Younger. But despite their tremendous political animosity, both men could agree on port. In the year beginning July 1784, Pitt purchased approximately 5,200 bottles of wine, of which port constituted nearly half (46 percent), and claret a mere 11 percent.[54]

The consumption of port in England among both the elite and middle ranks was clearly abetted by the Eden Treaty of 1786, which was promoted by Pitt as a way to diminish smuggling and expand legal trade, and hence, increase customs revenue. The Eden Treaty with France, and the Consolidation Act that resulted from it, both simplified and reduced the import duties on wine, so that Portuguese and Spanish wines paid £31 per tun, French wines £47, while Rhenish wines moved into the most expensive category at £51 per tun. The result was a sharp rise in Portuguese wine imports, from roughly 11,000 tuns to 15,000 tuns between 1786 and 1787. However, this dramatic increase in the absolute amount of port constituted a small decline in the relative amount. To be precise, Portuguese wine constituted 76 percent of all English wine imports in the decade 1777–86, and 73 percent during the five years in which the Eden Treaty operated without hindrance (1787–91). Meanwhile, French wine imports, which constituted 3 percent of all English wine imports in the decade prior to the Eden Treaty, increased to 4.3 percent during the next five years.

In other words, the major effect of the Eden Treaty upon the wine trade in England was to increase the overall volume of imports by 88 percent from the six years before the treaty to the five years after.[55] However, the actual contours of English taste changed very little. The elite were still the only significant consumers of French wine after 1786, but like the middle ranks, they also drank more port. A surviving wine bill from the London vintner's Christie and Barrow in 1790 for Spencer Perceval, one of Pitt's political protégés and a future Tory prime minister, reveals a predilection for port, which comprised 61 percent of Perceval's total purchases.[56] In the period 1792 to 1804, Henry Gage (3rd Viscount Gage)—a prominent Sussex landowner and son of General Thomas Gage, the last royal governor of Massachusetts—purchased the equivalent of nearly 19,000 bottles of wine, of which port constituted 48 percent. Sherry and madeira ranked next in volume, while claret accounted for only 3 percent of the total. Similarly, in the years 1796 to 1806, port was the most prominent wine in the cellars of the senior common room at Christ Church College at Oxford. In fact, at that time, sherry was the only other wine to be found in what was perhaps the most aristocratic of Oxford colleges.[57] A quote from an article in *The Times* in February 1798 confirms port's preeminent status among the future leaders of the nation:

"To which University," said a lady, some time since, to the late sagacious Dr. Warren, "shall I send my son?" "Madam," replied he, "they drink, I believe, near the same quantity of port in each of them."[58]

While some of the elite predilection for port after 1793 can be attributed to the war against revolutionary France, which began in that year (and which officially annulled the Eden Treaty), most cannot. As the evidence shows, the aristocratic and elite move toward port began as far back as the 1760s, a full generation before the war began. Instead, the change in elite taste from claret to port had everything to do with maintaining political power. As middle-ranking charges of elite "effeminacy" took hold in the late 1750s, members of the besieged elite looked to address their critics. One way to do so was to drink a symbolically middle-ranking wine like port. After all, according to the middle-class critics who needed to be placated, to drink port was to drink a glass of true English masculinity. Without this form of masculinity, the elite, especially the aristocrats among them, would no longer be politically legitimate. After all, to be less than a man was to be womanly or childlike, and hence politically disqualified.

With so much at stake, the gradual switch from claret to port was by no means the only politically motivated change in taste made by the besieged and anxious English elite. For example, fashion historians have identified a shift in men's clothing beginning around 1750, from brightly colored, flamboyant clothing to darker, simpler men's suits.[59] John Carl Flugel, a pioneer of fashion history, referred to this trend as the "Great Masculine Renunciation." And just like the shift from claret to port, elite male renunciation of silk and lace for worsted and cambric mirrored the fashion of the middling sorts.[60] Similarly, architecture and decorative arts historians have shown how simple, neo-classical designs began to replace more ornate rococo styles around the mid-eighteenth century.[61] In short, for the English elite to maintain power over the increasingly assertive middle-ranks of society, they had, symbolically at least, to adhere to middle-ranking tastes. In this sense, there was an embourgeoisement of English elite taste, even if the elite consumed better-quality port, more expensively tailored clothing, and larger and better-quality houses and objects with which to fill them.

What's in a bottle?

The increased demand for port from the English elite coincided with—and no doubt helped to propel—a technological change that made port a markedly finer wine. That technological change was the development of the cylindrical bottle. The wine writer and antiquarian André Simon opined that,

> Port could not be drunk with any degree of satisfaction from the cask, when quite young, like Claret, Moselle or even Sherry, and its consumption did not increase appreciably until the cylindrical bottle had evolved purposely to make binning possible: until binning became possible Vintage Port was impossible.[62]

Despite Simon's own feelings on the matter, most port in the eighteenth century was consumed with very little if any bottle age, and within a year or two of production. Most English consumers enjoyed it fiery and tannic, but no doubt they noticed a difference when the wine had time to mellow.

However, before the invention of the cylindrical bottle, bottle ageing was highly impractical. In the seventeenth-century bottles were generally globe- or onion-shaped, and by the eighteenth century they were usually mallet-shaped. In both cases the form supplied the function, which was to transport the wine from the cask to the table, and once on the table to provide a solid container that would not tip easily on frequently uneven surfaces. Some expensive French, Italian, and Rhenish wines were bottled, corked, and sealed during the eighteenth century; but bottling generally took place once the wine in cask was deemed ready to drink. Bottling was a way to slow down the ageing process that occurred while the wine was in wood. The result for these luxury wines was that the amount of time in bottle was often less than the amount of time in cask. And when bottle ageing did occur, it was a highly impractical use of space. Neither globe nor onion nor mallet-shaped bottles could easily be stacked on top of one another, so storing bottles required an awkward stacking frame or baskets full of sawdust for packing.

While bottle ageing was impractical, cask-ageing was extremely expensive for shippers in Portugal. Ageing required enough capital for the shipper not to need to sell his wines immediately, lodges for the wine to age in, and a ready supply of wine with which to keep the casks topped up. Thus, throughout the eighteenth century most port shipped to England was less than a year old; however, toward the end of the century increasing amounts of older wine (two and three years old) were blended in with the new wine before shipping.[63] This type of blending would have helped to mellow a fiery young port; but as the amount of brandy in port was also increasing as the century wore on, blending with older wines would not have been as efficacious as ageing the wine in bottle for many years.

Similarly, for consumers in England to cask age their wines, they needed both the space in their cellars in which to keep the large casks, as well as the capital with which to purchase them. This was a common enough practice, but not all consumers could afford an entire pipe of port. However, once the cylindrical bottle was available, all that the consumer needed, assuming he could afford the wine, was a small cellar and time. In other words, the cylindrical bottle enabled producers, shippers, and merchants to shift the cost of ageing wine on to a greater number of consumers. These consumers, in turn, did not need to buy an entire pipe of port, although those who could afford it often did.

The stackable, cylindrical bottle allowed wines efficiently to be stored on their sides for many years. A bottle laid on its side kept the cork moist and tight, and therefore the wine in and the oxygen out. One historian of port wine dates the development of the cylindrical bottle precisely to 1768, but evidence from antique bottles suggests that the cylindrical bottle did not come to prominence in one year, but developed gradually during the third quarter of the eighteenth century.[64] Corks, or course, were also necessary for the ageing process, but these had been used as bottle stoppers in England since at least the sixteenth century.[65] Even more importantly, the invention of the corkscrew sometime in the mid-seventeenth century allowed corks to be driven flush with the rim of the bottle.[66] Thus, during the third quarter of the eighteenth century all the technological

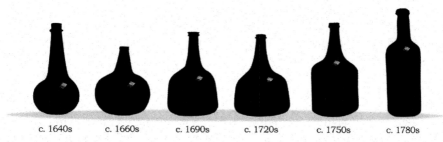

c. 1640s   c. 1660s   c. 1690s   c. 1720s   c. 1750s   c. 1780s

Figure 8.4   Evolution of the English wine bottle, c. 1640s–1780s[67]

conditions were right for wine to be bottle-aged, and the strongest wines benefitted from this ageing most of all (Figure 8.4).

The results of these new conditions were almost immediate, and are seen in the emergence of vintage port, the first mention of which comes from a Christie's sale in April 1773. The vintage was 1765, and the port came from the cellar of a "Gentleman's house" on Mortimer Street near Cavendish Square.[68] Top-quality claret, champagne, burgundy, and Rhenish wine had been sold by the vintage throughout much of the eighteenth century, but port had not been considered worthy of such careful production and marketing. So, while the late eighteenth century is too early to speak of modern port, it is not too early to speak of luxury port, and that new type of port was on the English market to stay.

The fact that luxury port existed by the third quarter of the eighteenth century should not blind us to the fact that some, perhaps most, port in England was still coarse, adulterated or counterfeit. Writing in 1775, Barry stated that port wines, although now preferred to claret, "are frequently adulterated here, which is not to be imputed to the Portugal merchants; and it is well known, that large quantities of nominal port wines are made here, without any Port wine in them."[69] A French visitor in 1765, Pierre-Jean Grosley, was even more explicit, saying that the port wine drunk in taverns was a combination of turnip juice, wild berries, beer, and litharge (lead oxide), and this he had learned from a vintner.[70] But he also said that one of the only two good bottles of wine he had during his six-week stay in England was a bottle of port imported directly from Lisbon by a French banker living in London; the other was a bottle of Macon brought directly from Burgundy. The former wine, which he called port in its "pure and natural state," was of a "deep colour, but lively, and of a very high spirit." It "resembled the best claret in right order, such as is drank at Bourdeaux itself."[71]

If a Frenchman living in London could procure an excellent bottle of port, surely savvy and well-to-do English consumers, who drank a great deal more port than the French, knew where to go in London to find a superior bottle. For the most part, though, wealthy English consumers purchased their wine from high-end merchants; they did not go to the tavern looking for top-quality wine.

Nevertheless, the peripatetic John Byng, nephew of the unfortunate admiral, said that it *was* possible to find a good bottle of port in a London tavern if you were known by the proprietor. He himself thought the "light [King's] Lynn" kind of port found in East Midlands taverns better than the "London heavy cut."[72]

***

Byng's remarks remind us that while the quality and style of port continued to vary, by the later eighteenth century the overall quality was improving enough that, at its best, port could compete with French wines for the most discerning English palates. In contrast, early eighteenth-century port had little to recommend it but its cheapness, its strength, and for some, its reputation as a patriotic wine. These factors had been enough to make port popular among the middle ranks, but not enough to make port fashionable wine among the English elite, be they Whig or Tory. During the later eighteenth century, however, elite fashion began to change; port was made with greater care and the quality of wine shipped to Britain and Ireland improved. This qualitative improvement coincided with a need among the English elite to behave in a way that the middle classes defined as more "English" and "manly," and less "effeminate" and "French." This demand on English elite men meant adopting certain middle-class habits and tastes; it meant drinking less claret and more port. In turn, elite men demanded a type of port in their own self-image: high-quality, aged and refined, but strong and manly nonetheless. With quality port available, the elite could behave like the middling-sorts without actually having to drink a middling-sort wine. To a casual observer of Englishmen, the socially divided society did not look so divided after all. From the middle-ranks up, everyone was a John Bull now.

To be sure, even at the end of the eighteenth century only a small amount of port was fine wine, and none of it was modern port. As late as 1824 the reputable Scottish physician and historian of wine Alexander Henderson wrote that port was a dry wine, and the debate over whether port should be dry or sweet, neat or fortified, continued until the mid-nineteenth century.[73] But whatever port tasted like on the palate—and apparently this taste varied as much as the quality—in the late eighteenth century it was appreciated by the entire spectrum of English wine drinkers for the solid English manliness that its consumption represented. So much was this the case that in 1787 Croft could write: "An Englishman of any descent [*sic*] condition, or circumstances, cannot dispense with it after his good dinner, in the same manner as he uses a piece of Cheshire cheese for digestion [*sic*] sake."[74] Precisely because port had been such a prominent symbol of middle-ranking men, it became, by the last decades of the eighteenth century, the Englishman's wine.

9

"That other liquor called port"

Port and the Creation of British Identity in
Scotland, 1770s–1815

In a codicil to his will, written in 1776, the Scottish philosopher and historian
David Hume added the following bequest:

> I leave to my friend John Home of Kilduff, ten dozen of my old claret, at his
> choice; and one single bottle of that other liquor called port. I also leave to him
> six dozen of port, provided that he attests under his hand, signed John *Hume*,
> that he has himself alone finished that bottle at two sittings. By this concession,
> he will at once terminate the only two differences that ever rose between us
> concerning temporal matters.[1]

This particular joke, besides indicating that Hume's sense of humor remained
steady to the end, reveals his fondness for port. His good friend Home, however,
was more traditionally Scottish in his taste for wine. He preferred claret, and was
the author of the epigram that asserted the Scottishness of claret, while denigrat-
ing port as a toxic English imposition. Indeed, it was almost certainly in response
to Home's famous epigram that Hume made his jocular offer.

Like Home, Hume was a proud Scot who ultimately preferred the cozy provin-
cialism of the Scottish capital to the bustle of the British metropolis. Thus, while
Hume wrote a monumental *History of England*, he was no fawning anglophile.
"John Bull's prejudices are ridiculous, as his insolence is intolerable," wrote
Hume in a fit of pique.[2] And that was not the only time that his cultural critique
of South Britons descended into invective.[3] Clearly, then, his predilection for
port cannot be explained by a desire to mimic the English. In fact, Hume had
not always liked port. In an essay written in 1752, he criticized the Methuen
Treaty on the grounds that Britain "lost the French market for our woolen manufactures, and transferred the commerce of wine to Spain and Portugal, where
we buy much worse liquor at a higher price."[4] As we have seen, most port was a
rough drink in 1752, but as it improved so did Hume's fondness for it. Moreover,
as Hume's will indicated, he never stopped enjoying claret; he had at least 120
bottles of "old claret" in his cellar at the time of his death, and among his
friends in Edinburgh he was famous for serving claret and mutton at his dinner
parties (where he did the cooking!).[5]

Hume's changing taste for wine mirrored a broad shift in Scottish taste that occurred in the second half of the eighteenth century. Wine-drinking Scots entered the post-1745 period still clinging to vestiges and symbols of their independent Scottish identity, one of which was consuming inexpensive, fraudulently declared or smuggled claret.[6] And yet, during the last quarter of the eighteenth century popular Scottish taste for wine switched from claret to port. Wine no longer divided the kingdom of Great Britain, but united it. Of course, shared taste in wine, or any other product, does not necessarily indicate a shared national identity or allegiance. However, because claret and port had such staunchly opposite political meanings in Scotland for much of the eighteenth century, the taste for wine in this instance provides a sensitive barometer to the questions of when, how, whether and what form of British identity emerged in Scotland.[7]

Most historians of Britain have come to agree that sometime in the second half of the eighteenth century a majority of politically and historically aware Scots began to embrace a British identity that was founded upon a sanitized, if not entirely overlooked Scottish past, and upon allegedly ancient English liberties.[8] These Scots, such as Hume and Home, were dedicated to a future within the Union even if, as in Home's case, they declared it to be a Faustian bargain in which Scotland's manly independence was forsaken for the sake of economic prosperity. But overall, the Scottish elite and middle ranks increasingly adopted and promoted a British identity, which was held in conjunction with more localized Scottish identities.[9] This British identity was decidedly Anglo-British, in that generally speaking English norms prevailed.[10] Nowhere was the emergence of this Anglo-Britishness more evident than in the taste for wine.

But if the taste for wine in Scotland reflected a change in Scottish identity, it also helps to reveal how that change occurred. Specifically, it shows that for the Scottish to become British they had to learn to hate the French and appreciate the English. This was a process and not an event, and it was largely completed by 1780. As a result, Scots who saw themselves as loyal Britons could no longer defiantly drink illegally imported claret. Instead, the only possible wine with which to assert a British identity was that which the Englishman offered. That wine was port.

Wine, war, and taxes

In 1778 the British Parliament turned once again to wine as a way to help finance a war, this time with Britain's rebellious colonists in North America. For four out of the next five years the import duty on wine was increased, and by the end of 1782 import tariffs stood at £96 per tun on French wine, which was almost twice as much as for Rhenish wines (£51), and more than twice as much as for Spanish (£46) and Portuguese wine (£45).[11] As had been the case since the creation of Great Britain in 1707, French wines were taxed the most, Portuguese wines the least.

The result of these duty increases was not necessarily what the government hoped. Instead, as Adam Smith remarked in his *Inquiry into the Nature and Causes*

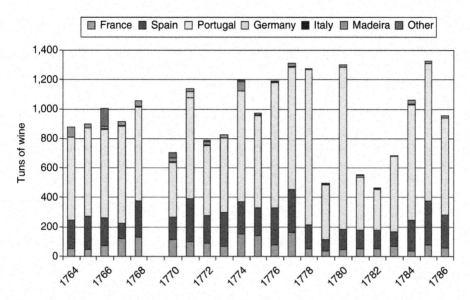

Graph 9.1 Official Scottish wine imports, 1764–86
Source: NA, Customs 14, Scottish Customs Accounts. Figures for 1769 were destroyed in a Customs House accident.

of the Wealth of Nations, which was published two years prior to the tariff hike of 1778:

> The high duties which have been imposed upon the importation of many different sorts of foreign goods ... have in many cases served only to encourage smuggling; and, in all cases have reduced the revenue of the customs beyond what moderate duties would have afforded.[12]

This was broadly true, as official Scottish wine imports were abnormally low in 1779, 1781, 1782, and 1783. With no more new tariffs on wine, merchants felt more secure and wine imports returned to their pre-1779 levels in 1784–5, even though the higher duties remained. But within this unsteady wine trade one thing was clear: the legal trade in Portuguese wine, or at least what was declared as such, dominated the Scottish market.

The Trade Commissioners' Report

As expected, a report delivered in December 1783 to William Pitt's fledgling government asserted that smuggling and fraud of many imported commodities not only continued unabated despite greater government investment in revenue gathering officers and boats, but in many parts of the kingdom, London and Scotland especially, illicit trade was increasing.[13] Among these commodities, of course, was wine. Between the periods 1769–73 and 1778–82, seizures of illegally imported wine increased by 122 percent in London, by 24 percent in English and Welsh outports, and by 55 percent in Scotland. The commissioners had no doubt that the amount of smuggling and fraud in the wine trade was vast, and that the result was tens of thousands of pounds lost to the revenue each year. Consequently, a government that was in massive debt owing to two long and costly wars since the mid-1750s could not even raise the money granted to it by Parliamentary statute.

The Scottish Trade Commissioners who contributed to the report stated that fraud and smuggling prevailed between Kirkcudbright and the Firth of Clyde in the southwest, and between St Abb's Head and Tarbat Ness in what they called the "South East Coast." This latter area, however, comprises nearly the entire east coast of Scotland. Nor did the commissioners imagine that smuggling was anathema in the Highlands and Islands of the north and west, they simply had no idea about the extent to which it was practiced: "these places being so thinly peopled that they cannot defray the Charges of Officers of the Revenue stationed to collect the Duties."[14] This opinion concurred with Samuel Johnson's experience ten years earlier, in 1773, when he found that the Western Islands were curiously well provisioned.

> I forgot to inquire how they were supplied with so much exotic luxury [mused Johnson back in London]. Perhaps the French may bring them wine for wool, and the Dutch give them tea and coffee at the fishing season, in exchange for fresh provisions. Their trade is unconstrained; they pay no Customs; for there is no officer to demand them, whatever therefore is made dear only by impost, is obtained here at an easy rate.

Upon further reflection, the sometimes Scottophobic Johnson conceded that the islanders were very liberal with the wine and brandy, "for they get them cheap, but as there is no Custom House on the Island [of Skye] they can hardly be considered as smugglers."[15]

Pitt takes charge: The Eden Treaty and the Consolidation Act of 1786

Clearly, fraud and smuggling of wine and other commodities were problems for a government in desperate need of revenue, and this is what spurred the new Prime Minister into action.[16] Pitt began by immediately pushing through Parliament many of the proposed laws that enhanced the powers of Revenue officers and made smuggling more difficult. This he followed with the Commutation Act, which dramatically lowered the duty on tea, in the belief that depriving the smuggler of the "principal article in the assortment of his illegal cargo" would reduce the quantities of other illicitly imported goods.[17]

The combined effect of these laws was almost immediate, such that in September 1785 an effusive Pitt could boast in a letter to William Wilberforce, "the produce of our revenues is glorious."[18] With momentum behind him, Pitt then succeeded where Walpole had failed in 1733, by transferring part of the duty on wine and tobacco to the more efficient Excise office. In the case of wine, he annulled all the customs duties placed on wine beginning in 1745, and replaced these with a single excise tax.[19] This law simplified tax assessment, and, of course, it permitted Excise officers to interrogate wine merchants even after their wine had cleared Customs and been placed safely in their vaults.

While these changes in wine duties took place at home, Pitt's government was actively negotiating a commercial treaty with France. The French called for most-favored-nation status on French wines; however, reducing the duty on French wines was one thing, giving them parity with the wines of Portugal was something else altogether, as such an agreement would have entailed violating the Methuen Treaty of 1703.[20] Parliament was not prepared to end the treaty in 1713, nor was it prepared to do so in 1786. Therefore, the British delegation under William Eden proposed a compromise, agreeing to import French wines at a rate no higher than those *now* paid by Portuguese wines.[21] This meant that in order to maintain the Methuen Treaty, the duty on Portuguese wine had to be lowered to one-third less than the duty on French wine. In fact, having recently read and been influenced by Adam Smith's *Wealth of Nations*, Pitt wanted to reduce the duty on all wines in the belief that this would undermine smuggling and fraud in the wine trade and thereby increase revenue by as much as £280,000 per year.[22] Now Pitt had his excuse to reduce wine duties, and he could get trading concessions from the French in return.

The so-called Eden Treaty was concluded on September 26, 1786, whereupon Pitt consolidated all of the remaining Customs duties on wine—thereby having one Customs duty and one Excise duty—and reduced the total duties to levels that complied with both the Eden Treaty with France and the Methuen Treaty with Portugal. The rates resulting from this act, known as the Consolidation Act,[23] cut the duty on French wine by approximately half of what it had been in 1785 (to £47 per tun), on Iberian wines by roughly 30 percent (Portuguese and Spanish duties were also equalized at £31 per tun), while the duty on Rhenish wines remained the same (£51 per tun).[24]

The substantially reduced tariff rates of the Consolidation Act had an immediate impact on legal wine importation into Great Britain, and Scotland was particularly affected; in the period 1787–92, total wine imports in Scotland jumped 128 percent from their post-1764 average. The annual average of imported tuns in the Eden Treaty era was 2,172 per year. French wine imports increased most of all—by 241 percent—while the amount of Spanish wine more than doubled and Portuguese wines nearly did so. Nevertheless, during the entire period 1787–92, French wine imports into Scotland averaged only 13 percent of the total annual amount, while Spanish wines accounted for 23 percent and Portuguese wines 60 percent (Graph 9.2).[25]

By comparison, in the five-year period beginning in 1787, England and Wales imported an average of 25,400 tuns of wine per year, which was 56 percent greater than the post-1764 average. However, French wine remained a mere 4.3 percent of total, while Spanish wine comprised 17 percent, and Portuguese wine 73 percent.[26] In that sense, Scottish drinkers were slightly more Francophile than their

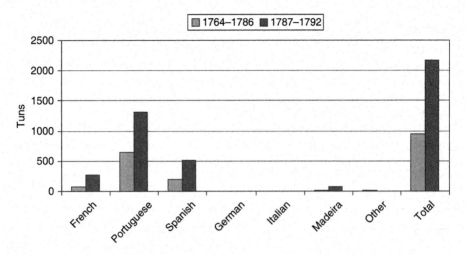

Graph 9.2   Scottish wine import averages, 1764–86 and 1787–92

countrymen to the south, but an overwhelming preference for Portuguese wines bound all the British together.

From claret to port

It is impossible to ascertain the degree of accuracy of official import figures for wine in Britain during the Eden Treaty regime, although clearly they are more accurate than the statistics from the previous period, especially when one considers the miraculous 102 percent increase in Scottish wine imports between 1786 and 1787. But despite the obvious increase in legal trade, French wine still accounted for only 13 percent of the overall Scottish total during the period 1787–92, while Portuguese wines accounted for 60 percent. In other words, however inexact Scottish import statistics were prior to 1787, by that year—and I believe some years earlier—a majority of Scottish wine drinkers were drinking far more port than claret.

However, what was true for middle-ranking consumers who constituted the majority of Scottish wine drinkers and who were more sensitive to price was not necessarily true for the Scottish elite, who had the means to manifest their preferences and make political statements through their consumption habits. According to Johnson and Boswell, Sir Alexander Macdonald, 9th Baronet of Sleat, consumed a hogshead of claret every week at his table, where as clan chieftain he was still expected to provide for a large retinue. That said, port was also to be found in the Highlands and Islands; Boswell discovered first hand that Lochbuie of Mull, chief of the Lochbuie Maclaines, had "admirable port," a bottle of which served as a prelude to a bowl of punch and, not surprisingly after so much alcohol, a night of vomiting.[27]

But during Boswell's years in Edinburgh, where he lived and worked as a law-yer for most of the 1770s, claret was his usual wine.[28] He was hardly alone in his preference within the late Georgian Scottish legal community, which was famously attached to red wine of Bordeaux. The Scottish law lords Monboddo, Hermand, Newton, Braxfield, and Gardenstone (a.k.a. the "Prince of Jolly Livers") were all, according to their collective biographer, well-known devotees of claret—and almost exclusively claret.[29] Forbes Gray recorded that on one occa-sion, when being entertained at Douglas Castle, Lord Braxfield (1722–99) was offered a bottle of port, to which he asked: "Is there was nae claret in the castle?" "I believe there is," came the reply, "but my butler tells me it is not good." That was not enough to discourage the claret-loving judge, who beseeched his host: "Let's pree't" (i.e. pry it open).[30]

Elite Scottish devotion to claret is even more clearly seen in a 1779 account of wine sent by David Ogilvy, 7th Earl of Airlie, to Airlie Lodge in Angus, one of the earl's many residences.[31] Claret constituted 45 percent of the total, and French wines in general accounted for 72 percent of all wines in the Airlie Lodge cellar, at a time when, according to official statistics, they represented roughly 8 percent of all wine imported into Scotland (Graph 9.3).[32]

Of course, one cellar inventory alone cannot provide more than a highly personal record of taste, and the 7th Earl of Airlie might have had exception-ally Francophile taste. After all, he had fought for Prince Charlie in 1745–6 and escaped to Sweden. He later commanded a Scottish regiment in the French army

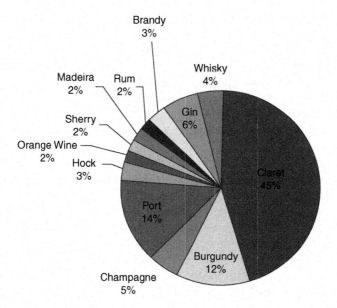

Graph 9.3   Airlie Lodge wine cellar, 1779
Source: NAS, General Register House, GD 16/33/41, Account of the wine sent from Cortacky, Auchterhouse and Newgrange, and put into the cellar at Airly Lodge, Dec. 1779.

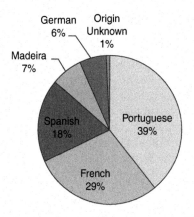

Graph 9.4 Dysart House wine cellar, 1789
Source: NAS, GD 164/818, Dysart House wine books, 1786–1792 (item 10).

and only returned to Scotland in 1778 after being pardoned by the king. However, what seems to have the case was that Airlie was holding back the tide of change; his preference for claret was increasingly exceptional.

Henry Cockburn stated in his memoirs that claret was the "ordinary beverage" of Scotland until 1780, when the "exemption of Scotch claret from duty" was removed.[33] As we have seen, there was no legal "exemption from duty," but the evidence for a shift in Scottish taste in and around 1780 seems to bear Cockburn out. For instance, if we return to the claret-loving Boswell, and specifically to the "Book of Company" he kept at Auchinleck, in Ayrshire, we see the shift from claret to port in the early 1780s. Boswell had become Lord Auchinleck upon the death of his father in 1782, and by the summer of 1783 he and his family were ensconced in their new home, where they were deeply if somewhat reluctantly involved in the custom of playing host to a never-ending stream of Scottish notables, and in the Boswells' case, friends from England and Ireland. During the most socially active period of their time at Auchinleck, from mid-August through the end of October 1783, the Boswells served 230 bottles of wine and 38 bottles of spirits. Of the wines, 88 bottles were port, 77 were claret, 44 were white Lisbon, 13 were madeira, and ten were Mountain from Malaga.[34] Port, therefore, was slightly more favored on Boswell's table than claret, and Portuguese wines as a whole (not including madeira), constituted 57 percent of all the wines served.

Boswell's changing taste represented a broad trend among elite Scottish wine consumers. For example, the prominent army officer and Whig Member of Parliament Sir James St Clair-Erskine (1762–1837) also favored port over claret by the 1780s, and unlike Boswell, whose purchases may have been influenced by a declining bank account, St Clair-Erskine had no reason to stint on wine. In fact, his star was on the rise in 1789 when the cellar at Dysart House in Fife, which he had just inherited, contained 6,168 bottles of wine and another 408 bottles of spirits, cider, and perry. Of the leading wines, 38 percent was port, 25 percent was claret, 13 percent was sherry, 7 percent was madeira and 6 percent was "old" hock. Overall, Portuguese wines (not including madeira) comprised 39 percent of the total, French wines 29 percent and Spanish wines 18 percent.[35] In sum, by 1780, some 13 years before Britain went to war against Revolutionary France, it seems that claret had lost its place to port as the dominant wine among even the wealthiest Scottish consumers (Graph 9.4).

The war with France, 1793–1815

In February, 1793 republican France declared war on aristocratic Britain and the British government reciprocated. No embargo was declared against French wines, nor was the tariff on French wines increased until 1795. However, all Eden Treaty agreements were annulled at the outset of war, and trade between the warring nations declined precipitously. For instance, French wine imports into Scotland dropped from their post-treaty average of 13 percent per annum to 9 percent in 1793, and then to 0.6 percent in 1794. Meanwhile, Portuguese wines jumped from roughly 60 percent of the Scottish total while the Eden Treaty was in effect, to nearly 74 percent of the total imports in 1794, with Spanish wines making up most of the difference. The result was a dearth of newly arrived claret in Scotland. Furthermore, smuggling of wine and other goods was greatly reduced by wartime naval activity.[36]

The pre-war predominance of port throughout Britain was further enhanced by seven Customs and Excise duty increases between 1795 and 1805. By the end of the latter year, the combined duty rate on French wines was roughly £144 per tun, compared to £47 when the war began. At the other end of the scale, the duty on Portuguese and Spanish wines in 1806 stood at £96 per tun.[37] Not surprisingly, Iberian wines dominated the British market in this fiscal environment, and just as in England the favorite Iberian wine in Scotland was port.[38] In other words, the taste for wine in Scotland was essentially the same as aggregate taste in Great Britain as a whole (Graph 9.5).[39]

Not that all Scottish consumers were pleased about the dominance of port. The author of the entry on "wine" in the 1797 edition of the *Encyclopaedia Britannica*— which was published in Edinburgh—wrote:

> A great proportion of the wine consumed in this country is brought from Spain and Portugal; government has always [sic] discouraged the importation of French wines by heavy taxes. We are not sure how far such conduct is founded on good policy, as the French wines are confessedly the best and might be the cheapest.[40]

Nevertheless, the author reluctantly conceded that the

> advantages which Britain derives from the Portuguese trade are very great, and it would not be easy to secure them on any other terms [than the Methuen Treaty].[41]

In other words, as Britons, it is for our country's sake we drink port.

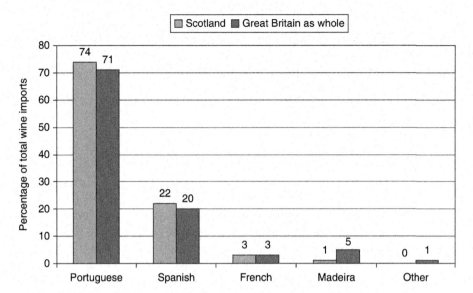

Graph 9.5   Scottish and British taste for wine, 1793–1802
Source: NA, Customs 14, Scottish Customs Accounts; Schumpeter, *Trade Statistics*, Table XVII.

The author of the *Encyclopaedia Britannica* might also have noted that tax increases during the war had made all wines expensive. In fact, by the time the war finally ended in 1815 the rate of duty on all wine was far more than it had been even prior to Pitt's tariff reductions of 1786–7. One result of these massive tariff increases, and the war itself, was that wine imports in Scotland decreased by 19 percent from the period 1786–92 to 1793–1802, and then another 20 percent in the period 1803–15.[42] Moreover, up to a quarter of the wine that was imported during the war years was re-exported to Northern Europe and North America because of the high wartime profits that could be made by Scottish middlemen.[43] Clearly, then, less wine arrived directly into Scotland during the war, but of the wine that did arrive, most of it was port (Graph 9.6).

Port and British identity

Another result of direct wine imports into Scotland during the war years was an increase in the trade and consumption of domestically produced whisky. Specifically, Lowland farmers and urban workers began for the first time to drink legally distilled Lowland whisky, while the wine-drinking middle and upper classes turned increasingly to the charms of small Highland stills.[44] Officially, Highland whisky was supposed to be for local consumption only, so that it had to be smuggled into the fashionable neighborhoods of Edinburgh, Glasgow, Aberdeen, and Dundee. Thus, the fraud and smuggling of imported goods in Scotland was to some degree replaced by internal smuggling in the form of whisky. But during the Napoleonic Wars whisky was not yet a broadly accepted symbol of Scottish

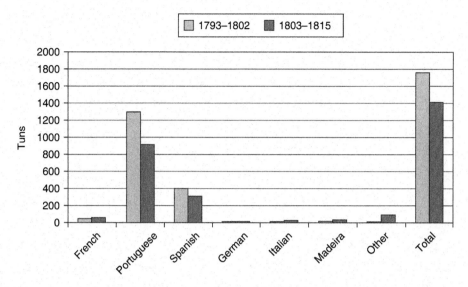

1793–1802 1803–1815

Graph 9.6 Scottish wine imports, 1793–1802 and 1803–15
Source: NA, Customs 14, Scottish Customs Accounts.

identity. That symbolism would be part of the Highlandization of Scottish identity that began after the fighting had ended. Claret had been a recognized symbol
of Scotland, and whisky would become one, but during the many years of fighting
against France in the late eighteenth century—1778–81, 1793–1801, 1803–15—
British identity was paramount. And the best way to express that identity with
alcohol was by consuming port.

Take, for instance, the case of Laurence Oliphant of Gask, an erstwhile
Jacobite who along with his father of the same name fought at Falkirk and
Culloden with Bonnie Prince Charlie in the '45, and then fled Scotland for exile
in France. Father and son were pardoned by George III and returned to Scotland
in 1763. The younger Laurence's wine records are incomplete, but from what
evidence is available, he was still purchasing claret, along with other wines,
in 1791. However, surviving wine receipts for 1793 show not a single drop of
claret; instead, he purchased sherry, rum, and "best old port," from the wine
merchants Montgomery and Stute, and 1785 vintage port from Adam Bisset
of Leith.[45] And this was before the wartime tax increases. While claret would
once have expressed Oliphant's Jacobite sympathies, the revolution in France
turned him emphatically against his former ally and more than ever before
toward Great Britain.[46] Based on the amounts purchased, the liquors that helped
Oliphant to form his loyal British identity were rum, brandy, sherry, and, most
of all, port.

Port's status as a symbol of British identity can be seen in James Gillray's satirical
print *The Death of the Great Wolf* (1795), which was itself a parody of Benjamin
West's great nation-building painting, *The Death of General Wolfe* (1770).[47] In this

Figure 9.1   The Death of the Great Wolf (1795), by James Gillray
Note: Port, a "British" detail like the Union Jack itself.

political cartoon, Gillray satirized the Pitt administration's draconian clampdown on free speech; he was clearly not immortalizing a fallen British hero. But, like West, Gillray exploited the symbols of British identity for didactic effect. Where West places the dying General Wolfe in the center of the original painting, Gillray places Prime Minister Pitt. And where West depicts a British officer stanching the flow of blood from Wolfe's mortal wound with a clean, white handkerchief, Gillray depicts a kilted Scotsmen, Henry Dundas (Secretary of War and Pitt's frequent drinking companion), on his knees, handing a glass of port to his dying friend.[48] In this instance, port is a self-consciously "British" detail, like the careful placement of the Englishman Pitt between the Scotsman Dundas and the Irishman Edmund Burke, all of whom are centered, tellingly, beneath a half-furled Union Jack (Figure 9.1).

Port's iconic British status increased throughout the Napoleonic Wars for a variety of reasons, although perhaps none more so than its affiliation with Britain's victorious warriors. For instance, according to a popular story that circulated in the aftermath of Horatio Nelson's epic victory off Cape Trafalgar on October 21, 1805, just a few hours prior to the opening cannonade Nelson gathered his captains on the HMS *Victory*, dipped his finger in a glass of port, and then sketched his battle plan on a table top for all his captains to see.[49] Nelson, of course, went down in victory, but in his heroic martyrdom, anything he touched—or was said to have touched—in his life, was enhanced by his death. Port, like the navy itself, was an iconic symbol of British military success.

Similarly, Wellington's victories in the Peninsular Campaign enhanced port's reputation as a symbol of triumphant Britain. There was little fighting in the Douro valley, where the grapes for port are grown; but the city of Oporto (including Vila Nova de Gaia), where port wines are aged and from which they are shipped, was captured twice briefly by the French, first in 1808 and then again in 1809.[50] Excepting these occasions, there were British soldiers in and around Oporto throughout the Peninsular Campaign. Many of the officers, and perhaps even some of the soldiers, became port aficionados in their spare time. The letters of Joseph Camo, an American wine merchant who as a "neutral" ran the British firm of Webb, Gray, Campbell and Camo after British nationals were expelled from Oporto in 1808, testify to the ubiquity of British troops in and around the port wine lodges.[51] According to Camo, officers would come by to taste the wines and then usually place an order for shipment back home.[52] It seems safe to speculate that port's "Britishness" was enhanced by the prestige of the victorious officers who returned home with talk of both battles and bottles.

Scottish merchants in the port trade

While Britishness was of course a transcendent identity that could encompass the Scottish, English, Welsh, and even some of the Irish, this chapter has focused on the emergence of British identity in Scotland. I have argued that a British identity emerged in Scotland even before the wars against Revolutionary and Napoleonic France, but that these wars hastened and strengthened that identity. It should also be noted that just prior to, during, and after the wars, Scottish merchants entered what had been an entirely English-run port wine trade. For example, in 1790 George and David Sandeman, natives of Perth, left their home for London, and with a loan of £300 from their father, rented a wine vault in the City. Initially, the Sandemans operated as importing agents for firms in Oporto and Cadiz, and as wholesale merchants within Britain. In fact, their first important contract came from a fellow Scotsman, James Duff, the British consul at Cadiz and a major sherry exporter. In 1796 the Sandeman brothers had an amicable parting, with George retaining the wine business and David becoming a banker in the City of London. It was at this point that George began making frequent trips to northern Portugal and Andalusia to source his own port and sherry. His reputation as a wine merchant within Britain grew so quickly that he was presented with the freedom of the city of Perth in 1797, although he continued to be based in London. By 1809 the firm had agents established in Cadiz, and in 1813, George Glas Sandeman, nephew of the founder, was working full-time in Oporto.[53]

In 1814, another Scotsman named Robert Cockburn arrived in Oporto with similar ambitions. Cockburn was brother of the famous Scottish law lord, and first came to Portugal to fight under Wellington. Having learned about port while tasting wine in the lodges of Vila Nova de Gaia, Cockburn returned to Portugal with a fortune in mind. With the help of the Leith-based wine merchant

Robert Wauchope, he established Cockburn and Wauchope, a firm that in 1828 was joined by another Scotsman in Oporto, William Greig.[54] Also in the 1820s, William and John Graham of Glasgow established their company in Oporto, originally as traders of dry-goods and textiles. However, when they were left with a bad debt that was paid in wine, they found themselves in the port shipping business and never looked back.[55]

British taste for wine

The convergence of Scottish and English taste around port during the final quarter of the eighteenth century reflected the successful development of the British state and helped to construct that state both politically and culturally. Perhaps not surprisingly, this British state, and the British identity that grew along with it, was most highly pronounced among Scots who made their fame and fortune in England. And there was no better example of such a Scotsman and in the eighteenth century than Alexander Wedderburn (1733–1805). Ironically, Wedderburn began his career as a lawyer in Scotland defending David Hume against church censure, and John Home—at that time a Presbyterian minister—against removal from office. Wedderburn was successful on both counts. But after an incident at court in 1757, for which Wedderburn refused to apologize, he left Edinburgh for London and the English bar. By 1768 he had an English wife and represented an English constituency in Parliament, and ten years later he was Attorney-General of England and a Privy Councilor. In 1780 he was made Lord Loughborough. Two years later he married for the second time, another English woman, and in 1793 he was appointed Lord Chancellor. It was a meteoric rise for this son of a Scottish advocate, and it did not stop there. In 1801 Wedderburn's Scottish origins were acknowledged with a Scottish title, the Earl of Rosslyn, and upon his death in 1805 he was given a "splendid incarceration" in St Paul's Cathedral.[56]

Wedderburn's taste in wine both reflected his outstandingly successful journey from Scot to British, and helped to solidify his new identity once he arrived at the latter. Indeed, Wedderburn's butler had the arduous task of maintaining thousands of bottles of wine at multiple residences (notably, all in England), and his organizational and clerical skills suggest that had he been born to a higher station in life or had different ambitions, he could have joined his lordship in a highly successful professional career. As it was, he was kept very busy in the subterranean vaults that enhanced and reflected his lordship's ability to shine in the world above. The uninterrupted records that Wedderburn's butler so meticulously kept date from 1775 to 1800, which was precisely the period during which Scottish elite taste for wine, like Wedderburn himself, became British.

In 1779, just prior to gaining his English peerage, Wedderburn's Scottish proclivities still showed. Of the wines consumed at his table that year, 34 percent were French (19 percent claret), 22 percent Portuguese (18 percent port), and 14 percent Spanish. Lesser amounts of madeira and hock also featured on his table. Ten years later, with his career still on the rise and the Eden Treaty with France still in place, Wedderburn's household drank nearly twice as much wine (over 930 bottles), but

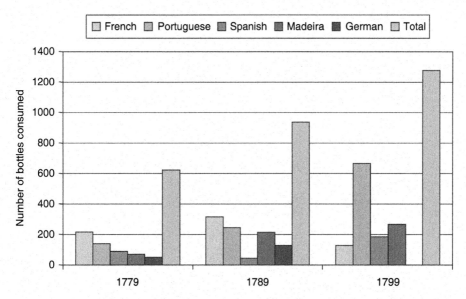

Graph 9.7   From Scot to Briton: Wedderburn's wine cellar, 1779, 1789, 1799
Source: NAS, GD 164/1034, "State of Lord Loughborough's wines, 1 Jan. 1775 to 6 June 1800."

now 22 percent of it was port, and 20 percent claret. The war, however, increased the ratio of port to claret. In 1799, as Lord Chancellor and wealthier than ever, Wedderburn's household consumed over 1,250 bottles, 44 percent of which was port, 21 percent madeira, 14 percent Spanish wine, and only 10 percent French wine.[57] Unlike Scots and Englishmen of lesser fortune, Wedderburn's taste for French wine was not deterred by high cost. He could have continued to be a claret drinker. Instead, by the end of the eighteenth century he chose to represent and constitute himself as a port-drinking Briton (Graph 9.7).

It could be argued that Wedderburn was an exceptionally anglicized Scot, and that, more than anything else, in the 25 years he kept his cellar records his taste conformed to English aristocratic norms. Certainly his taste for wine was elite— few people could afford all that high-quality port, claret, madeira, burgundy, and champagne. However, his taste was not simply that of a wealthy Englishman. It was elite *British* taste. And that is precisely the point: English and Scottish tastes for wine were no longer distinct. British taste for wine was certainly divided by class, with wealthier wine drinkers throughout Great Britain drinking a higher percentage of French wine than the members of the middle-ranks, who drank almost exclusively Portuguese and Spanish wines. But then again, by the end of the eighteenth century just about everyone who drank wine was drinking more Iberian wine than French wine, and more port than anything else.

To emphasize this point, we might return to the cellar of James St Clair-Erskine, who just happened to be Wedderburn's nephew and who inherited Wedderburn's Scottish title as the 2nd Earl of Rosslyn in 1805. As a high-ranking officer in the British army, eventually climbing to general, Erskine was stationed in England

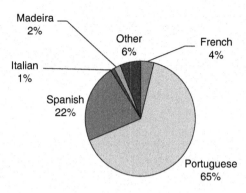

Graph 9.8   Percentage of Scottish wine imports, 1803–15
Source: NA, Customs 14, Scottish Customs Accounts.

and Ireland during the Napoleonic Wars, and campaigned in France, Corsica, Portugal, Spain, and Denmark. In 1796 he was elected MP for Dysart in Fife, and it was there, at Dysart House, that he had his principal residence. We have already seen that port was the dominant wine in St Clair-Erskine's cellar back in 1789, but claret followed close behind. Twenty-one years later, in 1810, port constituted fully half of the wine in his cellar, while claret, the erstwhile symbol of Scotland, amounted to less than 2 percent.[58] This was hardly exceptional; Scots as a whole had long since forsaken claret for port (Graph 9.8).

***

The change in Scottish taste for wine from claret to port reflected the successful establishment of a British identity in Scotland. This British identity was based largely, but not entirely, upon English tastes and norms, and its emergence was not the result of a single event such as the Jacobite rebellion of 1745–6, the Seven Years' War, or the long wars against Revolutionary and Napoleonic France. Instead, the creation of British identity in Scotland was a slow process that was accepted, at least by the majority of middle-ranking and elite men, by around 1780, although it never displaced a more localized Scottish identity. The protracted struggle against Revolutionary and Napoleonic France reinforced this British identity, and may have served to heighten its acceptance among Scottish women and push it farther down the social scale, although the taste for wine cannot help us in this regard.

Ultimately, then, shared Protestantism had made a British identity possible, and for the Scots, profits within England's empire made it attractive, as did England's more sophisticated political institutions. But, most of all, it was the century-long series of wars against France that taught the Scottish and English (and even some Irish) to be British. After all, the English brought to the Union a deep fear and dislike of the French "other," the Scottish did not. In fact, for the early eighteenth century, England served as Scotland's "other." Acceptance of the English and hatred of the French only arrived after years of fighting the French. But arrive it did, and in time for, not because of, the Revolutionary and Napoleonic Wars. Thus port, a fortified, often blood-red, and ostensibly English wine, was a particularly apposite drink for a people who found a common identity for a variety of reasons, but most of all because of war with France.

Coda: A British wine story

The "golden age" of vintage port coincided with the height of British imperial power and prestige, and thus occurred in the second half of the nineteenth century.[59] But the apotheosis of port as a symbol of British identity occurred well before that time, and is wonderfully illustrated in a "vintage port story"—the sort that became so popular among middle- and upper-class British men in the late nineteenth century. This story was recounted by a retired army officer named John Fowler and published in his memoirs in 1894. As one might expect, Fowler thought it to be the best wine story he ever heard (or told), and it went like this.

When the British army was safely encamped behind the defensive lines at Torres Vedras near Lisbon in 1809, George Sandeman, the Scottish port shipper, was a frequent guest at Wellington's dinner table. At one dinner, Sandeman expanded upon the superior qualities of his 1797 vintage port, which he thought was the "finest port ever known." General Harry Calvert, who was also present, requested that Sandeman ship two pipes of this celebrated wine to England. Calvert gave one pipe as a gift to the Duke of York, and the other pipe he bottled for himself. It was some of this latter wine that survived for Fowler's enjoyment and formed the basis for his story.[60]

However, as with many wine stories some of the details of this one may have become sketchy over time. The defensive lines at Torres Vedras were only begun in November 1809 and completed in September 1810, and by all accounts 1797 in the Douro was a wretched vintage, the wines being rated "very bad, tawny" by members of the British Factory at Oporto.[61] No matter, the importance of the story was, and is, not to be found in the details of the wine in question. For Fowler, the point of the story was to regale his audience with tales of an "ancient" vintage whose sublimity was enhanced by its associations with Wellington, Calvert, the Duke of York, and the war. But for us, the story is about port's symbolic role in the creation and reflection of British identity. To wit, there, in the midst of a long, drawn-out battle with the French, a Scottish-born merchant discoursed politely with an Irish-born field marshal and an English-born general upon the particular virtues of the "Englishman's wine" (which, one might add, was a product of Portugal).

Part IV
Drunkenness, Sobriety, and Civilization?

10

"By G–d, he drinks like a man!"

Manliness, Britishness, and the Politics of Drunkenness, c. 1780–1820s

In his memoirs, published in 1858, the Reverend Edward Bannerman Ramsay of the Scottish Episcopal Church recounted a story that was told to him by his friend, the author Henry Mackenzie (1745–1831). As the story goes, Mackenzie was involved in "a regular drinking party" sometime around the turn of the nineteenth century, and "was keeping as free from the usual excesses as he was able." After hours of imbibing wine, Mackenzie noticed "companions around him falling victims to the power of drink," so he "dropped off under the table among the slain, as a measure of precaution. Lying there, his attention was called to a small pair of hands working at his throat; on asking what it was, a voice replied, 'Sir, I'm the lad that's to lowse the neck-cloths.'" "Here, then," remarked Ramsay, "was a family where, on drinking occasions, it was the appointed duty of one of the household to attend, and when the guests were becoming helpless, to untie their cravats in fear of apoplexy and suffocation."[1]

This was not atypical behavior. Indeed, the period from roughly 1780 to 1820 witnessed a dramatic increase, if not even a historical apex, in British elite and middling male drunkenness, much of which came from wine. There were of course many reasons to drink wine during the late Georgian era, just as there had been in previous epochs. For those who could afford it, wine remained a customary adjunct to celebration and bereavement, a medicine, a stimulus, a facilitator, a release, and a sign of aristocratic, gentle, and middling social status. However, none of these reasons, even in the aggregate, can explain the marked increase in drunkenness of the late Georgian era. This increase was abetted by the popularity of alcoholically potent port, as well as the general rise in consumption of brandy, rum, whiskey, and whisky, often consumed in the form of punch. But to understand and explain why so many middling and elite men—including the most politically, culturally, and socially powerful men in the land—frequently drank themselves stupid and under the table, we must look to the broader contexts of Britain's many eighteenth-century wars against France, and to the still widely accepted belief that the willingness and ability to drink a great deal of alcohol was proof of one's masculinity.

Manliness, war and drinking

We recall that during the early going of the Seven Years' War middle-ranking social reformers lay the blame for British military and political impotence on the supposed effeminacy, corruption, and essential "Frenchness" of the British ruling elite. According to this same critique, the polite behavior that had given social and cultural distinction to its practitioners for much of the eighteenth century was actually a form of effeminacy. As this charge of effeminacy gained force because of initial British naval and military losses in the war, politeness as a model of male behavior began to disintegrate. One result was that by the 1760s and 1770s polite claret was less and less helpful in constructing elite male identity, because symbols of politeness such as luxury claret invited charges of effeminacy. Port, however, had the manly and British connotations that the ruling elite needed in order to keep their middle-ranking critics at bay and maintain their political legitimacy. Thus, port became the most popular wine among all wine-drinking classes, and the strength of port contributed to—but was not the primary cause of—the staggering amount of drunkenness of the late Georgian era.

That said, neither politeness nor the Reformation of Manners movement (which in any event fizzled out by the 1730s[2]) had ever provided more than a minor check on inebriety. The revelers at Walpole's "Norfolk Congresses" of the 1730s used the finest lead-crystal stemware and sat beneath the host's stunning collection of Great Master paintings hung from carved marble walls while getting drunk on Chateau Haut Brion and other polite French wines.[3] Nor was this behavior among polite men exceptional. Early and mid-eighteenth-century English and Scottish records abound with evidence of intoxication among elite and middling men, the very sort for whom polite behavior and aesthetics mattered most.[4] Most famous of all, at least to posterity, was William Hogarth's print, *A Midnight Modern Conversation* (1733), which satirized but also celebrated what often happened to polite gentlemen as the evening wore on. Specifically, Hogarth depicts a group of well-to-do men at St John's Coffee-house in Temple Bar, London, in various stages of intoxication (Figure 10.1).

Those who see a strident condemnation of drunkenness in Hogarth's print would be wrong. Instead, the print is a laughing satire, or as one art historian has described it: the "most deliberately good-humoured seeming of [Hogarth's] satirical prints."[5] In fact, *A Midnight Modern Conversation* was Hogarth's contribution to the 1733 Excise Debate, and he seems to have been gently chiding the consumers of wine and tobacco for their oft-excessive behavior, while also celebrating that behavior as an example of "lusty English 'freedom.'"[6] In other words, Hogarth was arguing for the ability to drink and enjoy oneself, come what may as a result. Certainly that is how the print was perceived by the public, because it sold as an anti-Excise print throughout the crisis of 1733.

So, inasmuch as politeness was intended to polish away men's allegedly natural barbarism, it did little if anything to reduce drunkenness; it merely made it more decorous. What the late Georgian era witnessed, therefore, was not a return to some pre-polite era of wild-eyed intoxication, but a dramatic increase in

Figure 10.1   A Midnight Modern Conversation (1733), by William Hogarth
Note: While polite conversation may have slowed down the pace of drinking it did not prevent drunkenness, and that was Hogarth's joke.

drunkenness within a society that already took for granted heavy drinking among all classes, and among men in particular.

***

Despite British victory, indeed the humiliation of France by the end of the Seven Years' War, the charge of elite effeminacy not only stuck, but the outcome of the war was seen as an affirmation of aggressive, physically courageous, and supposedly British manliness over the alleged effeminacy of the losing French. It is telling that Scottish Highland soldiers, deemed "barbarians" by the Hanoverian elite during the Jacobite rebellion of 1745–6, were increasingly seen as models of British masculinity. By the early 1770s the authors of the popular *Town and Country Magazine* voiced the view that true British masculinity was derived from a

> manly … ancient nobility and gentry … rough, bold and handy to pursue the sports in the field, or wield the spear and battle ax against the enemies of their country.

The authors compared such men favorably to the

> weak, sickly ... puny successors, who know no toils but those of the toilet ... a motley kind of beings who have caught the contagion of every vice and folly on the continent ... [and] import them on their return to contaminate the principles and customs of their native country.[7]

When the Thirteen Colonies of North America were lost in 1781, middle-ranking criticism of the aristocracy grew louder still, and the aristocracy had every right to be concerned. As Linda Colley writes:

> A British army led by a succession of patrician generals, Burgoyne, Howe and Cornwallis, and an administration under the leadership of the eldest son of a peer, Frederick, Lord North, had suffered a humiliating defeat, as had the monarch who had persistently supported the war, George III.

This was not the end of the line for the old British ruling class, but "the blow to the ruling order's pride and reputation was immediate and immense."[8]

In particular, the military defeat to what is now a largely forgotten alliance of allegedly backwoods Americans, effeminate Frenchmen, washed-up Spaniards and washed-out Dutch, precipitated, if not a full-blown crisis in British elite masculinity, then an ever-greater need for elite men to prove they were "true" Britons and not some pathetic hybrid of Channel-straddling fops.[9] In fact, men of the British ruling elite needed to prove both to themselves and to their critics that they could still lead the nation; they needed to prove that they were just the sort of men their critics said they were not. To do this, they made a recuperative move—no doubt only half-consciously—related to the one they had already made by drinking less claret and more port. Specifically, they turned to a code of conduct that had never entirely disappeared, even when politeness was dominant. This code was derived from the warrior societies of Britain's ancient and medieval past. The preferred activities of this "warrior" masculinity were drinking heavily with other men, fighting, hunting, gambling, and what among themselves men called many things, but most often "fucking." Crucially, this behavior was both respected and where possible practiced by middle-ranking men, for whom sober domesticity was not yet an established value.[10] As a result, men who wanted to maintain or gain political legitimacy and power drank massively, and the result was the extreme intoxication of the age.

***

Before moving on to a discussion of the perceived manliness of drinking in the late Georgian era, we must pause to consider both the claim that drunkenness was considered manly, and that the period from 1780 until 1820 constituted a zenith in British elite and middling male drunkenness. Regarding the first claim, we have already seen that in the 1650s Republicans ridiculed Royalist drunkenness as a form of effeminacy.[11] In fact, the belief that drunkenness caused men to become unreasonable, and thus to behave like women, antedated the Interregnum and continued long past the Restoration era. Some scholars even argue that drunkenness was always considered effeminate behavior by a majority of men in early modern England.[12] However, this claim is only partially correct because it fails to draw a distinction between how men got drunk. If we recall, Royalists were equally convinced that they were the real men because their drunkenness resulted from honorable drinking—that is, drinking with other men while scrupulously following rules regarding toasting, purchasing of drinks, and drinking equal amounts. Meanwhile, men who rejected alcohol altogether or got drunk without following the rules of the group were dishonorable and unmanly, because they disregarded the social bonds created by adhering to rules of behavior. Thus, while specific notions of what constituted honorable behavior changed over time, the evidence overwhelmingly indicates that drinking large amounts of alcohol with male companions and according to specific rules was considered by a majority of elite and middle-ranking men to be a highly honorable and manly activity until the end of the Napoleonic Wars. And even then the concept did not die out entirely. Indeed, reports of the demise of honor-based drinking among young men would strike many observers of twenty-first-century Britain as woefully premature.

My second claim, that the late Georgian era was especially dissolute, requires significant evidence and explanation given the keen competition from so many other eras of British history. Such evidence and explanation are especially necessary in light of comments by prominent contemporary observers who suggested that drunkenness in the 1770s was on the wane. Our "drinking less than our ancestors," proclaimed Samuel Johnson to James Boswell during their voyage to Scotland in 1773, in Boswell's account, was

> owing to the change from ale to wine. "I remember," continued Johnson, "when all the *decent* people in Lichfield got drunk every night, and were not the worse thought of. Ale was cheap, so you pressed strongly. When a man must bring a bottle of wine, he is not in such haste."[13]

There is little reason to doubt Johnson's recollection, but what he was probably noticing was the difference between a Lichfield ale house and a London tavern, and most especially on the different habits of provincial townsmen and his new metropolitan and culturally elite friends. Nevertheless, Johnson's point was that among his friends who drank wine the sort of drunkenness he was familiar with in Lichfield was rare.

Adam Smith incorporated a similar observation into his larger economic argument, postulating in *The Wealth of Nations* (1776) that were

> the duties upon foreign wines, and the excise upon malt, beer and ale, to be taken away all at once, it might, in the same manner, occasion in Great Britain a pretty general and temporary drunkenness among the middling and inferior ranks of people, which would probably soon be followed by a permanent and almost universal sobriety. At present drunkenness is by no means the vice of

the people of fashion, or of those who can easily afford the most expensive liquors. A gentleman drunk with ale, has scarce been seen among us.[14]

Looking back in 1819, the artist and author Joseph Farrington (1741–1821) said of the 1770s:

At this time a change in the manners and habits of the people of this country was beginning to take place. The coarse familiarity so common in personal intercourse was laid aside, and respectful attention and civility in address gradually gave a new and better aspect to society. The profane habit of using oaths in conversation no longer offended the ear, and bacchanalian intemperance at the dinner-table was succeeded by rational cheerfulness and sober forbearance.[15]

With hindsight, it appears that Johnson and Smith spoke on the cusp of an era, while Farrington, who lived through the entire drunken epoch, may have been gilding the past so as not to offend contemporary sensibilities. He may also have been overly influenced by Boswell's *Life of Johnson* for his recollection of conversational style in the 1770s. Discussions within Johnson's Literary Club were full of "rational cheerfulness and sober forbearance." But everything is relative. Johnson's friends certainly drank a good deal of wine when together, and they spoke frequently of drunkenness, suggesting that there was a lot of it even if they imagined it to be more of an issue for others than for themselves.[16] Boswell, sadly, might have disabused them of their delusions. He began many days slowly and with a headache.

Moreover, if some contemporaries were convinced that society was becoming more rather than less sober in the 1770s, that perspective was not maintained by most middle- and upper-class Britons in the 1820s, who looked back on the previous forty years with conspicuous embarrassment. We are "a much better people now than we were," wrote the tailor, political radical, and social observer Francis Place, "better instructed, more sincere and kind hearted, less gross and brutal, and have fewer of the concomitant vices of a less civilized state."[17] Likewise, the Edinburgh memorialist Robert Chambers reflected in 1824:

In the early part of the [eighteenth] century, rigour was in the ascendant; but not to the prevention of a respectable minority of the free and easy, who kept alive the flame of conviviality with no small degree of success. In the latter half of the century—a dissolute era all over civilized Europe—the minority became the majority, and the characteristic sobriety of the nation's manners was only traceable in certain portions of society. ... In Edinburgh ... intemperance was the rule to such an [sic] degree that exception could hardly be said to exist.[18]

The Welsh army captain Reese Howell Gronow (1794–1865) was more concise in describing the situation among London "society" during the Regency era (1811–20): "Drinking," he wrote, "was the fashion of the day."[19] Like Place and Chambers, Gronow spoke not from hearsay, but from personal experience.

Lastly, we can turn to the statistical evidence for further proof of heavy drinking. Certainly it is true that official English wine imports declined for much of the eighteenth century; between the decades 1717–26 and 1777–86, wine imports into England and Wales dropped by one-third, while during the same period the population grew from roughly six to roughly eight million people.[20] Nevertheless, one recent study based upon cellar and purchasing records shows that wine consumption of the gentry and aristocracy actually increased from the mid-seventeenth to the mid-eighteenth century.[21] More certainly, annual legal wine imports into England and Scotland more than doubled from the decade before the Eden Treaty of 1786 to the decade after, and while Scottish wine imports declined after 1800, British imports as a whole remained far above their pre-Eden Treaty levels. For instance, in the ten years up to and including 1786, the average annual amount of wine imported into England was 14,914 tuns and into Scotland 943 tuns, or 15,857 tuns for all of Great Britain. During the relatively untroubled years of 1787–91, that amount increased to 27,572 tuns for all of Great Britain, a 74 percent increase over the previous era. And during the period 1792–1808, the annual British average increased to 31,105 tuns, a jump of 96 percent increase over the pre-1787 decade.[22] In some war years as much as one quarter of the wine imported into Great Britain was re-exported, but even subtracting that amount from overall imports gives a net increase in wine retained for domestic consumption compared to the period before the Eden Treaty. So, while Scottish wine imports decreased during the Napoleonic Wars, and wine retained for home consumption in the entire United Kingdom began a slow if inconsistent downward trend in 1811, that decline began at a historical zenith.

In sum, the overall trend beginning from the 1780s until the 1820s was more wine rather than less. Moreover, consumption of spirits in England and Scotland also increased beginning in the 1780s.[23] True, per capita beer consumption in Britain declined during this period, but this had a greater impact upon the laboring classes than it did upon the middling sorts and elite for whom beer was rarely a recreational drink.[24] Thus, when the statistical evidence is added to the anecdotal, there is no gainsaying the assertion that during the late Georgian era, the British elite and middle ranks drank more alcohol than at any other time during the long eighteenth century. The result was a stupendous level of stupefaction.

Drink and the historians

Interestingly, most historians interested in drunkenness as a social or political "problem" in Britain have tended to overlook the late Georgian era. Instead, they have focused on the periods just prior to and after it, thereby implying a valley of sobriety between two mountains of crapulence.[25] But by focusing on the gin-mania of the early eighteenth century and the gin-palaces of the Victorian era, these historians have merely reflected and perpetuated the concerns of the ruling elite and middle ranks of those times, who saw working-class drunkenness as a threat to the social order. When it was the ruling elite and middle ranks themselves who were frequently and fashionably intoxicated, these same groups could hardly consider it an issue of great social concern. Furthermore, the extreme drunkenness of the ruling elite in the late Georgian era was intended to *preserve* the social order, precisely because the challenge to the ruling elite came from middle-ranking critics who admired hard drinking as part of a broader code of masculinity. Therefore, until the end of the Napoleonic Wars only a small number of medical doctors, social reformers, or Christian moralists did much complaining about elite and middling drunkenness. And since the late Georgian drunkenness was not much in the news at the time, it has not been much in the history books ever since. Only recently has this oversight begun to be addressed.[26]

Politeness, chivalry, and drunkenness

Recent scholarship has also addressed the related issue of masculine behavioral models that impacted attitudes toward heavy drinking. For instance some historians claim that as a model of behavior politeness broke down because it came to be seen as false, unctuous and overly affected, especially after the publication of Lord Chesterfield's *Letters to His Son* (1774). As a result, politeness gave way to the related, but supposedly more sincere and natural code of "sensibility."[27] Others claim that politeness did not disappear at all among men. Instead, it became increasingly redundant as its values were naturalized by upper- and middle-class men, and could still be seen in the model of Victorian "gentlemanliness."[28] Michèle Cohen asserts, as I do, that public opinion turned against male politeness beginning in the 1760s because of its "incompatibility with a masculine national character."[29] According to Cohen, the rejection of polite behavior among men continued until the 1780s, when the remnants of politeness finally gave way to a revitalized conception of chivalry that "provided a vocabulary for refashioning the gentleman as masculine, integrating national identity with enlightenment notions of progress and civilization."[30] Moreover, while men ultimately rejected politeness as a behavioral model, women continued to follow the polite precept of being pleasing to others, as this quality was considered natural to their being.

More recently, Vic Gatrell has attacked the very notion that politeness *ever* constituted a model of hegemonic masculinity, arguing instead that if eighteenth-century cultural history is properly understood, it is "impoliteness that becomes the baseline subject, and social disciplining that is the chronically challenged reaction."[31] This argument does not deny the presence and impact of politeness upon elite men's behavior. Indeed, says Gatrell, it was understood by a "man of good breeding" that he "might move in and out of polite venues and postures as he chose, affecting contempt for their over-refinement while retaining his social investment in them." The result was a man who could be "highly mannered among ladies," while "in tavern and club he could laugh and lech with the lowest."[32] The shortcoming of this argument, however, is that by focusing on the period 1780–1820, Gatrell denies the possibility that politeness had ever been the dominant model of elite male behavior, which for much of the eighteenth century it was.

It is my belief that, by the 1760s the hegemony of polite masculinity began to break down. In its wake, some men promoted and practiced sensibility, and still others turned to chivalry (or at least a late eighteenth-century version of it) to fashion new roles for, and between, men and women. But, for the ruling elite, whose manliness was being questioned, neither sensibility nor chivalry could maintain the healthy middle state between the extremes of effeminacy and barbarism. Instead, sensibility, as with politeness before it, collapsed into effeminacy, while neo-chivalry was transformed into a more aggressive form of warrior masculinity. Not that these men behaved like warriors all the time. Politeness or some variant of it was still practiced by elite and middling men from time to time, especially when in the company of women. But by 1780 or so the scales no longer wavered. Instead, they tipped in favor of warrior masculinity, whose core activity was heavy drinking.

Three-bottle men

"Drunk as a lord" was a socially charged phrase that emerged in late seventeenth-century England, and by the late eighteenth century the hard-drinking British aristocracy and gentry surpassed even their own formidable standards.[33]

> The Prince, Mr. Pitt, Dundas, the Lord Chancellor Eldon, and many others, who gave the tone to society, [wrote the aged Captain Gronow from the perspective of the 1860s] would, if they now appeared at an evening party, "as was their custom of an afternoon," be pronounced fit for nothing but bed. A three-bottle man [as in per diem consumption of wine] was not an unusual guest at a fashionable table; and the night was invariably spent in drinking bad port-wine to an enormous extent.[34]

Such heavy drinking could not help but leave behind a trace; in fact there is a torrent of evidence beginning at the very top of the social ladder. The Prince of Wales, known to his admiring contemporaries as the "First Gentleman of Europe," was perhaps first in more ways than one. There were few men anywhere, in Britain, Ireland, or on the Continent, who could challenge the future King George IV in the realm of drunkenness. Indeed, his sober parents had every right to be concerned.

> Intoxication in the most extensive sense, [reported an assistant toper] commonly followed the banquets of Carlton House, the effects of which have more than once nearly proved fatal. His Royal Highness has been, I know, critically rescued from suffocation, when the delay of half an hour or even a shorter time would have rendered unavailing all assistance.[35]

At his wedding to Caroline of Brunswick in 1795, George had to be held up by two dukes (i.e. his brothers); and the rest of his life, even as regent and king (1811–30), was full of similarly drunken antics. Such behavior could not be concealed from

THE ROYAL SOCIETY.

Figure 10.2   The Royal Society (1786), by George Stubbs or Henry Kingsbury
Note: George was outrageous, but not yet pathetic.

the public; news of his debauches filled the London and provincial papers without end. More famously still, political cartoonists found the Prince's behavior funny, at least at first, because it was so completely undisciplined. *The Royal Society*, an engraving from 1786 by George Stubbs or Henry Kingsbury, shows the drunken Prince of Wales climbing on to the dinner table and imploring his "Royal Crew" to "Drink! Drink!").

The Royal Society was but a gentle prelude to what was to come in the years ahead. For instance, James Gillray's *A voluptuary under the horrors of digestion* (1792) shows the Prince the morning after a very long night (Figure 10.3). In this print, the Prince sits picking his teeth with a fork, while surrounded by "empty wine bottles, gnawed bones, purgatives and pills for venereal disease," a "vomit or shit-brimming chamber pot," dice, and a record of unpaid bills.[36] The satire here was not to be found in the Prince's hangover *per se*, but in his inability to resist any form of sensual indulgence. His drinking, therefore, was not the manly sort, for like everything else George did, it knew no rules. Had the Prince of Wales cared less about his image and all the trappings of royalty, his behavior may have made him manly in the eyes of the public. As it was he became the prime example an "effeminate" drunkard, caring more about himself than the honor of the group. More broadly though, George was a prime example of the fashionableness of heavy drinking.

Figure 10.3 A Voluptuary under the Horrors of Digestion (1792), by James Gillray
Note: Over-indulgence in everything was decidedly unmanly and easy to mock.

One of the Prince's early drinking companions was the Irish playwright and theater owner Richard Brinsley Sheridan, who showed signs of severe intemperance from the time of his arrival in London. According to his friend and contemporary Nathaniel Wraxall, Sheridan's penchant for drink only increased after he left the theater and became a leading Whig politician.[37] When the young Lord Byron befriended the prematurely aging Sheridan, he declared him to be a wonderful drunk.[38] Indeed, during his later years Sheridan showed all the signs of an inveterate dipsomaniac: a carbuncled red nose and vein-struck cheeks. Most

Figure 10.4   The Feast of Reason and the Flow of the Soul, i.e. The Wits of the Age Setting the Table in a Roar (1797), by James Gillray
Note: Fox (second from left) and Sheridan (third from left) were easy to laugh at because of their physical signs of dipsomania.

tellingly of all, as Byron happily noted: "Poor Fellow! He got drunk very thoroughly and very soon."[39]

The Prince's and Sheridan's friend Charles James Fox was also a heavy drinker and one who was deeply devoted to warrior masculinity. He cheerfully acknowledged in a letter to a friend that dining, gambling, and "fucking in cundums frigging etc. was my chief employment in Town," and by his thirties he was physically inflated by the constant application of alcohol.[40] Gillray mercilessly depicted both Sheridan's nose and Fox's jowls on numerous occasions, and in some instances even together, with both men happily drunk. *The feast of reason and the flow of the soul* (1797), for instance, shows Sheridan, Fox, and fellow Whigs John Courtenay, Captain Charles Morris, and Colonel George Hanger trading bawdy stories over numerous bottles of wine (Figure 10.4).[41]

By the 1790s Whig political leaders thought the Tories reactionary, while Tories believed that the Whigs were closet republicans. But all sides could agree on drinking. Sheridan's and Fox's inveterate political foe William Pitt the Younger enjoyed his bottle so much that more than once did he stammer from drink while attempting to deliver a speech in the House of Commons. On one occasion in March 1787, after getting completely drunk at a ball the night before, Pitt said

Figure 10.5 *Auspicium Melioris Aevi* [Omen of a Better Age] (1788), by James Gillray
Note: On at least one occasion, Pitt was unable to speak in Parliament.

to his opponent Fox that he was "so much oppressed by indisposition" that he could not reply to Fox's questions.[42] As a result of this and other antics, Pitt's heavy drinking was public knowledge. Gillray, for example, used the news of Pitt's "indisposition" to depict the Prime Minister in a state of complete stupefaction (Figure 10.5).

But this print and others like it were ambivalent about drunkenness; viewers were meant to laugh at the leader's behavior, not to condemn it. Like Hogarth's attitude in *A Midnight Modern Conversation*, one could agree that a man drank too much in an evening, but simultaneously admire him for the freedom from over-refinement that his behavior revealed. Moreover, Gillray's depictions were not entirely satirical exaggerations. There are no surviving cellar books from Pitt's days at Downing Street, but those from his country house at Holwood reveal a conscientiously well-stocked cellar from which sometimes as many as five or six bottles of port, three or four of madeira, and two or three of claret were consumed in an evening. The number of guests on these occasions is unknown, and some evenings witnessed smaller amounts of wine consumed, namely two or three bottles of port, one of madeira and sometimes one of claret or another type of wine.[43] It is also important to note that Pitt, like previous prime ministers, had to entertain nightly as a matter of professional survival. Nevertheless, there is no doubting that the youngest prime minister ever to serve in Great Britain was also one of the drunkest. According to John Ehrman, Pitt's most encyclopedic biographer, by contemporary standards the amount of wine consumed at Holwood was "nothing much." But Ehrman goes on to say that "it may have been that he drank more in London, and when he was with those who set out to get drunk."[44]

In fact, "nothing much" in the late Georgian era was more than enough to get one drunk. If Pitt's wine purchases during the year beginning in July 1784 (over 5,100 bottles) are merely the beginning of an upward trend, then he was clearly attempting to surpass the convivial standards of his most illustrious predecessor in Number 10 Downing Street, the great Sir Robert Walpole.[45] Ehrman, however, overlooks prime ministerial precedent and places the blame for Pitt's frequent over-indulgence with the bottle on Henry Dundas, who "certainly sat down to [get drunk]." The tragedy of this friendship, says Ehrman, "was that Pitt became accustomed to sessions on a scale which was exceptional even by the practices of the day. For Dundas brought to London the habits of the Scottish Bench and Bar, the hardest drinking fraternity in the British Isles."[46] Gillray had a great laugh at Pitt and Dundas's debauchery, suggesting in one memorable print that it was a thrice-weekly occurrence (Figure 10.6).

Whether the reigning Scottish law lords were the most accomplished drinkers in the British Isles is impossible to say, but certainly some among them could have vied for the title. The encyclopedic English jurist Sir William Blackstone is said to have kept a glass of port as his constant companion while writing *Commentaries on the Laws of England* (published 1765–9),[47] but such an indulgence hardly compares to the heroic feats of Scotland's chief judges. Henry Cockburn, a Scottish law lord himself, and brother of the port-wine shipper of the same name, was privy to the activities of some of these Scottish jurists during the final days of their illustrious careers. According to Cockburn, two particularly notable members of this bibulous fraternity were Charles Hay, Lord Newton (1747–1811) and George Fergusson, Lord Hermand (1743?–1827). Cockburn describes Newton as "a man famous for law, paunch, whist, claret and worth. ... His daily flowing cups ... made him worthy of having quaffed with the Scandinavian heroes."[48] Newton, who was known as "The Mighty" for his drinking prowess, would often drink all night at the Ante-Manum Club and then go directly to the court for a full day of work, although, Cockburn noted, he was apt to be tired as a result. When, toward the end of his life, Newton sensed the approach of the dark cloud of temperance over the young generation of

Figure 10.6 God Save the King, in a Bumper. Or an Evening Scene, three times a week at Wimbleton (1795), by James Gillray
Note: Dundas may have taught even Pitt a thing or two about hard drinking.

lawyers in Edinburgh, he exclaimed to Cockburn in despair, "What shall we come to at last! I believe I shall be left alone on the face of the earth—drinking claret!"[49] Newton's crony Hermand also gloried in his cups, and Cockburn describes him as being "fond of the pleasures, and not the least of the liquid ones, of the table; he had acted in more of the severest scenes of old Scotch drinking than any man at last living." Like Newton, he was apt to drink wine all night and work all day, although such behavior had its consequences. The judicial circuit over which Hermand pre-sided, from Ayr to Jedburgh, was known by some wits as the "daft circuit."[50]

Even James Boswell may have paled in comparison to the leading wine drinkers of the Scottish legal community, although he certainly tried to keep the pace. During the three-month period of August to October 1783, which was immedi-ately after Boswell became 9th Laird of Auchinleck, Boswell's small household consumed roughly three bottles of wine and a half bottle of spirits per day.[51] This does not seem an astonishing amount for a man who as a lawyer in Edinburgh could polish off three bottles of wine by himself.[52] Nor is this figure remarkable given the number of guests the Boswells often entertained. But daily averages are misleading in that they tend to undervalue the amount of wine consumed at any given sitting because they do not include days in which the family was absent and, more than likely, being entertained by someone else.

Boswell's "Book of Company," however, gives us some specific consumption figures. On Thursday, October 16, 1783, the Boswells had six guests for dinner and overnight. Their tally from the cellar was 18 bottles of wine and one of rum, for an average of two-and-a-quarter bottles of wine per person, as well as an untold number of glasses of punch. The very next day, with one more male guest added, they drank 17 bottles of wine and three of rum, for an average of nearly two bottles of wine per person and three bowls of punch. There were two women present on both days, Margaret Boswell and a Miss Preston. In all likelihood they would have left the dining room after the first round of post-prandial toasts, leaving the men to get on with the serious drinking. As a result, the daily average for this gathering was closer to three bottles of wine per man, per day, as well as a significant amount of rum punch. Boswell wrote in his diary of these two days: "I drank a great deal of wine," to which he was able to add, "without feeling any bad effect."[53]

The fact that Boswell remarked upon the heavy consumption suggests that he drank an exceptional amount of alcohol over these two autumn days. However, it also seems to reveal a melancholy awareness of what we would today call "alcoholism." Heavy drinking for Boswell was the rule more than the exception. "I several times drank too much wine," he wrote in his diary, "and suffered severe distress after it. I was quite averse to writing. I was exact only in keeping my Book of Company and Liquors."[54] True, Boswell did not consume three bottles of wine plus punch every day; however, the impression one gets from his "Book of Company" and his simultaneously written diaries is that of a man who could, and often did, reach the three-bottle standard that helped define and uphold the masculine ideal of late Georgian Britain.

To get a better perspective on Boswell's wine and spirit consumption, one might contrast it with evidence from Seaton-Delaval Hall (near Newcastle) in the 1780s and 1790s. Simultaneous cellar and guest records from Seaton-Delaval reveal what was probably a very moderate-drinking aristocratic household. When Lord and Lady Delaval dined alone, their standard daily consumption of wine usually consisted of two bottles of port and one bottle of madeira or "frontignac" (a sweet wine from southern France).[55] How much of that wine was consumed by Lady Delaval is impossible to know; but, if typical for her sex and class at the time, it was probably no more than a quarter of the total. In other words, John Delaval (1st Baron Delaval) was at least a two-bottle man. Of course, as aristocrats, dining alone was neither often possible nor desired; hosting dinner parties, like heavy drinking, was an important way to uphold and enforce the local social and political hierarchy. Hence, during most weeks the wine cellar at Seaton-Delaval disgorged more than 21 bottles. For example, in one unexceptional week during the historically exceptional month of July 1789, the Delavals and their various guests consumed 26 bottles of port, three bottles of madeira, and two bottles of frontignac (31 total). In addition, the stewardess, Miss Hicks, received seven bottles of port (a bottle per day), while the cook was given three bottles of port, and the cook's agent one bottle of port.[56] Dinner party records from the same period reveal that per capita consumption at dinner was roughly one-and-a-half bottles of wine per person, along with punch and ale.[57] As usual, however, these averages are misleading because much of the wine and punch was consumed by the men after the ladies had withdrawn for tea.

Heavy-drinking leaders of British society included army officers, for whom warrior behavior was a requirement. To be sure, officers had too much responsibility to be drunk all the time, and they were still required by their peers to be polite among ladies of similarly exalted social standing.[58] But none of this precluded the sort of heavy drinking that had long been a part of martial masculinity and was particularly critical for the elite in the late Georgian era. For instance, on April 15, 1783, there were two festive gatherings of officers in Aberdeen. At the first, a midday meal hosted by the Duke of Gordon, 31 officers drank more than two bottles of wine and nearly two bottles of ale each. At the second, an evening entertainment, 19 officers drank more than two-and-a-half bottles of wine and more than two bottles of beer per person.[59] Scottish smugglers and "fair traders" must have still been active in Aberdeenshire, because on both occasions the amount of claret exceeded the amount of port. Wine purchases of the officers of the Prince of Wales' Own Fencibles suggest that they too combined bacchic festivities with the art of soldiering. Stationed on the Anglo-Norman island of Guernsey, a noted wine and wine-smuggling entrepot, they provisioned themselves in 1799 with no fewer than 732 bottles of port, 144 bottles of claret, and 48 bottles of gin.[60] How long these lasted is unclear.

Staying within the category of societal leaders but moving away from those for whom martial masculinity was a job requirement, we find that heavy drinking was also fashionable among clerics. Dr Alexander Webster (1722–1805), minister of Edinburgh's Tolbooth Kirk and Boswell's relation by marriage, was reportedly a five bottle-a-day-of-claret man. So prodigious was his capacity for wine that he was nicknamed Dr Bonum Magnum (after the extra large bottles).[61] However, according to his colleague and contemporary Dr Alexander Carlyle, who was also fond of the bottle, Webster was never "indecently the worse of liquor, and a love of claret, to any degree, not being reckoned in those days a sin in Scotland, all his excesses were pardon'd."[62]

In England, political cartoonists of the era constantly mocked the purported thirstiness of Anglican clergymen—from bishops to parsons—questioning whether Bacchus was not in fact their preferred god. In one memorable engraving by the precocious caricaturist Richard Newton entitled "Fast Day," four obscenely fat and ugly parsons sit around a table on which rests a gigantic joint of beef (Figure. 10.7). While the clerics on the far right and left of the picture carve into the meat, the two in the center raise their glasses of wine for a toast. "Here's to our old friend," proposes the first. To which the second asks: "You mean the Church, I suppose?"[63] How many clergymen actually fit this depiction is impossible to say, but the image of the beef-filled and port-soaked parson recurs often enough in the late Georgian era prints to suggest that it was more than simply a cliché of Enlightenment anti-clericalism.[64] Certainly, if Parson James Woodforde's parish life in Norfolk was at all exemplary of a late eighteenth-century Anglican priest, conviviality among and between clerics and parishioners in an English village was the rule rather than the exception.[65] But what Newton and others mocked was not

Figure 10.7   *Fast Day* (1793), by Richard Newton
Note: Hypocrites, not drunks.

shared conviviality; rather, it was the hypocrisy of clerics who drank and feasted while preaching the virtues of restraint and moderation to their flock.

***

Heavy drinking may have been strongest among the ruling elite—after all, it was their masculinity and authority that was being challenged—but the reason it was so fashionable among the elite was because it was still admired and practiced by middle-ranking men. In fact, the "alcoholic enthusiasms" of elite and middling men were the same.[66] In their much-lauded study of the English middle ranks, Leonore Davidoff and Catherine Hall remark that sobriety was not an established value until the 1840s.[67] This date seems a bit late, but it is clear that the idea of the serious and sober middle ranks did not pertain to the late Georgian era. In fact, evidence of frequent drunkenness among middle-ranking men during this period is easy to come by. For instance, the diary of Elizabeth Shackleton, a member of the minor gentry in late Georgian Lancashire, reveals a spectacularly disappointed—and at times beaten—woman, whose husband and friends drank heavily almost every time they were together. "Whitaker Riotous to a degree. Barton Dumb. Cunliffe Moralizing. Shackleton [her husband] sulky, quarrelsome, Cross," wrote Elizabeth of an all-too-common evening. Male sociability among the Lancashire gentry "was usually propelled by alcohol," and as a result, "drunken disorder was latent in almost all evening gatherings."[68] There is no reason to believe that Lancashire was an exceptional British county.

Picture engravers in London, a lower-middling group of artisans, enjoyed a hard-drinking cultural milieu. According to Gatrell, the most famous engravers of the late Georgian era "lived for liquor, enjoyed the easy ways of the girls of their class, and found much of their material in the city's lively streets and casual violence."[69] Gillray, Rowlandson, and the Cruikshanks, father and sons, all drank compulsively. Isaac Cruikshanks, the father (1764–1811), even shortened his life by what his son George called "the fashion of the day." He accepted a challenge to a drinking match that sent him into an irreversible coma.[70]

But the greatest evidence of all for middle-class drunkenness comes from what we know about male behavior in clubs. There were some 25,000 clubs in the English-speaking world during the eighteenth century, the greatest number in London. On any given night some 20,000 men in the metropolis spent the evening in a club.[71] The number of informal tavern-based clubs probably makes this number far too low, although how high it needs to go to be accurate is impossible to say. While clubs varied in purpose and social composition, most catered to the urban middling-sorts and had little purpose but all-male conviviality. In fact, the activity that bound them all together as clubs, even the philosophical and philanthropic clubs, was "heavy boozing." [72] The "essence of club fellowship," says the historian Peter Clark,

> was in most cases uncomplicated and conventional, marked by convivial rites of heavy drinking and drunkenness, swearing and obscene songs, activities which men felt increasingly uncomfortable about in the presence of women. Here clubs served as bastions of traditional male perceptions of sociable behaviour, against new, more refined notions of manners favoured by women and increasingly coloured by the culture of sensibility.[73]

As Francis Place asserted, the clubbishness famously recommended by Joseph Addison and Richard Steele at the beginning of the eighteenth century was nothing but a "delightful ideal." In reality—and Place was speaking of the late Georgian era—clubs were full of men "without understanding" who "substituted brutality and drunkenness for exhilaration and pleasant enjoyment."[74] Or, as the French visitor François de La Rochefoucauld wrote in 1784, English clubs were "nothing more than associations for debauchery and expense," wherein the wretched members devote themselves to "wine and gaming and women."[75] La Rochefoucauld may have exaggerated things just a bit, as some clubs devoted themselves to genuinely learned or benevolent activities *before* the drinking began. But when the drinking did begin, it was heavy, and the wine consumed was usually port. As the German pastor Friederich Wendeborn observed in his travel diary published in 1791, many English clubmen "will drink anything that is red [and called port], and will praise it the more as it is mixed with brandy to make it fiery."[76]

The athletes of liquor

As the war against revolutionary France dragged on into the nineteenth century and became the war against Napoleonic France, the amount of drinking seems only to have increased. After all, war promoted "warrior" masculinity in a variety of ways. For instance, one in ten men was being exposed to the habits of the army or navy, wherein warrior masculinity was an order and not an option. And what was learned in camp or on shipboard was brought home to civilian life. Captain Gronow allows that by the time of Waterloo in 1815 the well-known appellation, "three-bottle man," may not have been adequate to describe the standard bearers of conviviality. "Many men still living must remember the couple of bottles of port *at least* which accompanied his dinner in those days," recounts Gronow, who suggested that three bottles was routinely attained. What Gronow does not say is whether three bottles included post-prandial consumption, although it must have. According to Gronow there were four-, and even five-bottle men.

> [T]he only thing that saved them was drinking very slowly, and out of very small glasses. The learned head of the law, Lord Eldon, and his brother, Lord Stowell, used to say that they had drunk more bad port than any two men in England; indeed, the former was rather apt to be overtaken, and to speak occasionally somewhat thicker than natural, after long and heavy potations. The late Lords Panmure, Dufferin and Blayney, wonderful to relate, were six-bottle men at this time.[77]

Doubt has been expressed by some readers of Gronow and other late Georgian memorialists about whether these feats of alcohol consumption could actually have occurred.[78] It is perfectly understandable that later generations would refuse to believe the bottle figures, and dismiss the testimonials as the braggadocio of nostalgic, old men whose tales were exaggerated by a port-soaked haze. However, it is a popular misconception of wine aficionados and observers of the eighteenth-century that bottles were smaller and the wine significantly less potent, and therefore the amount of consumption was less formidable than it actually was.[79] In fact, the old quart bottle (32 pre-imperial/US fluid ounces) was larger than the modern 75 centiliter wine bottle (equivalent to 25.36 US fluid ounces/26.66 UK fluid ounces). Of course, pre-industrial glass-makers did not produce exactly uniform bottles; but an examination of wine bottles from the collection at the Ashmolean Museum in Oxford found that bottles produced between 1660 and 1817 ranged between 27 and 33 (US) fluid ounces.[80] Thus, even if there was considerable sediment in the bottle, the amount of liquid would have remained equal to if not greater than the amount of liquid in a standard 75 centiliter wine bottle of today.[81]

Just as eighteenth-century bottles were similar in size to the bottles of today, so too was the strength of port similar to today's standards. For example, we know that eighteenth-century port was frequently fortified, and the chemist Henry Vizetelly's investigations in the late nineteenth century found that perfectly fermented (i.e. unfortified) port could reach levels between 16 and 18 percent alcohol.[82] Of course, most port was *not* perfectly fermented, but was laced with brandy during and after fermentation, and this amount of brandy increased as the eighteenth century went on.[83] So while all port might not have reached the modern level of approximately 20 percent alcohol, some port did reach that level and some exceeded it. Wine samples tested in the early 1820s—the earliest-known examples of such testing—show that export-quality port ranged between 20 and 23 percent alcohol, while sherry and madeira ranged between 16 and 24 percent.[84] French wines, in Britain at least, had alcohol levels similar to those of today.[85]

In short, a "three-bottle man" was a formidable drinker of wine, and a four-, five- or six-bottle man was stupendous if not also wildly self-destructive. Asked whether the prowess of Georgian wine drinkers has been exaggerated, the wine historian William Younger, who clearly spent some time contemplating the question, said he thinks not. "In fact I think," said Younger, "we underestimate their rollicking capacity."[86] In a memorable turn of phrase, the wine historian A. D. Francis called the heroic drinkers of the Georgian era "athletes of liquor," adding, "just as a few men can run a hundred yards in ten seconds, so a few trained drinkers can perform prodigies."[87] It must also be remembered that drinking sessions could last for ten or 12 hours, and that "relief in the Roman manner" (i.e. self-induced vomiting) was neither uncommon nor impolite.[88] In fact, it was often necessary if a man was to continue being convivial.

Manly drinking and drinking for manliness

While the reasons for drinking wine in the late Georgian era were many, the primary impetus for the practice and acceptance of such a spectacular amount of drinking was the belief that it proved manliness, and this was true for both the ruling elite and the middle ranks of men. We know this to be true, first, because contemporaries said as much; second, because the activities with which this heavy drinking were associated were all part of the same masculine code of behavior; and third, because most of the heaviest drinking and the rituals surrounding it were exclusively and explicitly male.

"There was a sort of infatuation," recollected Ramsay about late Georgian Scotland, "in the supposed dignity and manliness attached to powers of deep potation. ... I have known persons who held that a man who did not drink must have a degree of feebleness and imbecility of character."[89] Lord Hermand, for example, thought drinking a virtue, and not only because it had the potential to stimulate conversation and make one jolly. "But beyond these ordinary attractions," writes Cockburn, "he had a sincere respect for drinking, indeed a high moral approbation, and serious compassion for the poor wretches who could not indulge in it; with due contempt of those who could, but did not."[90] Similarly, Ramsay recounts a story about George Cranstoun, later Lord Corehouse, who on one occasion fell an early victim to the evening's drinking. Upon seeing the prostrate Cranstoun, an old Selkirk writer who had been dictating the pace of consumption, turned to Walter Scott, the novelist, who had himself kept up with each bumper of wine.

"I'll tell ye what, Maister Walter," said the old man, "that lad Cranstoun may get to the tap o' the bar, if he can; but take my word for't, it's no be by drinking."[91] Nor was it only men who admired a man who could drink. Dr Lindsay Alexander of St Augustine's Church, Edinburgh, once overheard a "servant lassie" remark upon his fellow Presbyterian divine, Dr Alexander Carlyle: "there he ga'ed, dacent man, as steady as a wall after his ain share o' five bottles o' port."[92]

Other examples of the perceived manliness of drinking abound. William Hickey, a prominent Hiberno-English rake in late eighteenth-century London, wrote in his memoirs: "That fact is, I was always ambitious of sitting out every man at the table when I presided." This achievement made Hickey a "capital host" and confirmed his manly strength to himself, to those present, and, also importantly, to anyone who heard the tales of the evening.[93] Similarly, despite the fact that Hickey did not enjoy fox-hunting, a decidedly "manly" activity in the minds of late Georgian Britons, he was able to maintain his reputation as a real man because of his ability to consume great amounts of wine. "When at table," said Hickey of a weekend in the country, "the men often remarked that, although I shunned the [fox] chase, over the bottle I was as keen a sportsman as the best of them."[94] When the noted fox-hunter "Cheeks" Chester complimented Lord Byron by proclaiming in front of another male guest at a party, "By G–d he *drinks like a Man!*", the poet nearly swooned with pride.[95]

Fox-hunters were among the manliest men in late Georgian Britain; but perhaps more surprisingly from a twenty-first-century perspective, poets and writers like Byron were too. Robert Burns, Charles Lamb, Samuel Taylor Coleridge, and Byron could go head-to-head over the bottle with any group in the kingdom, fox-hunters, military officers, or otherwise.[96] Accordingly, they too were "real" men. Byron, an aristocrat, was particularly obsessed with his own warrior masculinity, and on one occasion humorously contrasted a "failed" man with a "real" man by recounting an event he had witnessed:

A beau (dandies were not then christened) came into the P[rince] of W[ales] and exclaimed— "Waiter bring me a glass of Madeira Negus with a Jelly—and rub my plate with a Chalotte. [sic]" This in a very soft tone of voice. —A Lieutenant of the Navy who sat in the next box immediately roared out the following parody—"Waiter—bring me a glass of d----d stiff Grog—and rub my a--e with a brick-bat."[97]

Martial themes

Heavy drinking had long been associated with real battlefield warriors, who were, not surprisingly, the epitome of manly men. Homer's *Iliad*, with which even moderately educated British men were familiar (thanks to Alexander Pope's popular translation), drew explicit connections between drinking and combat. And while the *Iliad* and the even more familiar Bible emphasized both the dangers and virtues of wine, the former lesson was often overlooked in favor of the latter. After all, getting drunk according to rules was seen as a form of battle, and therefore, offered a chance for men to be brave. Like armed combat, drinking could be physically challenging; to fight and defeat the bottle, or a fellow drinker, one had to be courageous in the face of assault, persistent over the course of many hours, steady when impaired, and finally, indifferent to pain.[98]

So linked were the ideas of drinking and battle in late Georgian Britain that the attitudes, the language, the rules, and the spaces used for drinking were all imbued with the spirit of Mars. And if drinking large amounts of alcohol was like entering combat, so too were the results. Empty bottles were "dead men," casks were "killed," and to get drunk was "to declare victory for the jolly god."[99] Byron, always a good source for alpha-male attitudes in the Regency Era, even used martial language to describe the differences between two of his favorite bottle companions. "I have got very drunk" with Sheridan and George Colman (both dramatists), writes Byron,

> but if I had to choose—and could not have both at a time—I should say—"let me begin the evening with Sheridan and finish it with Colman."—Sheridan for dinner—Colman for Supper—Sheridan for Claret or port—but Colman for every thing—from the Madeira and Champagne—at dinner—the Claret with a layer of port between the Glasses—up to the Punch of the Night—and down the to the Grog—or Gin and water of day-break—all these I have threaded with both the same—Sheridan was a Grenadier Company of Life Guards—But Colman a whole regiment of light Infantry to be sure—but still a regiment.[100]

Along the same lines, the Edinburgh drinking club known as the Crochallan Fencibles not only chose a regimental name for themselves ("fencibles" were full-time, home-based army regiments), but also used military titles for each member. Lord Newton was Major General of the Corps, and even the hard-drinking Robert Burns struggled to keep up with the training regimen. Upon being introduced to the Crochallans in 1787, Burns declared that he had "never been so abominably thrashed" in all his life.[101] Whether Burns already conceived of hard drinking as a battle is unknown, but certainly he began to after that. On August 16, 1789, Burns was invited to witness a drinking contest between Sir Robert Lawrie of Maxwelton, Robert Riddel of Glenriddel, and Alexander Ferguson of Craigdarroch. The resulting poem, "The Whistle" (1789), uses military combat as its central trope.

> Six bottles apiece had well wore out the night,
> When gallant Sir Robert, to finish the fight,
> turn'd o'er in one bumper a bottle of red,
> And swore 'twas the way that their ancestors did.

> Then worthy Glenriddel, so cautious and sage,
> No longer the warfare, ungodly, would wage;
> A high ruling-elder to wallow in wine!
> He left the foul business to folks less divine.

Ferguson, however, was the last man standing, and thus Burns put the following words in the defeated Lawrie's mouth.

> Thy line, that have struggled for freedom with Bruce,
> Shall heroes and patriots ever produce:
> So thine be the laurel, and mine be the bay;
> The field thou has won, by yon bright god of day![102]

For Burns, a champion drinker was a great warrior and a great Scot.

Not surprisingly, artists like Rowlandson, Gillray, and the Cruikshanks depicted the drunken debauchery in London clubs as akin to battle. No doubt influenced by Hogarth's *A Midnight Modern Conversation*, Rowlandson produced a drawing in 1801 entitled *The Brilliants*. It was based upon an actual club of that name, which met at The Swan tavern on Chandos Street in Covent Garden. Rowlandson's depiction shows a large group of men around a table in the tavern club room who are well into the evening's battle with the bottle (Figure 10.8). All the members of the club are drunk, some shout, some protest, some nurse their wounds quietly, and still others vomit (in one case directly onto a member who is prostrate on the floor). Unopened wine bottles, like unused ammunition, stand neatly in a massive wine cooler in the corner; while the empty bottles, like used artillery shells, are tossed nearby. More wine is being opened and a bowl of punch arrives to fuel the liquid combat.[103] As with Hogarth's print and title, *The Brilliants* was meant to be ironic because the drunken clubmen were anything but. And just like Hogarth, Rowlandson was satirizing and celebrating simultaneously. After all, he "had no reason to castigate their festive pleasures. This louche and boozy territory was his own, shared with downmarket bohemians like himself."[104] In fact, the Brilliants was his very own club!

Of course, prints like *The Brilliants* were not exact depictions, but as the nineteenth-century art historian Joseph Grego commented:

> allowing for the exaggeration of burlesque, we are far from denying that it is founded on actual observation, in an age notoriously given to conviviality, which was carried, in all phases of society, beyond the bounds of discretion, and, in some instances, to a degree incredible in our times.[105]

For example, William Hickey spoke of many nights in the late 1770s and 1780s when he and his friends in London resembled the figures in Rowlandson's print. On one occasion Hickey got so drunk that he did not notice his pocket being picked (by his evening companions!). At 5 a.m. (or so he was later told) he was carried to the Cross Keys bagnio in Little Russell Street. When he awoke at midday, he staggered into a hackney coach to go home, and then "vomited out of the coach window the whole way, to the great entertainment of the foot passengers."[106] Rowlandson would have been among those who found the scene funny. He was, in the words of modern art historians, "a painter of the absurdities of the human condition," "a reporter of daily life," someone whose "humorous

THE BRILLIANTS.

Figure 10.8   The Brilliants (1801), by Thomas Rowlandson
Note: A self-deprecating pun, not a condemnation.

caricatures … depicted his own sense of the ridiculous. … He made no attempt
to moralize." Instead, he had "a love of comic incident," and "his world was the
ordinary world and the ordinary man's response to it."[107]

Six days after *The Brilliants* was published, Gillray unleashed one of his greatest
pictorial efforts, *The Union-Club*, which was indebted to both Rowlandson and
Hogarth. In Gillray's depiction of the Whig-dominated Union Club (founded
to commemorate the Union with Ireland), the Prince of Wales and his friends
are seen in full drunken riot, celebrating the queen's birthday (Figure 10.9). The
prince himself is passed out under the table; portly Fox has fallen asleep from too
much drink; the red-nosed Sheridan holds a bottle of wine above his head and
another bottle waits in front of him, while a host of other Whig political leaders,
army officers, and dandies drink, sing, shout, vomit, and hold their heads in pain.
Empty bottles lie in piles while half-full bottles of wine spill their not-so-precious,
red liquid here, there, and everywhere. In the background a band attempts to
play, chairs and chamberpots fly through the air and a fight breaks out. There
is no evidence that the queen's birthday party (an actual event) was actually so
riotous, and Gillray was on Pitt's payroll from 1797 until 1801, so he would have

208

Figure 10.9 The Union Club (1801), by James Gillray
Note: A joyous celebration of a riotous age.

had a reason to mock the drunken Whigs.[108] However, Gillray's attitude toward the scene he depicts is ambivalent; he "seems half in love with what he mocks ... one might be tempted to say that the Whigs' manic enthusiasms are close to his own."[109] Indeed, if any single print can depict the love of drinking in the late Georgian era, surely this is it.

Some art historians have argued that prints like *The Brilliants* and *The Union-Club*—of which there are dozens from the late Georgian era—are satirical to the point of being radical condemnations of elite drunkenness.[110] But satire implies a moral judgment that is generally not present in such drawings. As Gatrell correctly observes, these drawings "were 'laughing' not 'savage' satires—or less satires than celebrations." Engravers like Rowlandson, Gillray, and the Cruikshanks were not political or social iconoclasts. In fact, they subscribed to the same code of warrior masculinity that they so often depicted.[111] Moreover, prints by the leading engravers were not cheap; they "were aimed at a sophisticated, educated and monied class."[112] In fact, the Prince of Wales, Fox, and Sheridan all purchased Gillray's prints, even ones in which they were the butt of the joke. In other words, prints like *The Union-Club* were as much comedy as satire, and the comedy was directed toward, and meant for, the very people who bought the prints.[113]

Upholding honor

As we recall, manly drinking had to be done socially and according to strict rules; nor could one bow out early in the competition. All of this can be seen in *The Brilliants*. On the wall behind the drunken men who occupy the center of the engraving a list of "Rules to be observed in this Society." It reads:

1st. That each Member shall fill a half Pint Bumper to the first Toast.
2nd. That after Twenty-four Bumper toasts are gone round, every [man] may fill as he pleases.
3rd. That any Member refusing to comply with the above Regulations to be fine[d] a bumper of Salt and Water.

Presumably, this last punishment would make a man thirsty again. But as much as we are supposed to laugh at the list, it was not entirely fanciful.

In fact, the rules of drinking were complex and serious business meant to uphold the honor of each man and bond the group together through the application of uniform standards in the face of a physically challenging task. The anglophile German Prince Herman von Pückler-Muskau said of English drinking practices in the mid-1820s: "Certainly, many of the customs of the South Sea islanders, which strike us most, are less ludicrous."[114] Pückler-Muskau noted that one never took wine at dinner without drinking to someone's health, and therefore there was a problem of redundancy if one dined with only one or two other people. However, the bigger problem arose when there were many people at dinner, as all "healths" had to be returned with the same salubrious wishes, and of course, another emptied glass. Thus, at a table of 12, one was liable to drink at least 12 full glasses of wine, less than full glasses being deemed unmanly and disrespectful. After dinner, though, is when the serious drinking began. Each post-dinner toast was responded to by all, which meant draining another glass.[115] Sticking to these rules ensured that everyone's manhood was tested fairly and equally, and like regimental discipline, rules provided a form of mutual support in the heat of battle. Rules that enforced heavy drinking also rationalized it to those who partook, and enhanced the effect of social bonding in communal drinking. With rules, everyone was in the struggle together. And, of course, with this much drinking, it was a struggle.

As in the military too, those who transgressed the rules and made choices independent of the group were brought into line or punished. Hickey, who spent most of his career working for the East India Company in Calcutta and Madras, spoke of an evening in the former city when he sat with a variety of Company officials and military officers through 22 bumper (full-glass) toasts before his friend Colonel Sherbrooke, the "President" for the evening, said that everyone might fill his glass at his own discretion. Prior to that moment Hickey had tried to slow down his pace, only to be upbraided by Sherbrooke, who said, "I should not have suspected you, Hickey, of shirking such a toast as the Navy." Hickey's immediate neighbor at the table, with bottle in hand, acted quickly to uphold his friend's honor, saying, "It must have been a mistake," and filled the empty glass to the brim. Hickey then kept up the rest of the way, but allowed that even after the declared cessation of enforced conformity, the pride and honor of every man maintained bumpers (i.e. full glasses) as the standard. Drinking anything less would have invited accusations of effeminacy and disrespect. As a result of that evening, Hickey suffered a 48-hour hangover and admitted, "a more severe debauch I never was engaged in any part of the world."[116]

Betting and gambling

If drinking heavily together helped to prove one's masculinity to oneself and others ("We are all men here"), drinking *against* someone was a way of establishing a hierarchy within a group of men ("I am more of a man than you"), or even denying someone the status of true manliness ("You are not a man at all"). Consequently, drinking contests were popular among men who sought to learn just where they and others stood on the scale of manliness. Charles James Apperley (whose *nom de plume* was "Nimrod") acknowledged that as an officer in the British Army he had partaken in many such drinking contests. But his severest test came in Ireland, where he was an officer in the British Army.

Nimrod's regiment, the "Ancient British," had gone to quash the United Irishmen uprising of 1798. To his credit, he did not like to talk about his military experiences in Ireland, which he felt were tarnished by the needless cruelty of the British Army. However, when speaking about punishment taken rather than given, he said this about his army experience: "Much as my regiment suffered by the sword, I have reason to believe that, among the officers, about equal slaughter was committed by the bottle." At 20 years of age and eager to prove he was a "real" man, Nimrod nearly fell victim to the latter. His drinking competitor in

Ireland was a fellow officer "twice my size, and as thoroughly seasoned as an old port wine cask." Moreover, the other officer had three more years of this particular aspect of military training already under his belt, and before that had established himself as the hardest drinker at Trinity College, Oxford. "Twas the sapling to the oak," writes Nimrod, "But at it we went, foot to foot, in a Dublin hotel, to prove," in Nimrod's telling phrase, "which was the better man."[117]

The result of this contest was 34 empty bottles of port, sherry, madeira, and claret, along with "cherry brandy in the morning at Anderson's fruit shop, and whisky-punch after our oysters at night," and all of this in four days. While the Oxford champion showed not a hint of stress, Nimrod succumbed to Bacchus and was bed-ridden for a month and three days, "head shaved—brother sent for express—given over by the doctor—prayed for by the chaplain." And, in what might have been a wine-induced simile, he writes: "to give you some idea of the fever I brought upon myself ... when the bedclothes were turned down, I smoked like a coach-horse at the end of a ten-mile stage on a frosty morning in November."[118] Amazingly, this result did not cure Nimrod of these "trials of strength," as he calls them. "I would not have yielded to Alexander himself, much less to a brother-officer, after this one defeat." There were several more "struggles for the victory" that Nimrod never gained.[119] Alas, in his own eyes, and presumably those of his regiment, he was the lesser man, although his bravery in battle against the Ancient British champion meant that his own manhood was unquestionable.

The colonial location of Hickey's severest debauch, and the quasi-colonial location of Nimrod's greatest test of manhood, no doubt heightened their symbolic importance. In both instances, the participants' very reason for being in the country was to assert, maintain, or restore physical control to the advantage of Britain. But such activities were no less frequent in Britain itself. After all, the intended audience of these drunken occasions was not so much Britain's colonial subjects; instead, it was the drinkers and their friends, as well as anyone who would either witness or hear about the event. Thus, heavy drinking and drinking contests were just as important, and for obvious reasons even more frequent, within Britain, than in India, Ireland or any other colonial outpost. We recall that the engraver Isaac Cruikshanks accidentally killed himself as the result of a drinking contest in London, while Nimrod had somewhat better luck in Cheltenham than in Dublin, when he accepted the challenge of drinking an entire bowl of punch in one sitting. He succeeded, made £50 in the process, and presumably, impressed all witnesses with his manly prowess.[120]

If men often bet on drinking contests, they also drank while betting on a host of other things. Gambling, as many late eighteenth-century social historians have pointed out, was a veritable obsession for elite and middling British men.[121] The most famous gambler of all was the Prince of Wales, who drank and bet his way to a mountainous debt on numerous occasions. In 1783, Parliament reluctantly gave him £30,000 to pay off his debts, and his father gave him a further £50,000 annually just to keep him in the black. This amount was insufficient, and he owed £400,000 in 1795 when he agreed, at the cost of removing his debt, to marry Caroline of Brunswick.[122]

The prince's friend Charles James Fox was equally fond of gambling, which he too combined with heavy drinking, and the results were similar. In the 1770s Fox's father paid off £120,000 of his gambling debts. In the 1780s Fox was twice bankrupted by gambling, and in 1793 his friends agreed to raise a subscription to relieve him; Fox asked for £70,000. But gambling was not only an upper-class sport. Rowlandson's many gambling prints depict middle-ranking men losing their shirts, and more, while gambling and drinking. In fact, Rowlandson himself was a dangerous gambler and in one protracted sitting lost 2,000 hard-earned pounds.[123]

Whoring

Chasing, coercing, and "conquering" women was another activity associated with warrior masculinity, and it too entailed a great deal of drinking by both men and women alike. Cock and Hen clubs, essentially informal gatherings of small tradesmen, artisans and the like, along with female prostitutes, were notoriously boozy places. More elite men like Hickey often preferred the bagnios of Covent Garden or the brothels around St James. In either case, the class dividing lines were not so strict, especially since many elite men liked to slum. And whatever the particular circumstances of the sexual act between paying men and female prostitutes, alcohol was usually part of the equation. Drinking together served as a prelude to sex; it heightened anticipation, reduced inhibitions, and symbolically sealed the deal before the act occurred. Boswell's London diaries are full of instances wherein he buys a prostitute a drink before their arrangement is consummated.[124]

So intertwined were wine and women within warrior masculinity that one could literally symbolize the other. In a late-eighteenth-century ballad entitled *The Bottle of Claret*, the bottle is anthropomorphized into a particular notion of an ideal woman:

> In spite of love, at length I've found
> A mistress that can please me,
> Her humour free and unconfin'd,
> Both night and day she'll ease me;
> ...
> But best of all she has not tongue;
> Submissive she obeys me;
> She's fully better old than young,
> And still to smiling sways me;
> ...
> If you her excellence would taste,
> Be sure you treat her kind, sir;
> Clap your hands around her waist,
> And raise her up behind, sir;
> As for her bottom never doubt,
> Push but home, you'll find it out;

> Then drink and never spare it,
> 'Tis a bottle of good claret.[125]

One suspects in this instance that claret, not port, was used for the sake of rhyme. Tellingly, male discourse about sex, like that about drinking, was infused with metaphors suggesting dauntless male courage and hopeless female resistance. Rakes in the late Georgian era spoke of "taking" a women, says Anna Clark, as if she were "a precious jewel rather than a person desiring sexual pleasure herself." More aggressively still, a "libertine discourse permeated slang and masculine popular culture, glorifying rape as a sort of amusement, or a way of proving their masculinity to other men."[126] Lines from one burlesque ballad on drunken male behavior in the late eighteenth century are particularly revealing of the way in which military metaphors were intertwined with acts of heavy drinking and aggressive misogyny:

> Soldiers obey commanders,
> But we stand not in fear;
> When drunk we're Alexanders,
> Fighting in front and rear.
> Quite full of whims and fancies,
> Break windows, lamps, and doors,
> Kick Jennies, Dollies, Nancies,
> With all the other whores.[127]

None of these attitudes or behaviors was new to Britain in the late-Georgian era and it is unclear whether violence against women peaked during the period c. 1780–1820s. It would probably be impossible to discern such a trend from the evidence given the changing policing methods of the late Georgian era.[128] However, it would not be surprising if such an upward trend did occur given the strong links between warrior masculinity and women as mere sexual objects. Similarly, one would expect violence against male homosexuals, or "mollies" as they were called in eighteenth-century Britain, to have increased during the reign of warrior masculinity. After all, men who were not exclusively and even aggressively heterosexual were considered a standing affront to the warrior ideal.[129]

Marriage and homosociability

Sex with prostitutes was an important component of warrior masculinity because it provided men with the possibility for aggressive sexual behavior. But marriage, as it had been for centuries, was still a prerequisite for male adulthood. Nevertheless, for late Georgian warriors, too much time around a wife was thought to make a man effeminate. As the Scottish philosopher William Alexander wrote in his *History of Women* (1779), men need to spend some time with women lest they become too rough. But "to retain the firmness and constancy of the male," they must also spend time "in the company of [their] own sex."[130] The English historian John Andrews wrote in 1782 that though Englishmen "might gain in delicacy and refinement" if they spent as much time in the company of women as Frenchmen supposedly did, they "might lose in manliness of behaviour and liberty of discourse, the two pillars on which the edifice of our national character is principally supported."[131] "Firmness," "constancy," and "pillars"? The phallic imagery of this masculine discourse was so ingrained that it could not be avoided.

Even dinner parties that began with mixed company rarely ended that way, as the ladies withdrew to the "drawing" room once the meal was finished. In other words, after spending some polite time with the ladies, the men had had enough and now wanted to talk impolitely, which was not something they could do with their wives present. Tellingly, this custom of separating after dinner did not become widespread until the latter part of the eighteenth century, clearly linking it to the decline of politeness and the rise of warrior masculinity.[132] Barthélemy Faujas de Saint-Fond, the French mineralogist and Louis XVI's Commissioner for Mines, traveled around Britain in the 1780s, and found that in "England the ladies leave the table as soon as the moment arrives for the toasts." However, in the Western Isles of Scotland it was different. There

> they stay for half an hour at any rate, and rightly share the gaiety where, ceremony being set aside, the Scots openheartedness and friendliness can show. It is certain the men gain by it, while the ladies do not lose. The health of each lady is drunk; to the guests each in turn by name, to the *patrie*, to liberty, to the happiness of mankind, to friendship. ... The ladies then go order tea.[133]

François de La Rochefoucauld, whom we have already met, also found it peculiar that the women would leave the table so soon after dinner in England. He noted with an air of bewilderment: "There is not an Englishmen who does not feel contented at that moment." Equally odd to La Rochefoucauld was the drinking that ensued after the women departed, which he described as "quite alarming." "Every man," observed the Frenchman,

> has to drink in turn, for the bottle goes continually round the table, and the master of the house makes sure that no one misses a turn. When one has been drinking for some time ... the drinking of 'toasts' is begun. The master of the house begins by naming a lady and drinking to her health: everyone does likewise. Another 'toast' follows, and everyone drinks to the health of everyone's lady. Then everyone names a man, and the ceremony is repeated.[134]

Versions of this ritual abounded in Britain; in late Georgian Edinburgh it was known as "Saving the Ladies." After dinner and sentimental toasts, women were escorted home, and therefore "saved" from the debauchery of the evening that ensued when the men returned to the host's house. Robert Chambers, who was privy to some of these occasions, describes how the evening usually progressed:

> One gentleman would give out the name of some lady as the most beautiful object in creation, and, by way of attesting what he said, drink one bumper.

Another would then enter the field, and offer to prove that a certain other lady, whom he named, was a great deal more beautiful than she just mentioned—supporting his assertion by drinking two bumpers ... and so on, in geometrical progression, till one or other of the heroes fell under the table; when of course the fair Delia of the survivor was declared the queen supreme of beauty by all present.[135]

Here, in a drinking game, is a perfect example of how chivalry could collapse into warrior masculinity. A man would devote himself to a woman and uphold her honor by becoming utterly intoxicated. In his mind, he may have been inspiring her love through his valorous deeds of strength and devotion, which kept him away from her rather than in her company. But his valorous deeds did not entail real fighting and real arms; they entailed braggadocio, large amounts of wine, and in all likelihood, vomiting. Headache aside, the end result may have made the victor feel good about himself as a man, although it is uncertain if the object of his love was impressed by the claim that his hangover was the necessary price for her honor.

If there were differences between the postprandial practices of the elite and middle ranks it is difficult to discern them. In both cases the women would leave the table and the men would stay on to drink. A broadsheet ballad entitled *Port and Sherry, or Britons be Wise and Merry* (1797), actually allowed men and women to act out the words they were singing:

> The Glass is filled the Toast goes round
> With Wine and sparkling Eyes
> The Ladies leave the Gentlemen
> And beg they will be wise

As the song progresses, the ladies "now to music go" and then drink tea or coffee. The men, meanwhile, "regale themselves below, with good old port and sherry." Eventually, the "ladies now retire to rest. ... But highly pleased with what has pass'd." The men "with firmness keep their stand," and continue to drink.

> But now alas! Completely trim'd,
> With good old Port and Sherry,
> Then let us drink our Loves and Wives
> And all the charming Ladies,
> The pride of Troy, Man's greatest joy
> For many hundred Ages,
> So pretty, so witty, we all adore the Ladies,
> God Bless the Ladies, God Bless the Ladies, etc.[136]

Nothing could be more explicit about the manly nature of drinking than the fact that when it was time to imbibe heavily, women were not welcome. "To the trade of Glasgow and the *outward bound*," was the clever pun that informed wealthy Clydeside women that it was time to go, while the men braced themselves for vinous combat.[137] Recalling his younger days in Edinburgh, Ramsay said:

> In many houses, when a party dined, the ladies going away was the signal for the commencement of a system of compulsory conviviality. No one was allowed to shirk—no daylight, no heeltaps was the wretched jargon in which were expressed the propriety and the duty of seeing that the glass, when filled, must be emptied and drained. We have heard of glasses having the bottoms knocked off, so that no shuffling tricks might be played with them, and that they could only be put down empty.[138]

Of course, men could have quit drinking after dinner and joined the ladies for tea or a parlor game, or the ladies could have stayed in the dining room and continued conversing with the men. But the men did not want that. Instead, the men wanted to be left alone at the table. Women's continued presence would only undermine the purpose of the men's activity, which was to be manly by getting drunk while talking about politics and local affairs, and telling stories about hunting, war, sex, and previous drunken escapades.

An anonymous French artist lampooned these after-dinner rituals of the English—although clearly he should have used the term "British"—in two prints

LES DAMES ANGLAISES APRÈS-DINÉ.
Scenes e Anglaises dessinées à Londres,
par un français prisonnier de Guerre
à Paris chez Martinet, Libraire, Rue du Coq St. Honoré

Figure 10.10 Les Dames Anglaises Après-Diné (c. 1810 or 1816), Anonymous
Note: Unattractive English wives taking tea among themselves.

Figure 10.11 *L'Après-Dinée des Anglais* (c. 1810 or 1816), Anonymous
Note: To French visitors, this behavior was a mystery.

drawn around the end of the Napoleonic Wars. In the first print the ladies (along with a young boy in a gown) are shown taking tea in the drawing room. They are being served by a handsome black butler who presents the tea on a platter that is drawn to look like a giant, protruding penis. The ladies, however, are too desexualized to be titillated (Figure 10.10).

Meanwhile, in the second print, the men are straight out of Rowlandson's "The Brilliants," but in this instance there is no jollity, no celebration of "lusty English freedom," just an air of heavy drunkenness (Figure 10.11). One of the men is so sodden with wine that he completely misses the chamber pot in the corner cupboard and urinates on the floor. No one notices, and nor would anyone seem to care. Here, then, is vicious satire. But even this French point of view is not meant to moralize; rather, it is meant to ridicule the English.

From boys to men

So deeply ingrained was the late Georgian connection between manliness and drinking that public schools, whose explicit purpose during the late Georgian era was to produce manly British men, were precisely where many elite boys first learned to drink.[139] "The drinking career of an English gentleman's son in my youthful days," wrote Nimrod in his autobiography,

> too often commenced at a public school, as mine did. How often have I been hoisted over a wall at night, and rehoisted by the same means with a bottle of wine under my greatcoat, from *Master* Lamley, as we used to call him, of the "Spread Eagle," or old Brummage of the "Black Bear." The price of the bottle was half-a-crown, and what it was composed of mattered not; it was black and strong, and called "port."[140]

Nimrod attended Rugby, which according to him "was what may be called a loose place in my time [1789–c. 1796], and especially so as to drinking, in which some boys indulged to a great excess." Some of Nimrod's school-fellows "did not spend less than £200 pounds [on wine] in the town in the course of the year." For example, one fellow for whom Nimrod often served as a "fag" (i.e. servant to a senior boy) usually had two or three different types of wine on offer. His indulgences mattered little, noted Nimrod, because he was a nobleman's son, "and could do without either Latin or Greek."[141]

Proof that public school drinking was very much about a certain conception of masculinity is seen in the fact that the pupils' other favorite extra-curricular activity was fighting. Neither activity was exactly promoted by the masters but, as Nimrod says, they were both generally ignored unless deemed excessive. And, of course, the fighting was the "manly" sort, "not the pulling, hauling and scratching style," insisted Nimrod, far from it.

> A ring was formed and each boy had his second and bottle-holder, and all the ceremonies of the fistic art were punctiliously observed ... and when once a lad had shown himself a good one in the ring he was generally respected in the school.[142]

To Nimrod's knowledge, Rugby was not an exceptional case, Eton and other schools being equal in "devotions to Bacchus and Apollo."[143] Not surprisingly, the prestige activities of Britain's most prestigious public schools reflected elite and middle-ranking male values. It was these men who fetishized pugilism from the 1770s to the 1820s, precisely because it was considered an overtly manly sport. In fact, until the 1820s elite men sponsored most of the formal boxing matches, while middle-ranking men were the bulk of paying customers. Like the warrior masculinity to which it was related, boxing lost its social luster in the late 1820s and moved downscale to become the province of the working classes.[144]

From manhood to death

If so many elite and middling men began drinking so young and drank hard for so long, it must be asked how they were physically able to do so. Practice and perseverance helped, but in most instances, constant applications of the bottle took its toll. Gout was endemic among upper-class men, and as the letters of Horace Walpole (1717–97) show, it could confine men to home for days, even weeks on end.[145] Walpole tried to control his gout by drinking very moderately, but others did not even bother, believing that gout, like occasional constipation, was an inevitable fact of life.[146] While gout was a problem, the ultimate consequence of heavy drinking, death, could and often did come early to the warriors of wine. "I could name two or three ... hard drinking men who started at Rugby as if they thought life was a race, and who never pulled up until arrested by death at an early age," offered Nimrod.[147]

Similarly, Cockburn described Edinburgh's Ante Manum Club, whose uncrowned king was Lord Newton, as "a jovial institution which contained and helped to kill, most of the eminent topers of Edinburgh for about sixty years preceding 1818, when the degenerate temperance of the age at last destroyed it."[148] Captain Gronow suggests that the temperate spirit did not creep in to London until a decade later, but he certainly agreed with Cockburn regarding the effects of frequent debauches upon the human frame. "I never knew but one person to whom it was said that smoking was the cause of his death," said Gronow, "But, alas, I have known thousands who have been carried off owing to their love of the bottle; ay, some of the noblest and famous men in our land, splendid in youth, strength and agility."[149] Pitt the younger died at 46, Boswell at 55, and Fox at 56, in all cases abetted by the bottle. Sheridan made it to 65 and his erstwhile drinking partner George IV carried on to the age of 68, but both men showed signs of physical grossness and decrepitude from a much earlier age. Socially more humble men such as Isaac Cruikshanks passed on at 48 and James Gillray at 59, while somehow Thomas Rowlandson made it to the proverbial three-score and ten. No doubt these lives too, were shortened by the bottle. The irony of this heavy drinking is that so many men killed themselves to prove that they were "manly," a reputation that surely had less value in the grave. Nevertheless, manliness is what they were after and in many cases manliness is what they got, even if their glory was also their ultimate undoing.

***

But other than poor health, headaches, and proof of masculinity, what did all of this drunkenness add up to? Clearly, in an already heavy-drinking nation such as Great Britain the extraordinary drunkenness of the period 1780–1820 should not be blamed solely on the popularity of port, or reduced to a 40-year drinking contest between competing social classes. But just as clearly, the popularity of port contributed to the phenomenal amounts of drunkenness, and class-based claims to political legitimacy helped drive alcohol consumption to new heights. Class boundaries were never static or clearly defined, but all participants, whether elite, middling, or somewhere in between, were agreed that heavy drinking was a critical measure of masculinity, and masculinity was the coveted prize because it was the prerequisite for political legitimacy. And lest we forget, the ruling elite were the winners. When the smoke cleared from the battlefields of the Continent and the club rooms of Britain, elite men may have been wobbling, but they were still standing. They had proved themselves to be real men in the eyes of their critics and their doubters, and those elite men who had died from battle or the bottle were class martyrs. One result was that there was no shift in political power from the ruling elite to the middle ranks of men during the long reign of George III (1760–1820).

But the old order was not to last, at least not without sharing political power. In the aftermath of war, a new generation of middle-ranking—now self-described "middle class"—critics emerged to challenge the ruling order and the warrior masculinity that had helped them to maintain their lofty status. These new reformers championed a form of masculinity that valued hard work, moral rectitude, domesticity, and sober self-control. They denied that the old measure of masculinity was manly and British, and argued instead that it was boyish and brutish. And as the changing taste for wine reveals, by the 1820s that view was taking hold.

11

"Happily, inebriety is not the vice of the age"

Sobriety, Respectability, and Sherry, 1820s–1850s

In 1835, Charles James Apperley, known only to his legions of readers as Nimrod, published a biography of a recently deceased friend, Squire John Mytton of Halston Hall, Shropshire. Mytton's fame, indeed infamy, derived from the fact that he was a hard-fighting, hard-gambling, fox-hunting, womanizing squire, who drank between four and eight bottles of port per day. He began drinking in the morning with a bottle of port on his toilet as he shaved, and proceeded from there, a glass or two at a time, until he had completed what Nimrod called the "Herculean task."[1] According to one of Mytton's friends, who signed an affidavit regarding the matter, Mytton was drunk without interruption for the last 12 years of his life.[2] He drove his carriage at high speeds, fox-hunted nearly naked, rode a bear into the drawing room at Halston Hall, and at one point he was so occluded by drink that he lit his shirt on fire to scare away the hiccups. He died penniless and insane in a Southwark debtors' prison in 1833 at the age of 38.

What is interesting about Squire Mytton is not so much his behavior, but Nimrod's attitudes toward him. Had Mytton been born a generation before, he would have been a leading rake, an alcoholic superstar, and among the manliest of men. However, by the 1820s Mytton's behavior was scandalous. And from the perspective of British upper- and middle-class society in 1835, when the biography of Mytton was first published, the hard-drinking squire was a reminder of just how much the manners of society had "improved" in one generation. Indeed, Nimrod's biography of Mytton was popular because it made its readers feel so wonderfully superior to their recent forebears. It was printed eight times by the end of Queen Victoria's reign in 1901.

But just as Shakespeare's Marc Antony came to bury Caesar, not to praise him, the whole point of Nimrod's biography of Mytton was to defend his type of masculinity from the calumnious judgments of a less-manly age. Nimrod writes:

> I offer no excuses for his drinking ... his drinking—for men are tried by wine, says the proverb, as metals are by fire—furnishes excuses, I should rather have said apologies, for his conduct. ... Many of his acts were not the acts of

Figure 11.1 Fair Play's a Jewel. Mytton shows fight, from Nimrod, *Memoirs of the Life of the late John Mytton* (1835)
Note: Sadly for Mytton, drunken fisticuffs were no longer in fashion.

John Mytton, but of a man *mad, half by nature, and half by wine*, and I think his best and dearest friends are decidedly of my opinion.[3]

In other words, Nimrod had no intention of condemning an honest and honorable man who represented the masculine ideal of the previous era, albeit in the extreme. To Nimrod, British society in the 1830s may have been more civilized, but it was also less manly, and the measure of that weakened manliness was people's disgust and embarrassment over the aggressive, hard-drinking behavior of a man like "Mad Jack" Mytton (Figure 11.1).

The era that began in the aftermath of the Napoleonic Wars in Britain witnessed a precipitous decline in drunkenness among all wine-drinking classes, as well as the rise of sherry, first to a position of parity with port by 1840 and then to primacy by the 1850s. Both of these changes in taste reflected the new values of the British middle classes, which emphasized the importance of "respectability" above all else.[4] As with the politeness and the warrior ethos, respectability was deeply political; it helped to define the middle ranks as one large, coherent "middle class," a class that valued hard work, thrift, domesticity and sobriety.[5] In so doing, the middle classes claimed themselves to be a culturally unified group that was morally superior to the supposedly dissolute aristocracy and irresponsible poor.[6]

Having unsuccessfully tried since the mid-eighteenth century to "out-masculine" the elite using the warrior code, a new generation of middle-ranking men changed the rules of the game. Sober respectability, not martial masculinity, was the new hallmark of allegedly proper manhood, and sober respectability was going to bring middle-class men the political voice for which they had long been striving. Sherry's importance in this new equation was that it was thought to be a feminine wine, appropriate for women, but not effeminizing to the men who drank it, especially if they continued to drink masculine port. Thus, post-war and early Victorian British middle-class men needed two kinds of wine to represent their virtues and constitute their power: sherry and port. Notably, both were fortified and neither was French.

A much "improved" age

Writing in the *Examiner* in December 1817, the American-born poet and essayist Leigh Hunt declared the "Death of Merry England."[7] This obituary was premature to say the least, and was certainly influenced by the fact that Britain was experiencing a post-war economic depression. Nevertheless, Hunt was on to something. Less sensitive observers might not have noticed a change in their country just yet, and in retrospect it is clear that Hunt spoke in the middle of a transitional era. Certainly "Merry England" and its sottish Scottish equivalent did not die overnight, but British society, especially among the middle classes, was becoming more decorous, more serious, and more sober. For example, wine imports retained for domestic consumption in the United Kingdom dropped from their wartime average of nearly 29,000 tuns per annum to just under 23,000 tuns for the period 1816–25; spirit consumption in the United Kingdom declined in the decade after Waterloo; and beer consumption in England, already waning, fell below 30 Imperial gallons, per head, per year.[8]

Some of the decline in alcohol consumption can be attributed to the economic depression, because these downward trends reversed course by 1825, or 1830 in the case of beer; but British culture was also changing. The taverns and clubs that had once welcomed in so many British men as the evening began and spewed them out drunk onto the streets in the wee hours, were either gone or changing. No longer bastions of intoxicated revelry, by the 1820s and 1830s clubs were transformed into learned societies where men might come to dine quietly, hear a lecture, or discuss ways to "improve" their towns, their cities, or themselves.[9] "Happily," wrote the prominent port shipper James Warre in 1823, "inebriety is not the vice of the age."[10] One year later, the Scottish physician and wine historian Alexander Henderson wrote:

A generation has scarcely passed away since it was no uncommon thing to see men of high intellectual acquirements, and of irreproachable character in other respects, protracting the nightly feast, till not only their cares, but their sense, were completely drowned in wine. ... It was once the boast of many that they could indulge in these deep potations with impunity.[11]

Similarly, in 1833 the journalist, wine writer, and social critic Cyrus Redding declared that the

> practice of drinking largely of wine has much decreased of late years, and though "Attic taste with wine" may be as rare a union as before in any class of society, it is certain that among the upper and middling classes wine was never less abused than in the present day, nor excess more generally avoided.[12]

British wine merchants and wine writers had more reasons than most to reflect upon people's diminishing wine consumption habits, but they were hardly alone in their observations. Recall that Francis Place wrote in the mid-1820s: "we [British] are a much better people" than a half-century before, "less gross and brutal," with "fewer of the concomitant vices of a less civilized state."[13] His words were echoed in 1829 by the fashionable fencing master Henry Angelo (the Younger), who observed that in "no period of our domestic history has so universal a change in the manners and habits of the people generally, taken place, as with the last half century." Angelo was born in 1780, and therefore may be forgiven for conflating the trajectory of his own life with the date at which British behavior began to "improve", but the essence of his remark was frequently repeated. "We may be said to be no longer the same people," continued Angelo, "doubtless, the manners of the middle class, in their evening amusements at least, are marked by a mighty change, in favour of general decorum."[14]

Sobriety was first fashionable among the broadly defined middle classes, but their ultimate success in promoting the idea of sobriety as a measure of morality and, therefore, political legitimacy, meant that eventually members of the aristocracy and working classes would have to follow suit if they wanted to maintain or gain political power.[15] As it happened, the aristocracy, who had long held the bulk of political power in Britain, as well as consumed a disproportionate amount of the wine wine, did not take long to sober up. A confidential report to the government in May 1853 cheerily stated: "It is a subject of notoriety and congratulations that a great change has taken place in the habits of the upper classes, as regards the use of wine, since the time of Mr. Pitt. ... The race of 'six bottle men' is extinct."[16] The same report also noted that from 1785 to 1794, per capita consumption of wine in Britain was three-and-a-half bottles per year, while from 1826 to 1853 that number had fallen to one bottle. In other words, even accounting for population growth, "those classes who can indulge in it to any extent," were drinking far less wine.[17] George B. Wilson, the author of the most comprehensive study of alcohol consumption trends in Britain, estimated that between 1801 and 1850, per capita wine consumption in the United Kingdom fell by 41 percent, and the decline in wine was not simply replaced by other forms of alcohol.[18]

Whether members of the working classes were more or less sober in the mid-nineteenth century than before is disputed by historians, but there was no doubt among the moralizing middle classes of the era that the working classes were all too frequently drunk. The statistical evidence is ambiguous. In 1825 spirit consumption began to increase, although it declined slightly in the 1840s, and then increased again in the 1850s.[19] And roughly three-quarters of all spirits were consumed by the working classes.[20] But beer was the favorite drink of the working classes, and excepting a brief rise in beer consumption following the Beer Act of 1830, consumption per head remained at roughly 30 gallons per annum from 1800 until 1860.[21] Perhaps even more surprisingly, tea consumption remained static from 1800 until the 1840s, when it began a dramatic rise, while coffee consumption increased slowly from 1820 until 1850 before stabilizing, although it never caught up to tea.[22] What all of this evidence points to is a fluctuation in the purchasing power of the working classes, including the purchasing and consumption of spirits, but a clear decline in alcohol consumption of any type among the middle and upper classes.[23]

Not that everyone was happy about the growth of a more sober society. Byron and a host of other conservative social critics saw increasing sobriety as part of a larger trend toward prudishness and false emotions. In 1821, Byron condemned the emerging era as the age of cant, "cant political, cant poetical, cant religious; but always cant, multiplied through all the varieties of life."[24] His epic poem *Don Juan* (1819–24) was a long and elaborate rejection of the ascendant morality, in which he famously wrote: "Man being reasonable, must get drunk;/ The best of life is but intoxication."[25] Walter Scott and Percy Shelley praised *Don Juan* for its honest description of human impulses, and the poem was immensely popular with the reading public; but it was also terribly scandalous. Rage against the cant as Byron and others did, these anti-reformers could not prevent the fading of the light. Drunkenness, like colorful men's clothing, libertinism, and laughter, was going out of fashion.[26]

Of course, the reformers would never have imagined that they were canting misanthropes. They believed they were doing God's work, so they were largely immune to the charges against them. To Byron and his ilk the older generation in England was free of pretension; they were more natural. But to the reformers the reverse was true. The older generation, like the libertine Byron, was enslaved by their animal instincts. True liberation came from being in control of one's instincts and emotions, and a large amount of alcohol was the quickest route to bestial behavior.[27]

Peace, wine, and taxes

There were many reasons for the decline in drunkenness after the Napoleonic Wars, but one reason was high taxes amidst an economic depression. Wartime taxes on both domestic and imported alcohol remained in place after the war ended. As a result, alcohol of all types was expensive; however, wine was particularly burdened. At the time of the Treaty of Vienna in 1815, duties on wine stood at the unprecedentedly high levels of more than £144 per tun for French wine, £118 for Rhenish wine, and £96 per tun for Portuguese, Spanish, and other

European wines. Put another way, the duty on French wine was almost 3 shillings per bottle, while the duty on Portuguese and Spanish wines was just under 2 shillings.

Consequently, there was no increase in the wine trade despite the peace; instead, trade continued its wartime decline. Not surprisingly, wine merchants were distraught. Warre's lengthy pamphlet, published in 1823, argued for an immediate reduction in the wine duties on the grounds that the "excess of duty is the principal cause of the diminished consumption" of wines.[28] In order to prove his point, Warre focused on the wine trade statistics for the years 1787–94, during which time Pitt's reduction of the wine duties had caused the volume of British wine imports to double. Likewise, the multiple wartime duty increases caused wine imports to revert to their pre-1787 level. "The goose was killed," said Warre, "the golden egg was lost."[29] He gave no credence to the "opinion entertained by some people, that wine is gone out of fashion, that our habits are changed, that soda water and ginger beer are now our only drinks." Instead, he insisted, "it is the price, not inclination, that compels abstinence."[30] Warre had a point; price mattered. But so too did changes in the cultural landscape, because in 1825 import duties on all wines were essentially cut in half, and except for a brief spike in port imports in that same year, port imports remained static. What did increase, however, was the amount of Spanish wine imported into and consumed in the United Kingdom, and most of that Spanish wine was sherry.

Respectability

Self-consciously Christian moralists—Anglican, Presbyterian, Methodist, and otherwise—began waging a war against drunkenness around 1800, although their message was generally dismissed or even mocked by the majority.[31] Nevertheless, these moralists achieved some successes in their broader goals to make Britain and its Empire more benevolent. The slave trade was ended in 1807 and prison reform was enacted in 1808. But calls for greater sobriety continued to fall on deaf ears. So long as a war was going on, alcohol-fuelled manliness was fashionable. However, in the aftermath of nearly twenty-five years of all-out war abroad and social turmoil at home, heretofore ignored calls for sobriety found purchase. The middle ranks, who emerged from the war in a position of relative economic power, wanted law and order along with the right to vote. If achieved, both of these goals would stabilize their position in what they had every reason to believe was an unstable world.[32]

One measure of newfound middle-class seriousness in the 1820s was that the formerly minority opinion that condemned drunken debauchery became a majority opinion. As a result, drunkenness, gambling, fisticuffs, and fornication—formerly both fun and funny to a majority of the middle classes—was now roundly condemned as the behavior that separated the respectable middle classes from the wretched poor and dissolute aristocracy. From this perspective, the sober and industrious middle classes merited their newfound wealth, while aristocrats were worthless parasites and the poor deserved their degraded lives. And there was nothing fun or funny about rich wastrels like Mytton, or poor beggars like the peg-legged black fiddler, Billy Waters, who had once been a popular sight in the streets of London. Instead, such people were to be condemned for their behavior and "improved," but not laughed at, and certainly not laughed with.[33]

Drunken behavior among the poor was the impetus for the Temperance movement that began in Ireland in 1828 and quickly made its way across the Irish Sea to Britain, where it made even bigger inroads. But it is important to say that it was at first a result, not a cause, of changing attitudes toward drunkenness. In other words, Temperance caught a wave and increased its size, it did not create it. At the outset of the movement, Temperance concerned itself with condemning spirits, while condoning beer and wine as useful, "temperate," beverages. Very quickly, however, a division arose within the Temperance movement between those who condoned the use of beer and wine, the Moderationists, and those who condemned all forms of alcohol, the Teetotalers.[34] But whatever the divisions within the movement, a majority of its leaders were Evangelical members of the middle classes. This included clergymen of various Christian stripes, whose objective was to improve the poor by spreading the middle-class gospel of sober respectability.[35]

While the thrust of the Temperance movement was initially directed from the middle classes downward, the emphasis on sobriety was also meant to send a message upward to the elite. Of course, the drunken aristocrat, just like the gin-soaked laborer, was a middle-class cliché, although George IV did his best to make the cliché true. But the key point is that the Temperance Movement was largely class-based and class-interested. The implicit argument of Temperance reformers was that the poor, as always, were too irresponsible to partake in politics, and the dissolute aristocracy had abdicated its leadership role. That left one social group standing with its moral reputation intact.[36]

As the tide of "respectable" behavior continued to rise, those who did not conform to the increasingly sober expectations were likely to be ostracized. Alexander Henderson wrote in 1824 that the excesses of six-bottle men, while not long disappeared, would in the new era "operate as an effectual and deserved exclusion from all respectable society." Such was the fate of Mytton, for example, who was considered a relic of the past and shunned by many men and women of his social class during the last decade of his life, from 1824 to 1833. Among works of fiction, the fate of Pierce Egan's *Life in London*, which was published in a dozen monthly parts beginning in 1821, demonstrates the same phenomenon (Figure 11.2).[37] Egan's book, lavishly illustrated by George and Robert Cruikshank, "contrasts the folly of the upper classes with the happiness of the lower and it aimed at a raffish readership long practiced in crossing social boundaries."[38] *Life in London*, in which the thinly disguised Tom, Jerry, and Logic (the Cruikshank brothers and Egan) perambulate throughout the town, carousing both day and night, high and low, became a best-seller and was frequently plagiarized; but the book's success could not have occurred a decade later; it looked backward to an era that was ending, not to the future in which there was nothing funny in the behavior of its characters. In the same decade that Britain built the world's first passenger train, Egan's

228

Figure 11.2 Frontispiece to Pierce Egan, *Life in London* (1820–1), illustrated by George Cruikshank
Note: Egan's book caught the last laugh out of town.

book caught the last laugh out of town. Later generations failed to get the joke.[39] Queen Victoria's famous disapproval of a ribald tale, "We are not amused," even if apocryphal, could stand as a mantra for nineteenth-century bourgeois respectability. And least amusing of all was the drunkenness that seemed to fuel the other forms of anti-social behavior.

A critical component of respectable behavior was a reverence for domesticity. Prior to the 1820s, middle-ranking men went to the tavern to assert and confirm their masculinity among other men, to escape their workplace (which for some was within or beneath their home), and to make or keep business contacts. In short, men were constructing a form of emotional and financial support network by socializing, and their socializing was abetted by alcohol. But by the 1820s, most middle-class men worked outside their homes. Home, therefore, became a refuge from work and the vicissitudes of the marketplace. Home was where the middle-class wife and children awaited the father's return, and where he, in turn, came to have his rough, manly edges smoothed by the soft unmanliness of women and children.[40]

Domesticity helped to prove respectability because what was private was ultimately meant for public consumption. To spend quiet and sober time in a well-appointed home with one's family, or with invited guests, was a public statement about one's moral probity.[41] And like sobriety itself, domesticity was a way for middle-class men to draw a clear distinction between themselves and the aristocracy on the one hand, and the lower orders on the other. To continue this cozy, middle-class narrative, aristocratic palaces were not even homes; rather, they were physically and emotionally cold buildings, which for all intents and purposes served as oversized breeding kennels for another generation of profligate peers. Meanwhile, working-class homes were also disqualified from true domesticity; they were neither physically comfortable nor orderly, as the man of the house was too often absent while drinking up his wages at the pub.[42]

Thus, the sobriety, seriousness, domesticity—the respectability—of the middle classes was an assertion of superior morality, which helped legitimize male, middle-class demands for a direct political voice. By 1820 there were some 30,000 middling households in London alone, and the middle-class men who presided over them, as was true throughout the United Kingdom, wanted the right to vote.[43] Respectability gave middle-class men a moral claim to join, if not displace, the old ruling order. Indeed, once the goal of expanding the franchise to include most middle-class men was achieved with the passage of the Reform Act of 1832, respectability continued to validate middle-class assertions of moral superiority and political legitimacy. And wine, sherry in particular, was part of the winning middle-class equation.

The rise of sherry

In the three decades from 1817 to 1846, Spanish wines retained for consumption in the United Kingdom increased from 22 percent, to 33 percent, to 38 percent of the overall total. Meanwhile Portuguese wines excepting madeira fell

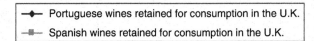

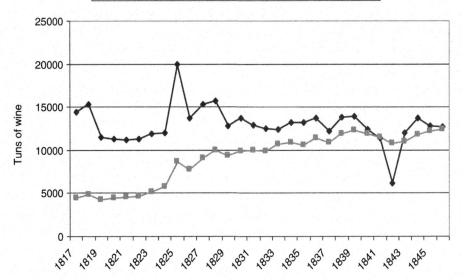

Graph 11.1   Sherry's rise to parity with port, 1817–46
Source: Parliamentary Report C.8706, *Customs Tariffs of the United Kingdom*, pp. 150–1.

from 51 percent, to 44 percent, to 40 percent in the same three decades.[44] In other words, by 1840 port and sherry were consumed in roughly equal amounts (Graph 11.1). In 1842, port actually dropped well below sherry because port shippers and importers waited to see if the proposed treaty with Portugal would substantially reduce the duty on Portuguese wines. However, the treaty was rejected by the British Parliament and port imports returned to essential parity with sherry for the rest of the decade.

Sherry's rise on the British market was dictated by middle-class consumers; after all, only the middle classes had the demographic numbers to impact import trends in such a dramatic fashion. As Warre wrote in 1823: "It is not, however, those who indulge in an occasional debauch, nor your three-bottle men, that affect the general consumption of wine, for they are but few in number; it is the daily, though perhaps small consumption of the middling classes of society."[45] And as Henderson wrote in 1824, the middling classes of society were "the drinkers of port and sherry."[46] These were the preferred wines, and often only wines, in middle-class homes. Even middle-class homes away from home, such as the Travelers Club in Edinburgh, served only port and sherry to the men who stayed there while on business.[47]

At least one Victorian-era commentator attributed the fashionableness of sherry to the fact that it was the Prince of Wales' favorite wine.[48] There were, in fact, few types of alcohol that George IV, as Prince, Regent and King, did not like. For instance, on his much-ballyhooed trip to Scotland in 1822—in which

George played the role of the king of Celts in his newly invented "Royal Stewart" tartan—a vast array of wines, spirits, beers, and liqueurs was ordered from Edinburgh wine merchants for the entertainment.[49] The variety and abundance of alcohol served—most of it wine—was meant to appeal to the broadest possible range of guests and to emphasize the splendor, generosity, and power of the monarch. But the king's favorite drink, in Scotland as in London, was sherry. For instance, among the wines sent to the royal yacht, the "Royal George," for the king's personal use while docked at Leith, were 120 bottles of claret, 216 bottles of port, and 288 bottles of sherry.[50] The wine was to be shared, of course.

George IV's preference for sherry may well have set in motion a new fashion among the British aristocracy, especially the generation that came of age during his reign.[51] For example, an 1824 cellar inventory of Ashburnham Place, the country residence in Sussex of George Ashburnham, 3rd Earl of Ashburnham and 5th Baron Asaph (1760–1830) showed that the ageing earl, like most of his contemporaries, still preferred port. His cellar contained 904 bottles of port, 501 bottles of madeira, 299 bottles of German wines, and 283 bottles of sherry, along with lesser numbers of other wines. The cellar was little changed in 1830 when the 3rd Earl died at 70.[52] However, an inventory of the cellar taken one year later shows that his eldest surviving son, Bertram Ashburnham (1797–1878), 4th Earl of Ashburnham, had dramatically different taste from his father. There were now 1,213 bottles of sherry, 805 bottles of madeira, 510 bottles of marsala, and 335 bottles of port among the leading wines in the Ashburnham cellar.[53] Similarly, in 1831–2, James Blair Oliphant, 10th Laird of Gask, purchased a variety of wines from the Edinburgh wine merchants Cockburn and Campbell; his favorites in descending order of preference were "superior" sherry, "East India" sherry, vintage 1822 claret, "old" port, and "white" champagne.[54]

But if George IV's preference for sherry swayed his fellow aristocrats, there is little reason to believe that a man so broadly despised by the middle classes would have influenced middle-class taste.[55] Instead, what seems more likely is that George IV, like his father's generation of aristocrats, latched on to a growing middle-class fashion for the purpose of enhancing his legitimacy and popularity among the social strata whose opinion mattered most. For all his desire to turn back the clock and create a magisterial monarchy along the lines of the former Bourbon kings of France, even George IV understood that it was the middle classes, not the aristocracy, who needed to be convinced of the king's majesty.[56] In fact, by the 1830s the British aristocracy as a whole seems to have been drinking proportionally more sherry than port. What George IV forgot, however, was that along with sherry, sobriety and self-restraint were integral to the respectable masculinity so admired by the middle classes.[57] In a wonderful print from 1820, John Marshall depicts the extremely fat king in a drunken stupor, being carried off to bed by two equally fat peeresses, while an inebriated courtier laughs and spills wine on the oblivious monarch. The king himself is represented, in his vacant chair, by an empty wine bottle (Figure 11.3).[58] While many of the turn-of-the-century satirical drawings of George laughed both with him and at him, Marshall's drawing does only the latter. There is no vicarious pleasure to be had

Figure 11.3 Our Fat Friend Going to Roost (1820), by John Marshall
Note: By this time George's behavior was no longer outrageous, it was odious.

here; the king may have had a fun evening, but there is no sense that Marshall wants to join him.

The new requirements of sobriety and self-restraint were not lost upon George IV's brother, the Duke of Clarence, who became King William IV in 1830. As one of William's biographers stated, the king's diet was frugal, simple, and rigidly adhering to "bourgeois standards."[59] One such standard was his preference for sherry. His physician, Dr William Beattie commented: "Sherry is his favorite, and I may say only wine. I never saw him taste port, and seldom French or Rhenish wines." Beattie added that the only other drink William consumed in quantity was barley water with lemon.[60] According to his son Adolphus FitzClarence, his father maintained his moderation and taste for wine in his final years. "After breakfast he devotes himself with Sir H. Taylor to business till two, when he lunches (two cutlets and two glasses of sherry)," wrote Adolphus; "then he goes out and drives til dinner; at dinner he drinks a bottle of sherry—no other wine—and eats moderately, and goes to bed soon after eleven."[61] In the twenty-first century some might regard William's bottle-and-a-quarter of sherry per day as immoderate, but even in the increasingly sober decade of the 1830s this was not an extravagant amount. In fact, it was a fairly average amount for a British middle-class gentleman, which, in practice, William was.

Similarly, Queen Victoria and Prince Albert were both moderate drinkers who enjoyed sherry more than any other wine in their numerous and well-stocked cellars. In the first quarter of 1838, before her marriage to Albert, Victoria's cellar master ordered eight hogsheads and four butts of sherry, and 16 hogsheads of

1834 Chateau Lafite claret for the queen's private table.[62] In other words, she had approximately 4,032 bottles of each wine for her personal use. As with her predecessors, Queen Victoria's cellars contained a startling range of wines, which did not diminish even after she married the cost-cutting Prince Albert. Nevertheless, of the myriad types of wine to be found in the royal cellars during the twenty years that Victoria and Albert presided over the British court together, sherry was the most common and the most commonly consumed by the Queen, the Prince Consort, and their many guests, as well as by the staff of the Royal Household.[63]

Admittedly, there were differences in the preferences of, and choices available to, the wine drinkers at court. The royal family and their guests drank mostly what the wine steward called "First Class" sherry, along with slightly lesser amounts of top-growth claret and sweet champagne, and, in distant fourth place, "First Class" port. This was true in 1841 and again in 1856.[64] As it happens, Victoria, and especially Albert, disliked port and the British ritual of men drinking port after dinner while the ladies withdrew to the drawing room for tea. Albert shortened the entire port-drinking ritual to roughly five minutes, disallowed any crass talk, and then went to join his wife and the ladies for singing.[65] Reluctantly, British aristocratic men followed Albert, both at court and eventually in their own homes and palaces.

To be sure, Victoria's and Albert's dislike of port was exceptional. Beyond the royal table, port remained popular, especially among the middle classes. For instance, in 1841 the members of the royal household, an economically lower-middling group, drank 7,450 bottles of "household" sherry, and 6,814 bottles of "household" port, and these were the two most popular wines.[66] Likewise, import figures for Britain as a whole show that sherry and port were essentially equal in popularity during the late 1840s and early 1850s. Only in the late 1850s did sherry become decidedly more popular than port.[67] Meanwhile, until 1860 the small amount of French wine that was imported was expensive and, therefore, consumed only by the very wealthy (Graph 11.2).

A feminine wine?

Historically, British consumers were quite familiar with sherry. It had been among the most fashionable of all wines in the Elizabethan and early Stuart eras, when it was known as "sack." But to understand why sherry returned to popularity in the second quarter of the nineteenth century, one must look to the changing perceptions of port. As we have seen, port had been a potent symbol of English middle-ranking men in the early and mid-eighteenth century because of its price, strength, and perceived patriotism. But the virtues of port in the eighteenth century became its weaknesses in the nineteenth. First, by the end of the century port's masculine and patriotic symbolism had been adopted by the English aristocracy in order to assert their own John Bull masculinity, and by Scottish wine drinkers of all ranks to claim their Britishness.[68] Thus, by the end of the Napoleonic Wars English middle-ranking men no longer had control over the symbolic meanings of port. Port was now a symbol of broadly defined British

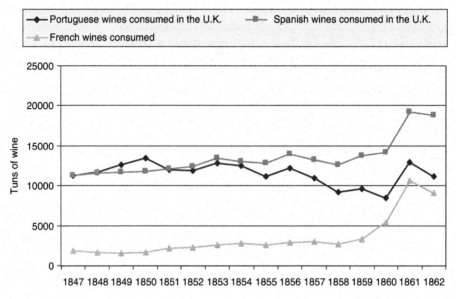

Graph 11.2   Portuguese, Spanish, and French wine consumed in the UK, 1847–62
Source: Parliamentary Report C.8706, *Customs Tariffs of the United Kingdom*, pp. 151–2.

masculinity, and in that sense it was no longer narrow enough in meaning to express the political aspirations of English middle-class men alone. Second, as a decidedly masculine wine, port was associated with the heavy drinking and war-rior ethos of the revolutionary era.

Sherry, however, was thought to be a delicate wine. Generally pale or brownish-yellow in color—although it can be dark brown—it did not have the fiery, tannic flavor of port. Sherry was fortified but not French, feminine but not effeminiz-ing. In the post-war era, it was a magical elixir. British middle-class men turned to sherry to express their respectability, which like politeness required taming aggressive masculinity with a dose of gentle refinement. But this did not mean that British men suddenly rejected port; instead, they saw sherry as a complement to port and drank both wines in nearly equal measure. As William Thackeray wrote in his 1855 novel, *The Newcomes: Memoirs of a Most Respectable Family*, a proper husband and father was "respected for his kindness and famous for his port wine."[69] But equally true is the fact that the respectable men in Thackeray's novel drink sherry and port (and a fair amount of claret as well). In other words, sherry gave respectable men the dose of refinement they needed to prevent a descent into barbarism that so obviously plagued their eighteenth-century forebears. So much were port and sherry linked together as a pair that specially labeled decanters were sold in tandem, suggesting that these two wines, like man and woman, husband and wife, Victoria and Albert, were made for each other by a beneficent God.[70]

If sherry helped British men to assert their own respectability by softening their rough masculinity, it was also considered an appropriate wine for respectable women. After all, it was both delicate and strong. Much work remains to be done on the history of women's taste for wine in nineteenth-century Britain, but literary evidence from the early Victorian era suggests that the rise in sherry consumption in Britain had as much to do with women as with men. In *Sketches of Boz*, a book of reportage about "every-day life and every-day people" in 1830s' London, Charles Dickens observed women drinking sherry at the theater as part of a regular occurrence.[71] Similarly, a story from *Fraser's Magazine for Town and Country* in 1838 speaks of the port being "placed on the table in its native black bottles for the gentlemen, and the two old-fashioned decanters for the sherry ladies."[72] The all but forgotten novelist Henry Cockton, in his forgettable novel *The Love Match* (1845), depicts the ladies and gentlemen drinking sherry with equal enthusiasm, whereas port is almost always for the men alone.[73] Robert Smith Surtees, a careful observer of English rural life, fox-hunting in particular, got the laugh in his novel *Mr. Sponge's Sporting Tour* (1853), when Mr Jawleyford insisted that "The ladies drink white wine—*sherry*," while only the men were offered any of his precious port (and they were lucky to have it!).[74] Continuing into the 1860s, when sherry was well ahead of port on the British market, a report on the wine trade in *The Edinburgh Review* in July 1867 declared that sherry, while still immensely popular, was declining in use among the higher classes. They were drinking more and more French wine. Nevertheless, the author went on to say,

> we fancy the ladies have something to do with maintaining from a rapid fall the highly alcoholised wines of Spain. They almost universally take either sherry or champagne at dinner, and if they take a glass after dinner, we observe it must be one of the old fashioned wines of early habit. They take but a glass, and that they like strong and sweet.[75]

Lastly, of course, there was Queen Victoria herself, a modest drinker, although voracious eater; she liked claret and champagne, but seems to have preferred sherry above all other wines. Prince Albert concurred.[76]

***

Sherry was not the first drink to be fashionable among or associated with women in Britain, but its rise in popularity in the post-war era of the early and mid-nineteenth century seems to mark the beginning of women as major wine consumers. Moreover, sherry was perhaps the first wine to be so overtly linked to women and, through them, to the idea and ideal of domesticity. One sees these links in a painting by William Powell Frith, entitled *Many Happy Returns of the Day* (1854) (Figure 11.4). In this painting, three generations of a prosperous middle-class family sit around a dining table. They are toasting the health of a young daughter on her birthday, hence the painting's title.[77] As one art historian has written, the painting is "a quintessential portrait of Victorian middle-class family life."[78] Not surprisingly, therefore, the scene is divided into a feminine sphere and a masculine sphere on either end of the table. Each of these two spheres has a wine decanter, one filled

Figure 11.4   Many Happy Returns of the Day (1854), by W. P. Frith
Note: A well-balanced family?

with a pale yellow wine, almost certainly sherry, and the other, a reddish-purple wine, almost certainly port. Quite clearly, the father and grandfather in the painting are drinking or about to drink the sherry, while the women and all but the youngest children are drinking or about to drink the port.[79]

In a bit of subtle symbolism that has eluded art historians, Frith seems to have painted the complementarity of port and sherry. For not only were port and sherry themselves masculine and feminine complements, but they complemented the men, women, and children who consumed them. In this instance, it seems that the women and children are being elevated to greater seriousness and maturity by drinking manly port, while the men are being softened and domesticated through their consumption of feminine sherry.

The family in Frith's painting, which was modeled on his very own,[80] has achieved a happy balance between generations and genders in part because of the wines they drink. Their wish for "Many happy returns of the day" is both a birthday wish for the little girl, as well as a wish for the continuity of happiness within the family. But as always, one generation dies off, one becomes old, one matures to adulthood, and another comes into being. Likewise, for gender, conceptions of masculinity and femininity that allowed for a temporary balance within a family are fleeting because they are constructed ideals that both reflect and instantiate power. Nothing is entirely fixed or certain. For instance, Frith himself had a mistress and seven bastard children living only a mile away from his "real" family.[81]

Likewise, the wines that helped the family achieve balance and harmony, at least in the painting, did not guarantee their popularity forever. In fact, even before sherry and port achieved their joint apotheosis as the perfect pair somewhere around the year 1840—the very year that Victoria and Albert got married—a handful of middle-class critics emerged to denounce all fortified wines as uncivilized. To these critics, the taste for wine was a measure of civilization, and fortified wines were nothing short of barbaric. If British civilization was to become truly civilized, they argued, the bulk of the population would need to drink unfortified wines. And among unfortified wines, French wines were undoubtedly the best.

12

"Taste is not an immutable, but a mutable thing"

British Civilization and the Great Nineteenth-Century Wine Debate

1851 was a momentous year in British history. On May 1, the Great Exhibition opened in Hyde Park, welcoming millions of visitors from throughout Britain, Ireland, the European continent, North America, and the British Empire. With the Crystal Palace as its showcase, Britain basked in the glory of its own industrial and technological superiority, the products of its unrivalled Empire, and its liberal economic policies—to which many attributed Britain's global dominance. "The products of all quarters of the globe are placed at our disposal," wrote Prince Albert, the man who was largely responsible for conceiving and promoting the Great Exhibition, "and we have only to choose that which is best and cheapest for our purposes, and the powers of production are entrusted to the stimulus of competition and capital."[1] But the Great Exhibition was not only a celebration of Britain's industrial, economic, and imperial might, it was also a celebration of British civilization. James Wilson, a Scotsman and founder of *The Economist* magazine, wrote in 1851 that Britain was vastly improved, materially, culturally, and morally, from the beginning of the century. This was the "golden age," said Wilson, and Britain was "the greatest nation that ever stood in the vanguard of civilization and freedom."[2]

But others were not so sure. Thomas George Shaw, another Scotsman and free-trade proponent who had found his way to London, where he worked his way up from a clerk at the wine docks to a prosperous wine merchant, wrote a short pamphlet in 1851 in which he expressed a vastly different view of Britain. "There is no country in the world," wrote Shaw, "where drunkenness and the crimes necessarily arising out of it, prevail to such an extent as among ourselves; for indeed, the consumption of spirits is nearly a gallon yearly for every man, woman and child."[3] Admittedly, civilization can be defined in many ways and does not preclude a high degree of intoxication. Moreover, the tendency among "freedom"-fetishizing imperialists like Wilson to delude themselves about the benevolence of their nation's endeavors is historically all too common, as is the doom and gloom of merchants like Shaw who just happen to have a cheer-inducing remedy to sell. Nevertheless, something *was* amiss in Britain, as these two views and their attendant realities could not easily be reconciled.

Attempts to understand how mid-nineteenth-century Britain was both immensely wealthy and yet full of human misery were referred to as the

"Condition of England" debate, or more broadly, the "Social Question," and within this debate the subject of alcohol was critical. To reform-minded liberals like Shaw, spirits were the villain, wine was the hero, and light French wines were best of all. The true method of eradicating British poverty and drunkenness, wrote Shaw, was not to place higher taxes on spirits, but "to place within reach of all, a wholesome and cheering beverage, which wine is, in its pure unadulterated state."[4] To achieve his goal of bringing wine to the masses, Shaw proposed lowering the duty on all wines so that a bottle could be had for as little as 1 shilling.

But just as there were those who disagreed about whether Britain had morally improved or declined since the beginning of the nineteenth century, and in what ways, there were people who did not believe that wine was the savior of British civilization. To begin with, the cultural optimists did not believe that Britain needed to be saved. Second, many of them believed that British taste for wine was already superior in that it centered on sherry and port, and for the very wealthy, the very best French wines. Related to this belief was the idea that taste was fixed; the middle classes would never renounce sherry and port for lighter wines, and the working classes would not drink much wine under any circumstances; they did not like it and never had.

Consequently, the mid-nineteenth-century wine debate hinged upon the questions of whether British taste was politically constructed or inherent, and whether it was potentially the same for all social classes. The social reformers and economic liberals, who eventually won the debate, believed that British preference for fortified wines like port and sherry was politically constructed (as was the taste for spirits among the working classes), that these preferences could be undone by lowering the duty on wines, that the mass of British consumers would turn to light wines once they became affordable, and that these wines would bring better health and morality to all levels of British society. In short, a British society that drank light, French wines would become, like the middle classes themselves—or at least the *soi-disant* enlightened ones among them—hard-working, healthy, and civilized.

The idea that British consumers of all social classes desperately needed French wines was, of course, a radical departure from the dominant political, cultural, and economic thought of the previous century-and-a-half. Indeed, the argument for French wine was a call for the government to roll back history, and return to the status quo of the seventeenth century, when claret was the least expensive and most popular wine in both England and Scotland. But this should not surprise us, for light French wines and free trade with France reflected the prevailing values of the mid-Victorian political order. What might surprise us, however, as certainly it surprised men like William Gladstone, is that the taste for wine in Britain, like the history it represented, was a stubborn thing.

The great nineteenth-century wine debate

When James Warre launched his scathing assessment of the wine trade in 1823, his subtitle said everything the reader needed to know about his argument: *Proving that an increase in Duty caused a decrease in Revenue; and a decrease of Duty, an increase of Revenue*. But nowhere in his attack did Warre imagine that British taste for wine would move away from port, the wine with which he was most involved as a merchant. In fact, Warre ended his analysis of the current problem in the port trade with a warning to Portugal, saying that should she be blind to her own interests and

> continue enhancing the price of her wines by unfair and improper regulations—
> it may be necessary to refer her to what has been stated on the effect of pro-
> tecting duties or to undeceive her that no other country can supply wines to
> the taste and general consumption of this country ... there are vineyards in the
> south of France, the wines of which, if England encouraged the importation by
> a reduction of duty, can be improved so as to meet the palates and taste of the
> inhabitants of the British Empire.[5]

In other words, Warre wondered whether the British might choose to procure their "port" from somewhere other than Portugal.[6]

Replies to Warre's essay ranged from a warning by Fleetwood Williams, an English lawyer, against a duty reduction until the Portuguese first corrected the "abuses at present existing in the Monopoly Wine Company," to an accusation by an anonymous Portuguese author that it was the British, not the Portuguese, who were in breach of commercial arrangements between the two countries because of the high import duties placed on Portuguese wines.[7] The Portuguese author challenged the "English" (his term) to find better port then that which was sent to Britain from Portugal,[8] and criticized the free-trade theories upon which the British made their complaints as a bunch of liberal nonsense. "Unrestricted liberty—liberty not regulated by law—liberty unprotected by inspection and the guardianship of the government," asserted the author, "are all chimeras and incompatible with the state of civil and political society, as constituted in modern times."[9] Nevertheless, the Portuguese author warned his fellow countrymen to be fair in their dealings with the British, as the taste for port was not inherent, he asserted, but subject to the caprice of fashion.[10]

All of these lengthy pamphlets, and still others, were distributed to Members of Parliament in hopes of swaying their opinions for or against a reduction of duty and a new commercial treaty with Portugal.[11] But importantly, everyone involved in this debate was hoping to increase the faltering port trade. No one wanted or really believed that British taste would shift to a different type of wine. For example, in "Supplementary Observations" added to the 1824 reprint of his pamphlet, Warre calmly claimed that port was the "staple Wine for British Constitutions: let it be but genuine, good and cheap, it will yet stand the test against all others."[12]

The debate and the post-war environment clearly had an impact because in 1825 a modified version of Warre's argument won the day. Parliament did not press the Portuguese to disband the Douro Company, which continued to restrict what wines could be exported to the United Kingdom; however, using the new "Imperial" measurement system, Chancellor of the Exchequer Frederick Robinson simplified and reduced the duties on all wines. First, the excise duty on wine was removed, and all wine duty collection was returned to the Customs Office. Second, the overall duty on Portuguese and Spanish wines was cut from 9s. 1d. to 4s. 9d. per imperial gallon, on Rhenish from 11s. 3d. to 4s. 9d. per imperial gallon, and on French wines from 13s. 9d. to 7s. 3d. per imperial gallon. Put in the terms that we have been using thus far, the duties on Portuguese and Spanish wines were cut from roughly £96 to £50 per tun, on Rhenish wines from £118 to £50 per tun, and on French wines from £144 to £78 per tun. Thus, Portuguese wines still paid roughly 36 percent less duty than French wines, thereby maintaining the terms of the Methuen Treaty.[13] The duties on Cape wines from South Africa, which were considered British wines by virtue of their colonial origin, were reduced from a mere three shillings to 2s. 5d. per imperial gallon (or £25 per tun). As appealingly low as that tax was, Cape wines were thought by most middle-class consumers to be inferior, and the working classes, who constituted the market for most Cape wines, drank very little wine of any sort. Consequently, Cape wines remained a small percentage of overall imports.

The intended beneficiary of the 1825 duty reductions was of course port. Wine merchants, free traders, and port drinkers of all persuasions no doubt pulled the corks on their favorite bottles to celebrate the duty reduction on their favorite wine. But in the pleasant intoxication of their celebration they may have overlooked the fact that another argument about wine was underway–and this argument was not about making port less expensive, but about whether port was compatible with true civilization. In 1824, Dr Alexander Henderson, a Scottish physician working in London, published *The History of Ancient and Modern Wines*.[14] Although Henderson spent many pages on Ancient Greek and Roman wines, thereby mimicking Sir Edward Barry's 1775 effort, he also described in detail the vineyards, production methods, and styles of modern European wines.[15] Above all, Henderson wrote as a doctor who was concerned about the relationship between wine and physical health, and it was this vantage point that caused him to condemn port. Portuguese wines, asserted Henderson, could at most "be placed on a level with the better sorts of Spanish wines and the secondary growths of France."[16] But the Methuen Commercial Treaty, he explained, "has in a manner compelled us to drink port wine."[17] Henderson the medical doctor was making a historical argument about the origins of contemporary British taste for wine:

> The impolicy of that [i.e. Methuen] treaty will not now be denied, especially as there is reason to believe, that its provisions have been less religiously observed by the Portuguese than by the British government. When it was formed (in the year 1703) there was certainly nothing in the wines of Portugal to entitle them to so decided a preference; and though, at first, it may have caused more care to be bestowed on their manufacture, yet its eventual tendency has been to retard the improvements in their quality, which a free competition with other countries would have produced. It has also checked the introduction of the wines of France, many of which are both better and cheaper; it has led to the importation of a large quantity of mixed liquors, under the name of Port wine, from other places than Oporto, especially from the island of Guernsey, and, what is

still worse, it has encouraged, in this country, the manufacture of various dele-terious compounds, of which the juice of the grape forms no part.[18]

Unlike his contemporaries, who were concerned about declining levels of port consumption, Henderson was worried about the very fact of port consumption. He showed that the "taste of the English [his term] in wine has varied consid-erably during the last two centuries," and claimed, with more optimism than evidence, that since the "peace of 1814, the renewal of our intercourse with the continent has tended to revive the taste for light wines, and to lessen materially the consumption of the growths of Portugal and Spain."[19] More heretical still, at a time when Britain was flush with military victory and enjoyed unparalleled esteem worldwide, Henderson drew an explicit connection between the taste for wine and British civilization. Indeed, Henderson's entire purpose in exploring the wines of the ancients was to show that the greatest civilizations of all in his mind, Greece and Rome, had no knowledge of fortified wines. The implicit connection was that unfortified wines were the mark of a civilized society, while fortified wines were the mark of a society that had some ways to go before achieving civi-lization. The British, therefore, should reject their favorite wine, port, which was a mediocre wine created by bad commercial policy, and spawned even more dele-terious imitations. Moreover, port's strength promoted drunkenness, a propensity for which, said Henderson, was "most prevalent among barbarous nations."[20] And while Henderson acknowledged that drunkenness from wine in Britain was wan-ing, it is clear that among the "barbarous nations" he included his own.

Henderson's book was beautifully printed and illustrated in a large, quarto vol-ume, and was never reprinted; production numbers are uncertain, but it probably reached a limited audience.[21] Nevertheless, the gauntlet had been thrown down, and Henderson's challenge would soon be supported by others. Moreover, the free-trade argument against both British fiscal policy and the restrictions of the Douro Company continued among policymakers and wine merchants despite the 1825 tariff reductions. In fact, to the growing number of British free-traders, import taxes on wine were still far too high, but, even more importantly, the Douro Company was blamed for maintaining artificially high prices on port.

Thus, in part to punish the Portuguese for maintaining the Douro Company's control over port production, the Whig Chancellor of the Exchequer, John Spencer (Viscount Althorp and later 3rd Earl Spencer), responded in 1831 with a slight increase in the duty on Portuguese, Spanish, and Rhenish wines, and a decrease in the duty on French wines, thereby equalizing the duty on *all* European wines at 5s. 6d. per imperial gallon, or just under £58 per tun. South African wines paid only half as much. After 127 years the Methuen Commercial Treaty was abrogated in a single stroke by a Whig Chancellor of the Exchequer, and, unlike in 1713, when abrogation was considered within the broader framework of the Treaty of Utrecht, this time around there were no major objections in Britain. In fact, the overwhelming response to the end of the Methuen Treaty in Britain was silence, and, therefore, "good riddance." Meanwhile, the Portuguese government could not protest the unilateral termination of the Methuen Treaty because Portugal had no settled government! Instead, Portugal was mired in a civil war and the British government was actively supporting the liberal faction under King Pedro IV, whose power base—perhaps not surprisingly—was in the city of Oporto.

The Whigs, having fully reversed their views on economic protectionism since the early eighteenth century, had once again carried the day regarding a grand decision about the British wine trade. Yet the debate over British taste for wine was not over. In fact, one result of the end of the Methuen Treaty was that Henderson's cultural critique of port began to gather steam, and was soon picked up by Cyrus Redding, a journalist from Cornwall. Redding's destiny as the first great wine writer in the English language and the leading voice in the great nineteenth-century wine debate was hardly preordained. He was born a Baptist, and by the time he became interested in wine many Baptists on both sides of the Atlantic were arguing that the wine in the Bible that made Noah drunk, that Jesus served to his disciples, and that is mentioned on dozens of occasions in the Old and New Testaments, was actually unfermented grape juice.[22] Nevertheless, serendipity overcame what may have been Redding's early prejudices, because in 1814 he was sent to Paris as correspondent for *The Examiner*, and remained there as editor of *Galignani's Messenger* until 1819. It was during his Paris years that Redding became interested in wine, and he travelled extensively in vineyards throughout Europe.[23] By the time he returned to Britain he was a passionate oenophile but a despiser of spirits. In that regard, his Baptist upbringing may have abided in him after all.

It is not certain when Redding began working on his encyclopedic study entitled *A History and Description of Modern Wines*, but there can be little doubt that he hoped for an immediate change in British taste for wine after the demise of the Methuen Treaty in 1831. When that did not happen, Redding unloaded his disappointment in his book. Ironically, Redding prefaced his study with a jab at Henderson for being too kind to his audience, saying: "It would never be thought that before 1581 the English were known for their sobriety." This was a possibility that Henderson had kindly offered his readers on the grounds that prior to the 1580s the English did not drink distilled alcohol. But Redding would have none of it, insisting that the English had always enjoyed getting drunk; however, he drew a critical distinction between drunkenness from wine and drunkenness from spirits. "There are few individuals comparatively, among the intemperate," said Redding, "who can lay the charge upon wine, in this country, if the pure juice of the grape be understood by that term. It is the produce of the still, mingled with wine, that operates the mischief."[24] It was clear what wine Redding had in mind, Britain's favorite, port. The national preference for port was, of course, precisely what Henderson had criticized; but, where the Scottish doctor was diplomatic, the English journalist was direct. And nothing made Redding angrier than port.

Like Henderson, Redding ranked French wines the best in the world, followed by Spanish wines. However, Redding could not discuss either of these nations' wines without insulting the wines of Portugal and their affluent, Northern European consumers: the British.[25] French wines, asserted Redding, "do not, like the wines of Portugal (which indeed, is not the fault of the growths, but of greedy traders), by being too strongly impregnated with brandy, carry disease into the stomach at the moment of social joy."[26] Similarly, the wines of Spain "deservedly rank high in the estimation of foreigners," although "this commendation is not to be drawn from the value in which the Spanish wines are held generally in England. It would be unjust to form an opinion of the wines from the taste of a people who think the adulterated and fiery wines of Portugal the best offspring of the grape."[27] These critiques were only the gentle prelude to Redding's discussion of the history and description of Portuguese wines, the opening sentence of which surely stands alone in the history of wine books for its damning allegations, and not so much against the producers of a wine, as against its consumers:

> The history of no country in the world furnishes an example of greater political absurdity than our own, in the conclusion with Portugal of what is commonly called the Methuen Treaty, better characterized as the Methuen, or wine merchants' job. By this treaty Englishmen were compelled to drink the fiery adulterations of an interested wine company, and from the coarseness of their wines, exposed to imitations without end, from materials some of which had never been in Portugal. ... The time the treaty was in full force, without any attempt to qualify or annul it, almost affords grounds for the belief, that Englishmen formerly never scrutinized beyond the surface of things. It is consolatory that this treaty is now gone to the tomb of the Capulets.[28]

Redding explained that Englishmen were "compelled" to drink such a pernicious and frequently adulterated beverage because of the prohibitively high duty laid upon French wines and the relative cheapness of Portuguese wines throughout the eighteenth century. From this he said: "It is evident ... that our taste for port wine was forced upon us by our rulers, out of jealously towards France. There is no necessity to search for any other reason why Port wine is now so generally drank in England."[29] This was the point in the argument where Henderson had asked his audience to connect the dots between the taste for fortified wines and the need for Britain to become more civilized, but Redding had no intention to be gentle with his readers. "No wine," proclaimed Redding as he contemplated Europe's wealthiest and most powerful imperial state, "is worthy to be drank in a highly civilized community which is not made of grapes alone, carefully selected from vines upon which practised labor has bestowed the proper culture, and that is not carried through the operations of the vintage and into the cellar with the most watchful attention."[30] By this definition, according to Redding, most port did not measure up. And this, said Redding, should be hugely embarrassing to every true Briton: "In the richest country in the world, it is mortifying to discover that every inn or tavern, where enormous prices are demanded for a bottle of wine, nothing is met with still, from Land's End to Caithness, but a coarse brandied product of the Oporto company, which in any other region but this would be flung into the still" (Figure 12.1).[31]

Redding's critique was imbued with free-trade arguments, but mostly it was a cultural critique meant to impress middle-class moralists who believed that the British middle classes lacked the civility and the civilizational achievements of

[Genuine Wine Manufactory.]

Figure 12.1 Frontispiece to chapter on "Adulteration," Cyrus Redding, *A History and Description of Modern Wines* (1833)
Note: Redding unfairly lumped all port together because most of it was fortified.

their erstwhile enemies across the Channel. *A History and Description of Modern Wines* sold well despite the fact that its central message was unflattering to its target audience, the port-drinking British middle classes. In fact, a substantially expanded second edition was published in 1836, and a lightly revised third edition followed in 1851. Insulted though they may have been, Redding's middle-class readers were receptive to the idea of being "improved," and they could console themselves with the knowledge that they were drinking less port than their forebears had done, and a good deal more "feminine" sherry. For Redding, however, this was not sufficient because sherry was also fortified, and in 1839 he published a book entitled *Every Man his own Butler*, whose title was a direct appeal to middle-class consumers. This book was intended to instruct members of the middle classes on what wines to purchase—mostly light, French wines, very little sherry and even less port—and how to store and serve wines, a task that the wealthy could assign to a butler. Significantly, even in this context Redding found room to repeat the crux of his earlier argument: "Port is the Englishman's wine, forced upon him by a minimum of duty, drank until became a habit and perpetuated exclusively, because, with honest John, habits, bad or good, always grow to become prejudices."[32]

While it can hardly be proven, it seems probable that the popularity of Redding's books contributed to port's relative decline on the British market. But of course, the major beneficiary of port's slumping sales was not light French wine, but sherry, which was often similar in alcohol content to port. Therefore, to reformers of Redding's mind who saw all fortified wines as a sign of debased civilization, sherry consumption was not a sign of improvement. But this argument hardly resonated with Redding's audience; sherry imports continued to rise throughout the 1830s, and during the 1840s sherry and port together reigned supreme on the British market. Clearly, then, Redding's work did not have an immediate impact.

Nevertheless, Redding's attack and the decline of port imports in the early 1840s did not go unnoticed by producers in Portugal. In 1842, the Portuguese government of Queen Maria II proposed a new version of the Methuen Treaty as part of a broader Anglo-Portuguese Treaty, in an attempt to increase port wine exports. However, this treaty was rejected by the British government.[33] More controversially, some prominent British port producers acknowledged that critics like Redding had a point: dubious production methods were being used. In a pamphlet written in 1844, the Yorkshire-born port producer and exporter Joseph James Forrester charged his fellow port shippers with adulterating their wines with sugar, elderberry juice, and *jeropiga*, a sweet syrup made from boiling down very young wines. Forrester also assailed his fellow producers for over-fortifying their wines, saying that port should be pure whenever possible, and only fortified when it was necessary to slow overly rapid fermentation or stabilize the wine.[34] Of course, Forrester offered his arguments and suggestions hoping that they would reverse the decline in British demand for port. However, the immediate result of his efforts was to incur the wrath of fellow producers. And while Forrester clearly lost the argument about whether port should be a fortified or unfortified wine, in responding to the criticisms of Redding and others he may have helped to improve the quality of port wine by calling for more stringent production practices.[35]

The wine debate heats up

Whatever the effects of Forrester's intervention, the wine debate in Britain continued because Redding and his followers stood four square against fortified wines, even well-made ones. These critics of British taste and civilization received a fillip in the late 1840s when free-trade proponents, formerly occupied in a successful struggle to repeal the Corn Laws (which had protected British wheat against foreign competition), turned their attention to wine, whose taxation they argued was still far too high. As a result, the small band of cultural critics led by Redding was now joined by an army of *laissez-faire* reformers. In this new alliance fortified wines were not only uncivilized, but also emblematic of a desperately misguided mercantilist fiscal policy that needed to be completely overturned. The absolute truth for eighteenth-century Whigs was replaced by the absolute truth for nineteenth-century Whigs—soon to be known as Liberals—who argued that a duty reduction on all wines would lead to greater competition among wine producers, the production of better-quality wines, a change in British taste to lighter wines, and ultimately, the improved health and morality of the British people. In short, the reform case was not only a cultural, medicinal, and economic argument, it was also a moral argument. The invisible hand of the marketplace was God's hand, declared the free-traders, and as such it would work its beneficent magic on all who followed the gospel of unfettered markets.

The alleged morality of wine duty reductions quickly emerged as the central plank in the reformist argument, and can be seen in a variety of written materials published in the late 1840s and early 1850s. For example, an anonymously published pamphlet from 1849, entitled *Eighteen Reasons why the Duty on Wine Should now be Very Largely Reduced, and Assumed Objections Answered why it should not*, invoked the Biblical command to drink wine, the improvement of personal health, and a massive increase in government revenue that would allow for a reduction in tax upon malt and hops, and hence, cheaper beer for the working man. To show that all this would happen if the duty were reduced, the author pointed to the increase in trade after Pitt's tariff reductions in 1786. And to those who said that the British would not drink light wines because of the cold and damp climate, the author pointed out that in Holland, northern Germany, Denmark, Sweden, Norway, and Russia, where the climate is "worse than our own ... light wines are the rule, and spirituous wines the exception."[36]

Similarly, in 1851 Thomas George Shaw argued in three letters to *The Times* and then in a follow-up pamphlet, that high tariffs since the late seventeenth century had lowered the total revenue, promoted adulteration, limited frequent consumption to the wealthy, restricted wine's use among the middle class and denied it to the poor, who turned instead to insalubrious spirits.[37] Furthermore, Shaw, like Henderson and Redding, argued that the British taste for spirituous wines like port and sherry was a result of past political legislation, and that taste would find its natural course if the wine duty was reduced to one shilling per imperial gallon, or a mere four pence per bottle.

Of course, not everyone agreed with this analysis. An anonymous respondent to Shaw's pamphlet asserted that a reduction in duty to one shilling per imperial gallon would hurt the revenue because there was no direct link between taxation and consumption. Instead, a reduction would only succeed in bringing in thin French wines, which were not suited to British working-class taste, which was for beer and spirits. In other words, the current tariff system had the benefit of promoting the importation of the best-quality wines for those who could afford them, while those who could not afford them did not want them anyway. Finally, addressing the issue of past politics, the anonymous author said that port "has had the lead from the appreciation by the public of its fine and wholesome qualities, not from any treaties with foreign countries, and no wine has hitherto been discovered which will take the place of the produce of the favored wine district of the Alto Douro."[38]

***

By 1851, then, the terms of the wine debate were set, and the central questions regarding inherent or politically constructed taste and the merits or demerits of fortified wine were clear. If the anti-reform argument was correct, then a duty reduction would discredit the wine trade by forcing unwanted wines upon consumers, decrease the revenue, and hurt the poor, who would turn to spirits more than ever before because the tax on beer would have to remain high to offset the loss from wine revenue. However, if the reform argument was correct, than a duty reduction would increase the consumption of light wines, increase the revenue, and all the benefits to the wine trade, the revenue, and the nation's health and morals would flow forth. The latter argument was of course what Redding had been arguing all along, and in 1851 he published the third edition of his *History and Description of Modern Wines*. This edition was more strident than ever, proclaiming: "Legislation alone caused the change in our relations with France, and the rejection of her delicate for coarser wines."[39] Redding and other reformers spoke loudly enough to have the new, Conservative government of Lord Derby pay attention to the wine duty debate when they came to power in February 1852. However, Chancellor of the Exchequer Benjamin Disraeli decided that the best method to avoid making any quick change was to feign interest; he appointed a committee under Thomas Chisholm Anstey to investigate the question.[40]

Hearings before the committee were held in London in May and June 1852, and the results proved disappointing to all sides. Among witnesses called to testify, most of whom were wine merchants, it was agreed that taste for wine in Britain among the majority of consumers, that is, the middle classes, was primarily for sherry, port, and to a much lesser degree marsala, the fortified wine from Sicily made popular during the Napoleonic Wars. But there was no consensus regarding whether this taste for fortified wines would change upon the introduction of inexpensive light, French wines to the British market. Conservative wine merchants like W. C. Carbonell believed that middle-class taste was fixed on fortified wines, and would not switch to lighter wines even if their price was diminished, while the working classes would not drink much wine at any price: "a greater delusion than that of believing the lower or middle classes will drink the common wines of Spain, Italy, Portugal, France or Germany, never entered the brain of man," uttered a disgusted Carbonell.[41]

On the other side of the debate George Richardson Porter, former Secretary to the Board of Trade and author of the best-selling *Progress of the Nation*, a statistical account of Britain in the early nineteenth century, asserted to the committee that much would change should the duty on wine be lowered, especially among the lower classes:

> The great mass of the people are not consumers of wine: because the duties are so high, it is placed beyond their reach. There is a large class of people who would gladly consume wine with their families, if it was put within their reach, who at present do not consume it, but have recourse to a very much worse thing to take; namely ardent spirit. I have little hesitation in giving it as my opinion, that to introduce the consumption of wine to the great mass of the people of this country would prove a great moral blessing.[42]

Similarly, when Thomas George Shaw was asked by the committee if "respectable tradesmen, mechanics getting good wages, shopkeepers, and so on," would reject spirits for wines if the price on wines were lowered, he responded:

> I would point to any place where wine is plentiful and cheap, there people do not consume spirits, but drink wine, and as far as we can trace the history of the habits of our ancestors, as described by Shakespeare, Walter Scott and others, we find constant allusion to wine, but never to spirits.[43]

But the situation remained complicated because even pro-duty reduction wine merchants like W. E. Tuke believed that the growing desire for wines among the "better class of artisans" was essentially a desire for port and sherry. Tuke referred to a customer named Barker who had gin palaces in Holborn, and another in Bishopsgate Street. According to Tuke, Barker "has commenced the system of selling a gill glass of Port and Sherry for 4d." The main customers for this wine were "small tradesmen and respectable artisans, men who will not drink ardent spirits, and who find beer too weak and washy for their stomachs; they want a pleasant exhilarating stimulant." If the price of port and sherry were reduced to 2d per glass, Barker predicted that he could sell a pipe of wine a day.[44]

Obviously, none of this testimony settled the issue of whether the working classes would drink more wine if the duty was lowered, and what kind of wine they would drink. In the end, Anstey drafted a report recommending a reduction of duties to one shilling per imperial gallon on all wines, in the belief that there was a massive untapped market for wine in Britain both among the middle classes and the "respectable" working classes. However, Anstey's report was so contested among committee members that it was never forwarded to the House of Commons.[45]

As a result of this anticlimax, some of the angry committee members went public with their opinions. Led by Redding, who was quite comfortable airing his thoughts in public, reform-minded committee members compiled an abstract of the evidence, to which Redding added an introduction that included his well-rehearsed arguments about the barbarity of British taste and the historical way in which it was constructed. Redding also included a copy of the suppressed committee chairman's report, which suggests that Anstey had given his tacit approval.[46]

Likewise, the free-trade proponent William W. Whitmore published a pamphlet in 1853 called simply *The Wine Duties*, in which he considered the subject in terms of free trade, the health, comfort, and morals of the people, and as a matter of general commercial policy. On all counts Whitmore came out for a reduction of the duty to one shilling per imperial gallon. The people, which he defined as the artisans, shopkeepers, and "respectable" members of the laboring classes, were becoming

> more civilized, their tastes more pure. Mechanics' Institutes—lectures on subjects of general literature or science—a love for music, for flowers, for parks, for gardens, for exhibitions, or baths and washhouses, for travelling, all proclaim that an advance in education and refinement is gradually, if not rapidly, taking place.[47]

But civilizing the working classes, for that matter civilizing all British people, was by no means a *fait accompli* for men like Whitmore who associated French wine with civilization. Consequently, a lower duty on wines was imperative. "I believe nothing, after religious instruction and secular education," he wrote, "would have a greater effect in improving the character of the people, than placing within their reach a light and wholesome beverage" such as French wine. Having made that argument, Whitmore felt it necessary to address an issue that had been implicit in many of the anti-reform pamphlets: that French wine and British masculinity were incompatible.

> I have already stated that previous to the Revolution of 1688, French wines were in general use, and Spanish and Portuguese rarely, or at least sparingly imported. This was surely not a period when true English habits did not exist. At no period of our history were the soldiers more brave—the yeomanry more sturdy—the thoroughly British character more developed, than during the first half of the Seventeenth Century; and yet this vigour of body and sturdiness of mind required neither Port, nor Sherry, nor other strong drinks to sustain it.[48]

Whitmore could easily deny the effeminizing effects of French wine at a time when Britain and France, along with the Ottoman Empire, had gone to war in the Crimea to halt Russian encroachment in the Balkan Peninsula. In this context, an argument about the alleged effeminacy of French wines was difficult to make, especially since the French army was having more luck than the British army in ousting the Russians from Sevastopol. But the old arguments about inherent British taste for strong wines stood firm. In 1855, Sir James Emerson Tennent, Secretary to the Board of Trade, MP for Belfast, and member of the Wine Duty Committee, denied that British, or Irish taste for that matter, had ever favored light wines. In a book that explicitly responded to Whitmore, Tennent asserted that

> without determining whether the preference be spontaneous or produced artificially by political or fiscal adjustments, it is sufficient for the purposes of the

present inquiry to advert to the uncontested fact, that from a very early period the people of these countries [i.e. Great Britain and Ireland] have *rejected light wines,* and drunk only those which, along with high flavour, combined a large proportion of *body and spirit.*[49]

This, of course, was false; however, what Tennent pointed out that was true, was that Pitt's tariff reductions did not cause a substantial growth in French wine imports in the few years that they were in operation. Likewise, the 1831 tariff equalization had a similarly insignificant effect.[50] From this, Tennent concluded that the "public taste in England has been, from a very remote time, in favour of strong and spirituous wines," and as such, it is unlikely to be changed.[51] If one took a very short view of what constitutes "remote times," Tennent had a point.

W. Bosville James, however, had no desire to let Tennent's weak historical assertions stand unchallenged. A wine merchant with 24 years' experience, James had testified to the Wine Duties committee, and he responded directly to Tennant with a book of his own.[52] He dismissed Tennent's historical argument as false, and then offered a liberal economic justification for duty reductions. The best course for the government, wrote James, "would be, by judicious and moderate duties, to encourage the freer use [of wine], and obtain a larger revenue from the consumption of the many than from the excessive indulgence of the few."[53] In particular, James had in mind the middle classes, who he believed would begin to drink wine with the same frequency of the aristocracy, should the duty be lowered. James asserted that if the "upper-classes" constituted the only wine drinkers in Britain, then there would be no need to lower the wine duties, because they could afford to buy the wines anyway, and because the high cost of wine encouraged them to be relatively thrifty in their consumption habits. However, he argued,

there are other classes, worthy of a like consideration—classes creating wealth, and by their industry, intelligence, education, and refinement, linked to the aristocracy, rising to equal importance, and far exceeding that class in numbers, intelligence, and influence. Those classes will not long be excluded from the use of wine, because legislation of high duties, grossly violating free trade principles, declare it a luxury.[54]

James's argument amounted to a mild threat: the respectable middle classes demand to have light French wines and, therefore, the wine duty might as well be lowered now, because the sooner it was done, the sooner the revenue from wine would begin to flow. But James was hardly content to let his argument rest on economic grounds alone; as a good Victorian liberal he also had a moral case to make. Wine, said James,

increases enjoyment, cements domestic habits, and precludes the injurious resort to the use of ardent drink. While it has these advantages, its use refines the taste and elevates the social feelings in the same degree as dram drinking degrades them.[55]

Yet none of these assertions or counter-assertions ended the debate. When Benjamin Oliveira, MP, put a motion before the House of Commons to consider a reduction in duty on July 15, 1856, it was quickly dismissed.[56] With the expensive war in Crimea having ended only months before, a majority of the House of Commons believed that a reduction in the wine duty was imprudent, as even proponents of the idea acknowledged that it would take some years before the lower rate provided greater returns through dramatically increased consumption.

However, when the second Palmerston administration came to power in July 1859, it was on surer financial footing and had ambitious plans for restructuring the nation's taxes. This new government was a coalition of Whigs, Peelites, and radicals, who could all agree on the idea of greater economic liberalism, hence the name of the new political bloc: the Liberal Party. The Liberal Chancellor of the Exchequer was William Gladstone, and he immediately cast his eye on wine duties as part of a potentially sweeping free-trade treaty with Britain's new ally, France.

Gladstone, whose own preference was for a bottle of champagne each evening, immediately embraced the commercial, moral, and political dimensions of the reformist argument and constructed his policy accordingly.[57] First, he made a wine duty reduction central to the terms of the 1860 commercial treaty with France (the Cobden–Chevalier Treaty). Second, he set about selling the idea of a wine duty reduction to Parliament. Speaking to the House of Commons on February 10, 1860, Gladstone proposed setting the duty on all wines to three shillings per imperial gallon, and on spirits to 8s. 2d. per imperial gallon. Further reductions on wine would follow in 1861, he said, once the delineation between wine and spirits was settled upon by merchants, importers, and Customs officials. Once these measures were in place, Gladstone believed that government coffers would begin to fill because the new duties would help the sale of wine at all prices, and therefore, to all classes.

Between common and coarse wine and the fine wines, [said Gladstone] there are ten thousand intermediate shades, and there is an immense capacity for producing wines fitted for the English market and for the taste of the middle and lower middle classes in the country, which capacity is at present entirely stifled by the operation of the wine duty.

But Gladstone's argument, like that of so many participants in the wine debate, was not only based on a specific conception of political economy, it was also based on an interpretation of history:

Of late years, a notion has gone abroad, that there is something fixed and unchanging in an Englishman's taste with respect to wine. You find a great number of people in this country who believe, almost like an article of Christian faith, that an Englishman is not born to drink French wines. Do what you will, they say; argue with him as you will; reduce your duties as you will; endeavour even to pour the French wine down his throat; but still he will reject it. Well, these are, without doubt, most worthy members of the community; but they form their judgment from the narrow circle of their own experience, and they will not condescend for any consideration to look beyond that narrow circle. What they maintain is absolutely the reverse of the truth; for nothing is more certain than the taste of English people at one time, and that, too, a prolonged period, for French wine. In earlier periods of our history, French wine was the great article of consumption here. Taste is not an immutable, but a mutable thing.[58]

Sentimental as Gladstone was, and as he knew his audience to be, he could not avoid finishing with moral arguments for wine duty reductions. First, said Gladstone, the current high duties encouraged fraud and adultery in the wine trade among wine merchants who served the middle classes. And second, there were the issues of health and the poor.

There is a time which comes to all of us, [Gladstone intoned] I mean the time of sickness—when wine becomes a common necessary. What kind of wine is administered to the poor man in this country? We have got a law which makes it impossible for the poor man when he is sick to obtain the comfort and support derived from good wine, unless he is fortunate enough to live in the immediate neighbourhood of some rich and charitable friend.[59]

Lowering the wine duties would, therefore, increase revenue, eradicate dishonest practices, and improve the health of the poor. For Liberals like Gladstone who believed in extending the franchise to all male heads-of-household, wine had the added symbolic appeal of conferring political legitimacy upon those who drank it. Gladstone never directly articulated this argument, perhaps because it was so divisive even among Liberals in 1860. But a man as clever as Gladstone undoubtedly understood that a wine-drinking man, whatever his social status, could hardly be denied a political voice.

Disgusted by Gladstone's logic and no doubt frightened by the prospect of greater democracy, the Conservative MP for North Essex, Charles Du Cane, responded:

For the sake of a speculative theory [i.e. that the working classes would drink wine] ... we are to be asked to supersede our native beverage [i.e. beer] by taking off duties upon wine which was and must for some time continue to be emphatically a luxury of the rich.[60]

This was the standard line of opposition to Gladstone's proposals, and in a wonderfully ironic historical moment, the Conservative Party was supported by both beer brewers *and* teetotalers in an attempt to kill Gladstone's budget.[61]

Nevertheless, Gladstone had spoken to a mostly Liberal House of Commons, which was duly persuaded by his arguments. The result was that Parliament passed Act 23 Victoria, c. 22, on February 29, 1860, which immediately lowered the duty on all wines to three shillings per imperial gallon. Furthermore, on

January 1, 1861, the new scale according to strength took effect, just as Gladstone had proposed. Thus, beginning in 1861, all wine imported in bottles, regardless of strength, was taxed at two shillings per imperial gallon. However, the vast majority of wine imported into Britain still arrived in casks, and of this wine, anything over 13 percent alcohol was also charged two shillings per imperial gallon, while wines between 12.9 and 7.5 percent alcohol were taxed at 1s. 6d., and all wines below 7.5 percent alcohol at one shilling. At the other end of the spectrum, any wine above 20 percent alcohol (which included some ports and sherries) was to be taxed as brandy, at 8s. 2d. per imperial gallon.

In July of 1861, duty on brandy was raised to 10s. 5d. per imperial gallon, but by 1862, the entire scale of duties on imported wines and brandies was deemed impractical because it required Customs officers to spend so much time gauging alcohol content. Consequently, in 1862, the wine duties were "simplified" at one shilling per imperial gallon on all wines below 13 percent alcohol, and 2s. 6d. all on wines between 13 percent and 20.9 percent alcohol, as well as all wines in bottle. Wines between 21 percent and 22.5 percent paid 2s. 9d. per imperial gallon, and anything above 22.5 percent was charged as brandy. In other words, nothing was really simplified at all; instead, the Customs Office and wine merchants had to tinker with the alcohol cut-off points in order to accommodate the alcohol contents of different wines. Almost all French wine was less than 13 percent alcohol, and most ports and sherries were around 20 percent alcohol, although some were a few degrees stronger. But clearly, unfortified wines received a preferential rate.

Finally, along with lowering the duties in order to democratize the taste for wine, Gladstone sought to democratize the distribution of wines. Beginning in 1860, the Refreshment Houses Act made all restaurants and "eating houses" eligible to purchase an annually renewable license to sell wine on premises. Gladstone hoped to link wine-drinking with eating among all classes of society, and France of course was the model. Then in 1861, the Single Bottle Act enabled shopkeepers to purchase an annually renewable license to sell wine for consumption off premises, which was referred to as an "off-license." These acts, said Gladstone, were intended "first, to open some new and cleaner channels for consumption, secondly, not to create a new monopoly."[62] "Gladstone's Claret," as inexpensive red Bordeaux wine was soon called, was now available in grocery stores and corner shops.

Conclusion: Old wine, new bottles?

Clearly, the legislation of 1860–2 was different from past legislation in that it explicitly rejected the mercantilist fiscal policies that had held sway since the late seventeenth century. Moreover, the new legislation was meant to undo two centuries of fiscal prejudice against French wines in particular. Where English Whigs once successfully argued that large-scale French wine consumption was against the national interest because it would hurt the economy and because France posed an existential threat, British Liberals now successfully argued that socially broad-based consumption of French wine would benefit government revenue and make the British people healthier. In a similar attempt to undo history, the new legislation was explicitly meant to make wine, and especially French wine, available to all but the indigent. The taste for inexpensive claret, it was hoped, would elevate the behavior of the beer and spirit-drinking working classes, and bring an even greater degree of civilization to the port- and sherry-drinking middle classes. Wine consumption would no longer draw a symbolic line between the upper, middle, and lower classes; instead, all respectable Britons would be united in French wine.

But in some ways the new wine legislation was similar to that which it tried to undo. Most obviously, the legislation that was passed both reflected and constructed political power; lower, but still graduated tariff levels were enacted in the name of free trade, sobriety, and improved morality, all of which were touchstones of British middle-class identity. This is not to say that the British bourgeoisie had overthrown the landed elite, far from it. Certainly middle-class values had conquered much of the elite by 1860, but these groups now shared political power. On a political level this new dynamic was exemplified on the one hand by Gladstone, who claimed always to belong to the "middle class," and on the other hand by the prime minister whom he served as chancellor of the exchequer when the momentous wine legislation was passed.[63] That man, one of many aristocrats who still stood atop the commanding heights of political power in Britain, was Henry John Temple, 3rd Viscount Palmerston, Knight of the Garter (KG) and Knight Grand Cross of the Order of the Bath (GCB).

The mid-nineteenth-century ruling elite was yet another hybrid of new and old money, commercial and landed wealth, and middle- and upper-class men. It needed a wine to represent its legitimacy and its values, and French wine was the perfect fit. It was a temperate form of alcohol, a product of free(er) trade, and because of its past affiliation, it had a noble pedigree. It represented the prosperity, good health, and morality, of the ruling classes. To the optimists, French wine even promised to bring these same qualities to working-class families, thereby justifying the participation of working-class men in the political process. Consequently, the time was ripe once again for French wine, claret in particular, to be the taste of power. This is not to suggest that anyone imagined the elite, the middle classes, and the working classes would all drink the same type of claret and be equally political powerful; but drinking claret or another light French wine would allow all men, regardless of class, to represent themselves as socially respectable and politically legitimate.

***

Only one year into the changed fiscal regime, Gladstone was able to celebrate a smaller loss of revenue from wine than anticipated thanks to a much larger increase in wine imports than expected: imports for the 1860–1 fiscal year were up 36 percent from the previous year, and by far the greatest percentage increase came from French wines.[64] Between calendar year 1860 and 1861, French wine retained for home consumption in the United Kingdom jumped by 98 percent.[65]

It mattered little to Gladstone that the import figures for Spanish wines increased most in absolute terms, and that sherry and port still dominated the British market. Clearly, the Great Nineteenth-Century Wine Debate was over, and with it the nefarious effects of so much ill-considered legislation and fortified wine. The desired change, so it seemed, was clearly underway.

Alas, for Gladstone and his fellow reformers, a free market in wine did not lead to a dramatic change in British taste. Moreover, the free market of the economic liberals was not (and never would be) free. Instead, the legislation of 1860–2 reversed eighteenth-century fiscal policy by favoring light wines—which meant mostly French wines—over the heavier wines of Portugal and Spain. In essence, the fiscal policies of the British government had returned to the fiscal policies of the English and Scottish governments of the mid-seventeenth century: French wine held a privileged position, while sweet wines from Southern Europe paid more. This situation was too much for those who had grown up on fortified wines and the thick gruel of Francophobia. A letter to the *Bristol Times*, from "Anti-Acid," published on August 3, 1861, declared that the mania for cheap claret would be the undoing of British masculinity:

> I am for old fashions in drink as in everything else, and I do believe when the British middle class man and squire give up their Port and Sherry for those "bodiless creations" coming in under Cobden's treaty, and the workman takes another newfangled folly called "Bitter Beer," instead of his Burton [i.e. strong ale], there will be an end of national manhood. ... I am no Sybarite, asking for fine or expensive wines; but I don't want to see brave Britishers Frenchified out of all their bone, muscle, and good temper by this "flimsy fermentation."[66]

Crotchety conservatives like "Anti-Acid" need not have been so worried; British taste did not suddenly return to where it was during the Restoration, and tumescent British manhood, such as it was, was not shriveled by French claret. To be sure, French wine imports into Britain surpassed those of Portugal in 1866, and those of Spain in 1876,[67] but port and sherry together continued to account for over half of all British wine imports into the early twentieth century.[68] In fact, by 1913 port was once again the most popular wine in Britain. One might speculate that with war on the horizon, manly port was once again the wine of choice. More certain is the fact that the lingering taste for port and sherry meant that politically constructed though it was, the taste for wine was not therefore artificial, as Redding, Gladstone, and others had argued; rather, it was as real and as much a part of British culture—of history—as the politics that helped to create it.

Appendix: Wine Duties

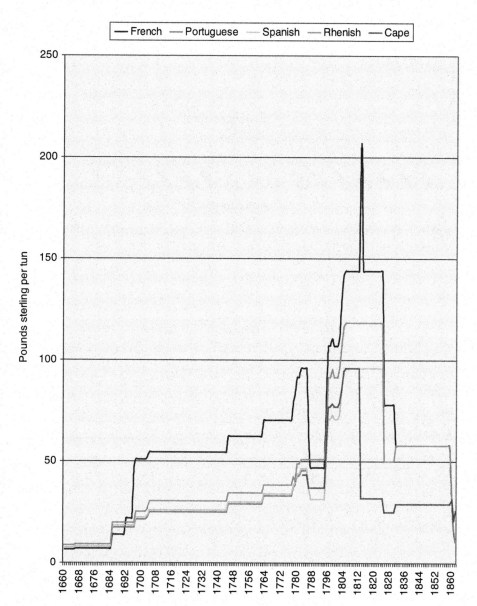

Graph A.1 Duties on wine in England (from 1660), Great Britain (from 1707), and the United Kingdom (from 1814) until 1862

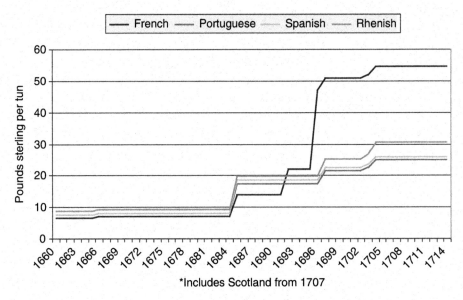

Graph A.2 Duties on wine in England, 1660–1714 (includes Scotland from 1707)

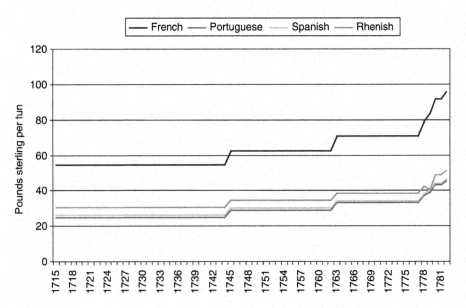

Graph A.3 Duties on wine in Great Britain, 1715–82

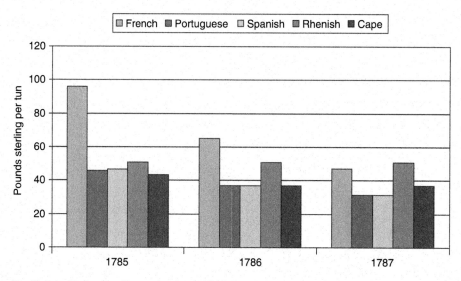

Graph A.4   Pitt's wine duty reductions, 1785–7

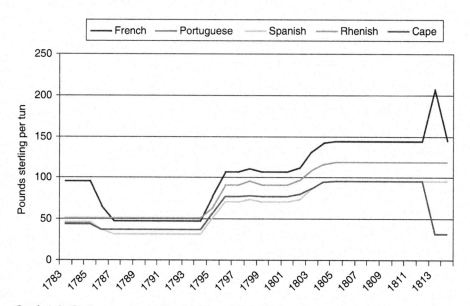

Graph A.5   Duties on wine in Great Britain, 1784–1814

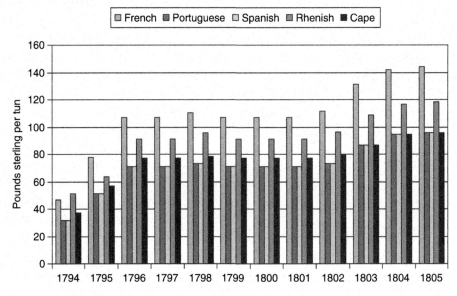

Graph A.6   The effects of war on wine duties, 1794–1805

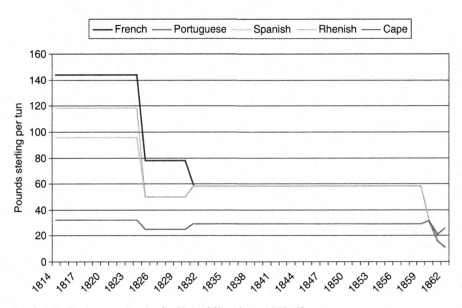

Graph A.7   Duties on wine in the United Kingdom, 1815–62

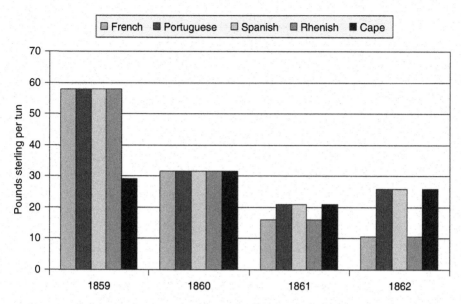

Graph A.8 Gladstone's changes to the wine duties, 1859–62

Table A.1 Wine duties in England (from 1660), Great Britain (from 1707), and the United Kingdom from (1814) until 1862

	French	Portuguese	Spanish	Rhenish	Cape
1660	6.5	7.5	7.5	8.75	
1661	6.5	7.5	7.5	8.75	
1662	6.5	7.5	7.5	8.75	
1663	6.5	7.5	7.5	8.75	
1664	6.5	7.5	7.5	8.75	
1665	6.5	7.5	7.5	8.75	
1666	7	8	8	9.25	
1667	7	8	8	9.25	
1668	7	8	8	9.25	
1669	7	8	8	9.25	
1670	7	8	8	9.25	
1671	7	8	8	9.25	
1672	7	8	8	9.25	
1673	7	8	8	9.25	
1674	7	8	8	9.25	
1675	7	8	8	9.25	
1676	7	8	8	9.25	
1677	7	8	8	9.25	
1678	7	8	8	9.25	
1679	7	8	8	9.25	
1680	7	8	8	9.25	
1681	7	8	8	9.25	

(continued)

Table A.1   Continued

	French	Portuguese	Spanish	Rhenish	Cape
1682	7	8	8	9.25	
1683	7	8	8	9.25	
1684	7	8	8	9.25	
1685	14	17.5	18.5	19.75	
1686	14	17.5	18.5	19.75	
1687	14	17.5	18.5	19.75	
1688	14	17.5	18.5	19.75	
1689	14	17.5	18.5	19.75	
1690	14	17.5	18.5	19.75	
1691	14	17.5	18.5	19.75	
1692	22	17.5	18.5	19.75	
1693	22	17.5	18.5	19.75	
1694	22	17.5	18.5	19.75	
1695	22	17.5	18.5	19.75	
1696	47	17.5	18.5	19.75	
1697	51	21.5	22.5	25.25	
1698	51	21.5	22.5	25.25	
1699	51	21.5	22.5	25.25	
1700	51	21.5	22.5	25.25	
1701	51	21.5	22.5	25.25	
1702	51	21.5	22.5	25.25	
1703	52	22.5	23.5	27	
1704	54.5	25	26	30.5	
1705	54.5	25	26	30.5	
1706	54.5	25	26	30.5	
1707	54.5	25	26	30.5	
1708	54.5	25	26	30.5	
1709	54.5	25	26	30.5	
1710	54.5	25	26	30.5	
1711	54.5	25	26	30.5	
1712	54.5	25	26	30.5	
1713	54.5	25	26	30.5	
1714	54.5	25	26	30.5	
1715	54.5	25	26	30.5	
1716	54.5	25	26	30.5	
1717	54.5	25	26	30.5	
1718	54.5	25	26	30.5	
1719	54.5	25	26	30.5	
1720	54.5	25	26	30.5	
1721	54.5	25	26	30.5	
1722	54.5	25	26	30.5	
1723	54.5	25	26	30.5	
1724	54.5	25	26	30.5	
1725	54.5	25	26	30.5	
1726	54.5	25	26	30.5	
1727	54.5	25	26	30.5	
1728	54.5	25	26	30.5	

(*continued*)

Table A.1   Continued

	French	Portuguese	Spanish	Rhenish	Cape
1729	54.5	25	26	30.5	
1730	54.5	25	26	30.5	
1731	54.5	25	26	30.5	
1732	54.5	25	26	30.5	
1733	54.5	25	26	30.5	
1734	54.5	25	26	30.5	
1735	54.5	25	26	30.5	
1736	54.5	25	26	30.5	
1737	54.5	25	26	30.5	
1738	54.5	25	26	30.5	
1739	54.5	25	26	30.5	
1740	54.5	25	26	30.5	
1741	54.5	25	26	30.5	
1742	54.5	25	26	30.5	
1743	54.5	25	26	30.5	
1744	54.5	25	26	30.5	
1745	62.5	29	30	34.5	
1746	62.5	29	30	34.5	
1747	62.5	29	30	34.5	
1748	62.5	29	30	34.5	
1749	62.5	29	30	34.5	
1750	62.5	29	30	34.5	
1751	62.5	29	30	34.5	
1752	62.5	29	30	34.5	
1753	62.5	29	30	34.5	
1754	62.5	29	30	34.5	
1755	62.5	29	30	34.5	
1756	62.5	29	30	34.5	
1757	62.5	29	30	34.5	
1758	62.5	29	30	34.5	
1759	62.5	29	30	34.5	
1760	62.5	29	30	34.5	
1761	62.5	29	30	34.5	
1762	62.5	29	30	34.5	
1763	70.5	33	34	38.5	
1764	70.5	33	34	38.5	
1765	70.5	33	34	38.5	
1766	70.5	33	34	38.5	
1767	70.5	33	34	38.5	
1768	70.5	33	34	38.5	
1769	70.5	33	34	38.5	
1770	70.5	33	34	38.5	
1771	70.5	33	34	38.5	
1772	70.5	33	34	38.5	
1773	70.5	33	34	38.5	
1774	70.5	33	34	38.5	
1775	70.5	33	34	38.5	

(*continued*)

Table A.1 Continued

	French	Portuguese	Spanish	Rhenish	Cape
1776	70.5	33	34	38.5	
1777	70.5	33	34	38.5	
1778	79	37	38	42.5	
1779	83.5	39	40	40.5	
1780	91.5	43	44	49	
1781	91.5	43	44	49	
1782	96	45.5	46.5	51	
1783	96	45.5	46.5	51	43.5
1784	96	45.5	46.5	51	43.5
1785	96	45.5	46.5	51	43.5
1786	65	37	37	51	37
1787	47	31.5	31.5	51	37
1788	47	31.5	31.5	51	37
1789	47	31.5	31.5	51	37
1790	47	31.5	31.5	51	37
1791	47	31.5	31.5	51	37
1792	47	31.5	31.5	51	37
1793	47	31.5	31.5	51	37
1794	47	31.5	31.5	51	37
1795	77.5	51	51	63.5	57
1796	107	71	71	91.5	77
1797	107	71	71	91.5	77
1798	110.5	73	73	95.5	78.5
1799	107	71	71	91.5	77
1800	107	71	71	91.5	77
1801	107	71	71	91.5	77
1802	111.5	73.5	73.5	96.5	79.5
1803	131	86.5	86.5	108.5	86.5
1804	142	94.5	94.5	116.5	94.5
1805	144	96	96	118.5	96
1806	144	96	96	118.5	96
1807	144	96	96	118.5	96
1808	144	96	96	118.5	96
1809	144	96	96	118.5	96
1810	144	96	96	118.5	96
1811	144	96	96	118.5	96
1812	144	96	96	118.5	96
1813	207	96	96	118.5	32
1814	144	96	96	118.5	32
1815	144	96	96	118.5	32
1816	144	96	96	118.5	32
1817	144	96	96	118.5	32
1818	144	96	96	118.5	32
1819	144	96	96	118.5	32
1820	144	96	96	118.5	32
1821	144	96	96	118.5	32
1822	144	96	96	118.5	32

(*continued*)

Table A.1 Continued

	French	Portuguese	Spanish	Rhenish	Cape
1823	144	96	96	118.5	32
1824	144	96	96	118.5	32
1825	78	50	50	50	25
1826	78	50	50	50	25
1827	78	50	50	50	25
1828	78	50	50	50	25
1829	78	50	50	50	25
1830	78	50	50	50	25
1831	58	58	58	58	29
1832	58	58	58	58	29
1833	58	58	58	58	29
1834	58	58	58	58	29
1835	58	58	58	58	29
1836	58	58	58	58	29
1837	58	58	58	58	29
1838	58	58	58	58	29
1839	58	58	58	58	29
1840	58	58	58	58	29
1841	58	58	58	58	29
1842	58	58	58	58	29
1843	58	58	58	58	29
1844	58	58	58	58	29
1845	58	58	58	58	29
1846	58	58	58	58	29
1847	58	58	58	58	29
1848	58	58	58	58	29
1849	58	58	58	58	29
1850	58	58	58	58	29
1851	58	58	58	58	29
1852	58	58	58	58	29
1853	58	58	58	58	29
1854	58	58	58	58	29
1855	58	58	58	58	29
1856	58	58	58	58	29
1857	58	58	58	58	29
1858	58	58	58	58	29
1859	58	58	58	58	29
1860	31.5	31.5	31.5	31.5	31.5
1861	16	21	21	16	21
1862	10.5	26	26	10.5	26

Source: All graphs and charts in the Appendix are derived from Parliamentary Report, C.8706, *Customs Tariffs of the United Kingdom from 1800 to 1897, with some notes upon the history of the more important branches of receipt from the year 1660* (London, 1897), pp. 137–48.

Note: All figures are given in pounds sterling per tun and rounded to the nearest .25 decimal (exact figures in pounds, shillings, and pence can be found in the text).

Notes

Preface

1. In theory, if all of the customs returns for England prior to 1675 still existed, which they do not, one could divide the amount of wine from each entry by the duty paid upon it in order to derive the country of origin, or in most cases since some wines were taxed the same amount, the possible countries of origin.
2. Davenant's report is divided into two accounts, "An Account of Wines Imported annually into the Port of London from the year 1674 to the year 1696, wherein French wines and those of other countries are distinguished," and "An Account shewing the Quantity of Wines imported in to London and the Outports of England, in Sixteen Years and one quarter, from Michaelmas 1696, to Christmas 1712," JHC, XVII, 363–5.
3. NA, E 190/62–154 (various), Port books for London regarding imported wines, 1675–1696.
4. Alexander Henderson, M.D., *The History of Ancient and Modern Wines* (London, 1824), Appendix VIII; and Cyrus Redding, *A History and Description of Modern Wines* (London, 1871 edn), pp. 383–414.
5. Parliamentary Report, C.8706, *Customs Tariffs of the United Kingdom from 1800 to 1897, with some notes upon the history of the more important branches of receipt from the year 1660* (London: Her Majesty's Stationery Office, 1897), pp. 153–7.
6. See, for example, H. E. S. Fisher, *The Portugal Trade: A Study of Anglo-Portuguese Commerce, 1700–1770* (London, 1971); Lorna Weatherill, *Consumer Behaviour and Material Culture in Britain, 1660–1760,* (London, 2nd ed. 1996); Patrick K. O'Brien, "The Political Economy of British Taxation, 1660–1815," *Economic History Review*, 2nd ser., 41 (1988), 1–32.
7. T. C. Smout, *Scottish Trade on the Eve of Union, 1660–1707* (Edinburgh, 1963), p. 285; Bruce Lenman, *An Economic History of Modern Scotland, 1660–1976* (London, 1977), p. 38.
8. NA, Customs 14.
9. For a extended discussion of the problems faced by Customs and Excise officers in measuring gallons and casks, see William J. Ashworth, *Customs and Excise: Trade, Production, and Consumption in England, 1640–1845* (Oxford, 2003), pp. 290–8.

Introduction

1. Jonathan White, "A World of Goods?" The 'Consumption Turn' and Eighteenth-Century British History," *Cultural and Social History*, 3 (2006), 93–104; Grant McCracken, *Culture and Consumption: New Approaches to the Symbolic Character of Consumer Goods and Activities* (Bloomington, 1988).
2. See, for example, Hugh Johnson, *Vintage: The Story of Wine* (New York, 1989), pp. 220–9; A. D. Francis, *The Wine Trade* (London, 1972), pp. 99–142; Barbara Bradford, *The Englishman's Wine: The Story of Port* (London, 1969), pp. 34–45; André L. Simon, *Bottlescrew Days: Wine Drinking in England during the Eighteenth Century* (London, 1926), pp. 54–66 and 144–50.
3. No doubt the most influential reference to the supposed link between party affiliation and personal taste comes from G. M. Trevelyan's immensely popular and often reprinted *English Social History: A Survey of Six Centuries from Chaucer to Queen Victoria*, 4 vols (London, 1944), III, 21. Speaking of the early and mid-eighteenth century, Trevelyan referred to the "endless Whig toasts in port and Tory toasts in French claret and champagne." In fact, the Whig elite also toasted in claret and champagne, and not in port.
4. For evidence of the port–claret divide in the nineteenth and twentieth centuries, see Charles Petrie, "Politics and Wine," *Quarterly Review*, 93 (1953), 445–56. In this article,

Petrie said that in Scotland it was "generally possible to tell a host's politics from the wine he gave his guests after dinner: if he was a Liberal he would provide Port, but if he was a Tory he would produce Claret. That tradition still lingers on, or at any rate did until a very recent date." He offered a similar example for England, saying that at Corpus Christi College, Oxford, a college with a strong Jacobite tradition, "the Claret has always been greatly superior to the Port." Petrie, "Politics and Wine," p. 445.

5. Charles C. Ludington, "'Be sometimes to your country true': The Politics of Wine in England, 1660–1714", in Adam Smyth, ed., *A Pleasing Sinne: Drink and Conviviality in 17th-Century England* (Woodbridge, 2004), pp. 89–106.

6. Billy Kay and Cailean Maclean, *Knee Deep in Claret: A Celebration of Wine and Scotland* (Edinburgh, 1983); James Crichton-Browne, "Claret in Scotland," *National Review*, 80 (1922), 397–407.

7. Charles C. Ludington, "'To the King o'er the Water': Scotland and Claret, c. 1660–1763," in Mack Holt, ed., *Alcohol: A Social and Cultural History* (Oxford, 2006), pp. 163–84.

8. Kay and Maclean, *Knee Deep in Claret*, Chapter 14.

9. William Younger, *Gods, Men and Wine* (Cleveland, OH, 1966), p. 378.

10. Thorstein Veblen, *The Theory of the Leisure Class* (1899; repr. New York, 2001). Neil McKendrick, John Brewer and John Harold Plumb, *The Birth of a Consumer Society: The Commercialization of Eighteenth-Century England* (London, 1982) is broadly in line with the Veblerian view of an emulation-driven economy. For rejections of Veblen's theory in recent British historiography, see Lorna Weatherill, *Consumer Behavior and Material Culture in Britain, 1660–1760* (New York, 1988); Weatherill, "The meanings of consumer behaviour in late seventeenth- and early eighteenth-century England," in John Brewer and Roy Porter, eds, *Consumption and the World of Goods* (London, 1993), 206–227; Ben Fine and Ellen Leopold, "Consumerism and the Industrial Revolution," *Social History*, 15:2 (May, 1990), 151–79; Beverly Lemire, *The Business of Everyday Life* (Manchester, 2005); Maxine Berg, *Luxury and Pleasure in Eighteenth Century Britain* (Oxford, 2005); John Styles and Amanda Vickery, eds, *Gender, Taste, and Material Culture in Britain and North America* (New Haven, 2006); Colin Campbell, *The Romantic Ethic and the Spirit of Modern Consumerism* (Oxford, 1987); Carole Shammas, *The Pre-industrial Consumer in England and America* (Oxford, 1990).

11. Pierre Bourdieu, *Distinction: A Social Critique of the Judgment of Taste*, trans. Richard Nice (Cambridge, MA, 1984).

12. J. A. W. Gunn, *Beyond Liberty and Property: The Process of Self-Recognition in Eighteenth-Century Political Thought* (Kingston, 1983), pp. 260–315; idem, "Public Opinion," in Terence Ball, James Farr, and Russell L. Hanson, eds, *Political Innovation and Conceptual Change* (Cambridge, 1989), pp. 247–65; Kathleen Wilson, *The Sense of the People: Politics, Culture and Imperialism in England, 1715–1785* (Cambridge, 1995).

13. See, most notably, R. H. Tawney, "The Rise of the Gentry, 1558–1640," *Economic History Review*, II (1941), 1–38; Christopher Hill, *The English Revolution of 1640* (London, 1940); idem, *The Century of Revolution, 1603–1714* (London, 1961); E. P. Thompson, *The Making of the English Working Class* (Harmondsworth, 1968); Eric Hobsbawm, *Industry and Empire: From 1750 to the Present Day* (Harmondsworth, 1969); idem, *The Age of Capital, 1848–1975* (London, 1975); Harold Perkin, *The Origins of Modern English Society, 1780–1880* (London, 1969); Asa Briggs, *The Age of Improvement, 1783–1867* (London, 1959).

14. Geoffrey Holmes, *Augustan England: Professions, State and Society, 1680–1730* (London, 1982); John Brewer, *The Pleasures of the Imagination: English Culture in the Eighteenth Century* (London, 1997); Peter Borsay, *The English Urban Renaissance: Culture and Society in the Provincial Town, 1660–1760* (Oxford, 1989); Paul Langford, *A Polite and Commercial People: England, 1727–1783* (Oxford, 1789); idem, *Public Life and the Propertied Englishman, 1689–1798* (Oxford, 1991).

15. J. A. Cannon, *Aristocratic Century: The Peerage in Eighteenth-Century England* (Cambridge, 1984); J. V. Beckett, *The Aristocracy in England, 1660–1914* (Oxford, 1986); J. C. D. Clark, *English Society, 1688–1832: Religion, Ideology, and Politics during the Ancien Régime*

(Cambridge, 1985); Lawrence Stone and Jeanne Fawtier Stone, *An Open Elite? England, 1540–1880* (Oxford, 1984); David Cannadine, *The Decline and Fall of the British Aristocracy* (New Haven, 1990); idem, *Aspects of Aristocracy* (Harmondsworth, 1995).

16. Roy Porter, "Georgian Britain: An Ancien Régime?," *British Journal for Eighteenth-Century Studies*, XV:2 (1992), 141–4.

17. Charles C. Ludington, "Drinking for Approval: Wine and the British Court from George III to Victoria and Albert," in Daniëlle de Vooght, ed., *Royal Taste: Food, Power and Status at the European Courts after 1789* (Farnham, 2011), pp. 57–86; Cannadine, *Aspects of Aristocracy*, pp. 9–36.

18. Wilson, *Sense of the People*, pp. 84–136.

19. The literature here is vast, but for some of the most recent assessments of the middling sorts/ranks/classes, and attempts at definition, see: Jonathan Barry, "Introduction," in Jonathan Barry and Christopher Brooks, eds, *The Middling Sort of People: Culture, Society and Politics in England, 1550–1800* (New York, 1994), pp. 1–27; Margaret Hunt, *The Middling Sort: Commerce, Gender and the Family in England, 1550–1800* (New York, 1994), pp. 15–18; Peter Earle, *The Making of the English Middle Class: Business, Society and Family Life in London, 1660–1730* (Berkeley, 1989), pp. 1–14; Alan Kidd and David Nicholls, "Introduction: History, Culture and the Middle Classes," in Kidd and Nicholls, eds, *Gender, Civic Culture and Consumerism: Middle Class Identity in Britain, 1800–1940* (Manchester, 1990), pp. 1–11; Alan Kidd and David Nicholls, "Introduction: The Making of the British Middle Class?," in Kidd and Nicholls, eds, *The Making of the British Middle Class? Studies of Regional and Cultural Diversity since the Eighteenth Century* (London, 1998), pp. xv–xl.

20. Nicholas Rogers, "The Middling Sort in Eighteenth-Century Politics," in Jonathan Barry and Christopher Brooks, eds, *The Middling Sort of People: Culture, Society and Politics in England, 1550–1800* (New York, 1994), p. 162.

21. This point is made in both Leonore Davidoff and Catherine Hall, *Family Fortunes: Men and Women of the English Middle Class, 1780–1850* (London, 1987); and Anna Clarke, "Manhood, Womanhood, and the Politics of Class in Britain, 1790–1845," in Laura L. Frader and Sonya O. Rose, eds, *Gender and Class in Modern Europe* (Ithaca, 1996), pp. 264–7.

22. Dror Warhman, "'Middle Class' Domesticity Goes Public: Gender, Class, and Politics from Queen Caroline to Queen Victoria," *Journal of British Studies*, 32 (October, 1993), 396–432.

23. Penelope Corfield, "Class by Name and Number in Eighteenth-Century Britain," *History*, 72:234 (February, 1987), 38–61; David Cannadine, *The Rise and Fall of Class in Britain* (New York, 1999), p. 28.

24. Kidd and Nicholls, "Introduction: The Making of the British Middle Class?," pp. xxiii–xxviii.

25. Dror Wahrman, *Imagining the Middle Class: The Political Representation of Class in Britain, c. 1780–1840* (Cambridge, 1995).

26. Cannadine, *Rise and Fall of Class*, pp. 16–35.

27. For this debate on what New Cultural History is or should be, see: Lynn Hunt, ed., *The New Cultural History* (Berkeley, 1989); Victoria Bonnell and Lynn Hunt, eds, *Beyond the Cultural Turn: New Directions in the Study of Society and Culture* (Berkeley, 1999); Ronald Grigor Suny, "Back and Beyond, Reversing the Cultural Turn?," *American Historical Review*, 107:5 (December, 2002), 1476–99; Patrick Brantlinger "A Response to *Beyond the Cultural Turn*," ibid., 1500–12; Richard Handler, "Cultural Theory in History Today," ibid., 1513–20; Peter Mandler, "The Problem with Cultural History," *Cultural and Social History*, 1 (2004), 94–117; William H. Sewell Jr, *Logics of History: Social Theory and Social Transformation* (Chicago, 2005).

28. R. W. Connell, *Masculinities*, 2nd edn (Cambridge, 1995), pp. 76–86.

29. John Tosh, "Hegemonic Masculinity and History of Gender," in Stefan Dudink, Karen Hagemann, and John Tosh, eds, *Masculinities in Politics and War: Gendering Modern History* (Manchester, 2004), pp. 53–4.

1 "A Health to our Distressed King!"

1. Christopher Hibbert, *Charles I: A Life of Religion, War and Treason* (Basingstoke, 2007), pp. 275–80.
2. For the major theoretical work on the theater of politics, see Clifford Geertz, *The Interpretation of Cultures* (New York, 1973) and Geertz, "Centers, Kings and Charisma: Reflections on the Symbolics of Power," in J. Ben-David and T. N. Clark, eds, *Culture and Its Creators: Essays in Honor of E. Shils* (Chicago, 1977), pp. 150–71. For studies of the English and British courts, see Sydney Anglo, *Spectacle, Pageantry and Early Tudor Policy* (Oxford, 1969); Roy Strong, *The Cult of Elizabeth: Elizabethan Portraiture and Pageantry* (London, 1999); Jayne Elisabeth Archer, Elizabeth Goldring, and Sarah Knights, eds, *The Progresses, Pageants and Entertainments of Queen Elizabeth I* (Oxford, 2007); David Cannadine, "The Context, Performance and Meaning of Ritual: The British Monarchy and the 'Invention of Tradition', c. 1820–1977," in Hobsbawm and Ranger, eds, *Invention of Tradition*, pp. 101–64.
3. For a summary of historians reception of Charles I, see Mark Kishlansky, "Charles I: A Case of Mistaken Identity," *Past and Present*, 189:1 (2005), 41–80.
4. The so-called Little Ice Age lasted from roughly A.D. 1300 to A.D. 1850, and witnessed cold winters and undependable summers throughout Northern Europe for much of this period.
5. John Burnett, *Liquid Pleasures: A Social History of Drink in Modern Britain* (London, 1999), p. 142.
6. John Grove, *Wine, Beere, and Ale, together by the Eares* (London, 1629).
7. For wine and Royalist literature, see Marika Trebusek, "Wine for Comfort: Drinking and the Royalist Exile Experience, 1642–1660," in Adam Smyth, ed., *A Pleasing Sinne: Drink and Conviviality in 17th-Century England* (Woodbridge, 2004), pp. 55–68; Lois Potter, *Secret Rites and Secret Writing, Royalist Literature, 1641–1660* (Cambridge, 1989); Earl Miner, *The Cavalier Mode from Jonson to Cotton* (Princeton, 1971). For Royalists songs, see Angela McShane, "The Politicisation of Drink and Drunkenness in Political Broadside Ballads from 1640–1689," in Smyth, ed., *Pleasing Sinne*, pp. 69–87.
8. Brome, "The Royalist" (1646), *Poems*, ed. Roman R. Dubinski, 2 vols. (Toronto, 1982), I, 117–18.
9. "Cavalier" (from *caballero*, or horseman), was meant to slander Royalists by linking them to Spanish, Catholic aristocrats with all the negative connotations of being foreign and tyrannical that such figures entailed. Meanwhile, "Roundhead," like its modern American equivalent "redneck," was a socially charged term used to insult Parliamentarians, based upon an allegedly common feature among English male laborers, in this case a utilitarian, "round" haircut. Both these originally pejorative terms were adopted by those whom they were meant to insult.
10. Brome, "The New Courtier" (written in 1648), *Poems*, I, 129; Trebusek, "Wine for Comfort," p. 58; Malcolm Smuts, *Culture and Power in England, 1588–1688* (New York, 1999), p. 120.
11. "A Royall Health to the Rising Sun" (1649), *Manchester Ballads*, vol. I. (44).
12. McShane, "Politicization of Drink," p. 73.
13. Ibid., p. 74.
14. Richard Flecknoe, "In Small Beer," *Miscellania. Or, Poems of all sorts, with Divers other Pieces* (London, 1653), p. 29. "Small" beer refers to weak beer, as opposed to "strong" beer, so it seems that Flecknoe was trying to allow for the possibility that some beer drinking could be Royalist.
15. Brome, "The Answer," *Poems*, I, 216. Trebusek points out that some poets made an exception for good-quality beer, perhaps because beer was already associated with England. Trebusek, "Wine for Comfort," p. 56, fn. 9.
16. "Canary's Coronation," from Thomas Jordan, *Fancy's Festival, a Masque* (London, 1657). This song was reprinted in *The Loyalist Garland* (London, 1673) and elsewhere.

17. Keith Thomas, *The Ends of Life: Roads to Fulfilment in Early Modern England* (Oxford, 2009), p. 155.
18. The literature on the history and consumption of beer in England is vast, but for a good place to start, see Burnett, *Liquid Pleasures*, pp. 111–40.
19. Anna Bryson, *From Courtesy to Civility: Changing Codes of Conduct in Early Modern England* (Oxford, 1998), pp. 217–18.
20. See Chapter 11 for the emergence of teetotalers.
21. Paul M. Hunneyball, "Cromwellian Style: The Architectural Trappings of the Protectorate regime," in Patrick Little, ed., *The Cromwellian Protectorate* (Woodbridge, 2007), pp. 53–81; Aileen Ribeiro, *Fashion and Fiction: Dress in Art and Literature in Stuart England* (New Haven, 2005); Roy Sherwood, *Oliver Cromwell: King in all but Name* (Stroud, 1997).
22. André L. Simon, *A History of the Wine Trade in England*, 3 vols. (London, 1909), I, 65.
23. Ibid., pp. 66–9.
24. Ibid., pp. 69–73.
25. Ibid., p. 76.
26. "Prisage" was a duty to be paid to the king in wine of one tun of any ship importing between 10 and 20 tuns, and two tuns for any ship importing 20 tuns or more. Prisage was part of the *Antiqua Custuma* (Old Custom), which was acknowledged to be ancient even at the time of Edward I. By the seventeenth century, prisage was usually paid in money, not in kind. Prisage was not abolished until the early nineteenth century; Parliamentary Report, C.8706, *Customs Tariffs of the United Kingdom from 1800 to 1897, with some notes upon the history of the more important branches of receipt from the year 1660* (London, 1897), p. 131.
27. Simon, *A History of the Wine Trade in England*, pp. 76–81.
28. Abraham Cowley, "Anacreontics" (Second Canto: "Drinking"), *Poems*, ed. A. R. Waller (Cambridge, 1905), p. 51.
29. Cowley, "Ode upon His Majesty's Restoration and Return," *Poems*, p. 430.
30. John Evelyn, *The Diary of John Evelyn*, 6 vols., ed. E. S. de Beer (Oxford, 1955), III, 281.
31. "The Royal Entertainment" (London, 1660), possibly written by Thomas Jordan.
32. McShane, "The Politicisation of Drink," p. 75.
33. Trebusek, "Wine for Comfort," pp. 61–3; Robert Ashton, *The Second Civil War and its Origins* (New Haven, 1994), pp. 199–200.
34. Charles II, 'Proclamation against Vicious, Debauched, and Prophane Persons, May 30th', in John Somers, ed., *A Collection of Scarce and Valuable Tracts*, Second edition, edited by Sir Walter Scott, 13 vols. (London: Cadell and Davies, 1812), vol. VII., 423.
35. Samuel Pepys, *The Diary of Samuel Pepys, a new and complete transcription*, 10 vols., ed. Robert Latham and William Matthews (Berkeley, 1970–1983), June 4, 1660.
36. Charles II, *A Proclamation for Publishing a former Proclamation of the 30th of May last (entituled, A Proclamation against Vicious, Debauch'd and Prophane Persons) in all Churches and Chappels throughout England and Wales, 13th of August* (London, 1660).
37. Pepys, *Diary*, April 23, 1661.
38. Bryson, *From Courtesy to Civility*, p. 256. See pp. 243–75 for a brilliant study of the attitudes and practises of libertines.
39. *Remarques on the Humours and Conversations of the Town. Written in a letter for Sr. T. L.* (London, 1673), p. 40.
40. The *Calendar of State Papers, Domestic Series*, of the reign of Charles II, 1660–85, are full of records regarding the arrival of wine from various European ports. See, for example, vol. X (Jan.–Dec., 1670), 3, 21, 62, 79, 82, 99, 146, 173, 182, 193, 199, 204, 212, 241, 292, 506, 551, 566, 579, 592.
41. Pepys, *Diary*, July 7, 1665, VI, 151. For a more general description of Pepys's drinks and drinking habits, see Pepys, *Diary*, ed. Latham and Matthews, X, "Drink," 104–8; and in particular Mendelsohn, *Drinking with Pepys* (London, 1963).
42. Mountain was the name for a popular, usually sweet white wine from Malaga; it was also known as Malagoes.

43. In Sunderland's cellar record, madeira is spelled "Madra," cyprus is spelled "Ciprus," and côte-rôtie is spelled "Quoterots." British Library (BL), Add. MS 61490, f. 203, "An Account of Lord Sunderland's Wine Cellar, 14 October 1666."

44. This wine is unidentified, but its name suggests that James Stewart, 2nd Earl of Galloway, imported the wine and gave or sold some to his friends, including Sunderland. Among seventeenth- and eighteenth-century male aristocrats, it was common for one person, when abroad, to purchase a large amount of wine and have it sent to back to England or Scotland, thus saving his friends the difficulties involved in importing. This favor was then expected in return. For poorer noblemen, it was a respectable form of business to make a bit of a profit on each sale.

45. Spencer's records do not indicate how much more wine he had in cask, but the amount was probably even greater, as prior to the late eighteenth century wine usually was purchased and stored in cask until a few months or weeks before being consumed.

46. *Journal of the House of Commons* (JHC, XVII, *An Account Shewing the Quantity of Wines imported in to London and the Outports of England, in Sixteen Years and one quarter, from Michaelmas 1696, to Christmas 1712* (report submitted by Charles Davenant, May 21, 1713), p. 363. The report includes figures for London alone, beginning in 1675.

47. 12 Car. II, c. 4, "First Tonnage and Poundage Act."

48. The two permanent duties, referred to as the "Additional Duty" and the "Coinage Duty," were derived from 12 Car. II, c. 4 (1660), and 18 Car. II, c. 5 (1666), respectively. The expired duties derived from 22 Car. II (1670), c. 5 and 30 Car. II, c. 2 (1678).

49. Fortrey, *England's Interest and Improvement; Consider'd in the Increase of Trade in this Kingdom. In which is an account of our commerce with several nations in Europe* (London, 1663), pp. 23–4.

50. The noted nineteenth-century free-market theorist J. R. McCulloch called Fortrey's estimations "vague" and "worthless." McCulloch, ed., *Early English Tracts on Commerce* (London, 1856; reprint, Cambridge, 1952), p. ix.

51. Fortrey, *England's Interest*, pp. 235–6.

52. The republication dates of Fortrey's book coincide with heated debates in Parliament about economic relations with France.

53. Simon, *A History of the Wine Trade in England*, III, 93–4.

54. Customs duties and wine licenses were forms of hereditary revenue to which the king was entitled in order to receive his annual income of £1,200,000. When this amount was not raised through these and other hereditary sources, the king would ask Parliament to vote for special taxes, or parliamentary supply, such as the various wine acts. During his 25-year reign, Charles II received his income only five times. *CSP, Dom. Ser.*, V, lxv.

55. Simon, *The History of the Wine Trade in England*, III, 100–1.

56. *Cobbett's Parliamentary History of England: From the Norman Conquest, in 1066, to the Year 1803.* 12 vols. (London, 1806–1812), VI, 1210.

57. Steven C. A. Pincus, "From Butterboxes to Wooden Shoes: The Shift in English Popular Sentiment from Anti-Dutch to Anti-French in the 1670s", *The Historical Journal*, 38:2 (June 1995), 333–61.

58. George Downing, *A Schedule of the Trade as it is at present carry'd on between England and France, in Commodities of the Native Product and Manufacture of each Country, calculated as exactly as possible, in Obediance to the Command of the Right Honourable the Lords Commissioners for the Treaty of Commerce with France, humbly tendered to your Lordships* (London, 1675). This report asserted that England lost 1 million pounds annually to France.

59. The Southampton duty for Mediterranean wines was granted by King Philip and Queen Mary, and not officially revoked until 1787.

60. Parliamentary Report, C.8702, *Customs Tariffs*, 138.

61. BL, Egerton MS 2882, "Proclamation for Prising Wines, 1 Feb. 1674."

62. "An Account of the Port[ugal] trade in relation to their wines" (c. 1677). This manuscript is in the possession of John Roberts of John Roberts Wine Books Ltd, London. It was once owned by the wine writer André L. Simon. Simon refers to the manuscript as a

"letter written to London by the English Commercial Agent at Oporto in 1677," and it is published in its entirety in Simon, *Bottlescrew Days*, pp. 113–14.

63. 19–20 Car. II, c. 1 (1678), "An Act for raising money by a poll and otherwise, to enable his Majesty to enter into an actual war against the French King, and for prohibiting several French commodities."

64. Pincus, "From Butterboxes to Wooden Shoes", pp. 358–9.

65. For discussion of the luxury debate, see Thomas, *The Ends of Life*, pp. 110–46; Maxine Berg, *Luxury and Pleasure in Eighteenth-Century Britain* (Oxford, 2005); Linda Levy Peck, *Consuming Splendor: Society and Culture in Seventeenth-Century England* (Cambridge, 2005); Woodruff Smith, *Consumption and the Making of Respectability, 1600–1800* (New York, 2002), pp. 63–104; Christopher Berry, *The Idea of Luxury: A Conceptual and Historical Investigation* (Cambridge, 1994); John Sekora, *Luxury: The Concept in Western Thought, Eden to Smollett* (Baltimore, 1977).

66. The literature on the Exclusion Crisis is vast, but for a good introduction, see J. R. Jones, *The First Whigs: The Politics of the Exclusion Crisis, 1678-1683* (Oxford, 1961); Tim Harris, *London Crowds in the Reign of Charles II: Propaganda and Politics from the Restoration until the Exclusion Crisis* (Cambridge, 1987); idem, *Politics under the Later Stuarts: Party Conflict in a Divided Society, 1660–1715* (London, 1993); Gary S. De Krey, *Restoration and Revolution in Britain: A Political History of the Era of Charles II and the Glorious Revolution* (Basingstoke, 2007).

67. The literature on party politics at the turn of the eighteenth century is extensive. For contemporary Whig and Tory views respectively, see Gilbert Burnet, *History of His Own Time from the Restoration of Charles II to the Treaty of Peace at Utrecht, in the Reign of Queen Anne* 2 vols. (London, 1840), and John Evelyn, *The Diary of John Evelyn*, ed. E. S. de Beer, 6 vols. (Oxford, 1955). For secondary literature, see Geoffrey Holmes and W. A. Speck, eds., *The Divided Society: Parties and Politics in England, 1694–1716* (London, 1967); J. H. Plumb, *The Growth of Political Stability in England, 1675–1725* (London, 1967); J. P. Kenyon, *Revolution Principles: The Politics of Party, 1689–1720* (Cambridge, 1977); Geoffrey Holmes, *British Politics in the Age of Anne* (London, 1987); Clyve Jones, ed., *Britain in the First Age of Party, 1680–1750: Essays Presented to Geoffrey Holmes* (London, 1987); Tim Harris, *Politics Under the Later Stuarts: Party Conflict in a Divided Society, 1660-1715* (Harlow, 1993); Gary S. De Krey, *A Fractured Society: The Politics of London in the First Age of Party, 1688–1715* (Oxford, 1985).

68. Harris, *London Crowds*, pp. 159–60, 187–8. The types of wine used by Whigs were rarely specified, although in one instance Harris records that an arrested Whig was sent a bottle of sack (pp. 187–8).

69. McShane, "Politicisation of Drink," p. 77.

70. John Oldham, *The Claret Drinker's Song; or, The Good Fellows Design* (London, 1680). This poem is also occasionally published as *The Careless Good Fellow*.

71. *The Wine Cooper's Delight, to the tune of "The Delights of the Bottle"* (London, 1681), possibly written by James Dean. The image comes from BL, C20, f. 9 (244).

72. McShane, "Politicisation of Drink," pp. 77–9.

2 "What's become of rich Burdeaux claret, who knows?"

1. JHC, XVII, 363.

2. This chapter focuses on fraud. See Chapters 4 and 6 for discussions of smuggling.

3. Having already been dismissed by Charles II, Parliament resolved that commissioners and officers of the customs had willfully broken the law prohibiting French wines, and that if they continued to do so, they would be questioned in Parliament when next it met. Chandler, Richard and Ceasar Ward, eds, *The History and Proceedings of the House of Commons of England*, 5 vols. (London, 1742), II, 97.

4. JHC, XVII, 363.

5. NA, C.O. 388/2, ff. 66–7, Memorial of the Portugal merchants of London, received by the Commissioners for Trade, August 9, 1692.

6. Davenant's estimate is substantiated by the ratio of London to outport figures after 1697.
7. *Calendar of Treasury Books*, VII, pt 1, xvi–xvii.
8. [Daniel Defoe] *Mercator, or Commerce Retrieved*, October 13, 1713.
9. Jonathan Scott, *Algernon Sydney and the Restoration Crisis, 1679–1683* (Cambridge, 1991); Melinda Zook, *Radical Whigs and Conspiratorial Politics in Late Stuart England* (University Park, PA, 1999).
10. Specifically, the new totals were over £14 per tun on French wine, over £17 per tun on Portuguese wine, and over £18 per tun on Spanish wine, and almost £20 per tun on Rhenish wine.
11. Francis, *Wine Trade*, p. 99.
12. That women had no "common draught" of wine was largely due to the fact that taverns, where most wine was consumed, were male-dominated.
13. Generally speaking, in seventeenth- and eighteenth-century England there was a tripartite division in drinking establishments, with inns, which provided food, drinks of all types and lodging, being the "elite of English victualling houses before 1800"; taverns for the more prosperous members of society (including the upper and the middling ranks), which provided food and wine but no lodging; and alehouses, for the laboring classes, which provided ale and occasionally food. Peter Clark, *The English Alehouse: A Social History, 1200–1830* (London, 1983), pp. 1–15. For contemporary evidence of tavern life, see Simon, *Wine Trade*, III, 204–52, which contains names, locations, and descriptions of many London taverns in the seventeenth century.
14. The literature on the glorious revolution is vast, but for a general introduction, see: Tim Harris, *Revolution: The Great Crisis of the British Monarchy, 1685–1720* (London, 2006); Steve Pincus, *1688: The First Modern Revolution* (New Haven, 2009); Gary S. De Krey, *Restoration and Revolution in Britain: A Political History of the Era of Charles II and the Glorious Revolution* (Basingstoke, 2007).
15. 1 Gul. et Mar., c. 34 (1689), "An Act for Prohibiting all trade and Commerce with France."
16. Although fighting ceased in 1696, the war was officially ended by the Treaty of Ryswick on September 20, 1697.
17. Between 1690 and 1696 Portuguese wine imports into London averaged 5,491 tuns annually, while Oporto wine exports to England rose to an average of 4,660 tuns. Warre, *Wine Trade*, appendix M.
18. For example, Portuguese and Spanish wine imports increased steadily almost every year until 1695, when they dropped for one year, before resuming the next year near their average level. Italian wine imports, although still minor, showed a marked increase over previous levels, suggesting that some of it, probably red wine from Tuscany, was being offered as a passable substitute for claret.
19. BL, Add. MS 23736, f. 18, An Account of the Kingdom of Portugal, c. 1701.
20. *The British Merchant, or, Commerce Preserv'd*, ed. Charles King, 3 vols (London, 1721, facs. edn New York, 1968), II, 277.
21. Ames may have lived near Lincoln's Inn, but there is no evidence that he was ever associated with the legal community.
22. Richard Ames, *The Search after Claret; or, a Visitation of the Vintners, a poem in two cantos* (London, 1691), 1.
23. Richard Ames, *A Farther Search after Claret; or, a Second visitation of the Vintners* (London, 1691); idem, *A Search after Wit; or, a Visitation of the Authors: In Answer to The Late Search after Claret; or, Visitation of the Vintners* (London, 1691); idem, *The Last Search after Claret in Southwark: or a Visitation of the Vintners* (London, 1692); idem, *The Bacchanalian Sessions, or the Contention of liquors, with a Farewell to Wine* (London, 1693); idem, *Fatal Friendship; or, the drunkards misery being a satyr against hard drinking by the author of The Search after Claret* (London, 1693).
24. Ames, *Bacchanalian Sessions*, 9.
25. For English consumers claret and port were not yet complements as they would become by the mid-nineteenth century, when, generally speaking, claret became

a "dinner" wine, and port an "after dinner" wine. Instead, claret and port were still strict substitutes.

26. Ames, *Bacchanalian Sessions*, 21.
27. Ibid., 22. "Lumber Pye" is a concoction of deer entrails, boiled in wine, sugar, mace, cloves, and other spices, then mixed with currents and baked in a pie crust. "Soporifrous methidrate" is unclear, but probably refers to a type of sleep-inducing medicine that contained some cheaply distilled spirits.
28. "Galliac" refers to wine from "Gaillac." As a French wine, this too would have been embargoed, but one assumes poetic license.
29. Ames, *Bacchanalian Sessions*, 23.
30. Francis, *Wine Trade*, III, 102.
31. Narcissus Luttrell, *Brief Historical Relation of the State of Affairs, from Sept. 1678 to April 1714*, 6 vols (Oxford, 1857), II, 314.
32. *Calendar of Treasury Papers*, I (1556–1696), March 7, 1696, pp. 492–3.
33. Madeira wine was generally taxed the same amount as wines from mainland Portugal, although in some years it was taxed a fraction more. Canary wine was almost always taxed slightly more than wine from mainland Spain.
34. These Acts were: "The Impost 1692–93," 4 Wm. and Mar., c. 5; "The Second 25 per cent," 7 and 8 Wm. and Mar., c. 20; "The Second Tonnage and Poundage Act", also known as the "New Subsidy," 9 and 10 Wm. and Mar., c. 23.
35. Christian Huetz de Lemps, *Géographie du Commerce de Bordeaux à la fin du règne de Louis XIV* (Paris, 1975), p. 119.
36. *Correspondance des Contrôleurs Généraux de Finances avec les Intendants des provinces*, ed. A. M. de Boislisle, 3 vols (Paris, 1874–93), I, 1727: "Vous avez approuvé pendant la guerre que l'on mist dans des futailles d'Espagne du vin de France pour l'Envoyer en Angleterre: cela a réussi. L'on y en a fait entrer tous les ans. Les Anglais en ont esté avertis. Ils ont envoyé des commissaries pour taster les vins d'Espagne afin de voir si'l y avait en Espagne des vins que l'on pust porter de la manière que l'on faisait en Angleterre. Les commissaires ont fait le rapport que l'on pouvait désirer: j'ay eu connaissance de la conduite que les négocians on tenue à l'égard de ces commissaries afin qu'ils fussent favorables ... L'on trouve moyen d'en faire porter une plus grosse quantité depuis la paix parce que la navigation estant libre d'icy a Saint-Sébastien et n'estant plus interrompue par des corsairs l'on envoye beaucoup plus de batimens en Angleterre avec des futailles d'Espagne. (My translation in text)
37. Archives National, Paris, G/7/138, Bazins de Bezons to Contrôleur Général, December 5, 1699.
38. *Calendar of Treasury Papers (CTP)*, 1697–1702, March 22, 1698, p. 146; January 29, 1700, p. 372.
39. *Calendar of Treasury Papers (CTP)*, 1697–1702, January 13, 1702, p. 557. *Calendar of Treasury Books (CTB)*, XXI, 2, June 26, 1707 and April 20, 1709; *(CTB)*, XXIII, 2, July 15, 1709, pp. 145 and 252.
40. Huetz de Lemps, *Géographie du Commerce*, p. 121.
41. Henri Kehrig, *Le Privilège des vins à Bordeaux, jusqu'en 1789* (Paris, 1886, facs. edn Bayonne, 1984), p. 36 n.
42. *The Constant Couple* was first performed at the Theatre Royal, Drury Lane, in November, 1699.
43. George Farquhar, *The Constant Couple, or a trip to the Jubilee* (1699), act I, scene 1, in Shirley S. Kenney, ed., *The Works of George Farquhar*, 2 vols (Oxford, 1988), I, 155.
44. Richard Ames, *A Dialogue between Claret and Darby-Ale, a poem* (London, 1691), 6.
45. Ames, *Claret and Darby-Ale*, 9.
46. Ames, *Bacchanalian Sessions*, 7.
47. Ward used this term in the title of a long poem he wrote, *Wine and Wisdom: or, the tipling Philosophers. A lyrick poem* (London, 1710). The poem was a humorous account of wine drinking among ancient philosophers, and Ward says in the preface that it was meant to be read aloud in the evening when wine was being consumed.
48. Edward Ward, *The London Spy*, vol. I, part 1 (London, 1698), 3.

49. Ames's known political works, all of them staunchly anti-Jacobite, are: *The Character of a Bigotted Prince, and what England may expect from the return of such a one* (London, 1691), which was republished the following year under the title, *Chuse which you will, Liberty or Slavery; or, An impartial Representation of the Danger of being Subjected to a Popish Prince; The Jacobite Conventicle, a poem* (London, 1692); *The Double Descent* (London, 1692). Ames, a 'student at Lincoln's Inn,' died in 1693.
50. Ames, *Double Descent*, 24.
51. "Hermitage Clarett" was probably Hermitage from the Rhône Valley near Tain. The term *clarett* may have been added by Hervey's wine merchant as a way to indicate a red wine from France, or as a way to make Hermitage sound more familiar. It may also have been Hervey's own description. Marketing terms were not yet agreed upon, to the occasional confusion of the wine historian.
52. Palm was simply another name for Canary wine (from Las Palmas in the Canary Islands), almost all of which was sweet malmsey.
53. Suffolk Record Office, Bury St Edmonds, 941/46/13/14, "Expense Book of John Hervey, first Earl of Bristol." Most of this information has been republished in *The Diary of John Hervey, First Earl of Bristol. With extracts from his book of expenses, 1688–1742*, ed. S. H. A. Hervey (Wells, 1894), "Wine," pp. 168–80.
54. Davenant, Charles, *set forth in a conversation between Mr. Whiglove and Mr. Double, two under-spur-leathers to the late ministry* (London, 1691).
55. John Brewer, *The Sinews of Power: War, Money and the English State, 1688–1783* (Cambridge, MA, 1990), pp. 66–8.

3   "The Cross ran with claret for the general benefit"

1. T. C. Smout, *Scottish Trade on the Eve of Union, 1660–1707* (Edinburgh, 1963), p. 170.
2. Alexander Fenton, "'Wyne Confortative': Wine in Scotland from the Thirteenth till the Eighteenth Centuries," in Christian J. Kay and Margaret A. Mackay, eds, *Perspectives on the Older Scottish Tongue: A Celebration of DOST* (Edinburgh, 2005), pp. 50–1.
3. S. G. E. Lythe and J. Butt, *An Economic History of Scotland, 1100–1939* (Glasgow, 1975), pp. 62–9.
4. Billy Kay and Cailean Maclean, *Knee Deep in Claret: A Celebration of Wine and Scotland* (Edinburgh, 1983), p. 9. For a general background on medieval Scottish wine trade and consumption, see Chapters 1–6.
5. F. Marian McNeill, *The Scots Cellar* (Moffat, 1992), p. 32.
6. Lythe and Butt, *Economic History of Modern Scotland*, p. 63.
7. Quoted in Robert Chambers, *Domestic Annals of Scotland: from the Reformation to the Revolution*, 2 vols (Edinburgh, 1858), II, 261.
8. Eighteenth-century clubs in Scotland should not be confused with their nineteenth-century English counterparts. Clubs, most numerous in Edinburgh, were not exclusive gentlemen's clubs; rather, they were informal gatherings of politically like-minded men who usually met in howffs to sing and drink wine. The howffs themselves were urban taverns, which were especially necessary in Edinburgh where kitchens were a rarity. For general descriptions of clubs and howffs, see Robert Chambers, *Traditions of Edinburgh* (1824; reprint, Edinburgh, 1980); Marie W. Stuart, *Old Edinburgh Taverns* (London, 1952).
9. Bruce Lenman, *An Economic History of Modern Scotland, 1660–1976* (London, 1977), p. 38.
10. Register of the Privy Council of Scotland, Ser. III, vol. vii, 697. Quoted in Smout, *Scottish Trade*, p. 170.
11. Smout, *Scottish Trade*, p. 170; Lenman, *Economic History of Modern Scotland*, p. 38, states that between 1660 and 1689, Leith received 60–70 percent of all wine imports, Glasgow a little less than 20 percent and no other port as much as 5 percent. Smout, *Scottish Trade*, p. 285, gives an exact breakdown of wine distribution within Scotland between 1686 and 1688. His figures concur with Lenman's. Leith continued its dominance of the Scottish wine trade long after the Union, consistently accounting for over two-thirds of all

legally imported wine; see National Archives of Scotland, Edinburgh (NAS), E 501 series, Comptroller General's account of customs, 1707–1830. From the production side of the equation, Bordeaux export figures from 1698 to 1716 reveal that Leith was far and away the principal Scottish destination for wine shipments to Scotland; see Christian Huetz de Lemps, *Géographie du Commerce de Bordeaux à la fin du règne de Louis XIV* (Mouton, 1975), pp. 110, 117.

12. NAS, E 72/15/15, Leith customs records, imported wine, 1672–1673. All customs records in this series begin on November 1 and end on October 31 of the following year. Of 15 total cargoes, which totaled over 817 tuns, only three came from elsewhere: two from Rouen in Normandy (often an entrepot for Bordeaux wines shipped to Northern Europe) and one from "France." It is therefore possible that 100 percent of the wine landed at Leith in 1672–3 was of Bordeaux origin.

13. NAS, E 72/15/22, Leith customs records, imported wine, 1680–1681. The total amount of wine imported during this year was 1,235 tuns.

14. NAS, E 72/15/27, 29, 33, and 38, Leith customs records, imported wine, 1682–1686.

15. This conclusion concurs with Smout's, *Scottish Trade*, p. 170: most "French wine" was "certainly red wine, and most of the red wine was claret from Bordeaux, the favourite drink of Scotsmen until well into the eighteenth century."

16. This figure is based on the percentage of wines arriving at Leith from Bordeaux. There is a paucity of seventeenth-century Scottish references to white wine that was not of Spanish origin, and Bordeaux records from the period show almost all of the exported white wine going to Holland. Huetz de Lemps, *Géographie du Commerce*, pp. 104–15, 181–213.

17. NAS, E 72/15/42, Leith customs records, imported wine, 1688–1689.

18. NAS, E 72 series (customs records) for other Scottish ports such as Aberdeen, Dundee, and Port Glasgow do not list wine independently, as do Leith records. However, a cursory perusal of these records suggests that most wine arriving at these ports came from Bordeaux. See also Smout, *Scottish Trade*, p. 285.

19. JHC, XVII, 363. For a complete breakdown of London wine imports from 1675 until 1697, see Chapter 1.

20. Sir John Foulis, *The Account Book of Sir John Foulis of Ravelston, 1671–1707* (Edinburgh, 1884). "Cummers" are female intimates, and "gossips" were close friends of either sex, usually godparents.

21. Rosalind K. Marshall, *The Days of Duchess Anne: Life in the Household of the Duchess of Hamilton, 1656–1716* (London, 1973), p. 100.

22. Michael Fry, *Scotland and the Treaty of Union* (Edinburgh, 2006).

23. NAS, GD 406/1/970, Campbell to Douglas, July 22, 1673. Since at that time all wine was made to be consumed within the year of production, it is likely that Campbell was advising Hamilton to drink the "Parisse wine" as quickly as possible. Paris wine was probably either wine from vineyards just outside of Paris, which were once plentiful and provided the city with a simple white wine, or just as likely, a wine from Orléans, which was at that time the primary source of wine for the densely populated Ile de France. See Roger Dion, *Histoire de la Vigne et du Vin en France des origines au XIXème Siècle* (Paris, 1959), Chapter 6; and M. Lachiver, *Vins, Vignes et Vignerons* (Paris, 1988), pp. 314–28. Finally, it is also possible that the wine came from another region but was purchased from a merchant in Paris, and hence the name.

24. At the end of the seventeenth century and just prior to the Union, the Scottish pound stood at 12:1 in relation to the English pound (Sterling). Thus, £37,000 (Scots) was approximately £3,083 Sterling.

25. Kay and Maclean, *Knee Deep in Claret*, p. 64.

26. *Acts of the Parliament of Scotland* (APS), IX, 457.

27. APS, IX, 460a–b.

28. Smout, *Scottish Trade*, pp. 170 and 253.

29. I William 8, n. 11 (1701), "Act discharging Wine, Brandy and all other Liquors of the growth of France," APS, X, 278–9.

30. Huetz de Lemps, *Géographie du Commerce*, table 7, p. 147.
31. APS, X, 278–9.
32. Rosalind Mitchison, *A History of Scotland*, 3rd edn (London, 2003), pp. 305–6.
33. Andrew Fletcher, "Speeches by a member of the Parliament," in *Political Works*, ed. John Robertson (Cambridge, 1997), p. 169.
34. APS, X, 102.
35. Mitchison, *History of Scotland*, p. 306; Smout, *Scottish Trade*, p. 306.
36. Fletcher, "Speeches by a member of the Parliament," in *Political Works*, ed. Robertson, p. 169.
37. APS, XI, 103a, 112a.
38. The exception here is T. C. Smout, who stated that when the Wine Act repealed the prohibition against French wines, "the French trade came to stand for defiance of English influence." Smout, *Scottish Trade*, p. 170.
39. Quoted in Kay and Maclean, *Knee Deep in Claret*, pp. 74–5.
40. NAS, GD 124/15/259/1, Clelland to Erskine, Lord Grange, November. 10, 1705.
41. Cited in Parliamentary Report, C. 8706 (LXXXV, 1897), *Customs Tariffs of the United Kingdom from 1800-1897. With some notes upon the history of the more important branches of receipt from the year 1660*, p. 21.
42. National Library of Scotland, MS 1520 (65), *Letter from a Scots Factor at London, to a merchant in Edinburgh, Concerning the House of Commons; to prevent the importation of wines and other Goods from Scotland* (London, April, 17, 1707), p. 1.
43. W. R. McLeod and V. B. McLeod, *Anglo-Scottish Tracts, 1701–1714* (Lawrence, KS, 1979), pp. 60–1, cannot identify the author of this pamphlet. They too conclude that the letter was spurious.
44. *Letter from a Scots Factor at London*, p. 1.
45. NAS, GD 124/15/537, Sir Samuel McClellan to the Earl of Mar, April 22, 1707. In this letter McClellan says that almost all wine coming in to Leith was from France.
46. NAS, GD 124/15/491/5, Grange to Mar, April 22, 1707.
47. NAS, GD 124/15/522/3, Northesk to Mar, May 26, 1707.
48. NAS, GD 124/15/513/13, Erskine to Mar, May 26, 1707. Erskine was possibly a relative.
49. NAS, GD 124/15/513/15, Erskine to Mar, June 7, 1707.
50. Kay and Maclean, *Knee Deep in Claret*, p. 75.
51. NAS, GD 124/15/491/12, Grange to Mar, June 10, 1707.
52. NAS, GD 124/15/491/15, Grange to Mar, June 20, 1707; and GD 124/15/513/21, David Erskine to Mar, June 28, 1707.
53. [Daniel Defoe], *The Trade of Britain Stated: Being the substance of two papers published in London on the occasion of the Importation of Wine and Brandy from North Britain* (London, 1708), pp. 2–7.
54. Ibid., p. 8.
55. *London Gazette*, no. 4417, March 11, 1708.
56. *The Times* (London), December 24, 1807.

4 "The interest of the nation lay against it so visibly"

1. For a detailed analyses of the debate surrounding the proposed Commercial Treaty with France in 1713, see D. A. E. Harkness, "The Opposition to the 8th and 9th articles of the Commercial Treaty of Utrecht," *Scottish Historical Review*, 21 (1924), 219–26; D. C. Coleman, "Politics and Economics in the Age of Anne: The Case of the Anglo-French Treaty of 1713," in D. C. Coleman and A. H. John, eds, *Trade, Government and Economy in Pre-Industrial England: Essays Presented to F. J. Fisher* (London, 1976), pp. 187–211; Geoffrey Holmes and Clyve Jones, "Trade, the Scots and the Parliamentary Crisis of 1713," *Parliamentary History*, 1 (1982), 47–77.
2. A. D. Francis, *The Methuens and Portugal, 1691–1708* (Cambridge, 1966), pp. 112–34.

3. JHC, XIV, 289–90, January 20, 1704. The official English name for this treaty was "The Treaty between England and Portugal, signed December 27th, 1703." The "Pragmatical Sanctions" were a series of laws enacted throughout the seventeenth century in Portugal that endeavored to restrict the consumption of luxury goods, especially of foreign manufacture, and to repair the Portuguese economy. These laws were deeply embedded in Counter-Reformation thought, so that austerity in dress had a spiritual underpinning as well. Most recently, a law prohibiting the use of English cloth had been decreed on January 25, 1675. See Francis, *Wine Trade*, pp. 82–9; and Francis, *Methuens and Portugal*, pp. 184–218.

4. G. M. Trevelyan, *England under Queen Anne*, 3 vols (London, 1948), I, 299–300.

5. Paul Duguid, "The Making of Methuen: The Commercial Treaty in the English Imagination," *História*, 3:4 (2003), 9–36.

6. 2 and 3 Ann., c. 18; and 3 and 4 Ann., c. 3.

7. Francis, *Methuens and Portugal*, p. 205.

8. 3 and 4 Ann., c. 12.

9. Bordeaux wine exports to the Anglo-Norman isles of Guernsey and Jersey, and to northern France—from the north coast of Brittany to Pas de Calais—were markedly higher before (and after) the War of the Spanish Succession than during the war itself, going from over 7,000 tuns per year to roughly 2,000 tuns per year. This suggests that much of the peacetime wine exports were intended for smuggling into England, an activity that was much more difficult when English corsairs on patrol intercepted whatever vessels they came across. Huetz de Lemps, *Géographie du Commerce*, pp. 161–2.

10. 9 Ann., c. 8.

11. While most surviving evidence from the late Stuart era suggests that wine fraud was carried on to a much greater extent than smuggling, the latter was nevertheless considered a problem—hence the Parliamentary committee of 1704. See also, *An Enquiry into the Causes of the Prohibition of Commerce with France, during the present War* (London, 1708). For recent assessments of smuggling, see Cal Winslow, "Sussex Smugglers," in Douglas Hay, Peter Linebaugh, John G. Rule, E. P. Thompson and Cal Winslow, *Albion's Fatal Tree: Crime and Society in Eighteenth-Century England* (New York, 1975), pp. 119–66; Paul Monod, "Dangerous Merchandise: Smuggling, Jacobitism, and Commercial Culture in Southeast England, 1690–1760," *Journal of British Studies*, 30 (April, 1991), 150–82; William J. Ashworth, *Customs and Excise: Trade, Production and Consumption in England, 1640–1845* (Oxford, 2003), pp. 63–93, 191, 197–8, 203, 379–83.

12. Adulteration of wines in England was as old as the English wine trade itself. However, the high cost of French wine by the 1690s and throughout the eighteenth century increased merchants' incentive to create or "lengthen" "French" wine in particular with native ingredients. Witness Joseph Addison's comments in *The Tatler*, no. 131, February 9, 1709: "There is in this city a certain fraternity of chymical operators who work underground in holes, caverns, and dark retirements, to conceal their mysteries from the eyes and observation of mankind. These subterraneous philosophers are daily employed in the transmigration of liquors, and by the power of magical drugs and incantations, raise under the streets of London the choicest products of the hills and valleys of France. They can squeeze Bourdeaux out of a slow, and draw Champagne from an apple." *The Tatler*, ed. Donald F. Bond, 3 vols (Oxford, 1987), II, 259–60. For a general discussion of wine adulteration in England and indeed throughout the world, see Rod Phillips, "Wine and Adulteration," *History Today* (July, 2000), pp. 31–7; and Phillips, *A Short History of Wine* (London, 2000). For a discussion of the adulteration of port, see Chapters 7 and 8.

13. Gilbert Burnet, *History of his own Time from the Restoration of Charles II to the Treaty of Peace at Utrecht, in the reign of Queen Anne*, 2 vols (London, 1840), II, 864.

14. *The Spectator*, ed. Donald F. Bond, 5 vols (Oxford, 1965), no. 43, dated Oxford, April 13, 1711, I, 181–2.

15. For a discussion of port's strength, see Chapter 7.

16. *The Guardian*, ed. John Calhoun Stephens (Lexington, KY, 1982), no. 170, September 25, 1713, pp. 552–6.

17. Chandler and Ward, *The History and Proceedings of the House of Commons of England*, IV, 128. See also BL, Add. MS 61541, f. 132, Dom Luis da Cunha to Queen Anne, February 24, 1708. In this letter da Cunha, the Portuguese envoy in London, suggests that an end to the embargo against French wines would impoverish Portugal and consequently necessitate an end to that country's participation in the war. Da Cunha also reminded the queen that Portugal paid hard cash for English goods while France would pay with her own goods and manufactures. There is a tone of desperation in da Cunha's letter that reveals how much the Portuguese needed British goods and military protection. Interestingly, this view runs contrary to later Portuguese interpretations of the Methuen Treaty, which stated that it was oppressive to Portugal and that only Britain benefitted by it. See A. D. Francis, *Some Reflections on the Methuen Treaties* (Coimbra, 1965), pp. 20–1; Francis, *Methuens and Portugal*, pp. 205–26.
18. *A Toast for A--e and Robbin in the French Wine* (London, 1711).
19. *O raree show; O brave show! Who see my fine pretty show: or the new raree show ballad, to a New Tune, much in Request* (London, c. 1712).
20. Most favored nation status means that all tariffs between the two signatories must be equal to or less than the lowest tariff granted on any commodity to any other nation.
21. Coleman, "Politics and Economics," pp. 188–9, 196–8.
22. Duguid, "The Making of Methuen," pp. 29–31.
23. Charles Davenant, *A Report to the Honourable Commissioners for Putting in Execution the Act, Intitled, An Act for the Taking, Examining, and Stating the Publick Accounts of the Kingdom*, 2 vols (London, 1712), II, 49. The information from this report was repeated and expanded in Davenant, *An Account of the Trade between Great Britain, France, Spain and Portugal, etc.*, 2 vols. (London, 1715).
24. Ibid., II, 25.
25. Ibid., II, 70.
26. Ibid., II, 58. My italics.
27. JHC, XVII, 365.
28. For general discussions of Davenant's economic philosophy and its historical context, see Joyce O. Appleby, *Economic Thought and Ideology in Seventeenth-century England* (Princeton, 1978); Istvan Hont, "Free Trade and the Economic Limits to National Politics: Neo-Machiavellian Political Economy Reconsidered," in *The Economic Limits to Modern Politics*, ed. John Dunn (Cambridge, 1990), pp. 41–120; Mark Blaug, ed., *Pre-Classical Economists*, 3 vols (Aldershot, 1991), I, 161–70, 189–226; Kustaa Multamäki, *Towards Great Britain: Commerce and Conquest in the Thought of Algernon Sidney and Charles Davenant* (Helsinki, 1999), pp. 149–207.
29. Davenant, *A Report to the Honourable Commissioners*, II, 58–60.
30. For this view, see in particular J. G. A. Pocock, *Virtue, Commerce and History: Essays on Political Thought and History, Chiefly in the Eighteenth Century* (Cambridge, 1985), pp. 103–23, 230–4; idem, *The Machiavellian Moment: Florentine Political Thought and the Atlantic Republican Tradition* (Princeton, 1975), pp. 423–61; Kenneth Morgan, "Mercantilism and the British Empire," in *The Political Economy of British Historical Experience, 1688–1914*, ed. Donald Winch and Patrick K. O'Brien (Oxford, 2002), pp. 165–8.
31. Appleby, *Economic Thought and Ideology*, pp. 158–279.
32. Davenant, *A Report to the Honourable Commissioners*, II, 72.
33. [Daniel Defoe] *Defoe's Review*, ed. A. W. Secord, 9 vols in 22 facsimile books (New York, 1938), July 18, 1706, III, 342.
34. Defoe, *Review*, May 16, 1713, in *Defoe's Review*, ed. Secord, IX, 191.
35. Defoe, *Review*, May 19, 1713, in *Defoe's Review*, ed. Secord, IX, 193.
36. *Queries Relating to the Importation of French Wines*, (London ?, 1713?). This document is in the possession of John Roberts, of John Roberts Wine Books Ltd, London. This very rare printed petition was once owned by André L. Simon. The only other extant copy of this printed petition is found at the Royal Irish Academy, Dublin [MS RRG, 20 A 12 (13)], where the publishing date is suggested as 1709. Simon dates it 1713, as do I. The petition is reprinted in its entirety in Simon, *Bottlescrew Days*, pp. 63–4.

37. Gary S. De Krey, *A Fractured Society: The Politics of London in the First Age of Party, 1688–1715* (Oxford, 1985), pp. 244–5.
38. *Reasons Humbly Offer'd by the Merchants Trading to Spain and Portugal against the Bill for suspending the Duty of £25 per Tun on French Wines* (London, 1713), reason no. VIII, n.p.
39. De Krey, *Fractured Society*, pp. 102–4, 125, 244–5.
40. As well as *Reasons Humbly Offer'd by the Merchants*, see *Reasons Humbly offer'd against opening the trade a trade with France for wines* (London, 1713?); and *Reasons Humbly offer'd by the Merchants trading to Italy, Spain and Portugal, against lowering the duties on French wines equal to those of Italy, Spain and Portugal* (London, 1713).
41. *A Vindication of the late House of Commons, in rejecting the bill for Confirming the Eighth and Ninth articles of the Treaty of Navigation and Commerce between England and France* (London, 1714), 17. Other examples of this admission regarding English preference for French wine can be found in *The Consequences of a Law for reducing the dutys upon French wines, Brandy, Silks and Linen, to those of other nations. With remarks on the Mercator* (London, 1713); *The British Merchant*, ed. King, I, 346–52.
42. Burnet, *History of his own Time*, II, 897.
43. Theodore Janssen, *General Maxims of Trade, particularly applied to the Commerce between Great Britain and France* (London, 1713).
44. Coleman, "Politics and Economics," pp. 194–6.
45. Steven C. A. Pincus, "From Butterboxes to Wooden Shoes: The Shift in English Popular Sentiment from Anti-Dutch to Anti-French in the 1670s," *The Historical Journal*, 38:2 (June 1995), 333–61.
46. *The Examiner*, August 7–14, 1712. The author of this article may have been Swift or Prior, both of whom wrote for *The Examiner* at this time.
47. *The Consequences of a Law for reducing the dutys upon French wines, Brandy, Silks and Linen, to those of other nations*.
48. *The Trade with France, Italy, Spain and Portugal, Considered: with some observations on the Treaty of Commerce between Great Britain and France* (London, 1713).
49. Julian Hoppit, *A Land of Liberty? England 1689–1727* (Oxford, 2000), p. 308.
50. JHC, XVII, 347–420, passim.
51. Burnet, *History of his own Time*, II, 898.
52. Defoe wrote in the *Review* on June 6, 1713: "I was going about [clarifying errors about the treaty of commerce] and had made a beginning in three papers, relating to the trade with France; when on a suddain I found my province invaded, and that work taken out of my hands, by an unexpected paper without an author, and call'd the *Mercator*. This work I soon discovered, if not done by the Government's direction, is so far encourag'd, as to have the help of Original Documents and Authorities to speak from, Things … which I never pretended to." *Defoe's Review*, ed. Secord, IX, 209.
53. JHC, XVII, 402.
54. Holmes and Clyve, "Trade, the Scots and the Parliamentary Crisis of 1713," p. 63.
55. *Cobbett's Parliamentary History*, VI, 1223.
56. *A Letter from a Member of the House of Commons to his Friend in the Country, Relating to the Bill of Commerce. With a true copy of the Bill, and an Exact List of all those who voted for and against Engrossing it* (London, 1713).
57. Holmes and Jones, "Trade, the Scots and the Parliamentary Crisis of 1713," pp. 68–70.
58. *Cobbett's Parliamentary History*, VI, 1223; Trevelyan, *England under Queen Anne*, III, 257; Geoffrey Holmes, *British Politics in the Age of Anne* (London, 1967), pp. 280–1.
59. Holmes and Clyve, "Trade, the Scots and the Parliamentary Crisis of 1713," p. 64.
60. For more on the demography and the Tory–Whig divide at the time of the debate, see Tim Harris, *Politics under the Later Stuarts: Party Conflict in a Divided Society, 1660–1715* (London, 1993), pp. 176–207.
61. For pamphlets, see *A Letter to the Honourable A——r M—re, Com———ner of Trade and Plantations* (London, 1714). Regarding the *British Merchant*, Henry Martin was the

principal author, but he was joined by a host of others, including Sir Charles Cooke, Theodore Janssen, James Milner, Nathaniel Toriano, Joshua Gee, and Christopher Haynes. Under King George I, Martin was rewarded for his services by being given Davenant's job as Inspector General of Customs.

62. Francis, *Wine Trade*, pp. 140–1; Francis, *Methuens and Portugal*, pp. 216–17.
63. Duguid, "The Making of Methuen," pp. 28–9.
64. J. H. Plumb, *The Growth of Political Stability in England, 1675–1725* (London, 1967), pp. 159–89; Julian Hoppit, *A Land of Liberty? England 1689–1727* (Oxford, 2000), pp. 383–417; Kathleen Wilson, *The Sense of the People: Politics, Culture and Imperialism in England, 1715–1785* (Cambridge, 1998), pp. 84–136.
65. Adam Smith, *The Wealth of Nations*, ed. Andrew Skinner (Harmondsworth, 1999), IV, Chapter 3, part 2, 72. For other economic liberals, see, for example, David Hume: "We lost the FRENCH market for our woollen manufactures, and transferred the commerce of wine to SPAIN and PORTUGAL, where we buy worse liquor at a higher price." *Of the Balance of Trade* (1752), in Hume, *Essays: Moral, Political and Literary*, ed. Eugene F. Miller (Indianapolis, 1987 edn), p. 315. W. E. H. Lecky wrote: had Bolingbroke "succeeded, he would have unquestionably added immensely both to the commercial prosperity of England, and to the probabilities of a lasting peace." *A History of England in the Eighteenth Century* (London, 1883 edn), I, 142. For claret connoisseurs, see Simon, *Bottlescrew Days*, p. 65. Simon's lament is somewhat misplaced. As we shall see in the next chapter, the failure to ratify the commercial treaty with France in 1713 was crucial for the continued improvement in the quality of claret.
66. Henry St John, Viscount Bolingbroke, *Letters and Correspondence, Public and Private, by the Lord Viscount Bolingbroke during the time he was Secretary of State*, ed. Gilbert Parke, 4 vols (London, 1798), IV, 137–8, 141, 149, 197, 264; Eric Schnakenbourg, "Les Interactions entre Commerce et Diplomatie au début du XVIIIe siècle: L'Example du Traité de Commerce Franco-Anglais de 1713," *Histoire, Economie et Société*, 23:3 (2004), 349–65.
67. Ralph Davis, "The Rise of Protection in England, 1689–1786," *Economic History Review*, 2nd ser., 19 (1966), 307; Davis, "The English Wine Trade in the Eighteenth and Nineteenth Centuries," *Annales Cisalpines d'Histoire Sociale* 3 (1972): 87–106; François Crouzet, *De la Supériorité de 1'Angleterre sur la France: 1'Economique et Imgaginaire, XVIIe–XXe Siècle* (Paris, 1985), chap. 5; John V. C. Nye, *War, Wine and Taxes: The Political Economy of Anglo-French Trade, 1689–1900* (Princeton, 2007); John Nye, and P. E. Dauzat, "Guerre, Commerce, Guerre Commerciale: L'Economie politique des échanges Franco-Anglais reéxminée," *Annales: Economies, Sociétés, Civilisations*, 47 (1992): 613–631 argue that France was more protectionist than Britain until 1860.
68. Kathleen Wilson argues that the conflation of English national interests with those of its merchants occurred in the 1720s and 1730s. *Sense of the People*, pp. 123–36. However, I think that convergence should be dated to the Commercial Treaty debate of 1712–14.
69. Joseph Addison, *The Late Tryal and Conviction of Count Tariff* (London, 1713), in *The Miscellaneous Works of Joseph Addison*, 2 vols, ed. A. C. Gutkelch (London, 1914), II, 265–72.
70. John Bull was invented in 1712 by John Arbuthnot, also at the time of the Treaty of Utrecht. Addison seems to have plagiarized much from Arbuthnot's caricature and plot, and may well have been responding to it. The original John Bull was a cloth dealer involved in a lawsuit against Lewis Baboon (i.e. Louis Bourbon). Bull was "an honest, plain dealing fellow, choleric, bold and of very unconstant temper." John Arbuthnot, *The History of John Bull* (London, 1712), p. 9. For a lengthy discussion of the career of John Bull, see Miles Taylor, "John Bull and the Iconography of Public Opinion in England, 1712–1929," *Past and Present*, 34 (1992), 93–128.
71. Addison, *Late Tryal*, pp. 267, 269.
72. *The Jovial Drinker* (Printed by Samuel Lyne, London, 1741). The date of the original ballad and print are uncertain, and clearly the lyrics could have been written some time between the 1640s and the Exclusion Crisis of 1679–81. However, according to Dr Angela McShane

and Prof. Chris Breward, print and costume experts respectively at the Victoria and Albert Museum, London, the illustration is from the time of the Treaty of Utrecht; the clothing and print style are c. 1710–20. Author's exchange with McShane and Breward, June 2010. Lyne must have reprinted this ballad and illustration in 1741 in response to the War of Jenkins' Ear, in which yet another embargo on wine was being considered. This print is not found in Frederick George Stephens and Mary Dorothy George, *Catalogue of Prints and Drawings in the British Museum: Political and Personal Satires*, 11 vols (1870–1954), but the British Museum does have a copy of the print. The Victorian mount on that print puts the date at 1699, but that date is not confirmed by the British Museum.

73. Lewis-Walpole Library (LWL), Print Number, 741.0.2, *The Jovial Drinker* (London, 1741).
74. *Mercator*, December 19, 1713.
75. Keith Thomas, *The Ends of Life: Roads to Fulfilment in Early Modern England* (Oxford, 2009), p. 180.
76. Steve Pincus, "Nationalism, Universal Monarchy, and the Glorious Revolution," in George Steinmetz, ed., *State/Culture: State Formation after the Cultural Turn* (Ithaca: Cornell University Press, 1999), pp. 182–210; idem, "From Butterboxes to Wooden Shoes," pp. 360–1.
77. Susannah Centlivre, *The Works of the celebrated Mrs. Centlivre*, ed. J. Pearson, 3 vols (London, 1872), *The Wonder: A Woman Keeps a Secret*, III, 67. *The Wonder* was set in Lisbon, which makes the lines about French wine equally fitting; however, the lines were fully intended for an English audience, and Lisbon was understood to be London. The comedy is about the attitudes of English men toward English women. It may have been set in Portugal for political reasons, or more likely to illustrate Centlivre's point that Englishmen were equally domineering (and foolish) as the Southern European men whose attitudes they mocked.
78. Centlivre, *Works, A Gotham Election*, III, 158.
79. Francis, *Wine Trade*, p. 131.
80. *Dictionary of National Biography*, 63 vols (London, 1875–1901), III, 1329–31.
81. Centlivre, *Works, A Gotham Election*, III, 165.
82. The exact percentage of Haut Brion and Margaux within Hervey's claret purchases during the War of the Spanish Succession was 79.26.
83. BL, Add. MS 61349, f. 83, f. 68, f. 69, f. 108; 61363, f. 48, f. 78, Wine bills and receipts of the first Duke of Marlborough.
84. Richard Steele, *The Englishman*, ed. Rae Blanchard (Oxford, 1955), 1st ser., no. 8, October 22, 1713.

5 "A good and most particular taste"

1. Henri Enjalbert, "Comment Naissent les Grands Crus: Bordeaux, Porto, Cognac," *Annales: Economies, Sociétés, Civilisations*, 8 (1953), 457; Enjalbert, "L'Origine des Grands Vins," in Charles Higounet, ed., *La Seigneurie et le Vignoble de Château Latour: Histoire d'un grand cru du Médoc (XIVe-XXe siècle)* (Bordeaux, 1974), 3–18; Paul Butel, "Grands Propriétaires et Production des Vins du Médoc au XVIIIe Siècle," *Revue Historique de Bordeaux* (1963): 129–141; Butel, *Les Dynasties Bordelaises: de Colbert à Chaban* (Paris, 1991); Jean-Louis Flandrin, "L'Invention des Grands Vins Français et la Mutation des Valeurs Oenologiques," *Eighteenth Century Life*, 23:2 (1999): 24–33; Robert Forster, "The Noble Wine Producers of the Bordelais in the Eighteenth Century," *Economic History Review*, 2d ser., 14 (1961): 18–33; Christian Huetz de Lemps, "L'Entrée de Latour dans le Grand Commerce," in Charles Higounet, ed., *La Seigneurie et le Vignoble de Château Latour* (1974), 199–207; René Pijassou, "Le Marché de Londres et la Naissance des Grands Crus Médocains (fin 17ème Siècle–debut 18ème Siècle)," *Revue Historique de Bordeaux*, 23 (1974): 139–150.
2. For broad discussions of polite culture and politeness, see Lawrence Klein, *Shaftesbury and the Culture of Politeness: Moral Discourse and Cultural Politics in Early Eighteenth Century*

England (Cambridge, 1994); Paul Langford, *A Polite and Commercial People: England, 1727–1783* (Oxford, 1989). For more on politeness, See Chapter 5, Footnote 63.

3. Terry Eagleton, *The Ideology of the Aesthetic* (Oxford, 1990), pp. 1–69; W. D. Smith, *Consumption and the Making of Respectability 1660–1800* (New Haven, 2002); Keith Thomas, *The Ends of Life: Roads to Fulfilment in Early Modern England* (Oxford, 2009), pp. 110–46. For broader theoretical background, see Pierre Bourdieu, *Distinction: A Social Critique of the Judgment of Taste*, trans. Richard Nice (Cambridge, MA, 1984).

4. For more on Old Whigs, see J. G. A. Pocock, "The Varieties of Whiggism from Exclusion to Reform," in his *Virtue, Commerce and History* (Cambridge, 1985), pp. 215–34.

5. J. H. Plumb, *The Growth of Political Stability in England, 1675–1725* (London, 1967), pp. 159–89; Julian Hoppit, *A Land of Liberty? England 1689–1727* (Oxford, 2000), pp. 383–417; Kathleen Wilson, *The Sense of the People: Politics, Culture and Imperialism in England, 1715–1785* (Cambridge, 1998), pp. 84–136.

6. René Pijassou, *Un Grand Vignoble de Qualité: Le Médoc*, 2 vols (Paris, 1980), I, 330–51.

7. National Archives (NA), L.S. 13/91, cellar book of Charles II, 1660–1661 (Vinum). The entire entry is in Latin. The fact that these wines were sold in bottles suggests that Pontac and/or Batailhe were well aware of the merits of bottle-ageing.

8. Samuel Pepys, *The Diary of Samuel Pepys: A New and Complete Transcription*, ed. Robert Latham and William Matthews, 10 vols (Berkeley, 1970–83), IV, 100.

9. Christian Huetz de Lemps, *Géographie du Commerce de Bordeaux à la fin du règne de Louis XIV* (Mouton, 1975), pp. 116–21 and 181–99; Pijassou, *Médoc*, I, 364–9, 409–10; *The Economist*, "Hedonism and Claret" (December 17, 2009), pp. 121–2, makes the explicit claim that Haut Brion was produced for the middle classes. It was not.

10. Jancis Robinson, ed., *The Oxford Companion to Wine* (Oxford, 1994), p. 242; René Pijassou, "Le Vignoble Bordelais. La Naissance des Grands Crus," in F.-G. Pariset, ed., *Bordeaux au XVIIIe Siècle*, Vol. V of Charles Higounet, ed., *Histoire de Bordeaux* (Bordeaux, 1968), p. 165.

11. For a discussion of wine rectifying and adulteration in early modern England, see Chapter 3, and, more generally, Rod Phillips, *A Short History of Wine* (London, 2000), passim, and idem, "Wine and Adulteration," *History Today* (June, 2000), pp. 31–7.

12. Pijassou, *Le Médoc*, I, 337. The English language has no equivalent of the French word *terroir*, which indicates a specific plot of land and the taste of the wine that is derived from it. Pontac's creation of Haut Brion seems to be the first attempt to use *terroir* as a selling point.

13. Ben Weinreb and Christopher Hibbert, eds, *The London Encyclopedia* (London, 1983), pp. 627–8. André Simon incorrectly gave the address of Pontac's Head as being behind the Old Bailey, in Christ Church Passage. *The History of the Wine Trade in England*, 3 vols (London, 1909), III, 222. Since that time the mistake has often been repeated. See, for example, Hugh Johnson, *Vintage: The Story of Wine* (New York, 1989), p. 203; and Andrew Barr, *Drink: A Social History* (London, 1998), p. 44.

14. Henri Misson, a Huguenot refugee in early eighteenth-century London, said of Pontac's Head, "those who would dine at one or two guineas per head, are handsomely accomodated at our famous Pontac's." *M. Misson's Memoirs and Observations on his Travels over England* (London, 1719), p. 147.

15. Weinreb and Hibbert, *London Encyclopedia*, pp. 627–8.

16. John Locke, "Observations upon the Growth and Culture of Vines and Olives: The Production of Silk: The Preservation of Fruits," *The Works of John Locke*, 10 vols (London, 1823), X, 329.

17. Locke, *Works*, X, 351.

18. Clive Coates, *Grands Vins: The Finest Châteaux of Bordeaux and their Wines* (Berkeley, 1995), pp. 310–15.

19. Bibliothèque Municipale de Bordeaux (BMB), Fonds Itié, carton 4, liasse 1689–1691. For a summary of these wine-making practices at Haut Brion, see Pijasou, *Medoc*, I, 346–7.

20. John Locke, *Locke's Travels in France 1675–1679*, ed. John Lough (Cambridge, 1953), p. 142. In listing the provenance of the Bordeaux region's finest wines, Locke was using two unequal terms: Médoc is a region to the immediate north of Bordeaux, while Pontac was a specific place just outside the old city walls to the southwest, in what is known as the Graves region (so named for its gravelly soil). Terminological confusion aside, what is interesting to the historian of wine is that these two districts had already in the late 1670s established their reputations for producing the finest clarets.

21. John Evelyn, *The Diary of John Evelyn*, ed. E.S. de Beer, 6 vols (Oxford, 1955), IV, 329.

22. Pijassou, *Médoc*, I, 340.

23. My friend and colleague Brian Cowan claims that the "presumption that Pontack [the restaurateur] was the son of Arnaud de Pontac (1599–1681), president of the parlement of Bordeaux, must be dismissed, for Pontack's only son, Francois Auguste de Pontac, died in 1694 and Pontack the tavern keeper was alive in London in 1695." Cowan, "Pontack" (fl. 1666–1711), *Oxford Dictionary of National Biography*, 60 vols (Oxford, 2004), ref: ODNB/22509. I disagree with this conclusion. François-Auguste de Pontac arrived in London in or around 1666 and returned to Bordeaux in 1689, when war between England and France began. Cowan denies the evidence of men such as John Evelyn who met Pontac in 1683 and referred to him as the son of the president of the parlement of Bordeaux (see text). What seems likely, therefore, is that upon the departure from London of François-Auguste de Pontac in 1689, the new proprietor of the tavern, if not an actual member of the Pontac family, used the name "Pontack" for commercial purposes.

24. Pijassou, *Médoc*, I, 347–50.

25. Richard Ames, *A Farther Search after Claret* (London, 1691), p. 9.

26. See Chapter 2 for more details on the increases of wine duties in the 1690s.

27. While the Dutch purchased a greater amount of wine from the Bordeaux region than the English in the 1690s and throughout the eighteenth century, they were famous among the Bordelais producers for purchasing the least expensive white wines. Théophile Malvezin, *Histoire du Commerce de Bordeaux depuis les Origines jusqu'à nos jours*, 3 vols (Bordeaux, 1892), III, 271–7, 318–21; Maurice Braure, "Quelques Aspects des Relations Commerciales entre la France et l'Angleterre au XVIIIe Siècle," *Annales du Midi* (1953), pp. 67–89; Christian Huetz de Lemps, "Le Commerce Maritime des Vins d'Aquitaine de 1698 à 1716," *Revue Historique de Bordeaux* (1965), pp. 25–43; Huetz de Lemps, *Géographie du Commerce*, pp. 105–16, 181–207.

28. Huetz de Lemps, *Géographie du Commerce*, pp. 148–50. In 1703–4, 85 tuns were exported from Bordeaux to England.

29. JHC, XVII, 365.

30. P. M. Handover, *A History of the London Gazette, 1665–1965* (London, 1965), p. 25.

31. *London Gazette*, no. 3963, November 4, 1703.

32. In this way, the use of generic or broadly geographical terms for French wines, such as "claret," "white Bordeaux," or "High Country" (from up the Dordogne and Garonne rivers) was similar to the nomenclature used for Spanish wines that were seized during the war. These were usually listed as "red" or "white," or occasionally by their general place of origin: Malaga, Sherris (Xerez), Palm-sack (Las Palmas) and Canary. For French wines, see, for example, *London Gazette*, no. 3952, October 11, 1703; no. 4087, January 11, 1705; no. 4097, February 15, 1705; no. 4100, February 26, 1705. For Spanish wines, see, for example, *London Gazette*, no. 3933, July 22, 1703; no. 4010, April 17, 1704; no. 4031, June 29, 1704; no. 4037, July 20, 1704.

33. *London Gazette*, no. 4040, July 31, 1704; no. 4055, September 24, 1704.

34. Pijassou, *Médoc*, I, 372–9.

35. *London Gazette*, no. 4123, May 12, 1705. With this notice we return briefly to the question raised earlier about the possible difference between Haut Brion and Pontac, and clearly the evidence here suggests two distinct wines, just as evidence elsewhere suggests that they were one and the same. Pijassou, who believed that they were the same wine, nevertheless offered that Pontac could have been the name of a wine from Margaux,

because the d'Aulède family, owners of Château Margaux, became co-owners of Haut Brion after the death of Arnaud de Pontac in 1682. Pijassou, *Médoc*, I, 375. However, we recall that Locke used the expression "vine de Pontack" when referring to wine made at Haut Brion in 1678.

36. *London Gazette*, no. 4128, June 4, 1705; no. 4132, June 18, 1705.
37. Johnson, *Vintage*, p. 208.
38. Ibid.
39. Ibid.
40. *London Gazette*, no. 4333, May 22, 1707.
41. According to the Classification of 1855, Chateaux Haut Brion, Margaux, Lafite, and Latour were the only "First Growth" wines. Chateau Mouton Rothschild was added to this group in 1973.
42. *London Gazette*, no. 4334, May 26, 1707.
43. NA, L.S. 13/96, Wine Order Book for the Royal Household, 1702–1709.
44. NA, L.S. 13/268, Wine Accounts of the Royal Household, 1719–1731.
45. NA, L.S. 13/46, Wine Accounts of the Royal Household, 1727.
46. NA, L.S. 13/269, Wine Accounts of the Royal Household, 1733–1752.
47. John Gay, *John Gay: Poetry and Prose*, ed. Vinton A. Dearing, 2 vols (Oxford, 1974), "Wine," I, 21–9.
48. Plumb, *Growth of Political* Stability, p. 153.
49. Juan Christian Pellicer, "*Wine* (1708) and the Whigs," *British Journal for Eighteenth-Century Studies*, 27 (2004), 245–55; J. A. Downie, "Gay's Politics," in *John Gay and the Scriblerians*, ed. Peter Lewis and Nigel Wood (London, 1988), pp. 44–61; David Nokes, *John Gay: A Profession of Friendship* (Oxford, 1995).
50. All citations regarding Hervey's wine cellar are taken from Suffolk Record Office, Bury St Edmunds, 941/46/13/14, "Expense Book of John Hervey, first Earl of Bristol." Most of this information has been republished in *The Diary of John Hervey, first Earl of Bristol. With extracts from his book of expenses, 1688–1742*, ed. S. H. A. Hervey (Wells, 1894), "Wine," pp. 168–80.
51. The origins of some wines are not specified, so all figures are based on what is known, and are, therefore, close approximations.
52. *Margaux* is variously spelled as *Margoose, Margous, Margoo*, and sometimes referred to as *Chateau Margou, Margou-Claret*, and *Chasteau Margoux*. Hervey's use of "Chateau" to denominate a Bordeaux winery is only used for Margaux, and was first written on September 29, 1716. This is the first use of which I am aware of the term "chateau" to designate a winery.
53. Hervey purchased wine from a number of different merchants and often already in bottles. His bottle purchases were part of a trend that began in England with Charles II, but which for most of the eighteenth century affected only a tiny percentage of wines. Significantly, it was wealthy English consumers who were the first to bottle-age luxury claret. A letter from a Paris-based merchant, M. Carme, to his correspondent in Bordeaux, M. Wischold, dated February 22, 1714, shows two French merchants playing catch-up in order to make a profit on the lucrative English market. Carme asked Wischold to purchase four hogsheads of "old, black and smooth" Margaux wine, which he said: "You must put [the hogsheads of wine] into wicker-covered bottles that are well stopped with cork, seal them with wax and put them in small cases as they do in Italy, of 50 bottles each, address them to our correspondent in London, Mr. Paul Hovard for our account. ... I believe this experiment will work wonders, after which we can send greater quantities" and make a profit of two shillings per bottle. (My translation.) Archives Départmentale de Gironde (ADG), Bordeaux, "Négociants," 7 B 3017.
54. Among the estate-grown clarets purchased by Hervey after 1702 the prices varied between roughly £40 and £50 per hogshead, while generic clarets purchased by Hervey cost between £25 and £40 per hogshead. Given that English import tariffs on all wines stayed the same from 1705 until 1745, price fluctuations in this instance can be attributed to the

varied results of each vintage and changing transport costs. On average, burgundy and Hermitage cost the same as luxury claret; however, champagne was consistently the most expensive wine of all. This is no surprise, for champagne, along with burgundy, had high transport costs to England. These wines, the most fashionable in Paris and Versailles, had to go overland and downriver before even arriving at a seaport, something that wines from Bordeaux did not have to do. For champagne, there was the added risk that the wine would re-ferment in the warm summer months or in the hold of a ship. Until the process of secondary fermentation was understood and controlled in the mid-eighteenth century, transporting champagne was a risky business as wine in casks or bottles could re-ferment and burst. Thus, part of the cost of champagne was paying for the wines that did not arrive successfully. Robinson, *Oxford Companion*, p. 210; Thomas Brennan, *Burgundy to Champagne: The Wine Trade in Early Modern France* (Baltimore, 1997), pp. 246–58.

55. BL, Add. MS 61664, f. 13, "An exact inventory of the late Earl of Sunderland's Cellars, 13 June 1722."
56. In the inventory of June 13, 1722, this wine is listed simply as "white wine," but later evidence reveals it to be white port. See, BL, Add. MS 61664, f. 60, and the discussion of the Countess of Sunderland's wines below.
57. Plumb, "Father and Son," p. 146.
58. Biographical material for Colonel Robert Walpole and Sir Robert Walpole is based upon Plumb, "Father and Son," in his *Men and Centuries* (London, 1963), pp. 121–46.
59. Plumb, "Father and Son," p. 141.
60. Each of these wines cost £45 per hogshead. The approximately 25 dozen (300) glass bottles that were eventually needed for each hogshead were included in the price of the wine, but added to the cost were charges for racking and bottling, corks for sealing the bottles, hampers for transporting them, and of course "porterage" itself, as in some instances the wine was delivered to Walpole in bottle and not in cask. Apparently, even high-volume orders from the Prime Minister did not merit free delivery.
61. Plumb, "Father and Son," p. 121.
62. John Hervey, *Lord Hervey and His Friends, 1726–1738: Based on Letters from Holland House, Melbury and Ickworth*, ed. Lord Ilchester (London, 1950), p. 73.
63. For the political uses of politeness in England, see Lawrence Klein, *Shaftesbury and the Culture of Politeness*; idem, "Shaftesbury, Politeness and the Politics of Religion," in Nicholas Phillipson and Quentin Skinner, eds, *Political Discourse in Early Modern Britain* (Cambridge, 1993); idem, "Liberty, Manners and Politeness in Early Eighteenth Century England," *Historical Journal*, 32 (1989), 583–605; idem, "Politeness and the Interpretation of the British Eighteenth Century," *Historical Journal*, 45 (2002), 869–98; idem, "Politeness for Plebes: Consumption and Social Identity in Early-Eighteenth Century England," in Ann Bermingham and John Brewer, eds. *The Consumption of Culture, 1600–1800: Image, Object, Text* (Abingdon, 1995), pp. 362–82; J. G. A. Pocock, "Virtue, Rights and Manners: A Model for Historians of Political Thought", in his *Virtue, Commerce and History*; in the same volume, see "The Varieties of Whiggism from Exclusion to Reform," esp. pp. 230–9; Nicholas Phillipson, "Politics and Politeness in the Reigns of Anne and the Early Hanoverians," in J. G. A. Pocock, *The Varieties of British Political Thought, 1500–1800* (Cambridge, 1993), pp. 211–45. For the general effects of politeness upon eighteenth-century English politics and society, see Paul Langford, *A Polite and Commercial People*; idem, "Politics and Manners from Sir Robert Walpole to Sir Robert Peel," *Proceedings of the British Academy*, 94 (1996), 103–25. For the influence of politeness upon expressions of English culture, see, John Brewer, *The Pleasures of the Imagination: English Culture in the Eighteenth Century* (London, 1997); Peter Borsay, *The English Urban Renaissance: Culture and Society in the Provincial Town, 1660–1770* (Oxford, 1989); Steven Shapin, *A History of Truth: Civility and Science in Seventeenth-Century England* (Chicago, 1994); Tom Williamson, *Polite Landscapes: Gardens and Society in Eighteenth-Century England* (Stroud, 1995). For the connection between politeness and

conceptions of masculinity, see Philip Carter, *Men and the Emergence of Polite Society, Britain 1660–1800* (Harlow, 2001); Tim Hitchcock and Michèle Cohen, eds, *English Masculinities, 1660–1800* (London, 1999). For a general overview of the scholarship on politeness, see the various contributions to a forum in *Transactions of the Royal Historical Society*, 6th ser., 12 (2002), 263–472.

64. Lawrence Klein, "Liberty, Manners, and Politeness in Early-Eighteenth-Century England," *Historical Journal*, 32 (1989), 583; John Styles, "Introduction to Georgian Britain, 1714–1837," in Michael Snodin and John Styles, *Design and the Decorative Arts, Britain 1500–1900* (London, 2001), p. 183.

65. See, for example, Philip Carter, "James Boswell's Manliness," in Tim Hitchcock and Michèle Cohen, eds, *English Masculinities, 1660–1800* (London, 1999), pp. 111–30; Vic Gatrell, *City of Laughter: Sex and Satire in Eighteenth Century London* (New York, 2006), pp. 15–19; Karen Harvey, "The History of Masculinity, circa 1650–1800," and Michèle Cohen, "Manners Make the Man: Politeness, Chivalry, and the Construction of Masculinity, 1750–1830," *Journal of British Studies*, 44 (April, 2005), 296–311 and 312–29; Klein, "Politeness and the Interpretation of the British Eighteenth Century," pp. 869–73, 896–8.

66. On "Old" and "Modern Whigs," see Pocock, "The Varieties of Whiggism," in *Virtue, Commerce, and History*, esp. pp. 230–9; On luxury, see Maxine Berg, *Luxury and Pleasure in Eighteenth-Century Britain* (Oxford, 2005); Linda Levy Peck, *Consuming Splendor: Society and Culture in Seventeenth-Century England* (Cambridge, 2005); Woodruff Smith, *Consumption and the Making of Respectability, 1600–1800* (New York, 2002), pp. 63–104; Christopher Berry, *The Idea of Luxury: A Conceptual and Historical Investigation* (Cambridge, 1994); John Sekora, *Luxury: The Concept in Western Thought, Eden to Smollett* (Baltimore, 1977).

67. Lawrence Klein, "Courtly *Politesse* and Civic Politeness in France and England," *Halcyon*, 14 (1992), 171–81.

68. Klein, "Liberty, Manners and Politeness," p. 588.

69. Margot Finn, "Men's Things: Masculine Possession and the Consumer Revolution," *Social History*, 25:2 (May, 2000), 133–55.

70. Styles, "Introduction," in Snodin and Styles, *Design and the Decorative Arts*, p. 184.

71. Klein, "Liberty, Manners," pp. 587–8: "In other words, in the language of politeness, the archetypal gentleman was envisioned in the company of his peers demonstrating good taste in the manner of his social interactions or in the character of his cultural predilections and activities." For in-depth discussions of taste in the eighteenth century, see Jules Lubbock, *The Tyranny of Taste: The Politics of Architecture and Design in Britain 1550–1960* (New Haven, 1995); George Dickie, *The Century of Taste: The Philosophical Odyssey of Taste in the Eighteenth Century* (Oxford, 1996); R. W. Jones, *Gender and the Formation of Taste in Eighteenth-Century Britain* (Cambridge, 1998); Carolyn Korsmeyer, *Making Sense of Taste: Food and Philosophy* (Ithaca, 1999), pp. 38–54; Denise Gigante, *Taste: A Literary History* (New Haven, 2005), pp. 47–67.

72. Thomas, *Ends of Life*, p. 129.

73. Lawrence Klein, "The Political Significance of 'Politeness' in Early-Eighteenth-Century Britain," in Gordon Schochet, ed., *Politics, Politeness and Patriotism* (Washington, DC, 1993), p. 76.

74. Klein, "Politeness and the Interpretation of the British Eighteenth Century," p. 886; Snodin, "'Style' in Georgian Britain," *Design and the Decorative Arts*, pp. 187–214; Borsay, *English Urban Renaissance*, pp. 235–306.

75. Charles Saumarez Smith, *Eighteenth-Century Decoration: Design and the Domestic Interior in England* (New York, 1993), pp. 70–3; Sacheverell Sitwell, *Conversation Pieces: A Survey of English Domestic Portraits and Their Painters* (London, 1936); London County Council, *The Conversation Piece in Georgian England* (London, 1965); Mario Praz, *Conversation Pieces: A Survey of the Informal Group Portrait in Europe and America* (University Park, PA, 1971); Ellen G. D'Oench, *The Conversation Piece: Arthur Devis and His Contemporaries* (New Haven, 1980); Jane Turner, ed., *The Dictionary of Art*, 34 vols (New York, 1996), VII, 784–7.

76. Sitwell attributes "The Brothers Clarke of Swakeleys and Friends" to Hogarth and offers a date of 1750, when Thomas Clarke purchased his property called Swakeleys, at Ickenham, Middlesex. Sitwell, *Conversation Pieces*, p. 92 and plate 19. Praz attributes the painting to Hamilton and gives a date of c. 1730. Praz, *Conversation Pieces*, pp. 99, 247 and plate 263. The evidence in Hamilton's favor lies primarily in the fact that Hogarth scholars do not claim the painting for him. See, for example, Frederick Antal, *Hogarth and His Place in European Art* (London, 1961), and Ronald Paulson, *Hogarth: His Life, Times and Art*, 2 vols (New Haven, 1971).

77. Ibid., p. 42, plate 32b. This painting is also known as "Mr. Dudley Woodbridge celebrates his call to the Bar in his chambers at Brick Court, Middle Temple," c. 1730, private collection, New York, NY.

78. Pijassou, *Medoc*, I, 404–5.

79. In the period 1707–11, "New French Clarets" accounted for 2,387 out of 3,370 hogsheads, or 71 per cent, of seized French wines. Pijassou, *Médoc*, I, 377.

80. *London Gazette*, August 4, 1711.

81. Thomas, *The Ends of Life*, p. 129; Eagleton, *The Ideology of the Aesthetic*, pp. 31–69.

82. Plumb, *Growth of Political Stability*, p. 163.

83. Susan Jenkins, *Portrait of a Patron: The Patronage and Collecting of James Brydges, 1st Duke of Chandos, 1644–1744* (Aldershot, 2007).

84. Huntington Library, ST vol. 60 (1–3): Brydges' wine books from Cannons and London, 1718–1728.

85. C. H. Collins Baker and Muriel Baker, *The Life and Circumstances of James Brydges, First Duke of Chandos: Patron of the Liberal Arts* (Oxford, 1949), pp. 188–9.

86. Baker and Baker, *Life of Brydges*, p. 188. For details of Cantillon's fascinating and varied life, see Antoine E. Murphy, *Richard Cantillon: Entrepreneur and Economist* (Oxford, 1986). Cantillon apparently had many English clients (p. 142, 196–8). For the extensive Irish involvement in the Bordeaux wine trade, see Renagh Holohan and Jeremy Williams, *The Irish Châteaux: In Search of Descendants of the Wild Geese* (Dublin, 1999).

87. Baker and Baker, *Life of Brydges*, pp. 188–91.

88. Ibid., p. 190.

89. 3rd. Earl of Shaftesbury, Anthony Ashley Cooper, *Characteristics of Men, Manners, Opinions, Times*, 2 vols, ed. John Robertson (Gloucester, MA, 1963), I, 79.

90. For a longer discussion of this argument, see Eagleton, *Ideology of the Aesthetic*, pp. 31–69; Klein, *Shaftesbury and the Culture of Politeness*, pp. 211–12.

91. Thomas, *Ends of Life*, p. 115.

6 "Firm and erect the Caledonian stood"

1. John Hill Burton, *The Lives of Simon Lord Lovat and Duncan Forbes of Culloden, from original sources* (London, 1847), p. 296. This letter was dated at Inverness, September 26, 1716.

2. Edward Burt, *Letters from a Gentleman in the North of Scotland to his Friend in London*, 2 vols (London, 1754), I, 15.

3. Burt and his companions were "very merry till the Clock struck Ten, the hour when everybody is at Liberty, by beat of the City Drum, to throw their Filth out at the Windows. The Company began to light Pieces of Paper, and throw them upon the Table to smoke the Room, and, as I thought, to mix one bad Smell with another." Burt, *Letters from a Gentleman*, I, 19–20.

4. Ibid., I, 138.

5. Ibid., I, 138–9.

6. This could be wine from the former independent principality of Orange in southern France, it could be an early name for Châteauneuf-du-Pape, or it could be a wine mixed with orange brandy and sugar.

7. NAS, GD 26/6/178, "Inventory of the wine cellar at Balgony, taken the 28th May 1726, and the key delivered up by Mr. Ker to the Earle of Leven."

8. "In praise of Claret," from McNeill, *Scots Cellar*, pp. 158–9: *dull draff-drink*, whisky; *dowff*, dull, spiritless; *yowff*, sharp yelling; *howff*, a haunt, resort, tavern; *chancy*, lucky, bringing luck; *gowff*, blow, hit.

9. From "To the Ph__, an Ode" (1721), in *The Works of Allan Ramsay*, ed. Burns Martin and John W. Oliver, 2 vols (Edinburgh, 1944–5), I, 223; *gash*, lively, talkative.

10. Kay and Maclean speak of the "reduced customs differential following the Union," *Knee Deep in Claret*, p. 75; however, there was no differential at all; François Crouzet, writing about exports to the British Isles, says, "It was Scotland and especially Ireland that were in fact the principal outlets for wines from Bordeaux; because the customs duties were less elevated, less prohibitive than in England, consumption of French wines was relatively greater." (My translation.) Crouzet, "Le Commerce de Bordeaux," in F-G. Pariset, ed., *Bordeaux au XVIIIème Siècle*, vol. V of Charles Higounet, ed., *Histoire de Bordeaux* (Bordeaux, 1968), p. 263. Crouzet's analysis is correct in the case of Ireland but not so for Scotland, where the Customs duty was the same as in England after 1707.

11. Writing about the "Early Hanoverian Years," A. D. Francis states: "In England Spanish wines were still well to the fore and still more so in Scotland. Scotland was a poor country and perhaps smuggled more than paid customs duty, but in these years it took over 1,000 tuns of Spanish wine, about 90% of its total imports of wine." *The Wine Trade* (London, 1972), p. 152. Unfortunately, Francis does not cite his Scottish sources, although in any case his analysis is wrong. Most Scottish wine imports at the time came directly or indirectly from France; Huetz de Lemps also errs in his analysis when he writes: "Le commerce des vins de Bordeaux vers l'Ecosse semble donc avoir reçu un coup mortel pendant la guerre [1702–13] du fait de l'Acte d'Union avec l'Angleterre. Les Ecossais perdirent l'habitude de boire du vin pour se 'reconvertir' à d'autres boissons comme la biere et le whisky!" *Géographie du Commerce*, p. 179. This statement is based on official export figures from Bordeaux for the years 1713–16, and not on Scottish import figures or knowledge of Scottish smuggling. In effect, he was speaking of the late eighteenth century, but not the early eighteenth century. Furthermore, Lowland Scots were not "reconverted" to the taste for whisky, they were converted to it; prior to the late eighteenth century very little whisky was consumed in Lowland Scotland at all.

12. Cambridge University Library (CUL), CH (H) 41/18/6, "Of the running of wine," a report to Walpole dated March 1733, shows that most French wine was smuggled into the south coast. This report includes CH (H) 41/18/7, "An account of the particular instances of frauds which have come to the knowledge of the commissioners of the Customs relating to wine in London and the outports." See also, CH (H) 41/29, "A memorandum concerning smuggling in the Isle of Guernsey, from Ventris Colombine, Customs officer, to Robert Walpole," c. 1733; André Simon, *Bottlescrew Days: Wine Drinking in England during the Eighteenth Century* (London, 1926), p. 85.

13. For an extensive discussion of Scottish Customs gathering before the Union, see Smout, *Scottish Trade*, pp. 32–46.

14. Parliamentary Report, C.8706, *Customs Tariffs*, p. 19. Reprinted letter from the Commissioner of Customs in England to the Treasury, April 22, 1707, and reprinted minute of the Treasury, April 22, 1707.

15. Parliamentary Report, C.8706, *Customs Tariffs*, pp. 19–20. Reprinted letter from the Commissioners of Customs in Scotland to the Treasury, July 15, 1707.

16. Parliamentary Report, C.8706, *Customs Tariffs*, p. 20.

17. T. M. Devine, *The Scottish Nation, 1700–2000* (Harmondsworth, 1999), pp. 56–7.

18. CUL, CH (H) 40/16, Report of Robert Paul, Richard Sankey, and Samuel Kettilby of their general survey of the ports of Scotland to the Lords Commissioners of HM Treasury, September 17, 1724; Kay and Maclean, *Knee Deep in Claret*, Chapters 9 and 12.

19. Simon, *Bottlescrew Days*, pp. 85–9.

20. John, Steuart, ed. *Letter Book of Baillie*, Mackay, June 22, 1756, p. 258.

21. CUL, CH (H) 40/16, Report ... general survey of the ports of Scotland, September 17, 1724.

22. Ibid.; Kay and Maclean, *Knee Deep in Claret*, Chapter 8.
23. CUL, CH (H) 40/16, Report … general survey of the ports of Scotland, September 17, 1724.
24. CUL, CH (H) 40/13, Report …general survey of the ports of Scotland, August 24, 1724.
25. CUL, CH (H) 40/14, Report … general survey of the ports of Scotland, August 24, 1724.
26. CUL, CH (H) 40/19, Report … general survey of the ports of Scotland, October 8, 1724.
27. CUL, CH (H) 41/18/6, "Of the running of wine, March 1733"; 41/18/7, "An account of the particular instances of frauds which have come to the knowledge of the Commissioners of the Customs relating to wine in London and the outports," March 1733; 41/29, "Memorandum concerning smuggling in the isle of Guernsey," c. 1733. For specific examples of smuggling in England, see Cal Winslow, "Sussex Smugglers," in Douglas Hay, Peter Linebaugh, John G. Rule, E. P. Thompson and Cal Winslow, *Albion's Fatal Tree: Crime and Society in Eighteenth-Century England* (New York, 1975), pp. 119–66; Paul Monod, "Dangerous Merchandise: Smuggling, Jacobitism, and Commercial Culture in Southeast England, 1690–1760," *Journal of British Studies*, 30 (April, 1991), 150–82; William J. Ashworth, *Customs and Excise: Trade, Production and Consumption in England, 1640–1845* (Oxford, 2003), pp. 199–200. See also *Report from the Committee of the House of Commons, Appointed to enquire into the Frauds and Abuses of the Customs, to the Prejudice of Trade, and Diminution of the Revenue* (London, 1733), reprinted in *House of Commons Sessional Papers of the Eighteenth Century*, ed. Sheila Lambert, 147 vols. (Wilmington, Del., 1975), XII, 323–425.
28. There was a great deal of debate surrounding Walpole's proposal in England; however, it had a distinct Scottish angle that was not much discussed at the time, nor has it been explored by scholars since. Paul Langford, *The Excise Crisis* (Oxford, 1975), pp. 140, 109, 140, says that Scottish voting constituencies were so small and the Earl of Islay in such control that opposition to the bill "never got off the ground." This is remarkable because the excise tax was proposed for tobacco and wine, which were the most valuable and probably the most smuggled or fraudulently declared imports of Glasgow and Leith respectively.
29. For general discussions of the Excise Crisis and why the bill failed, see Langford, *Excise Crisis*, passim; Ashworth, *Customs and Excise*, pp. 63–84; Kathleen Wilson, *A Sense of the People: Politics, Culture and Imperialism in England, 1715–1785* (Cambridge, 1995), pp. 117–36.
30. Kay and Maclean, *Knee Deep in Claret*, p. 151.
31. Burt, *Letters from a Gentleman*, I, 168.
32. Ibid., I, 168–70.
33. Mitchison, *History of Scotland*, p. 324.
34. J. H. Plumb, *The Growth of Political Stability in England, 1675–1725* (London, 1967), p. 181.
35. Burt, *Letters from a Gentleman*, I, 171–2.
36. Cited in Kay and Maclean, *Knee Deep in Claret*, p. 101.
37. NAS, E 504/22, Port of Leith, Collector's Quarterly Accounts.
38. NAS, E 504/22/1, Port of Leith, Collector's Quarterly Accounts, 1 Oct. 1742–31 December 1742.
39. NAS, E 504/22/1, Port of Leith, Collector's Quarterly Accounts, 1 Jan. 1745–31 March 1742.
40. Apparently, Norway's role in this deception went back to the seventeenth century at least. Smout, *Scottish Trade*, p. 158.
41. *Letter Book of Bailie John Steuart*, ed. Mackay, April 5, 1722, pp. 179–80.
42. National Library of Scotland (NLS), Adv. 82.3.3, ff. 23, 147, wine bills from M. Wood to Laurence Oliphant, Laird of Gask, 1723.
43. Negus was a drink made of wine, hot water, lemon juice, sugar, and nutmeg; it was named after Francis Negus, an English army officer (d. 1732).
44. NLS, Adv. 82.4.1, f. 47, wine and supper bill from Anne Hickson, to Oliphant of Gask, Perth, December 20, 1745.

45. NLS, Adv. 82.4.1, f. 141, wine and supper bill from Anne Hickson, to Oliphant of Gask, Perth, January 21, 1746.
46. Accounts of James Gib, quoted in Kay and Maclean, *Knee Deep in Claret*, pp. 139–40.
47. Louis M. Cullen, *Smuggling and the Ayrshire Economic Boom of the 1760s and 1770s*, Ayrshire Monograph no. 14 (Darvel, Ayrshire, 1994), pp. 10, 24.
48. Given the purpose of Oliphant's request, it is surprising that he wanted hogsheads. Since he specified Spanish casks, he probably meant a half-butt, which was roughly the equivalent in volume, although not in shape to a hogshead. The important thing was that a trained eye could tell the difference between French, Spanish, and Portuguese casks.
49. NAS GD 1/306/1 Letter book of Alexander Oliphant of Ayr, Oliphant of Ayr to Barry, January 14, 1767.
50. Archives Nationale, Paris, F12/1500, cited in Crouzet, "Commerce de Bordeaux," p. 264. Crouzet gives his figures in modern Bordeaux *tonneaux*, which means 900-litre barrels. I have therefore converted his figure from 2,500 tonneaux to 1,975 British tuns, by multiplying the former figure by .79. Interestingly, during the 1740s Crouzet gives annual averages of 1,000 tonneaux of wine from Bordeaux to England and 4,000 tonneaux to Ireland. Scottish figures are derived from NAS, E 504/22/1, Port of Leith, Collector's Quarterly Accounts, October 1, 1742–December 31, 1742.
51. Devine, *Scottish Nation*, p. 20.
52. [Robert Walpole?], *A Letter from a Member of Parliament to his Friend in the Country, Concerning the Duties on Wine and Tobacco* (London, 1733), p. 16.
53. See Chapters 7 and 8.
54. NAS, GD 124/15/513/21, Erskine to Mar, June 28, 1707; and GD 124/15/513/34, Erskine to Mar, October 28, 1707.
55. NAS, GD 124/15/513/34, Erskine to Mar, October 28, 1707.
56. *Lady Grisell Baillie's Household Book, 1692–1733*, ed. Robert Scott Moncrief (Edinburgh, 1911), p. 416.
57. For discussions of "politeness" in Scotland, see: Nicholas Phillipson, "Culture and Society in the Eighteenth-Century Province: The Case of Edinburgh in the Scottish Enlightenment," in Lawrence Stone, ed., *The University in Society*, 2 vols (Princeton, 1974), II, 407–48; idem, "Politeness and Politics in the Reign of Queen Anne and the Early Hanoverians," in J. G. A. Pocock, ed., *The Varieties of British Political Thought, 1500–1800* (Cambridge, 1993), pp. 211–45; idem, *Hume* (New York, 1989); John Dwyer, *Virtuous Discourse: Sensibility in Late-Eighteenth Century Scotland* (Edinburgh, 1987); idem, "Introduction—A 'Peculiar Blessing': Social Converse in Scotland from Hutcheson to Burns," in John Dwyer and Richard B. Sher, eds, *Sociability and Society in Eighteenth-Century Scotland* (Edinburgh, 1993), pp. 96–118; Rosalind Carr, "The Gentleman and the Soldier: Patriotic Masculinities in Eighteenth-Century Scotland," *Journal of Scottish Historical Studies*, 28:2 (2008), 102–21.
58. *Letter Book of Bailie John Steuart*, ed. Mackay, October 17, 1718, p. 97. For Gordon's Jacobitism, see Monod, "Dangerous Merchandise," p. 171 and n. 92.
59. *Letter Book of Bailie John Steuart*, ed. Mackay, July 17, 1721, p. 155.
60. Ibid., July 10, 1734, p. 382.
61. Kay and Maclean, *Knee Deep in Claret*, pp. 115–20.
62. For instance, John Ramsay (1736–1814) said, "if the old claret was very cheap, it had little strength. Judge Graham of Airth told Mr. Abercromby that the wine imported in his younger days drank very well from November or December that it came in, till the summer session." John Ramsay of Auchtertyre, *Scotland and Scotsmen in the Eighteenth Century*, 2 vols (London, 1888), II, 79fn.
63. For some of the major historiographical debates surrounding in Jacobitism in Scotland, see Bruce Lenman, *The Jacobite Risings in Britain, 1689–1746* (London, 1980); Murray Pittock, *Jacobitism* (New York, 1998).
64. The repeal of the unlucky Union.
65. Chambers, *Traditions*, esp. pp. 142 and 339; McNeill, *Cellar*, pp. 56–75; Kay and Maclean, *Knee Deep in Claret*, Chapter 7.

66. The literature here is extensive, but the principal assertions have been made by Linda Colley, *Britons: Forging the Nation, 1707–1837* (New Haven, 1992), who sees the Anglicization of Scotland, and the closely related construction of a truly British identity as a century-long process, but one that got a particular boost from the Jacobite rebellions of 1715 and 1745, and from the Seven Years' War. Colin Kidd, *Subverting Scotland's Past: Scottish Whig Historians and the Creation of an Anglo-British identity, c. 1689–1830* (Cambridge, 1993), focuses on the Anglicization of Scottish history, and also identifies the mid-eighteenth-century as the beginning of what he calls "Anglo-British" identity. See also, Kidd, "North Britishness and the Nature of Eighteenth-Century British Patriotisms," *Historical Journal*, 39:2 (1996), 361–82; idem, *British Identities Before Nationalism: Ethnicity and Nationhood in the Atlantic World, 1600–1800* (Cambridge, 1999); Murray Pittock, *Inventing and Resisting Britain: Cultural Identities in Britain and Ireland, 1685–1789* (New York, 1997), takes issue with Colley, and says that it was the Seven Years' War and the French Revolution in particular that finally created a united, Protestant, imperial Britain, although Pittock insists that significant fissures remained. See also, Pittock, *Scottish Nationality* (Basingstoke, 2001); Alexander Murdoch, "Scotland and the Idea of Britain in the Eighteenth Century," in T. M. Devine and J. R. Young, eds, *Eighteenth Century Scotland: New Perspectives* (East Linton, 1999), pp. 106–20; Richard J. Finlay, "Keeping the Covenant: Scottish National Identity," in T. M. Devine and J. R. Young, eds, *Eighteenth Century Scotland: New Perspectives* (East Linton, 1999), pp. 121–33; idem, "Caledonia or North Britain? Scottish Identity in the Eighteenth Century," in Dauvit Broun, R. J. Finlay, and Michael Lynch, eds, *Image and Identity: The Making and Remaking of Scotland through the Ages* (Edinburgh, 1998), pp. 143–56.
67. Public Record Office, Customs 14. These figures are based on my own tabulations and are explored in much greater detail in Chapter 5.
68. Paul Butel, "Le trafic européen de Bordeaux, de la guerre d'Amérique à la Révolution," *Annales du Midi*, 78 (1966), 74–81.
69. Cited in Kay and Maclean, *Knee Deep in Claret*, pp. 104–5.
70. John Home, *The Works of John Home, Esq., now first collected. To which is prefixed, an account of his life and writings, by Henry Mackenzie, Esq.*, 3 vols (Edinburgh, 1822), I, 164. Mackenzie gives no date for the epigram, but writes: "As to the port-wine, it is well known that Mr. Home held it in abhorrence. In his younger days, claret was the only wine drank by gentlemen in Scotland. His epigram on the enforcement of the high duty on French wine in this country, is in most people's hands." Given this evidence, I believe the epigram was probably written in the 1760s. An alternative date is offered by James Crichton-Browne, "Claret in Scotland," *The National Review*, 80 (1922), 404, who claims that Home wrote the epigram as a "protest against Pitt's Budget" (i.e. in the mid-1780s). This seems unlikely, however, as Pitt's budget reforms actually reduced the tariff on French wines (see Chapter 5). Furthermore, Home had a horseback riding accident in 1778 from which he suffered brain damage, after which time his literary output was minimal.
71. For Home's Britishness, see, for example, act I, scene 1 of his most famous play, *Douglas* (first performed in Edinburgh in 1756), wherein Lady Randolph asserts: "War I detest: But war with foreign foes, / Whose manners, language, and whose looks are strange, / Is not so horrid, nor to me so hateful, / As that which with our neighbours oft we wage. / A river here, there an ideal line, / By fancy drawn, divides the sister kingdoms. / On each side dwells a people similar, / As twins are to each other; valiant both: / Both for their valour famous through the world." Home, *Douglas* (London, 1757), p. 2.
72. What exactly Anglo-British identity entailed is a matter of great scholarly debate, but one clear result of its growth was that Scottish identity became more "local, symbolic, and limited in the statements it made and the challenges it offered to the superpower in whose success it played a disproportionate part." Pittock, *Scottish Nationality*, p. 80. Drinking claret had been a symbolic and ultimately unthreatening statement of defiance to the English since 1707, and it continued that role for some years after 1745.

73. For an exploration of some of the different types of Scottish identity in the eighteenth century, see Janet Adam Smith, "Some Eighteenth-Century Ideas of Scotland," in Nicholas Phillipson and Rosalind Mitchison, eds, *Scotland in the Age of Improvement: Essays in Scottish History in the Eighteenth Century* (Edinburgh, 1970), pp. 107–24.

7 "Port is all I pretend to"

1. Figures cited in André L. Simon, *Bottlescrew Days: Wine Drinking in England during the Eighteenth Century* (London, 1926), pp. 74–5.
2. Figures cited in ibid., p. 73.
3. BL, Add. MS 38854, f. 147, Slingsby Bethell, Esq. to Thomas Gordon, for wine delivered to the Old Bailey, October 21, 1751.
4. Worcestershire Record Office, City Centre Branch (St Helen's), BA 9504/1, 899:832, Petty Ledger of James Pardoe, Wine Sales, 1741–1746.
5. James Woodforde, *The Diary of a Country Parson, 1758–1802*, ed. John Beresford, 5 vols (Oxford, 1981), I, 12.
6. Ibid., I, 13.
7. Ibid., I, 17. Assuming that the bottles themselves were roughly uniform and that the cask was both its stated size and full, 150 bottles out of 31.5 gallons of wine renders the figure 1.68 pints (26.88 ounces), or 79.5 centiliters. The standard wine bottle used today is 75 centiliters, thus 4.5 centiliters smaller than the average size of Woodforde's bottles.
8. Peter Clark, *The English Alehouse: A Social History 1200–1830* (London, 1983), pp. 6–14.
9. Don Manuel Gonzales, *Voyage to Great Britain*, 1731, cited in F. A. King, *Beer Has a History* (London, 1947).
10. Clark, *English Alehouse*, pp. 11–14; idem, *British Clubs and Societies, 1580–1800: The Origins of an Associational World* (Oxford, 2000), pp. 94–140.
11. Clark, *English Alehouse*, pp. 11–14.
12. For Montesquieu's thoughts on England, see *The Spirit of Laws*. For Voltaire's observations, see his *Letters Concerning the English Nation*. More generally, see J. Churton Collins, *Voltaire, Montesquieu and Rousseau in England* (London, 1908). Recently, books by Ian Buruma, *Anglomania: A European Love Affair* (London, 1998) and Paul Langford, *Englishness Identified: Manners and Character 1650–1850* (Oxford, 2000), have both examined a vast number of the early modern accounts of England and Englishness that were written by foreign observers.
13. César de Saussure, *A Foreign View of England in the reigns of George I and George II*, ed. Madame Van Muyden (London, 1902), pp. 99–100.
14. For English descriptions of port, see the discussion later in this chapter.
15. Numerical estimates of the middle-ranks in eighteenth century England and Wales fluctuate according to the definition of the middle ranks themselves. For a discussion and summary of these estimates see, Jonathan Barry, "Introduction", in Jonathan Berry and Christopher Brooks, eds., The Middling Sort of People: Culture, Society and Politics in England, 1550-1800 (New York, 1994), pp. 1–27, and Endnote 5.
16. All import figures for this chapter are taken from E. B. Schumpeter, *English Overseas Trade Statistics, 1697–1807* (Oxford, 1960), Tables 16 and 17.
17. J. de Macedo, *A Situacao Economica no Tempo de Pombal* (Lisbon, 1951), p. 75, cited in H. E. S. Fisher, *The Portugal Trade: A Study of Anglo-Portuguese Commerce, 1700–1770* (London, 1971), p. 78 n. 1.
18. Sarah Byng Osborn, *The Letters of Sarah Byng Osborn, 1721–1773*, ed. John McClelland (Palo Alto, CA, 1930), p. 34.
19. James Henry Monk, *The Life of Richard Bentley, D. D.*, 2 vols (Cambridge, 1833), II, 401.
20. Alexander Pope, "The Dunciad," Book IV, *Poetry and Prose of Alexander Pope*, ed. Aubrey Williams (Boston, MA, 1969), p. 362.

21. Alexander Pope, *The Correspondence of Alexander Pope*, ed. George Sherburn, 5 vols (Oxford, 1956), Pope to Humphrey Wanley, July 1, 1725, II, 304.
22. Monçao is now in the heart of the Vinho Verde region of northernmost Portugal.
23. A hogshead of port cost Hervey £16. Two years before, in December 1709, Hervey paid over £39 for a hogshead of unnamed "Clarett."
24. See purchases made on January 12, 1710 and December 7, 1710. Suffolk Record Office, Bury St Edmonds, 941/46/13/14. Much of this information is published in *The Diary of John Hervey, first Earl of Bristol. With extracts from his book of expenses, 1688–1742*, ed. S. H. A. Hervey (Wells, 1894), "Wine," pp. 168–80.
25. Statistics are derived from figures cited in Simon, *Bottlescrew Days*, pp. 74–5.
26. BL, Add. MS 61664, ff. 13, "An exact inventory of all the wines in the late Earl of Sunderland's Cellars, June 13th, 1722."
27. BL, Add. MS 61664, f. 60, "Account of the wines taken by Wm. Davis out of the late Earl of Sunderland's Cellars for the use of the Gent. Countess dow[ag]er of Sunderland, June 30th, 1722, from the Honourable John Hooker, Steward to the said Earl." For a complete listing of Charles Spencer's cellar, and what Anne Spencer removed from it in 1722, see Chapter 2.
28. Marlborough's bill for the port was finally paid by his executor in 1725. BL, Add. MS 61349, f. 123b, bill paid by Mr Charles Hodges, executor of the late Duke of Marlborough's estate, to Samuel Braund, April 12, 1725. This delay had nothing to do with the quality of the wine, nor even with the fact that Marlborough died before payment was due. Most terms of credit to the purchaser were for six months, but eighteenth- and nineteenth-century household records are replete with entreaties from desperate merchants for overdue payments. For example, in 1751 Lord Egmont's bill for £161 9s. from the wine merchants Collingwood and Holford was two years overdue, BL, Add. MS 47014 B, ff. 39, 42; Sir Robert Walpole's wine bill from James Bennett in 1736 had not been paid for three years, Cambridge University Library (CUL), CH (H) "Vouchers, 1657–1745." This was simply one of the risks of being a wine merchant, and the principal reason that they—as well as wine shippers and wine producers—had to be well capitalized. Payments were slow throughout the industry, and credit had to be extended repeatedly.
29. C. H. Collins Baker and Muriel Baker, *The Life and Circumstances of James Brydges, First Duke of Chandos, Patron of the Liberal Arts* (Oxford, 1949), pp. 189–90.
30. Matthew Prior, "Alma: or the Progress of the Mind," in *The Literary Works of Matthew Prior*, ed. H. Bunker Wright and Monroe K. Spears, 2 vols (Oxford, 1959), I, 472, 515.
31. CUL, CH (H), "Vouchers, 1657–1745." These wine bills were first analyzed by J. H. Plumb in "Sir Robert Walpole's Wine," in his *Men and Places* (London, 1953), pp. 147–52; and upon Plumb's suggestion, by René Pijassou in *Médoc*, I, 391–7 (see also p. 416 n. 209). Consequently, my own analysis is indebted to both scholars, although my ultimate interpretation is somewhat different.
32. Plumb, "The Walpoles: Father and Son," in his *Men and Centuries* (Boston, MA, 1963), p. 121.
33. Ibid., p. 130.
34. All references regarding Col. Walpole's wine are derived from Plumb, "Walpole's Wine," and Pijassou, *Médoc*, I, 390–1, as the pertinent documents (i.e. Colonel Walpole's wine accounts) are now missing from CH (H) "Vouchers, 1657–1745" at Cambridge University Library. All references to Sir Robert Walpole's wine come from the original sources.
35. Notably, this was a very early use of the term "sherry," instead of "Sherris-sack" or just plain "sack," which were both in common use at the time. It suggests perhaps that "sherry" started as a regionalism before becoming the commonly used term by the late eighteenth century.
36. Prices at King's Lynn were similar to those in London. The red port cost £15 per hogshead and the white port £16 per hogshead. The sherry, if converted to the same volume, cost nearly £19.
37. Plumb, "Father and Son," pp. 126–30.

38. Ibid., p. 141.
39. For Walpole's political skills, and in particular his ability to act the role of the Norfolk squire, see Plumb, *Sir Robert Walpole*, 2 vols (London, 1956–60).
40. Tax on wine has been and remains a favorite way for the British government to raise revenue, war or no war. The frequency of duty increases on wine in the eighteenth century was a harbinger of early twenty-first-century British taxation policy, when consumers can expect an increase of a few pence per bottle of wine almost every fiscal year.
41. Motoko Hori, "The Price and Quality of Wine and Conspicuous Consumption in England 1649–1759," *English Historical Review*, cxxiii, 505 (December, 2008), 1457–69.
42. White Lisbon was generally more expensive than red port because of the simple laws of supply and demand. The area under vines around Lisbon was much smaller than the port-producing area of the Douro valley, especially after the earthquake of 1755. Therefore, less white Lisbon was produced.
43. Hervey, *Diary*, pp. 172–3; De Saussure, *Foreign View of England*, pp. 99–100; CUL, CH (H), "Vouchers, 1657–1745."
44. *Gentleman's Magazine* (December, 1731). Prices quoted in Simon, *Bottlescrew Days*, p. 74.
45. Lewis Walpole Library, MS, Augusta Princess Dowager of Wales, account book, 1755.
46. *A letter to the Honourable A——r M—re, Com———ner of Trade and Plantations* (London, 1714).
47. Schumpeter, *English Overseas Trade Statistics*, Table 16.
48. Joseph Forrester, *A short treatise on the unequal and disproportionate imposts levied on port-wine, shipped from Oporto to Great Britain* (London, 1850), Table A, p. 17.
49. *In Vino Veritas; Or, a conference betwixt Chip the Cooper, and Dash the Drawer, (Being both Boozy), Discovering some secrets of the wine-brewing trade. Useful for all sorts of people to save their money and preserve their health* (London, 1698), p. 11.
50. *Objections against the importation of French wine, Answer'd* (London, 1711).
51. *A Letter from a Member of the House of Commons to his Friend in the Country, Relating to the Bill of Commerce. With a true copy of the Bill, and an Exact List of all those who voted for and against Engrossing* (London, 1713), pp. 21–2.
52. [Daniel Defoe], *A Brief Case of the Distillers, and of the distilling trade in England, shewing how far it is the interest of England to encourage the said Trade, as it is so considerable an advantage to the landed interest, to the trade and navigation, to the publick revenue, and to the employment of the poor. Humbly recommended to the Lords and Commons of Great Britain, in the present Parliament assembled* (London, 1726), p. 46.
53. Ibid., pp. 46–7.
54. Ibid., p. 47.
55. Ibid., p. 18.
56. Peter Clark, "The Mother Gin Controversy in the Early Eighteenth Century," *Transactions of the Royal Historical Society*, 5th ser., 38 (1988), 64.
57. B. R. Mitchell and P. Deane, *Abstract of British Historical Statistics* (Cambridge, 1962), pp. 254–5.
58. Patrick Dillon, *The Much Lamented Death of Madam Geneva: The Eighteenth-Century Gin Craze* (London, 2002).
59. John Burnett, *Liquid Pleasures: A Social History of Drinks in Modern Britain* (London, 1999), pp. 160–78; Andrew Barr, *Drink: A Social History* (London, 1998), Chapters 1 and 2; Simon, *Bottlescrew Days*, pp. 15–50.
60. F. W. von Archenholz, *A Picture of England*, 2 vols (London, 1789), II, 110–11.
61. Simon, *Bottlescrew Days*, p. 52.
62. In the 1870s, the English wine writer Henry Vizetelly inquired about the strength of unfortified port, and was told by Mr M. J. Ellis of W. & J. Graham and Co., that "in years when the grapes have thoroughly ripened, perfectly fermented Alto Douro wine will develop 32 degrees of proof spirit and, when made exclusively from the bastardo grape as many as 34 degrees." This corresponds to 16 to 18 percent alcohol. Henry Vizetelly,

Facts about Port and Madeira, with Notices of the wines vintaged around Lisbon and the wines of Tenerife (London, 1880), p. 143.

63. Sarah Bradford, *The Englishman's Wine: The Story of Port* (London, 1969), pp. 30–42; Rose Macaulay, *They Went to Portugal* (London, 1946), "Port Wine," pp. 229–52.

64. Generally speaking, the higher the alcohol content the more stable the wine. This is one reason for the longevity of fortified wines such as port and madeira.

65. Filtering a wine and thereby removing the yeasts will also stabilize a wine, but this technique was not known in the seventeenth or eighteenth century.

66. The information on winemaking comes from conversations with and letters received from Natasha Robertson Bridge of Taylor, Fladgate & Yeatman, Vila Nova de Gaia, Portugal, in August 2000 and April 2001; and Daniel Munger of Santé Wine Importers, Durham, North Carolina, in May 2001.

67. William Younger, *Gods, Men and Wine* (Cleveland, OH, 1966), p. 380.

68. André Simon, who is often taken as an authority on this matter, dates the beginning of arrested fermentation from 1727 when the British shippers in Oporto formed an association in order to regulate the trade and to obtain better prices from the Portuguese farmers for their wine. Yet there is no evidence for this date, and it gives more credit to the British shippers than the Portuguese farmers who at that time would have been the ones to oversee fermentation of the wine. Simon, *Bottlescrew Days*, p. 119.

69. Richard Mayson, *Port and the Douro* (London, 1999), p. 11.

70. Bradford, *The Englishman's Wine*, p. 46.

71. Hugh Johnson, *Vintage: The Story of Wine* (New York, 1989), pp. 227–9.

72. NA, S.P. 89/31, Burnett to Newcastle, August 6, 1724.

73. NA, Chancery Master's Exhibits, C 110/19/20, Thomas Pratt to John Hitchcock, September 12, 1734.

74. Sir Edward Barry, *Observations Historical, Critical, and Medical, on the wines of the Ancients. And the Analogy between them and Modern Wines. With general observations on the principles and qualities of water, and in particular those of Bath* (London, 1775), p. 439.

75. John Wright, *An essay on Wines, especially on Port Wine; intended to instruct every person to distinguish between that which is pure, and to guard against the frauds of adulteration* (London, 1795), p. 21.

76. Johnson, *Vintage*, p. 225.

77. Richard Ames, *The Bacchanalian Sessions, or the Contention of Liquors, with a Farewell to Wine* (London, 1693), p. 22.

78. Port production is no longer the haphazard practice that it was in the eighteenth century. To make port today, roughly 20 gallons of brandy (or more properly, grape spirit) is added to every pipe of must at a precise moment in order to arrest fermentation, thereby creating a wine with a high degree of residual sugar. However, it was not until the nineteenth century that the practice became fully mastered or even agreed upon. Bradford, *The Englishman's Wine*, p. 47.

79. Circular letter from the English Factors at Oporto, called by them "New Instructions," September 1754. Reprinted in [A Portuguese], *The Wine Question Considered; or, Observations on the Pamphlets of Mr. James Warre and Mr. Fleetwood Williams, respecting the General Company for the Agriculture of the Vineyards on the Upper Douro, Known in England under the name of the Royal Oporto Wine Company* (London, 1824), appendix.

80. John Croft, *A treatise on the wines of Portugal; and what can be gathered on the subject of the wines, etc. since the establishment of the factory at Oporto, anno 1727: also, a dissertation on the nature and use of wines in general, imported into Great Britain, as pertaining to luxury and diet* (York, 1787), p. 7; Bradford, *The Englishman's Wine*, p. 25.

81. Ibid.

82. Francis, *Wine Trade*, p. 240.

83. G. N. Johnstone, "The Growth of the Sugar Trade and Refining Industry," in Derek Oddy and Derek Miller, eds, *The Making of the Modern British Diet* (London, 1976), p. 60. Sidney Mintz, "The Changing Roles of Food in the Study of Consumption," in

John Brewer and Roy Porter, eds, *Consumption and the World of Goods* (New York, 1993), p. 265. For a general discussion of the rise of sugar consumption in eighteenth-century Britain and a brilliant interpretation of its significance in British and Western history, see Sidney Mintz, *Sweetness and Power: The Place of Sugar in Modern History* (New York, 1985).

84. Peter Shaw, *The Juice of the Grape: or wine preferable to water. A treatise wherein wine is shewn to be the grand preserver of health, and restorer in most diseases. With many instances of cures performed by this noble remedy; and the method of using it, as well for prevention as cure, with a word of advice to the vintners* (London, 1724), p. 15.

85. [A Physician in the Country], *Vinum Britannicum: or an essay of the properties and effects of malt liquors; wherein it is considered, in what cases, and to what constitutions they are either beneficial or injurious, with a plain mechanical account of how they are serviceable or disserviceable to the human bodies* (London, 1727), p. 49. Possibly written by James Sedgwick or Thomas Short.

86. "Response of the Douro wine brokers," September 1754, reprinted in A Portuguese, *Wine Question*, appendix.

87. James Boswell, *Boswell's London Journal, 1762–1763*, ed. Frederick Pottle (New York, 1950), p. 303.

88. Pierre-Jean Grosley, *A Tour to London; or, New Observations on England and its Inhabitants*, 2 vols, trans. by Thomas Nugent (London, 1774), I, 87.

89. Barry, *Observations Historical, Critical, and Medical*, p. 439, states that port wines "certainly are more heavy and heating than they formerly were, and require more time, after they have been bottled, to bring them to a proper maturity."

90. John Byng, *The Torrington Diaries*, ed. C. Bruyn Andrews, 4 vols (New York, 1936). See, for example, I (1784–8), 367, 376; II (1789–91), 84; III (1792–3), 24, 35, 42, 56, 66, 237, 248, 319; IV (1790, NB: vol. IV is not in chronological order with other volumes), 160.

91. Croft, *Treatise on the Wines of Portugal*, pp. 5, 25, 26.

92. Younger, *Gods, Men and Wine*, p. 378. See also Barr, *Drink*, p. 84.

93. Elvin M. Jellinek, "The Symbolism of Drinking: A Culture-Historical Approach", *Journal of Studies on Alcohol*, 38 (1977), 852–66; Mary Douglas, ed., *Constructive Drinking: Perspectives on Drink from Anthropology* (Cambridge, 1987), pp. 3–15; Marianna Adler, "From Symbolic Exchange to Commodity Consumption: Anthropological Notes on Drinking as a Symbolic Practice," in Susanna Barrowes and Robin Broom, eds, *Drinking: Behavior and Belief in Modern History* (Berkeley, 1991), pp. 376–98; Dwight B. Heath, "Anthropological and Sociocultural Perspectives on Alcohol as a Reinforcer," in W. Miles Cox, ed., *Why People Drink: Parameters of Alcohol as a Reinforcer* (New York, 1990), pp. 263–90; Heath, *Drinking Occasions: Comparative Perspectives on Alcohol and Culture* (Ann Arbor, 2000), Chapters 5 and 6.

94. BL, Add. MS 32690, f. 140; 32717, f. 212; 32737, f. 529; 32857, f. 270, Newcastle Papers, wine bills and letters from wine merchants to Thomas Pelham-Holles, Duke of Newcastle.

95. BL, Add. MS 32737, f. 529, Hay to Newcastle, c. 1754.

96. Johnson, *Vintage*, p. 304.

97. *The Cellar-Book: or, the Butler's Assistant, in keeping a Regular Account of his Liquors* (printed for J. Dodsley in Pall Mall, 1766). The copy of this rare book that I consulted is at the National Archives of Scotland, GD 16/57/42.

98. Johnson, *Vintage*, p. 304.

99. Susannah Centlivre, *The Works of the celebrated Mrs. Centlivre*, ed. J. Pearson, 3 vols (London, 1872), A Gotham Election, III, 158.

8 "Claret is the liquor for boys; port for men"

1. The National Archives (NA), Wine Cellar Accounts of the Royal Household, L.S. 13/271, 1761–1766; L.S. 13/272, 1767–1770. For wine cellar accounts of George I and George II,

see L.S. 13/191, 1714–1719; L.S. 13/192, 1719–1725; L.S. 13/268, 1719–1731; L.S. 13/269, 1733–1752; L.S. 13/270, 1753–1761.

2. British Library (BL), Add. MS 61672, f. 130, "An account wines delivered to the Duke of Marlborough's Homes, 1763–1767."

3. The origins of this term are unclear. It has been attributed to Prof. George Saintsbury; however, in his *Notes on a Cellar-Book* (London, 1920), Saintsbury implies that the term had long been in use. What Saintsbury does say is that Port is "the Englishman's wine," for "it strenghtens while it gladdens as no other wine can do, and there is something about it which must have been created in pre-established harmony with the best English character." *Notes*, (London, 1920), pp. 40, 45.

4. Schumpeter, *Trade Statistics*, Table 16.

5. John Croft, *A Treatise on the Wines of Portugal; and What can be Gathered on the Subject of the Wines, etc. Since the Establishment of the Factory at Oporto, Anno 1727: also, a Dissertation on the Nature and use of Wines in General, Imported into Great Britain, as Pertaining to Luxury and Diet* (York, 1787), p. 7.

6. For a general discussion of the various methods used to rectify and adulterate wines in the medieval and early modern periods, see Rod Phillips, *A Short History of Wine* (London, 2000), passim; idem, "Wine and Adulteration," *History Today* (July, 2000), pp. 31–7. For specific examples of English rectifying manuals, see: *The Art and Mystery of Vintner's and Wine Coopers: Containing approved Directions for the Conserving and Curing all Manner and Sorts of Wines, whether Spanish, Greek, Italian or French, very Necessary for all Sorts of People* (London, 1682); Walter Charleton, *The Vintner's Mystery Display'd: or the whole Art of the Wine Trade laid open. In which are the necessary directions for rightly managing all sorts of wines, so as to render them bright and good; or to restore them when they prove defective in any way.* (London, 1705?).

7. See, for example, *Vinetum Angliae, or a new and easy way to make wine of English grapes and other fruit Vinetum Angliae: or a new and easy way to make wine of English grapes and other fruit, equal to that of France, Spain, &c. with their physical virtues. Also to make artificial wines, and to order and recover them when damaged. To make all sorts of cyder, mead, metheglin, rum, rack, and many other useful liquors. To gather, order and keep fruit in all seasons. The true art of distilling brandy, strong-waters and cordial-waters. To make all sorts of pickles, and sundry sorts of vinegars. The whole art and mystery of a confectioner. The compleat caterer, or how to know whether flesh, fish or fowl be old or young, new or stale. Rules for frugal, cheap and well living. To destroy all sorts of vermin; with divers other notable things, never before made publick. By D.S.* (London, 1690?); [Thomas Tryon?], *The way to get wealth: or, A new and easie way to make twenty three sorts of wine, equal to that of France. To which is added, A help to discourse, giving an account of trade of all countries by the author of The way to save wealth; and of One thousand notable things* (London, 1702).

8. Croft, *Treatise on the Wines of Portugal*, p. 7. Croft may have been familiar with this recipe because such wines were still being made in Britain during his lifetime.

9. [Robert Walpole?], *A Letter from a Member of Parliament to his Friend in the Country, concerning the Duties on Wine and Tobacco* (London, 1733).

10. *A Vindication of the Conduct of the Ministry, in the Scheme of the Excise on Wine and Tobacco, proposed last sessions of Parliament: with a General Examination of the Reasons which determined the said Ministry to it: the Consequences and Events it would have had* (London, 1734), pp. 11–12.

11. For a detailed discussion of why Walpole's 1733 Excise Bill failed, see Paul Langford, *The Excise Crisis* (Oxford, 1975).

12. Schumpeter, *Trade Statistics*, Table 16. For port export figures, see Joseph James Forrester, *A Short Treatise on the Unequal and Disproportionate Imposts Levied on Port-wine, Shipped from Oporto to Great Britain* (London, 1850), Table B, pp. 19–20.

13. H. E. S. Fisher, *The Portugal Trade: A Study of Anglo-Portuguese Commerce, 1700–1770* (London, 1971), p. 78.

14. Croft, *Treatise on the Wines of Portugal*, p. 7.
15. Ibid., pp. 11–16. Croft's work is the first history of port and the port trade to discuss the controversial Company.
16. Circular letter from the English Factors at Oporto, called by them "New Instructions," September 1754. Reprinted in [A Portuguese], *The Wine Question Considered; or, Observations on the Pamphlets of Mr. James Warre and Mr. Fleetwood Williams, respecting the General Company for the Agriculture of the Vineyards on the Upper Douro, Known in England under the name of the Royal Oporto Wine Company* (London, 1824), appendix, p. 2.
17. Ibid.
18. Ibid., p. 3.
19. Ibid.
20. Ibid,, p. 5.
21. "Response of the Douro wine brokers," September 1754, reprinted in [A Portuguese], *Wine Question*, appendix, p. 6.
22. Ibid., p. 8.
23. Ibid., pp. 11–12.
24. Ibid., p. 15.
25. A. D. Francis, *The Wine Trade* (London, 1972), pp. 207–24; Sarah Bradford, *The Englishman's Wine: The Story of Port* (London, 1969), pp. 49–54; André L. Simon, *Bottlescrew Days: Wine Drinking in England during the Eighteenth Century* (London, 1926), pp. 121–43; Croft, *Treatise on the Wines of Portugal*, pp. 11–14.
26. Croft, *Treatise on the Wines of Portugal*, pp. 10–11.
27. Trans., the General Company for the Agriculture of the Vineyards of the Upper Douro.
28. Section X of the laws establishing the Company, quoted in Croft, *Treatise on the Wines of Portugal*, p. 16.
29. See, for example, *Original Documents Respecting the Injurious Effects and the Impolicy of a Further Continuance of the Portuguese Royal Wine Company of Oporto* (London, 1813); James Warre, *The Past, Present and Probably the Future State of the Wine Trade; proving that an increase of duty caused a decrease of revenue; and a decrease of duty, an increase of revenue. Founded on parliamentary and other documents. Most respectfully submitted to the right honourable the President and Members of the Board of Trade* (London, 1823); Fleetwood Williams, *Observations on the State of the Wine Trade. Occasioned by the Perusal of a Pamphlet on the same subject, by Mr. Warre. Most respectfully submitted to his Majesty's Ministers* (London, 1824); [A Portuguese], *Wine Question*.
30. Henri Enjalbert, "Comment naissent les grands crus: Bordeaux, Porto, Cognac," *Annales: Economies, Sociétés, Civilisations*, 8 (1953), 466–9; Simon, *Bottlescrew Days*, pp. 123, 142; Bradford, *The Englishman's Wine*, p. 53; William Younger, *Gods, Men and Wine* (Cleveland, OH, 1966), p. 382; Johnson, *Vintage*, p. 229. Francis demurs on this point, saying "there is no evidence that the Pombaline legislation had much effect on the quality of the wine sold in England one way or another." Francis, *Wine Trade*, p. 214. Among historians of wine and wine writers, however, he stands alone in his assessment.
31. The exact figures here are 7,508, moving to 11,462 tuns per annum. Forrester, *A Short Treatise*, Table C, p. 21.
32. The exact figures here are 9,494, moving to 11,566 tuns per annum. Schumpeter, *Trade Statistics*, Table 16.
33. The decline of Lisbon area vineyards in 1755 was perpetuated by Portuguese laws that forbade the replanting of vines in areas around the capital where wheat could grow.
34. Francis, *Wine Trade*, p. 226.
35. Jessica Warner, *Craze: Gin and Debauchery in an Age of Reason* (New York, 2002); Peter Clark, "The Mother Gin Controversy in the Early Eighteenth Century," *Transactions of the Royal Historical Society*, 5th ser., 38 (1988), 63–84; Dorothy George, *London Life in the Eighteenth Century* (London, 1925).

36. Kathleen Wilson, "Empire of Virtue: The Imperial Project and Hanoverian Culture, c. 1720–1785," in Lawrence Stone, ed., *An Imperial State at War, Britain from 1689 to 1815* (London, 1994), p. 146.
37. Ibid., p. 144; Karen Harvey, "The History of Masculinity, c. 1650–1800", *Journal of British Studies*, 44 (April, 2005), 308.
38. Eliza Haywood, "Effeminacy in the Army Censured", in *The Female Spectator* (1744–6), ed. Gabrielle Firmager (London, 1993), p. 30.
39. Gerald Newman, *The Rise of English Nationalism* (New York, 1987), pp. 68–84.
40. Wilson, "Empire of Virtue", p. 145.
41. Kathleen Wilson, *The Sense of the People: Politics, Culture and Imperialism in England, 1715–1785* (Cambridge, 1995), p. 189.
42. *Newcastle Journal*, September 11, 1756. Quoted in Wilson, *Sense of the People*, p. 189.
43. Newman, *English Nationalism*, pp. 68–84; Philip Carter, *Men and the Emergence of Polite Society: Britain 1660–1800* (Harlow, 2001), pp. 124–38; Wilson, "Empire of Virtue", pp. 143–50; idem, *Sense of the People*, pp. 185–205; Matthew McCormack, *The Independent Man: Citizenship and Gender Politics in Georgian England* (Manchester, 2005); idem, "The New Militia: War, Politics and Gender in 1750s Britain", *Gender and History*, 19:3 (2007), 483–500.
44. Wilson, "Empire of Virtue", p. 145; see also, idem, "The Good, the Bad, and the Impotent: Imperialism and the Politics of Identity in Georgian England," in Ann Bermingham and John Brewer, eds, *The Consumption of Culture 1600–1800: Image, Object, Text* (London, 1995), pp. 237–62.
45. John Brown, *An Estimate of the Manners and Principles of the Times*, 2 vols (London, 1757), I, 66–7; II, 176, 40.
46. *The Imports of Great Britain from France: Humbly Address'd to the Laudable Associations of Anti-Gallicans, and the Generous Promoters of the British Arts and Manufactories* (n.p., 1757).
47. Michèle Cohen, "'Manners' Make the Man: Politeness, Chivalry, and the Construction of Masculinity," *Journal of British Studies*, 44 (April, 2005), 314–17. See also, idem, *Fashioning Masculinity: National Identity and Language in the Eighteenth Century* (London, 1996), pp. 99–101.
48. James Boswell, *The Life of Samuel Johnson*, ed. R. W. Chapman (Oxford, 1980), 1016.
49. Christie's, St James, London (company archives), catalogues for auctions held on March 28, 1768; May 18, 1772; April 2, 1778.
50. Edward Barry, *Observations Historical, Critical, and Medical on the Wines of the Ancients. And an Anology between Them and Modern Wines. With General Observations on the Principles and Qualities of Water, and in Particular those of Bath* (London, 1775), p. 439.
51. "Frontignac" (i.e. Muscat de Frontignan) is a sweet wine from southern France.
52. Durham County Record Office, D/X 101/3, Isabella Widdrington to Mrs Mills, July 8, 1777.
53. BL, Add. MS 44401, ff. 30–2, tavern bills from L. Reilly to R. B. Sheridan, March–June, 1777.
54. NA, P.R.O. 30/8/219, William Pitt's wine expenses, July 1784–June 1785.
55. Schumpeter, *Trade Statistics*, Table XVII.
56. BL, Add. MS 49186, ff. 1–2, Bill and receipt for wine order from Christie and Barrow to the Hon. Spencer Perceval, September 3, 1790.
57. Christ Church College, Oxford, Common Room Accounts, MS C.R.2.
58. "Theatre" (Drury Lane), *The Times* (London), February 19, 1798, p. 1.
59. John Carl Flügel, *The Psychology of Clothes* (London, 1930).
60. Ibid.; David Kuchta, *The Three-Piece Suit and Modern Masculinity: England, 1550–1850* (Berkeley, 2002), pp. 91–132; idem, "The Making of the Self-Made Man: Class, Clothing, and English Masculinity, 1688–1832," in Victoria De Grazia and Ellen Furlough, eds, *The Sex of Things: Gender and Consumption in Comparative Perspective* (Berkeley, 1996), pp. 54–77.

61. Michael Snodin, "'Style' in Georgian Britain, 1714–1837," in Michael Snodin and John Styles, *Design and the Decorative Arts, Britain 1500–1900* (London, 2001), pp. 198–203.
62. Simon, *Bottlescrew Days*, p. 52.
63. Fisher, *Portugal Trade*, p. 83. My own research in Vila Nova de Gaia shows that little had changed in the opening years of the nineteenth century. Most of the wine shipped to England was from the previous vintage, with older wines blended in. Taylor, Fladgate, and Yeatman (company archives), Vila Nova de Gaia, T/Z. 1808–12/C5.P5, letter book of Joseph Camo, 1808–1812.
64. Bradford, *The Englishman's Wine*, p. 54; Younger dates the emergence of the cylindrical bottle from "some time around 1760." *Gods, Men and Wine*, p. 352. For more detailed evidence, see R. Butler and G. Walkling, *The Book of Wine Antiques* (Woodbridge, 1986); D. C. Davis, *English Bottles and Decanters 1650–1900* (New York, 1972); and Jancis Robinson, ed., *The Oxford Companion to Wine*, 2nd edn (Oxford, 1999), pp. 96–8.
65. Johnson, *Vintage*, p. 195.
66. Ibid., pp. 196–8.
67. Bottle images are derived from André L. Simon, *History of the Wine Trade in England*, 3 vols (London, 1906-9), III, plates v, vii, xii; idem, *Bottlescrew Days*, p. 234.
68. Christie's (company archives), catalogue for an auction held on April 1, 1773.
69. Barry, *Observations Historical, Critical, and Medical*, p. 439.
70. Pierre-Jean Grosley, *A Tour to London; or New Observations on England and its Inhabitants*, trans. Thomas Nugent, 2 vols (London, 1774), I, 81–2.
71. Ibid.
72. John Byng, *The Torrington Diaries: Containing the Tour Through England and Wales of the Hon. John Byng (later Viscount Torrington) between the Years 1781 and 1794*, ed. C. Bruyn Andrews, 4 vols (New York, 1935), II, 49; III, 192.
73. Alexander Henderson, *The History of Ancient and Modern Wines* (London, 1824), p. 12.
74. Croft, *Treatise on the Wines of Portugal*, p. 5.

9 "That other liquor called port"

1. John Home, *The Works of John Home, Esq., now first collected. To which is prefixed an account of his life and writing by Henry Mackenzie, Esq.*, 3 vols (Edinburgh, 1822), I, 163.
2. David Hume, *The Letters of David Hume*, ed. J. Y. T. Greig, 2 vols (Oxford, 1932), Hume to John Home of Ninewells, March 26, 1748 (NS), I, 121.
3. For other examples, see Henry Gray Graham, *Scottish Men of Letters in the Eighteenth Century* (London, 1908), p. 51.
4. David Hume, *Of the Balance of Trade* (1752), in *Essays: Moral, Political and Literary*, ed. Eugene F. Miller (Indianapolis, 1987), p. 315.
5. Hume enjoyed cooking, and regarding his "old mutton" said "nobody excels me." Graham, *Scottish Men of Letters*, p. 54.
6. See Chapter 6.
7. For arguments about British identity in England and Scotland, see: Linda Colley, *Britons: Forging the Nation, 1707–1837* (New Haven, 1992); Douglas Hay and Nicholas Rogers, *Eighteenth Century English Society* (Cambridge, 1997); Lawrence Brockliss and David Eastwood, "Introduction," in Brockliss and Eastwood, eds, *A Union of Multiple Identities: The British Isles, c. 1750–c.1850* (Manchester, 1997), pp. 1–8; Adrian Hastings, *The Construction of Nationhood: Ethnicity, Religion and Nationalism* (Cambridge, 1997); J. E. Cookson, *The British Armed Nation* (Oxford, 1997); Brendan Bradshaw and Peter Roberts, eds, *British Consciousness and Identity: The Making of Britain 1533–1707* (Cambridge, 1998).
8. For arguments about Scottish identity in the eighteenth century, see: Colley, *Britons*, passim; Colin Kidd, *Subverting Scotland's Past: Scottish Whig Historians and the Creation of an Anglo-British Identity, 1689–c. 1830* (Cambridge, 1993), pp. 206–14; idem, "North Britishness and the Nature of Eighteenth-Century British Patriotisms," *Historical Journal*, 39:2 (1996), 361–82; Murray Pittock, *Inventing and Resisting Britain: Cultural Identities*

in Britain and Ireland, 1685–1789 (London, 1997), pp. 129–45; Alexander Murdoch, "Scotland and the Idea of Britain in the Eighteenth Century," in T. M. Devine and J. R. Young, eds, *Eighteenth Century Scotland: New Perspectives* (East Linton, 1999), pp. 106–20; Richard J. Finlay, "Keeping the Covenant: Scottish National Identity," in Devine and Young, eds, *Eighteenth Century Scotland*, pp. 121–33; Richard J. Finlay, "Caledonia or North Britain? Scottish Identity in the Eighteenth Century," in Dauvit Broun, R. J. Finlay and Michael Lynch, *Image and Identity: The Making and Re-Making of Scotland Through the Ages* (Edinburgh, 1998), pp. 143–56.

9. Murdoch, "Scotland and the Idea of Britain in the Eighteenth Century," p. 115.

10. Kidd makes a convincing case for the term *Anglo-British* (originally coined by Roger Mason, in reference to the sixteenth century) rather than *North British* or simply *British*, when describing the historical content upon which Scottish identity was based at the end of the eighteenth century. *Subverting Scotland's Past*, p. 214.

11. Parliamentary Report, C.8706, *Customs Tariffs of the United Kingdom, from 1800 to 1897, with some notes upon the history of more important branches of receipt from 1660* (London, 1897), pp. 131–57.

12. Adam Smith, *The Wealth of Nations*, ed. Andrew Skinner (Harmondsworth, 1999), V, Chapter 2, part 2, article 4, 476–7.

13. *First Report from the Committee, Appointed to Inquire into the Illicit Practices Used in Defrauding the Revenue* (December 23, 1784), p. 4. The second and third reports followed on March 1 and March 23, 1784. All three reports were presented to the House of Commons by William Eden.

14. *First Report from the Committee*, p. 9.

15. Samuel Johnson, *A Journey to the Western Islands of Scotland*, ed. J. D. Fleeman (Oxford, 1985), pp. 45, 181.

16. For discussions of Pitt's tariff reforms, see William J. Ashworth, *Customs and Excise: Trade, Production and Consumption in England, 1640–1845* (Oxford, 2003), pp. 348–67; Peter Mathias and Patrick O'Brian, "Taxation in Britain and France, 1715–1810," *Journal of European Economic History*, 5 (1967), 601–40.

17. George Rose, *A Brief Examination into the Increase of the Revenue, Commerce and Navigation of Great Britain, since the Conclusion of the Peace in 1783*, 4th edn (London, 1794), p. 24. The duty on tea was lowered from 119 percent to 12 percent *ad valorem*.

18. Pitt to Wilberforce, September 30, 1785, *The Correspondence of William Wilberforce*, 2 vols, ed. Robert I. Wilberforce and Samuel Wilberforce (London, 1840), I, 9.

19. 26 George III, c. 66. Effective July 5, 1786.

20. Marie Donaghay, "The Exchange of the Products of the Soil and Industrial Goods in the Anglo-French Commercial Treaty of 1786," *Journal of European Economic History*, 19:2 (1990), 380.

21. For the intricacies of the negotiations, see ibid., and J. Holland Rose, "The Franco-British Commercial Treaty of 1786," *English Historical Review*, 23 (October, 1908), 709–24; Léon Cahen, "Une Nouvelle Interprétation du Traité Franco-Anglais de 1786–1787," *Revue Historique* (July–December, 1939), pp. 226–85; W. O. Henderson, "The Anglo-French Commercial Treaty of 1786," *Economic History Review*, 2nd ser., 10 (August, 1957), 104–12; Jeremy Black, "The Marquis of Carmarthen and Relations with France, 1784–1787," *Francia*, 12 (1984), 283–303; Donald C. Wellington, "The Anglo-French Commercial Treaty of 1786," *Journal of European Economic History*, 21:2 (1992), 325–37; Jeremy Black, *British Foreign Policy in an Age of Revolutions, 1783–1793* (Cambridge, 1994), Chapter 3.

22. *Parliamentary History of England* (Hansard, London, 1815), XXV, 1433.

23. 27 George III, c. 13. Effective May 10, 1787.

24. Wine imported in British ships still paid a lower rate than wine arriving in foreign bottoms, the import rate for London was still roughly £3 higher than the outports, and prisage was still paid in all English and Welsh ports except for London and the remaining Cinque Ports. According to the authors of the 1897 Parliamentary Report,

while Pitt's "great Act of 1787 made an enormous simplification" of the previous state of affairs, the "officers still continued to find cause for the exaction of fees." Parliamentary Report C.8706, *Customs Tariffs*, p. 139.

25. NA, Customs 14.
26. Schumpeter, *English Overseas Trade Statistics*, Tables 16 and 17. Her English import statistics end in 1791, after which they are inclusive of all Great Britain; hence the discrepancy in the period under comparison.
27. James Boswell, *The Journal of a Tour to the Hebrides with Samuel Johnson, LL. D.*, ed. Frederick A. Pottle and Charles H. Bennett (New York, 1936), pp. 224, 344.
28. James Boswell, *Boswell for the Defense, 1769–1774*, ed. William K. Wimsatt, Jr and Frederick A. Pottle (New York, 1959), passim; Boswell, *Boswell: The Ominous Years, 1774–1776*, ed. Charles Ryskamp and Frederick A. Pottle (New York, 1963), passim; Boswell, *Boswell in Extremes, 1776–1778*, ed. Charles M. Weis and Frederick A. Pottle (New York, 1970), passim.
29. W. Forbes Gray, *Some Old Scots Judges* (London, 1914), passim.
30. Gray, *Old Scots Judges*, ibid., p. 109.
31. NAS, General Register House, GD 16/33/41, Account of the wine sent from Cortacky, Auchterhouse and Newgrange, and put into the cellar at Airly Lodge, Dec. 1779.
32. NA, Customs 14, Scottish Customs Accounts. This figure (8 percent) represents the annual average for French wines, 1777–9.
33. Henry Cockburn, *Memorials of his Time*, ed. Karl F. C. Miller (Chicago, 1974, originally published 1856), p. 32.
34. James Boswell, *James Boswell's "Book of Company" at Auchinleck, 1782–1795*, ed. Viscountess Eccles and Gordon Turnbull (Roxburghe Club, 1995), pp. 39–47.
35. NAS, GD 164/818, Dysart House wine books, 1786–1792 (item 10).
36. Gavin Daly, "English Smugglers, the Channel, and the Napoleonic Wars, 1800–1814", *Journal of British Studies*, 46 (January, 2007), 30–46; Patrick K. O'Brien, "The Political Economy of British Taxation, 1660–1815," *Economic History Review*, 2nd ser., 41:1 (1988), 25–6; Cullen, *Smuggling and the Ayrshire Economic Boom*, pp. 50–1. While smuggling diminished during the war, the importation of prize (i.e. captured) wines increased. See Francis, *Wine Trade*, pp. 266–85.
37. From 1805 through 1813, Spanish red wines actually paid slightly more than Spanish white wines (£107 compared to £96 per tun). This disparity was meant to favor imports from insurgent-controlled parts of Spain (which included Cadiz) over French-controlled parts of Spain. Most British imports were "white" Spanish wine from Cadiz: sherry.
38. The ten-year average for port production fell from by nearly 8,000 pipes (roughly 12 percent) between the decades 1792–1801 and 1802–1811. This included three successive vintages (1809–11) that produced less than 45,000 pipes. Because the United Kingdom received over 90 percent of all exported port wine, this drop in production had a statistically significant effect on British and Irish consumption. Figures come from Forrester, *A Short Treatise*, table A, p. 17.
39. During the war, England imported far more French wine than it had done previously, although roughly three-quarters of it was re-exported and sold for a high profit in Northern Europe. Parliamentary Report C.8706, *Customs Tariffs*, pp. 150–2, 155–7; Francis, *Wine Trade*, pp. 321–5. For a specific discussion of the wine with France during the war, see François Crouzet, "Les Importations d'eaux de vie et de vins Français en Grande-Bretagne pendant le Blocus Continental," *Annales du Midi*, 65 (1953), 91–106.
40. Quoted in Kay and Maclean, *Knee Deep in Claret*, p. 173.
41. Quoted in ibid., p. 173.
42. Specifically, annual averages declined from 2,172 tuns in 1787–92 to 1,768 tuns in 1793–1802, and to 1,413 tuns in 1803–15.
43. NA, Customs 14, Scottish Customs Accounts, see "Exports."

44. Vivien Dietz, "The Politics of Whisky: Scottish Distillers, the Excise, and the Pittite State," *Journal of British Studies*, 36 (January, 1997), 62–4.
45. National Library of Scotland, Adv. 82.3.9; Adv. 82.1.6, ff. 38 and 42, wine bills of the Oliphants of Gask.
46. Oliphant's wine purchases of 1793 are reminiscent of a more recent event among American wine consumers. In the winter of 2002–3, just prior to the American invasion of Iraq, some American consumers, who were angry at France for not supporting America's war, boycotted French wines, and in some cases even got rid of their French wines.
47. For more on West's "splendid fraud" and its role in British identity construction, see Colley, *Britons*, pp. 177–82.
48. James Gillray, *The Death of the Great Wolf* (engraving), published December 17, 1795, by H. Humphrey, 37 New Bond Street, London. BL no. 8704. Gillray was protesting over the "Two Acts" of 1795, which extended the definition of treason and prohibited mass meetings unless approved by a magistrate.
49. Six weeks before fighting his last battle at Trafalgar in 1805, Nelson purchased three pipes of port, for which he paid a total of £308 2s. 0d, an expensive wartime price even for Britain's least-taxed wine. Clearly, Nelson did not stint on port. This may have been the port that Nelson had on board the H.M.S. *Victory* at Trafalgar. Mayson, *Port*, pp. 22–3.
50. Norman Bennett, "The Vignerons of the Douro and the Peninsular War," *Journal of European Economic History*, 21:1 (1992), 7–29.
51. Webb, Gray, Campbell and Camo is today known as Taylor, Fladgate &Yeatman.
52. Taylor, Fladgate & Yeatman (company archives), Vila Nova de Gaia, T/Z 1808–1812/C5-P5. See, for example, Camo to Gray, March 17, 1809.
53. Norman Bennett, "Port Wine Merchants: Sandeman in Porto, 1813–1831," *Journal of European Economic History*, 24:2 (1995), 239–69; Bradford, *The Englishman's Wine*, pp. 194–5; Kay and Maclean, *Knee Deep in Claret*, pp. 175–9.
54. Bradford, *The Englishman's Wine*, pp. 190–1; Kay and Maclean, *Knee Deep in Claret*, pp. 181–4.
55. Bradford, *The Englishman's Wine*, p. 192; Kay and Maclean, *Knee Deep in Claret*, pp. 179–81.
56. Colley, *Britons*, p. 126.
57. NAS, GD 164/1034, "State of Lord Loughborough's wines, 1 Jan. 1775 to 6 June 1800."
58. NAS, GD 164/879 (item 17), inventory of Dysart House wine cellar, June–Aug. 1810. Madeira accounted for 7.3 percent of all wines, and German wine 4.6 percent.
59. Bradford, *The Englishman's Wine*, Chapter 6. Norman Bennett sees the late-eighteenth and early-nineteenth century as the golden age of the port wine trade, that is, when the port wine trade became financially stable and recognized for quality. See Bennett, "The Golden Age of the Port Wine System, 1781–1807," International History Review, 12 (1990): 221–248.
60. John Fowler, *Recollections of Country Life: Social, Political, Sporting and Agricultural* (London, 1894), pp. 152–4.
61. Alexander Henderson, *The History of Wines, Ancient and Modern* (1824), appendix 5,374; Warre, *State of the Wine Trade*, appendix M.

10 "By G–d, he drinks like a man!"

1. Edward Bannerman Ramsay, *Reminiscences of Scottish Life and Character* (Edinburgh, 1928 edn, first published 1858), pp. 78–9.
2. Margaret Hunt, *Commerce, Gender and the Family in England, 1680–1780* (Berkeley, 1996), pp. 101–24.
3. See Chapters 5 and 6 for more detail on Walpole's wine consumption.
4. See Chapter 5 for an extensive discussion of politeness.
5. David Brindman, *Hogarth and his Times: Serious Comedy* (Berkeley, 1997), p. 35.
6. Jenny Uglow, *Hogarth: A Life and a World* (New York, 1997), p. 230.

7. *Town and Country Magazine* (March, 1771), p. 134, quoted in Michèle Cohen, "Manliness, Effeminacy and the French: Gender Construction in Eighteenth Century England," in Tim Hitchcock and Michèle Cohen, eds, *English Masculinities, 1660–1800* (London, 1999), p. 60.

8. Linda Colley, *Britons: Forging the Nation, 1707–1832* (New Haven, 1992), p. 149.

9. Ibid., pp. 147–55. See also, Cohen, "Manliness, Effeminacy and the French," which explores the link between conceptions of English foppery, Frenchness, and effeminacy. Notably, Cohen concludes that by the 1780s (i.e. after the defeat in America), linguistic priorities had been "significantly altered." Bluntness among English men was now admired because of its supposed indication of manliness.

10. For a discussion of the changing modes of masculinity among middle-ranking men, see Leonore Davidoff and Catherine Hall, *Family Fortunes: Men and Women of the English Middle Class, 1780–1850*, 2nd edn (London, 2002), pp. 108–13.

11. See Chapter 1.

12. Elizabeth A. Foyster, *Manhood in Early Modern England* (Harlow, 1999), pp. 56–7; Foyster, "Boys will be Boys? Manhood and Aggression, 1660–1800," in Tim Hitchcock and Michèle Cohen, eds, *English Masculinities: 1660–1800* (London, 1999), 151–166; Anna Bryson, *From Courtesy to Civility: Changing Codes of Conduct in Early Modern England* (Oxford, 1998), p. 217; Alexandra Shepard, *Meanings of Manhood in Early Modern England* (Oxford, 2003); Keith Thomas, *The Ends of Life: Roads to Fulfilment in Early Modern England* (Oxford, 2007), p. 24.

13. Boswell, *Journal of a Tour to the Hebrides*, eds Pottle and Bennett, p. 39.

14. Adam Smith, *The Wealth of Nations*, ed. Andrew Skinner, 2 vols (Harmondsworth, 1999—Penguin edition of standard Oxford text), Book IV, Chapter 3, part 2, 71–2.

15. Joseph Farrington, *Memoirs of the Life of Sir Joshua Reynolds* (London, 1819), pp. 64–5. More recently, Gregory Austin, ed., *Alcohol in Western Society from Antiquity to 1800* (Santa Barbara, 1985), seems to accept this view, but the evidence he presents is consistent only in its contradictions: pp. 273–81, 321–8, 335–7, 342–3, 350–4, 366–9.

16. See, for example, Boswell, *Life of Johnson*, ed. Chapman, pp. 618, 851, 1022. J. S. Madden, "Samuel Johnson's Alcohol Problem," *Medical History* 11 (1967): 141–149.

17. Francis Place, *The Autobiography of Francis Place, 1771–1854*, ed. M. Thale (Cambridge, 1972), p. 82.

18. Robert Chambers, *Traditions of Edinburgh* (Edinburgh, 1980 reprint of 1868 edn, first published in 1824), p. 146.

19. Rees Howell Gronow, *The Reminiscences and Recollections of Captain Gronow, Being Anecdotes of the Camp, Court, Clubs and Society, 1810–1860*, 2 vols (London, 1892 edn, originally published 1862–5), II, 75.

20. Schumpeter, *English Overseas Trade Statistics*, Tables 16 and 17.

21. Motoko Hori, "The Price and Quality of Wine and Conspicuous Consumption in England, 1646–1759," *English Historical Review*, cxxiii, 505 (December, 2008), 1457–69.

22. Prior to 1792, the Scottish figures are derived from: NA, Customs 14, and the English figures from Schumpeter, *English Overseas Trade Statistics*, Tables 16 and 17. Schumpeter's figures for all of Great Britain begin in 1792 and end in 1808.

23. Wilson, *Alcohol and the Nation*, Table 2, p. 335.

24. John Burnett, *Liquid Pleasures: A Social History of Drink in Modern Britain* (London, 1999), pp. 119–26.

25. For drunkenness in the early eighteenth century, see M. Dorothy George, *London Life in the Eighteenth Century* (London, 1925), pp. 27–37; T. G. Coffey, "Beer Street and Gin Lane: Some Views of Eighteenth-Century Drinking," *Quarterly Journal of Studies in Alcohol*, 27 (1966), 669–92; James Watney, *Mother's Ruin: A History of Gin* (London, 1976); Peter Clarke, "The Mother Gin Controversy in the Early Eighteenth Century," *Transactions of the Royal Historical Society*, 5th ser., 38 (1988), 63–84. For Victorian drunkenness and the Temperance movement, see M. M. Glatt, "The English Drink

Problem: Its Rise and Decline through the Ages," *British Journal of Addiction*, 55 (July, 1958), 51–67; Brian Harrison, *Drink and the Victorians: The Temperance Question in England, 1815–1872*, 2nd edn (Keele, 1994).

26. Roy Porter, *English Society in the Eighteenth Century* (Harmondsworth, 1982), pp. 33–4; idem, "The Drinking Man's Disease: The Pre-History of Alcoholism in Georgian Britain," *British Journal of Addiction*, 80 (1985), 385–96; idem, "Introduction," in Thomas Trotter, M.D., *An Essay, Medical, Philosophical and Chemical on Drunkenness and its Effects on the Human Body*, ed. Porter (London, 1988); Anya Taylor, *Bacchus in Romantic England: Writers and Drink, 1780–1830* (London, 1999).

27. Philip Carter, *Men and the Emergence of Polite Society, Britain, 1660–1800* (Harlow, 2001), pp. 53–162, 209–17; idem, "Polite 'Persons': Character, Biography, and the Gentleman," *Transactions of the Royal Historical Society*, 6th ser., 12 (2002), 333–54; G. J. Barker-Benfield, *The Culture of Sensibility: Sex and Society in Eighteenth-Century Britain* (Chicago, 1992).

28. John Tosh, "Gentlemanly Politeness and Manly Simplicity in Victorian England," *Transactions of the Royal Historical Society*, 6th ser., 12 (2002), 455–72.

29. Michèle Cohen, "'Manners' Make the Man: Politeness, Chivalry, and the Construction of Masculinity, 1750–1830," *Journal of British Studies*, 44 (April, 2005), 314.

30. Ibid., p. 315.

31. Vic Gatrell, *City of Laughter: Sex and Satire in Eighteenth-Century London* (New York, 2007), p. 17.

32. Ibid., pp. 111–12.

33. Robert Hendrickson, ed., *Encyclopedia of Word and Phrase Origins* (New York, 1997), p. 219; Porter, *English Society in the Eighteenth Century*, p. 34.

34. Gronow, *Reminiscences and Recollections*, II, 75.

35. Sir Nathaniel Wraxall, *The Historical and Posthumous Memoirs of Sir Nathaniel William Wraxall*, ed. Henry B. Wheatley, 5 vols (London, 1884), V, 364.

36. Gatrell, *City of Laughter*, p. 216.

37. Wraxall, *Memoirs*, ed. Wheatley, IV, 3689 and 3803; See also Fintan O'Toole, *A Traitor's Kiss: The Life of Richard Brinsley Sheridan* (London, 1997), pp. 207–8, 458.

38. George Gordon, Lord Byron, *Byron's Letters and Journals*, ed. Leslie A. Marchand, 12 vols (Cambridge, MA, 1979), VI, 12.

39. Byron, *Byron's Letters*, ed. Marchand, IX, 15.

40. BL, Add. MS 47580, f. 15, Fox to R. Fitzpatrick, August 19, 1770, as quoted in L. G. Mitchell, *Charles James Fox* (Oxford, 1992), p. 14. As quoted in Mitchell, Charles James Fox (1992), 14.

41. James Gillray, "'The feast of reason and the flow of soul,'__i.e.__The Wits of the Age setting the Table in a roar" (February 4, 1797), *CPBM*, no. 8984.

42. March 5, 1787, *Parliamentary History*, XXVII, 115. The indisposition was a result of having been drunk at a ball with Dundas and the Duchess of Gordon on the previous night. "They must have had a hard night of it," wrote Lord Bulkeley to the Duke of Buckingham, "for even Dundas, who is well used to the bottle, was affected by it, and spoke remarkably ill, tedious and dull. ... No minister ever cut a more pitiable figure [than Pitt]." Duke of Buckingham and Chandos, *Memoirs of the Court and Cabinets of George III. From original family documents*, 4 vols (London, 1853), I, 361.

43. NA, PRO 30/8/203, Holwood wine cellar record, 1780s.

44. John Ehrman, *The Younger Pitt*, 2 vols (London, 1969), I, 586.

45. NA, PRO 30/8/219, part 6, f. 45, Pitt's wine purchases, July 1784–July 1785.

46. Ehrman, *The Younger Pitt*, I, p. 586.

47. Boswell, *Life of Johnson*, ed. Chapman, p. 1135.

48. Henry Cockburn, *Memorials of His Time* (1856), ed. Karl Miller (Chicago, 1974), pp. 209–10.

49. Ibid., p. 211.

50. Ramsay, *Reminiscences of Scottish Life*, pp. 73–4.
51. *James Boswell's "Book of Company" at Auchinleck, 1782–1795*, ed. Viscountess Eccles and Gordon Turnbull (Roxburghe Club, 1995), pp. 35–49.
52. See, for example, Boswell, *Boswell for the Defense*, ed. Wimsatt and Pottle, p. 224: on July 9, 1774, Boswell and Boswell and seven others, including Dr Webster, drank "eleven Scotch pints of claret, two bottles of old hock, and two of port, and drams of brandy and gin"; Boswell, *Boswell, The Ominous Years*, ed. Ryskamp and Pottle, p. 34: on November 4, 1774, Boswell drank half a bottle of port by himself, and then he went to Fortune's Tavern where he and Captain James Gordon of Ellon drank five bottles of claret "and were most profound politicians."
53. James Boswell, *Boswell: The Applause of the Jury, 1782–1785*, ed. Irma S. Lustig and Frederick A. Pottle (New York, 1981), pp. 162–3.
54. Ibid., p. 164.
55. "Frontignac" was a common British corruption of "Frontignan," and the wine in question was a sweet muscat.
56. Northumberland Record Office, Melton Park, Newcastle-upon-Tyne, 2/DE/31/9, Wine Book for Seaton-Delaval Hall, July 1789–June 1790.
57. Northumberland Record Office, Melton Park, Newcastle-upon-Tyne, 2/DE/30/15 and 2/DE/30/15/24, miscellaneous steward's records and accounts, Seaton-Delaval Hall, 1789 and 1795.
58. Catriona Kennedy, "John Bull into Battle: Military Masculinity and the British Army, 1793–1815," in Karen Hagemann, Gisela Mettele, and Jane Rendall (eds), *Gender, War and Politics: The Wars of Revolution and Liberation in Transatlantic Comparison, 1775–1820* (Basingstoke, 2009), pp. 127–46.
59. Kay and Maclean, *Knee Deep in Claret*, p. 160.
60. NAS, GD 21/551 and GD 21/640, miscellaneous wine bills, the Prince of Wales' Own Fencibles, while stationed at Guernsey, 1799.
61. Alexander Carlyle, *Anecdotes and Characters of the Times*, ed. James Kinsley (London, 1973), p. 122.
62. Ibid., p. 122.
63. Thomas Rowlandson, "Fast Day," published April 19, 1793, British Museum no. 8323. Below the title is the line: "Fasting and Prayer, attending the Church Bell, That, that's the way, good Christians, to live well!"
64. See, for example, John Collier (a.k.a. Tim Bobbin), *The Human Passions Delineated*, prints number 27 and 34 (1773); Anonymous, "Wolves in Sheeps Cloathing" (May 23, 1777); George M. Woodward, *Country Characters*, "Vicar" (September 10, 1799), see *CPBM*, nos 9482–7; Thomas Rowlandson, "Mounseer in Danger, or the Rector's Hopes Confirmed by John Bull's Discovery" (January 27, 1804).
65. See Chapter 7 for details of Parson Woodforde's wine consumption.
66. Gatrell, *City of Laughter*, p. 110.
67. Davidoff and Hall, *Family Fortunes*, p. 400.
68. Amanda Vickery, *The Gentleman's Daughter: Women's Lives in Georgian England* (New Haven, 1998), pp. 213–14. See also, pp. 75, 77.
69. Gatrell, *City of Laughter*, p. 94
70. Ibid., p. 103.
71. Peter Clark, *British Clubs and Societies 1580–1800: Origins of an Associational World* (Oxford, 2000), pp. 2, 89.
72. Ibid., pp. 164–5, 188, 191, etc.
73. Ibid., p. 202.
74. Place Papers, BL, Add. MSS 27828, f. 29, as cited in Gatrell, *City of Laughter*, p. 120.
75. François de La Rochefoucauld, *Mélange sur l'Angleterre* (Paris, 1784), p. 23.
76. G. F. A. Wendeborn, *A View of England towards the Close of the Eighteenth Century*, 2 vols (London, 1791), I, 205, 207.

77. Gronow, *Reminiscences and Recollections*, II, 33.
78. A. D. Francis, *The Wine Trade* (London, 1972), p. 241.
79. See, for instance, John Wain, *Samuel Johnson* (London, 1974), p. 240.
80. William Younger, *Gods, Men and Wine* (Cleveland, OH, 1966), p. 354.
81. Some historians have suggested that the bottles referred to when speaking of a "three-bottle man" were pint bottles (16 fluid ounces), but that was not the case. Contemporary cellar records are explicit in their differentiation between "bottles" meaning quart bottles, and "pints" meaning pint bottles. Byng's diaries also reveal that quart bottles were the standard point of reference. Whenever Byng drank a quart of port he stated he had a "bottle," whereas when he drank a pint of port he referred to it specifically by its size. John Byng, *The Torrington Diaries: containing the tour through England and Wales of the Hon. John Byng (later Viscount Torrington) between the years 1781 and 1794*, ed. C. Bruyn Andrews, 4 vols (New York, 1935), I, 340, 371; II, 315, 411; III, 20, 35, 66, 192, 194, 233, 314–15, 319. See also the facsimiles of Byng's dining and lodging bills reproduced throughout the text of this edition. What was true in England was also true in Scotland. Ironically, a "Scots pint" was actually an oversized bottle (equal to one-and-a-half to two quart bottles), the semantic inversion itself a testimony to the humor and bravado with which the Scots approached hard drinking, but a simple "bottle" in Scotland was a quart-bottle. One story regarding Doctor Webster (of five-bottle fame) illustrates the occasional confusion surrounding bottle sizes. When a friend promised to regale Webster with a "bottle" of a forty-year-old claret and produced what turned out to be a pint-bottle, the disappointed minister responded, "Dear me, it's unco wee for its age." F. Marian McNeill, *The Scots Cellar* (Moffat, 1992), p. 81.
82. Henry Vizetelly, *Facts about Port and Madeira, with Notices of wines vintaged around Lisbon and the wines of Tenerife* (London, 1880), p. 143.
83. Sir Edward Barry, *Observations Historical, Critical, and Medical on the wines of the Ancients. And the analogy between them and Modern Wines. With general observations on the principles and qualities of water, and in particular on those of Bath* (London, 1775), p. 439. For a discussion of this trend in port production, see Chapter 3.
84. Alexander Henderson, *The History of Ancient and Modern Wines* (London, 1824), Appendix II, pp. 363–4.
85. For example, the average amount of alcohol found in claret was 12.91 percent, champagne 12.61 percent, Côte Rôtie 12.32 percent, and remarkably, burgundy 14.57 percent, suggesting that the latter was heavily chaptalized (i.e. sugar was added to the fermenting juice): Henderson, *History of Wines*, Appendix II, p. 363.
86. Younger, *Gods, Men and Wine*, p. 354.
87. Francis, *Wine Trade*, p. 241.
88. Ibid.
89. Ibid., pp. 70–2.
90. Cockburn, *Memorials*, ed. Miller, p. 123.
91. Ramsay, *Reminiscences of Scottish Life*, p. 72.
92. Carlyle, *Autobiography* (1910 edn), ed. J. H. Burton, pp. 250–1,fn. †.
93. William Hickey, *Memoirs of William Hickey*, ed. Peter Quennell (London, 1960), pp. 299–300.
94. Ibid., p. 310.
95. *Byron's Letters*, ed. Marchand, IX, 445.
96. Taylor, *Bacchus in Romantic England*, Chapters 1–4, 7.
97. *Byron's Letters*, ed. Marchand, IX, 29.
98. For an anthropological approach on the ways in which alcohol consumption is used in some cultures as a measure of masculinity, see Dwight B. Heath, *Drinking Occasions: Comparative Perspectives on Alcohol and Culture* (Ann Arbor, 2000).
99. Nimrod (Charles James Apperley), *My Life and Times*, ed. E. D. Cuming (Edinburgh, 1927), p. 87.

100. *Byron's Letters*, ed. Marchand, IX, 48.
101. W. Forbes Gray, *Some Old Scotch Judges* (New York, 1915), pp. 183–4.
102. Robert Burns, "The Whistle," in *The Poems and Songs of Robert Burns*, 3 vols, ed. James Kinsley (Oxford, 1968), I, 484–8.
103. Thomas Rowlandson, "The Brilliants" (January 15, 1801), *CPBM*, no. 9784.
104. Gatrell, *City of Laughter*, p. 88.
105. Joseph Grego, *Rowlandson the Caricaturist: A Selection from his works, with anecdotal descriptions of his famous caricatuires and a sketck of his life, times and contemporaries*, 2 vols (London, 1880) II, 24.
106. Hickey, *Memoirs*, ed. Quennell, pp. 79–81.
107. Hugh Belsey, "Thomas Rowlandson: A Response to Necessity," in Lowell Libson, ed., *Beauty and the Beast: A Loan Exhibition of Rowlandson's Works from British Private Collections* (London, 2007), p. 14; Lowell Lisbon "Turns of the Wheel: Rowlandson and his Collectors," in Lisbon, *Beauty and the Beast*, p. 17; John Hayes, *The Art of Thomas Rowlandson* (Alexandria, VA, 1990), pp. 11, 20; idem, *Rowlandson, Watercolours and Drawings* (London, 1972), pp. 47, 60. For a broad discussion of Rowlandson's work, see Gatrell, *City of Laughter*, passim.
108. Katherine Hart and Laura Hacker, *James Gillray: Prints by the Eighteenth-Century Master of Caricature* (Hanover, NH, 1994), p. 11.
109. Gatrell, *City of Laughter*, p. 292.
110. See most prominently: Diana Donald, *The Age of Caricature: Satirical Prints in the Reign of George III* (New Haven, 1996).
111. Ibid., pp. 110–11.
112. Godfrey, *James Gillray*, "Introduction", p. 24.
113. For understanding the works of Gillray, see Gatrell, *City of Laughter*, pp. 258–92, and passim; Richard Godfrey, "Introduction," and Mark Hallett, "James Gillray and the Language of Graphic Satire," in Richard Godfrey, ed., *James Gillray: The Art of Caricature* (London, 2001), pp. 11–21, 23–37, 38–9.
114. Herman Ludwig Heinrich von Pückler-Muskau, *A Regency Visitor: The English Tour of Prince Pückler-Muskau Described in his Letters, 1826–1828*, trans. Sarah Austin, ed. E. M. Butler (London, 1957), p. 62.
115. Andrew Barr, *Drink: A Social History* (London, 1995), p. 344, believes that the "only practical justification for the survival of the practices of toasting and pledging had lain in the questionable allegiance loyalties of the Civil War and the Jacobite resistance of the late seventeenth and early eighteenth century."
116. William Hickey, *Memoirs of William Hickey*, ed. Alfred Spencer, 4 vols (New York, 1913–25), IV, 191.
117. Nimrod, *Life and Times*, ed. Cuming, pp. 236–7. "In other words, the greater beast," is what, from the vantage point of a Victorian gentleman, Nimrod felt compelled to add.
118. Ibid., p. 237.
119. Ibid., pp. 237–8.
120. Ibid., p. 226.
121. Roy Porter, *English Society in the Eighteenth Century* (Harmondsworth, 1982), pp. 255–6.
122. Gatrell, *City of Laughter*, p. 127.
123. Ibid., p. 153.
124. Boswell, *London Journal*, p. 138, etc.
125. *The Bottle of Claret* (Warington?, c. 1770–1800).
126. Anna Clark, *Women's Silence, Men's Violence: Sexual Assault in England, 1770–1845* (London, 1987), p. 6.
127. *The roaring bacchanal, a burlesque on How little do the Landsmen know* (Salisbury, c. 1750–1800), Fowler Collection (BL).
128. Personal correspondence with Anna Clark, September 3, 2007.

129. Randolph Trumbach, *Sex and the Gender Revolution: Heterosexuality and the Third Gender in Enlightenment London* (Chicago, 1998), pp. 3–65.
130. Cohen, "Manliness, Effeminacy and the French," p. 60.
131. Ibid., p. 58.
132. Leonore Davidoff and Catherine Hall, *Family Fortunes: Men and Women of the English Middle Class, 1780–1850* (Chicago, 1987), pp. 399–400.
133. As quoted in in McNeill, *Scots Cellar*, p. 111.
134. As quoted in Gatrell, *City of Laughter*, p. 122.
135. Chambers, *Traditions of Edinburgh*, p. 147.
136. J. Worgan, *Port and Sherry, or Britons be wise and merry, A favorite new song, Written and composed by J. Worgan* (London, 1797).
137. Ramsay, *Reminiscences of Scottish Life*, p. 69.
138. Ibid., p. 67.
139. Colley, *Britons*, pp. 167–70.
140. Nimrod, *Life and Times*, pp. 220–1.
141. Ibid., p. 221.
142. Ibid., pp. 147–8.
143. Ibid., p. 222.
144. Gatrell, *City of Laughter*, pp. 133–5. For more on the history of boxing in Britain, see Kasia Boddy, *Boxing: A Cultural History* (London, 2008); Dennis Brailsford, *Bareknuckles: A Social History of Prizefighting* (Cambridge, 1989).
145. Horace Walpole, *Horace Walpole's Correspondence*, ed. W. S. Lewis, 48 vols (New Haven, 1937–83), passim.
146. Porter, *English Society in the Eighteenth Century*, p. 34; and more specifically, Roy Porter and George Sebastian Rousseau, *Gout: The Patrician Malady* (New Haven, 1998).
147. Nimrod, *Life and Times*, p. 147.
148. Cockburn, *Memorials*, p. 210.
149. Gronow, *Reminiscences and Recollections*, II, 299–300.

11   "Happily, inebriety is not the vice of the age"

1. Nimrod, *Memoirs of the Life of the late John Mytton, by Nimrod. With numerous illustrations by Alken, reprinted from the New Sporting Magazine* (London, 1835), pp. 78–9.
2. Ibid., p. 71 fn.*.
3. Ibid., pp. 77–8.
4. For the long antecedents of nineteenth-century respectability, see Woodruff Smith, *Consumption and the Making of Respectability, 1600–1800* (London, 2002).
5. The literature here is vast, but for some of the most recent assessments of the middling sorts/ranks/classes, and attempts at definition, see: Leonore Davidoff and Catherine Hall, *Family Fortunes: Men and Women of the English Middle Class, 1780–1850* (London, 1987); Jonathan Barry, "Introduction," in Jonathan Barry and David Brooks, eds, *The Middling Sort of People: Culture, Society and Politics in England, 1550–1800* (New York, 1994), pp. 1–27; Margaret Hunt, *The Middling Sort: Commerce, Gender, and the Family in England, 1680–1780* (Berkeley, 1996), pp. 15–18; Peter Earle, *The Making of the English Middle Class: Business, Society and Family Life in London, 1660–1730* (Berkeley, 1989), pp. 1–14; Alan Kidd and David Nicholls, "Introduction: History, Culture and the Middle Classes," in Kidd and Nicholls, eds, *Gender, Civic Culture and Consumerism: Middle Class Identity in Britain, 1800–1940* (Manchester, 1990), pp. 1–11; idem, "Introduction: The Making of the British Middle Class?", in Kidd and Nicholls, eds, *The Making of the British Middle Class? Studies of Regional and Cultural Diversity since the Eighteenth Century* (London, 1998), pp. xv–xl; Dror Wahrman, *Imagining the Middle Class: The Political Representation of Class in Britain, c. 1780–1840* (Cambridge, 1995).

6. This idea is emphasized by Wahrman in *Imagining the Middle* Class. For a brilliant analysis of the gendering of "middle class," see Wahrman, "'Middle Class' Domesticity Goes Public: Gender, Class, and Politics from Queen Caroline to Queen Victoria," *Journal of British Studies*, 32 (October, 1993), 396–432.

7. *The Examiner*, December 21, 1817, as cited in Ben Wilson, *The Making of Victorian Values: Decency and Dissent in Britain, 1789–1837* (New York, 2007), p. 332.

8. Parliamentary Report C.8706, *Customs Tariffs of the United Kingdom from 1800–1897, with some notes upon the history of more important branches of the receipt from 1600* (London, 1897), pp. 150–1; George B. Wilson, *Alcohol and the Nation* (London, 1940), Table 2, p. 335; T. R. Gourvish and R. G. Wilson, *The British Brewing Industry, 1830–1980* (Cambridge, 1994), Table 2.3, p. 30.

9. John Tosh, *A Man's Place: Masculinity and the Middle-Class Home in Victorian England* (New Haven, 1999), p. 125.

10. James Warre, *The Past, Present, and Probably the Future State of the Wine Trade: Proving that an increase in Duty caused a decrease in Revenue; and a decrease of Duty, an increase of Revenue. Founded on Parliamentary and other authentic Documents. Most respectfully submitted to the Right Honourable the President of the Board of Trade* (London, 1823), p. 36.

11. Alexander Henderson, *The History of Ancient and Modern Wines* (London, 1824), pp. 346–7.

12. Cyrus Redding, *A History and Description of Modern Wines* (London, 1833), p. xxiii.

13. Francis Place, *The Autobiography of Francis Place*, ed. Mary Thale (Cambridge, 1972), p. 82.

14. Henry Angelo, *Reminiscences of Henry Angelo, with memoirs of his late father and friends*, 2 vols (London, 1828–30), I, 283–4.

15. Anna Clark, "Manhood, Womanhood, and the Politics of Class in Britain, 1790–1845," in Laura L. Frader and Sonya O. Rose, eds, *Gender and Class in Modern Europe* (Ithaca, 1996), pp. 272–3.

16. BL, Add. MS 44572, f. 33, p. 15, "Wine Duties," May 3, 1853, 16.

17. Ibid., pp. 15–16.

18. Wilson, *Alcohol and the Nation*, Table 1, pp. 331–3.

19. Ibid., Table 2, p. 335.

20. "Report of the Committee of the British Association on the Present Appropriation of Wages," 1882. Cited in Joseph Rowntree and Arthur Sherwell, *The Temperance Problem and Social Reform*, 3rd edn (London, 1899), p. 10. As quoted in John Burnett, *Liquid Pleasures: A Social History of Drinks in Modern Britain* (London, 1999), p. 167.

21. Gourvish and Wilson, *British Brewing Industry*, Table 2.3, p. 30; Burnett, *Liquid Pleasures*, pp. 125–6, 147.

22. Brian Harrison, *Drink and the Victorians: The Temperance Question in England, 1815–1872*, 2nd edn (Keele, 1994), Fig. 2, p. 39; Burnett, *Liquid Pleasures*, pp. 57–8, 79–83.

23. Burnett, *Liquid Pleasures*, pp. 58, 147–8, 184–5.

24. George Gordon Byron, Lord Byron, *Letter to **** ****** [John Murray] on the Rev. W. L. Bowle's Strictures on the Life and Writing of Pope* (London, 1821), pp. 16–17.

25. George Gordon Byron, Lord Byron, *Don Juan*, Canto the Second, stanza CLXXIX.

26. For the decline of libertinism and laughter, see Vic Gatrell, *City of Laughter: Sex and Satire in Eighteenth-Century London* (New York, 2006), Chapters 14–15 and Epilogue. For changes in clothing, see David Kuchta, *The Three Piece Suit and Modern Masculinity: England 1550–1850* (Berkeley, 2002), pp. 133–72.

27. Wilson, *Making of Victorian Values*, p. 384.

28. Warre, *The Past, Present, and Probably the Future State of the Wine Trade*, p. 3.

29. Ibid., p. 9.

30. Ibid., pp. 34–5.

31. See, for instance, John Bowles, *A View of the Moral State of Society* (London, 1804); Patrick Colquhoun, *A Treatise on Indigence; exhibiting a general view of the national resources for productive labour; with propositions for ameliorating the condition of the poor* (London, 1806); Thomas Trotter, M.D., *An Essay, medical, philosophical and chemical,*

on drunkenness, and its effects on the human body (London, 1804). For more recent assessments of the general failure of the early temperance advocates, see Anya Taylor, *Bacchus in Romantic England, 1780–1830* (London, 1999); Wilson, *Making of Victorian Values*.

32. Wilson, *Making of Victorian Values*, p. 308.
33. Gatrell, *City of Laughter*, p. 547.
34. Harrison, *Drink and the Victorians*, pp. 121–38.
35. Ibid., pp. 85–102, 139–66.
36. Charles Ludington, "Drinking for Approval: Wine and the British Court from George III to Victoria and Albert," in Danielle de Vooght, ed., *Royal Taste: Food, Power and Status at the European Courts after 1789* (Farnham, 2011).
37. Pierce Egan, *Life in London: The Day and Night Scenes of Jerry Hawthorn, Esq., and his Elegant Friend Corinthian Tom, Accompanied by Bob Logic, the Oxonian, in there Rambles and Sprees through the Metropolis* (London, 1821).
38. Gatrell, *City of Laughter*, p. 548.
39. Ibid., pp. 550–2.
40. For more on the topic of nineteenth-century domesticity, see Mary Poovey, *Making a Social Body: British Cultural Formation, 1830–1864* (Chicago, 1995); John Tosh, *Manliness and Masculinities in Nineteenth-Century Britain: Essays on Gender, Family, and Empire* (Harlow, 2005).
41. Tosh, *A Man's Place*, pp. 4–6, 138–41.
42. Ibid., p. 125.
43. Gatrell, *City of Laughter*, pp. 576–8.
44. Parliamentary Report C.8706, pp. 150–1.
45. Warre, *State of the Wine Trade*, p. 36.
46. Henderson, *Ancient and Modern Wines*, p. 316.
47. *Chamber's Edinburgh Journal*, vol. 11, no. 521 (January 22, 1842), p. 5.
48. *Report from the Select Committee on Import Duties on Wines, Together with the Proceedings of the Committee, Minutes of Evidence, Appendix and Index. Ordered by the House of Commons, to be printed, 18 June 1852* (London, 1852), p. 167.
49. NA, L.S. 8/320, Expenses of His Majesty's Visit to Scotland, 1822. For more on the king's trip to Scotland, see Hugh Trevor-Roper, "The Invention of Tradition: The Highland Tradition of Scotland," in Eric Hobsbawm and Terence Ranger, eds, *The Invention of Tradition* (Cambridge, 1983), pp. 15–42; John Prebble, *The King's Jaunt: George IV in Scotland, August 1822: "one and twenty daft days"* (London, 1988).
50. NA, L.S. 8/320.
51. A. D. Francis, *The Wine Trade* (London, 1972), p. 303.
52. East Sussex Record Office, Lewes, MS 2721, List of the Wine Cellar, Ashburnham Place, February 15, 1824; MS 2723, List of the Wine Cellar, Ashburnham Place, November 10, 1830.
53. East Sussex Record Office, Lewes, MS 2724, List of the Wine Cellar, Ashburnham Place, April 18, 1831.
54. NLS, Adv. 82.8.92, f. 110, 1831–32 bill from Coburn [sic] and Campbell for James B. Oliphant, Esq. of Gask. "Superior" sherry was probably dryer in style, like an Amontillado, while "East India" sherry was famously sweet.
55. Christopher Hibbert, *George IV, Regent and King, 1811–1830* (London, 1973), pp. 782–3.
56. Clarissa Campbell Orr, "The Feminization of the Monarchy, 1780–1910: Royal Masculinity and Female Empowerment," in Andrzej Olechnowicz, ed., *The Monarchy and the British Nation, 1780 to the Present* (Cambridge, 2007), pp. 79–81.
57. Ludington, "Drinking for Approval," p. 76.
58. John Marshall, *Our Fat Friend Going to Roost* (1820).
59. Philip Ziegler, *King William IV* (London, 1971), p. 130.
60. Ibid., p. 130.
61. As quoted in Ziegler, *William IV*, p. 271.

62. NA, LS 13/298, Board of the Green Cloth, Account of creditors not paid by salary, 1838, ff. 1–3.
63. BL, Add. MS 38372, f. 42, Stock of Wine (Royal Household), 31 Dec. 1841.
64. BL, Add. MS 76683, Summary of Monthly Returns made by the Gentleman of Her Majesty's Wine Cellar, April 1–December 31, 1856.
65. David Duff, *Albert and Victoria* (London, 1972), p. 238; Joanna Richardson, *Victoria and Albert: A Study of a Marriage* (London, 1977), p. 100; Stanley Weintraub, *Albert: Uncrowned King* (London, 1997), pp. 143–4.
66. BL, Add. MS 38372, f. 42.
67. Parliamentary Report C.8706, *Customs Tariffs of the United Kingdom*, pp. 151–2.
68. See Chapters 8 and 9.
69. William Makepeace Thackeray, *The Works of William Makepeace Thackeray*, Volume 7: *The Newcomes: Memoirs of a Most Respectable Family* (Cambridge, MA, 1907), p. 137.
70. Francis, *Wine Trade*, p. 310.
71. Charles Dickens, *Sketches of Boz: Illustrative of every-day life and every-day people* (London, 1836), "Miss Evans and the Eagle," p. 127.
72. *Fraser's Magazine for Town and Country*, vol. 18 (November 1838), "Passages from the Diary of the late Dolly Duster," p. 604.
73. Henry Cockton, *The Love Match* (London, 1845), passim.
74. Robert Smith Surtees, *Mr. Sponge's Sporting Tour* (London, 1853), p. 138.
75. *The Edinburgh Review*, "Wine and the Wine Trade," vol. 126, no. 257 (July, 1867), p. 202.
76. Ludington, "Drinking for Approval." pp. 79–85.
77. William Powell Frith, *My Autobiography and Reminiscences*, 3 vols.(London, 1887), I, 262–3.
78. Jane Sellars, "Frith's Women: William Powell Frith and the Female Model," in Mark Bills and Vivien Knight, eds, *William Powell Frith: Painting the Victorian Age* (New Haven, 2006), p. 137.
79. W. P. Frith, *Many Happy Returns of the Day* (1854).
80. Christopher Wood, *William Powell Frith: A Painter and His World* (Stroud, 2006), pp. 40–1.
81. Ibid.

12 "Taste is not an immutable, but a mutable thing"

1. As quoted in Asa Briggs, *A Social History of England* (Harmondsworth, 1983), p. 189.
2. James Wilson, "The First Half of the Nineteenth Century: Progress of the Nation and the Race," *The Economist* (February 1, 1851), pp. 109–11.
3. Thomas George Shaw, *The Wine Trade and its History* (London, 1851), p. 7. As quoted in Asa Briggs, *Wine for Sale, Victoria Wine and Liquor Trade, 1860–1984* (Chicago, 1985), p. 26.
4. As quoted in Briggs, *Wine for Sale*, p. 27.
5. James Warre, *The Past, Present, and Probably the Future State of the Wine Trade: Proving that an increase in Duty caused a decrease in Revenue; and a decrease of Duty, an increase of Revenue. Founded on Parliamentary and other authentic Documents. Most respectfully submitted to the Right Honourable the President of the Board of Trade* (London, 1823), p. 48.
6. Warre was probably referring to wine from Masdeu in Roussillon, which was beginning to be available on the British market.
7. Fleetwood Williams, *Observations on the State of the Wine Trade, Occasioned by the Perusal of a Pamphlet on the same subject, by Mr. Warre. Most respectfully submitted to His Majesty's Ministers* (London, 1824); [A Portuguese], *The Wine Question Considered, or, Observations on the Pamphlets of Mr. James Warre and Mr. Fleetwood Williams, respecting the General Company of the Agriculture of the Vineyards, of the Upper Douro, Known in England under the name of the Royal Oporto Wine Company* (London, 1824), p. 49.

8. [A Portuguese], *Wine Question Considered*, pp. 34–5.

9. Ibid., pp. 61–2.

10. Ibid., pp. 64–5.

11. See, for example, Warre's revised, 1824 edition of *State of the Wine Trade*, which included "Supplementary Observations," as well as Fleetwood Williams's follow-up to his initial pamphlet, *Further Observations on the Wine Trade, and on the Reduction of Duties, etc., in a letter addressed to the Right Honourable, the Chancellor of the Exchequer* (London, 1825).

12. Warre, *State of the Wine Trade* (1824 edn), pp. 99–100.

13. The Weights and Measures Act of 1824 instated Imperial Measurements on all measurable items. The Imperial gallon is 20 percent greater (5:6) than the previously used gallon, which is still the gallon used in the United States today.

14. Biographical material on Alexander Henderson, MD comes from James Gabler, *Wine Into Words: A History and Bibliography of Wine Books in the English Language* (Baltimore, 1985), p. 126.

15. While Henderson's book is often credited as being the first book in English about the production of modern wines, that title could also go to Robert Shannon, M.D., for his *Practical treatise on brewing, distilling and rectification, with the genuine process of making brandy, rum, and hollands gin ... With an appendix on the culture and preparation of foreign wine* (London, 1805). What distinguishes Henderson's book from Shannon's is that the former focuses on wine alone.

16. Alexander Henderson, *The History of Ancient and Modern Wines* (London, 1824), p. 197.

17. Ibid., p. 214.

18. Ibid., pp. 315–16.

19. Ibid., p. 319.

20. Ibid., pp. 346–7.

21. Gabler inquired into the number of copies of Henderson's book that were printed, but says that the London publishing company, Baldwin, Craddock and Joy, left little archival information about the book. *Wine into Words*, p. 126.

22. Norman Longmate, *The Waterdrinkers: A History of Temperance* (London, 1968).

23. Gabler, *Wine into Words*, p. 221.

24. Cyrus Redding, *A History and Description of Modern Wines* (London, 1833), p. xxiii.

25. Redding, like Henderson, used the term "English" synonymously with all the inhabitants of Great Britain. For evidence that the United Kingdom still constituted the primary market for port wine in the 1830s, see W. and J. Graham, "Orders for Wine," May 1835-December 1838.

26. Redding, *History and Description of Modern Wines*, p. 54.

27. Ibid., pp. 179–80.

28. Ibid., pp. 199–200.

29. Ibid., p. 213.

30. Ibid., p. 217.

31. Ibid., p. 221.

32. Cyrus Redding, *Every Man his own Butler* (London, 1839), pp. 11–12.

33. There was a brief flurry of debate surrounding a possible duty reduction in 1842–3, when a new commercial treaty with Portugal was being considered, but ultimately it was not enacted. In this instance, merchants were concerned primarily about receiving the "drawback" (the difference between the old and new tariff) from the government should the reduction take place. See *Report of the Committee, appointed at a general meeting of the wine trade, held at the Commercial Sale Rooms, Mincing Lane, London, on Tuesday, 26th July 1842, to take into consideration the measure to be adopted in consequence of the reduction in the duties upon wine, expected to take place, on the conclusion of the commercial treaty with Portugal* (London, 1842).

34. Forrester began this debate with his pamphlet *A Word of Truth on Port-wine: showing how, and why, it is adulterated, and affording some means of detecting its adulteration* (London,

1844), in which he said the decline in the port trade was due to the poor quality of most wine and the extreme degree of fortification. He was not against fortification in every instance, but suggested that when it had to be used, it should be done judiciously. His charge was that most of his rivals in the port-shipping trade added brandy and other ingredients in all instances. Forrester's pamphlet received many angry responses, including Thomas Whittaker's *A Word of Truth on Port Wine* (London, 1844), in which the fortification of port and the reputation of British port shippers was roundly defended. Forrester wrote and published many more pamphlets asserting his position. For a lengthy discussion of this debate, see: Sarah Bradford, *The Englishman's Wine: The Story of Port* (London, 1969), pp. 79–85; Francis, *Wine Trade*, pp. 305–9; and Hugh Johnson, *Vintage: The Story of Wine* (New York, 1989), pp. 327–9.

35. William Younger, *Gods, Men and Wine* (Cleveland, OH, 1966), pp. 382–3.
36. *Eighteen Reasons why the Duty on Wine Should now be Very Largely Reduced, and Assumed Objections Answered why it should not* (London, 1849), n.p., "Objection" no. 2.
37. *The Times*, November 6, 1850, January 30, 1851; Thomas George Shaw, *The Wine Trade and its History* (London, 1851). For Shaw's collected writings, see Thomas George Shaw, Wine in Relation to Temperance, Trade and the Revenue (London, 1854).
38. *Notes on the Wine Duty Question and Mr. Shaw's Pamphlet [Wine Trade and its History]* (London, 1851), p. 11.
39. Redding, *History and Description of Modern Wines*, 3rd edn (London, 1851), p. 387.
40. So sensitive was the issue among wine merchants that even the appointment of a committee to look into the question of a wine duty reduction brought forth criticism. See *A letter to the Right Honourable Benjamin D'Israeli, MP, Chancellor of the Exchequer, from a Wine Merchant* (London, 1852). See also, Briggs, *Wine for Sale*, pp. 24–6.
41. As quoted in Briggs, *Wine for Sale*, p. 30.
42. Quoted in W. Bosville James, *Wine Duties Considered Financially and Socially, being a reply to Sir James Emerson Tennent, on "Wine, Its Taxation and Uses"* (London, 1855), p. 77.
43. As quoted in Briggs, *Wine for Sale*, p. 28.
44. As quoted in Briggs, p. 27.
45. Benjamin Oliveira, ed., *Proceedings of the Wine Duties' Reduction Committee, since its formation in 1852, comprising reports, debates in the House of Commons, a list of the general committee, and other particulars connected with the reduction of the import duty upon wines, up to the dissolution of the committee when the measure was carried, through the Anglo-French Treaty, in 1860* (London, 1861).
46. Cyrus Redding, ed., *Wine Duties Reduction. An abstract of the evidence given before a select committee of the House of Commons upon the import duties on wines, in May and June, 1852, with a draft of the chairman's report* (London, 1852).
47. William Wolryche Whitmore, *The Wine Duties* (London, 1853), p. 18.
48. Ibid.
49. Sir James Emerson Tennent, *Wine, its Use and Taxation. An inquiry into the operation of the wine duties on consumption and revenue* (London, 1855), pp. 57–8.
50. Ibid., pp. 62–9.
51. Ibid., p. 69.
52. See James, *Wine Duties Considered*, and also J. R. McCulloch's hugely influential pro-free trade *A Dictionary, Practical, Theoretical, and Historical, of Commerce and Commercial Navigation*. McCulloch's *Dictionary* was first published in 1832, and revised and republished seven times in the 1840s and 1850s. In each instance, McCulloch's article on "wine" was a scathing critique of the Methuen Treaty and the political creation of English taste, saying: "This is the most striking example, perhaps in the history of commerce, of the influence of customs duties in diverting trade into new channels, and altering the taste of a people." McCulloch, *Dictionary of Commerce*, 3 vols (London, 1856), III, 1413.
53. James, *Wine Duties Considered*, p. vi.
54. Ibid., p. 159.
55. Ibid.

56. Benjamin Oliveira, ed., *Report of the Meeting of the Wine Duties Reduction Committee and the Anglo-French Free-Trade Association at the Crystal Palace, 9th July 1856; Debate in the House of Commons on Mr. Oliveira's Motion for the Wine Duties Reduction on the 15th July 1856; A list of the general committee; and other particulars connected with the reduction of the import duty on wines* (London, 1856).
57. Briggs, *Wine for Sale*, p. 34; Burnett, *Liquid Pleasures*, p. 149.
58. William Ewart Gladstone, *The Financial Statements of 1853, 1860–1863* (London, 1863), February 10, 1860, p. 152.
59. Ibid.
60. Hansard, February 20, 1860.
61. Briggs, *Wine for Sale*, p. 23.
62. Letter of Gladstone to Edward Baines, February 24, 1860, as quoted in Briggs, *Wine for Sale*, p. 11.
63. As quoted in David Cannadine, *The Rise and Fall of Class in Britain* (New York, 1999), p. 92.
64. Gladstone, *Financial Statements*, April 15, 1861, p. 203.
65. Parliamentary Report C.8706, *Customs Tariffs*, p. 152.
66. As quoted in Charles Tovey, *Wine and Wine Countries: a record and manual for wine merchants and wine consumers* (London, 1862), pp. 168, 170–1.
67. Parliamentary Report C.8706, *Customs Tariffs*, p. 152.
68. Ibid., p. 152; Wilson, *Alcohol and the Nation* (London, 1940), pp. 361–3.

Bibliography

Manuscripts

United Kingdom

British Library, London

Add. MS 23736, f. 18, An Account of the Kingdom of Portugal, c. 1701.

Add. MSS 32690, f. 140; 32717, f. 212; 32737, f. 529; 32857, f. 270, Newcastle Papers: Wine bills and letters from wine merchants to Thomas Pelham-Holles, Duke of Newcastle, 1730s–1750s.

Add. MS 38372, f. 42, Stock of Wine of the Royal Household, December 31, 1841.

Add. MS 38854, f. 147, Slingsby Bethell, Esq. to Thomas Gordon, for wine delivered to the Old Bailey, October 21, 1751.

Add. MS 44401, ff. 30–32, Tavern bills from L. Reilly to R. B. Sheridan, March-June, 1777.

Add. MS 44572, f. 33, p. 15, "Wine Duties," May 3, 1853.

Add. MS 47014 B, ff. 39, 42, Lord Egmont's first and second notice of an outstanding bill totaling £161.90 from the wine merchants Collingwood and Holford, 1751.

Add. MS 49186, ff. 1–2, Bill and receipt for wine order from Christie and Barrow to the Hon. Spencer Perceval, September 3, 1790.

Add. MS 61349, f. 123b, Bill paid by Mr Charles Hodges, executor of the late Duke of Marlborough's estate, to Samuel Braund, April 12, 1725.

Add. MSS 61349, f. 83, f. 68, f. 69, f. 108; 61363, f. 48, f. 78, Wine bills and receipts of the first Duke of Marlborough.

Add. MS 61490, f. 203, "An Account of Lord Sunderland's Wine Cellar," October 14, 1666.

Add. MS 61541, f. 132, Dom Luis da Cunha to Queen Anne, February 24, 1708.

Add. MS 61664, f. 1, "An exact inventory of the late Earl of Sunderland's Cellars, 13 June 1722."

Add. MS 61664, ff. 13, "An exact inventory of all the wines in the late Earl of Sunderland's Cellars, June 13th, 1722."

Add. MS 61664, f. 60, "Account of the wines taken by Wm. Davis out of the Late Earl of Sunderland's Cellars for the use of the Gent. Countess dow[ag]er of Sunderland, 30 June 1722, from the Honourable John Hooker, Steward to the said Earl."

Add. MS 61672, f. 128, "Stock of wine in the cellars at Blenheim taken June 7th, 1767."

Add. MS 61672, f. 130, "An account wines delivered to the Duke of Marlborough's Homes, 1763–1767."

Add. MS 76683, Summary of Monthly Returns made by the Gentleman of Her Majesty's Wine Cellar, April 1–December 31, 1856.

Egerton MS 2882, "Proclamation for Prising Wines," February 1, 1674.

Cambridge University Library, Cambridge

Cholmondeley (Houghton) MSS

CH (H), "Vouchers, 1657–1745."

CH (H) 41/18/6, "Of the running of wine," March 1733.

CH (H) 41/18/7, "An account of the particular instances of frauds which have come to the knowledge of the commissioners of the Customs relating to wine in London and the outports," March 1733.

CH (H) 41/29, "A memorandum concerning smuggling in the Isle of Guernsey, from Ventris Colombine, Customs officer, to Robert Walpole," c. 1733.

CH (H) 40/13–14, "Report of Robert Paul, Richard Sankey and Samuel Kettilby of their general survey of the ports of Scotland to the Lords Commissioners of HM Treasury, 24 Aug. 1724."
CH (H) 40/16, "Report of Robert Paul, Richard Sankey and Samuel Kettilby of their general survey of the ports of Scotland to the Lords Commissioners of HM Treasury, 17 Sept. 1724."
CH (H) 40/19, "Report of Robert Paul, Richard Sankey and Samuel Kettilby of their general survey of the ports of Scotland to the Lords Commissioners of HM Treasury, 8 Oct. 1724."

Christ Church, Oxford
Common Room Accounts, MS C.R.2.

Christie's, St. James, London
Auction catalogues, 1766–1800.

Durham County Record Office, Durham
D/X 101/3. Isabella Widdrington to Mrs Mills, July 8, 1777.

East Sussex Record Office, Lewes
MS A 741, S.A.S., Gage Account Book, 1792–1804.
MS 2721, List of the Wine Cellar, Ashburnham Place, February 15, 1824.
MS 2723, List of the Wine Cellar, Ashburnham Place, November 10, 1830.
MS 2724, List of the Wine Cellar, Ashburnham Place, April 18, 1831.

John Roberts, John Roberts Wine Books, Ltd., London
MS: "An Account of the Port[ugal] trade in relation to their wines," c. 1677.

National Archives of Scotland, Edinburgh
E 501 series, Comptroller General's Account of Customs, 1707–1830.
E 504/22/1, Port of Leith, Collector's Quarterly Accounts, October 1, 1742–December 31, 1742.
E 72/15 series, Leith Customs records, imported wine, 1672–1689.
GD 1/306/1, Letter book of Alexander Oliphant of Ayr, 1767–1768.
GD 16/33/41, "Account of the wine sent from Cortacky, Auchterhouse and Newgrange, and put into the cellar at Airly Lodge, Dec. 1779."
GD 21/551 and GD 21/640, miscellaneous wine bills, the Prince of Wales' own Fencibles, while stationed at Guernsey, 1799.
GD 26/6/178, "Inventory of the wine cellar at Balgony, taken the 28th May 1726, and the key delivered up by Mr. Ker to the Earle of Leven."
GD 124/15/259/1, William Clelland to James Erskine, Lord Grange, November 10, 1705.
GD 124/15/491 series, Correspondance of James Erskine, Lord Grange and the John Erskine, the Earl of Mar, 1707.
GD 124/15/513 series, Correspondance of David Erskine and the Earl of Mar, 1707.
GD 124/15/522/3, Earl of Northesk to the Earl of Mar, May 26, 1707.
GD 124/15/537, Samuel McClellan to the Earl of Mar, April 22, 1707.
GD 164/818, Dysart House wine books, 1786–1792.
GD 164/879 (item 17), Inventory of Dysart House wine cellar, June–August 1810.
GD 164/1034, "State of Lord Loughborough's wines, 1 Jan. 1775 to 6 June 1800."
GD 406/1/970, Hugh Campbell to John Hamilton, servitor to William Douglas, the Duke of Hamilton, July 22, 1673.

National Library of Scotland, Edinburgh
Adv. 82.1.6, f. 38, wine bill from Montgomery and Stute, wine merchants (location unknown), to Laurence Oliphant, Laird of Gask, 1793.

Adv. 82.1.6, f. 42, wine bill from Adam Bisset, wine merchant of Leith, to Laurence Oliphant, Laird of Gask, 1793.

Adv. 82.3.3, ff. 23, 147, wine bills from M. Wood to Laurence Oliphant the Younger of Gask, 1723.

Adv. 82.3.9, ff. 53, 108, wine bills from Patrick Stewart, wine merchant of Perth, to Laurence Oliphant, Laird of Gask, 1791.

Adv. 82.4.1, ff. 47, 128, 131, 141, 176, wine and food bills from Anne Hickson, tavern keeper at Perth, to Laurence Oliphant, Laird of Gask, 1745–1746.

Adv. 82.8.92, f. 110, wine bills from Coburn [sic] and Campbell for James B. Oliphant, Esq. of Gask, 1831–1832.

MS 1520 (65), *Letter from a Scots Factor at London, to a merchant in Edinburgh, Concerning the House of Commons; to prevent the importation of wines and other Goods from Scotland* (London, April 17, 1707).

Northumberland Record Office, Melton Park, Newcastle

2/DE/30/15 and 2/DE/30/15/24, miscellaneous steward's records and accounts, Seton-Delaval Hall, 1789 and 1795.

2/DE/31/9, Wine Book for Seaton-Delaval Hall, July 1789–June 1790.

National Archives, Kew

C.M.E. C 110/19/20, Thomas Pratt to John Hitchcock, September 12, 1734.

C.O. 388/2, ff. 66–67, Memorial of the Portugal merchants of London, received by the Commissioners for Trade, August 9, 1692.

Customs 14, Customs accounts for Scotland, 1755–1827.

E 190/62–54 (various), Port books for London regarding wine, 1675–1696.

L.S. 8/320, Expenses of His Majesty's Visit to Scotland, 1822.

L.S. 13/46, Wine Accounts of the Royal Household, 1727.

L.S. 13/91, Cellar book of Charles II, 1660–1661.

L.S. 13/96, Wine Order Book for the Royal Household, 1702–1709.

L.S. 13/191, Wine Accounts of the Royal Household, 1714–1719.

L.S. 13/192, Wine Accounts of the Royal Household, 1719–1725.

L.S. 13/268, Wine Accounts of the Royal Household, 1719–1731.

L.S. 13/269, Wine Accounts of the Royal Household, 1733–1752.

L.S. 13/270, Wine Accounts of the Royal Household, 1753–1761.

L.S. 13/271, Wine Accounts of the Royal Household, 1761–1766.

L.S. 13/272, Wine Accounts of the Royal Household, 1767–1770.

L.S. 13/298, Board of the Green Cloth, Account of creditors not paid by salary, 1838, ff. 1–3.

P.R.O. 30/8/203, Holwood wine cellar record, 1780s.

P.R.O. 30/8/219, William Pitt's wine expenses, July 1784–June 1785.

P.R.O. 30/8/219, part 6, f. 45, Pitt's wine purchases, July 1784–July 1785.

S.P. 89/31, Burnett to Newcastle, August 6, 1724.

Suffolk Record Office, Bury St. Edmonds

941/46/13/14, Expense Book of John Hervey, 1st Earl of Bristol.

Worcestershire Record Office, City Centre Branch (St. Helen's)

BA 9504/1, 899:832, Petty Ledger of James Pardoe, wine sales, 1741–1746.

France

Archives Départmentale de Gironde, Bordeaux

"Négociants," 7 B 3017. Carme to Wischold, February 22, 1714.

Archives National, Paris
G/7/138, Bazins de Bezons to Contrôleur Général, 5 December 1699, Archives National, Paris, G/7/138.

Bibliothèque Municipale de Bordeaux
Fonds Itié, carton 4, liasse 1689–1691.

Portugal
Taylor, Fladgate and Yeatman,, Vila Nova de Gaia
T/Z. 1808–12/C5.P5, Letter book of Joseph Camo, 1808–1812.

W. and J. Graham, Vila Nova de Gaia
"Orders for Wine," May 1835–December 1838.

The United States
Lewis-Walpole Library, Farmington, CT
MS, Augusta Princess Dowager of Wales, account book, 1755.

Huntington Library, San Marino, CA
ST vol. 60 (1–3): Brydges' wine books from Cannons and London, 1718–1728.

Government publications

Acts of the Parliaments of Scotland (APS), T. Thompson and Cosmo Innes, ed., 12 vols. (Edinburgh, 1814–1875).
Calendar of State Papers, Domestic Series, of the reign of Charles II (1660–1685), Mary Anne Everett Green, F. H. Blackburne Daniell and Francis Bickley, eds., 28 vols. (London, 1860–1939).
Calendar of Treasury Books (1666–1714), William A. Shaw, ed., 28 vols. (London, 1905–1955).
Calendar of Treasury Papers, vol. I (1556–1696), ed. Joseph Redington (London, 1868).
Customs Tariffs of the United Kingdom from 1800 to 1897, with some notes upon the history of the more important branches of receipt from the year 1660 (London, 1897). Parliamentary Report, C.8706.
First, Second and Third Report from the Committee, Appointed to Inquire into the Illicit Practices Used in Defrauding the Revenue (London, 1783–1784), reprinted in *House of Commons Sessional Papers of the Eighteenth Century*, ed. Sheila Lambert, 147 vols. (Wilmington, Del., 1975), XXXVIII, *First Report*, 215–278; *Second Report*, 279–331; *Third Report*, 333–389.
Journal of the House of Commons (JHC), XVII.
Report from the Committee of the House of Commons, Appointed to enquire into the Frauds and Abuses of the Customs, to the Prejudice of Trade, and Diminution of the Revenue (London, 1733), reprinted in *House of Commons Sessional Papers of the Eighteenth Century*, ed. Sheila Lambert, 147 vols. (Wilmington, Del., 1975), XII, 323–425.
Report of the Committee, appointed at a general meeting of the wine trade, held at the Commercial Sale Rooms, Mincing Lane, London, on Tuesday, 26th July 1842, to take into consideration the measure to be adopted in consequence of the reduction in the duties upon wine, expected to take place, on the conclusion of the commercial treaty with Portugal (London, 1842).
Report from the Select Committee on Import Duties on Wines, Together with the Proceedings of the Committee, Minutes of Evidence, Appendix and Index. Ordered by the House of Commons, to be printed, 18 June 1852 (London, 1852).

Printed primary sources

Addison, Joseph, *The Late Tryal and Conviction of Count Tariff* (London, 1713), in *The Miscellaneous Works of Joseph Addison*, ed. A. C. Gutkelch, 2 vols. (London, 1914), II, 264–272.
Addison, Joseph and Richard Steele, *The Guardian*, ed. John Calhoun Stephens, (Lexington, KY, 1982).
——, *The Spectator*, ed. Donald F. Bond, 5 vols. (Oxford, 1965).
——, *The Tatler*, ed. Donald F. Bond, 3 vols. (Oxford, 1987).
Ames, Richard, *The Search after Claret; or, a Visitation of the Vintners, a poem in two cantos* (London, 1691).
——, *A Dialogue between Claret and Darby-Ale, a Poem Considered in an Accidental Conversation between Two Gentlemen* (London, 1691).
——, *A Farther Search after Claret; or, a Second Visitation of the Vintners* (London, 1691).
——, *The Last Search after Claret in Southwark: or a Visitation of the Vintners* (London, 1691).
——, *A Search after Wit; or, a Visitation of the Authors: In Answer to The Late Search after Claret; or, Visitation of the Vintners* (London, 1691).
——, *The Character of a Bigotted Prince, and what England may expect from the return of such a one* (London, 1691).
——, *Chuse which you will, Liberty or Slavery; or, An Impartial Representation of the Danger of being Subjected to a Popish Prince* (London, 1692).
——, *The Jacobite Conventicle, a Poem* (London, 1692).
——, *The Double Descent, a Poem* (London, 1692).
——, *The Bacchanalian Sessions, or the Contention of Liquors, with a Farewell to Wine* (London, 1693).
——, *Fatal Friendship; or, the Drunkards Misery being a Satyr against Hard Drinking by the Author of The Search after Claret* (London, 1693).
Angelo, Henry, *Reminiscences of Henry Angelo, with Memoirs of his Late Father and Friends*, 2 vols. (London, 1828–1830).
Arbuthnot, Joseph, *The History of John Bull* (London, 1712).
Archenholz, Johann Wilhelm von, *A Picture of England*, 2 vols. (London, 1789).
The Art and Mystery of Vintner's and Wine Coopers: Containing approved Directions for the Conserving and Curing all Manner and Sorts of Wines, whether Spanish, Greek, Italian or French, very necessary for all Sorts of People (London, 1682).
Baillie of Mellerstain, Lady Grisell, *Lady Grisell Baillie's Household Book, 1692–1733*, ed. Robert Scott Moncrief (Edinburgh, 1911).
Barry, Sir Edward, *Observations Historical, Critical, and Medical on the wines of the Ancients. And the analogy between them and Modern Wines. With general observations on the principles and qualities of water, and in particular on those of Bath* (London, 1775).
Beowulf, trans. and ed. Seamus Heaney (London, 2000).
Boislisle, Arthur Michel de, *Correspondance des Contrôleurs Généraux de Finances avec les Intendants des provinces*, 3 vols. (Paris, 1874–93).
Bolingbroke, Henry St John, Viscount, *Letters and Correspondence, Public and Private, by the Lord Viscount Bolingbroke during the time he was Secretary of State*, ed. Gilbert Parke, 4 vols. (London, 1798).
Boswell, James, *The Journal of a Tour to the Hebrides with Samuel Johnson, LL. D.*, ed. Frederick A. Pottle and Charles H. Bennett (New York, 1936).
——, *Boswell's London Journal, 1762–1763*, ed. Frederick Pottle (New York, 1950).
——, *Boswell for the Defense, 1769–1774*, ed. William K. Wimsatt, Jr. and Frederick A. Pottle (New York, 1959).
——, *Boswell: The Ominous Years, 1774–1776*, ed. Charles Ryskamp and Frederick A. Pottle (New York, 1963).
——, *Boswell in Extremes, 1776–1778*, ed. Charles M. Weis and Frederick A. Pottle (New York, 1970).

——, *Boswell: The Applause of the Jury, 1782–1785*, ed. Irma S. Lustig and Frederick A. Pottle (New York, 1981).

——, *James Boswell's "Book of Company" at Auchinleck, 1782–1795*, ed. Viscountess Eccles and Gordon Turnbull (Roxburghe Club, 1995).

——, *The Life of Samuel Johnson*, ed. R. W. Chapman (Oxford, 1980).

The Bottle of Claret (Warington?, c. 1770–1800).

Bowles, John, *A View of the Moral State of Society* (London, 1804).

The British Merchant, or, Commerce Preserv'd, ed. Charles King, 3 vols. (London, 1721, facs. ed. New York, 1968).

Brown, John, *An Estimate of the Manners and Principles of the Times*, 2 vols. (London, 1757).

Brome, Alexander, *Poems*, ed. Roman R. Dubinski, 2 vols. (Toronto, 1982).

Buckingham and Chandos, Duke of, *Memoirs of the Court and Cabinets of George III. From original family documents*, 4 vols. (London, 1853).

Burnet, Gilbert, *History of his own Time from the Restoration of Charles II to the Treaty of Peace at Utrecht, in the Reign of Queen Anne*, 2 vols. (London, 1840).

Burns, Robert, *The Poems and Songs of Robert Burns*, ed. James Kinsley, 3 vols. (Oxford, 1968).

Burt, Edward, *Burt's Letters from the North of Scotland*, 2 vols. (Edinburgh, 1974, facs. ed. of 1754 ed. titled *Letters from a Gentleman in the North of Scotland to his Friend in London*).

Burton, John Hill, *The Lives of Simon Lord Lovat and Duncan Forbes of Culloden, from original sources* (London, 1847).

Byng, John, *The Torrington Diaries: Containing the tour through England and Wales of the Hon. John Byng (later Viscount Torrington) between the years 1781 and 1794*, ed. C. Bruyn Andrews, 4 vols. (New York, 1935).

Byron, George Gordon, Lord, *Letter to **** ****** [John Murray] on the Rev. W. L. Bowle's Strictures on the Life and Writing of Pope* (London: John Murray, 1821).

——, *Byron's Letters and Journals*, ed. Leslie A. Marchand, 12 vols. (Cambridge, MA, 1979).

——, *Don Juan* (Harmondsworth, 2004).

Jordan, Thomas, *Fancy's Festival, a Masque* (London, 1657).

Carlyle, Alexander, *Autobiography of the Rev. Dr. Alexander Carlyle, Minister of Inveresk* (Edinburgh, 1910).

——, *Anecdotes and Characters of the Times*, ed. James Kinsley (London, 1973).

The Cellar-Book: or, the Butler's Assistant, in keeping a Regular Account of his Liquors (London, 1766).

Centlivre, Susannah, *The Works of the Celebrated Mrs. Centlivre*, ed. J. Pearson, 3 vols. (London, 1872).

Chambers, Robert, *Traditions of Edinburgh* (1824; reprint, Edinburgh, 1980).

——, *Domestic Annals of Scotland: From the Reformation to the Revolution*, 2 vols. (Edinburgh, 1858).

Chandler, Richard and Ceasar Ward, eds., *The History and Proceedings of the House of Commons of England*, 5 vols. (London, 1742).

Charles II, *A Proclamation against Vicious, Debauch'd, and Prophane Persons, 30th May* (London, 1660).

Charles II, *A Proclamation for Publishing a former Proclamation of the 30th of May last (entituled, A Proclamation against Vicious, Debauch'd and Prophane Persons) in all Churches and Chappels throughout England and Wales, 13th of August* (London, 1660).

Charleton, Walter, *The Vintner's Mystery Display'd: or the Whole Art of the Wine Trade laid open. In which are the necessary directions for rightly managing all sorts of wines, so as to render them bright and good; or to restore them when they prove defective in any way* (London, 1705?).

Cobbett, William, ed., *Cobbett's Parliamentary History of England: From the Norman Conquest, in 1066, to the year, 1803*, vols. 1–12 (London, 1806–1812). This series continues as T. C. Hansard, ed., *The Parliamentary History of England from the Earliest Period to the Year 1803*, vols. 13–36 (London, 1812–1820).

Cockburn, Henry, *Memorials of His Time* (1856), ed. Karl Miller (Chicago, 1974).

Cockton, Henry, *The Love Match* (London, 1845),

Colquhoun, Patrick, *A Treatise on Indigence; exhibiting a general view of the national resources for productive labour; with propositions for ameliorating the condition of the poor* (London, 1806).

The Consequences of a Law for reducing the dutys upon French wines, Brandy, Silks and Linen, to those of other nations. With remarks on the Mercator (London, 1713).

Cowley, Abraham, *Poems*, ed. A. R. Waller (Cambridge, 1905).

Croft, John, *A Treatise on the Wines of Portugal; and what can be gathered on the subject of the wines, etc. since the establishment of the factory at Oporto, anno 1727: also, a dissertation on the nature and use of wines in general, imported into Great Britain, as pertaining to luxury and diet* (York, 1787).

Vinetum Angliae: or a new and easy way to make wine of English grapes and other fruit, equal to that of France, Spain, &c. with their physical virtues. Also to make artificial wines, and to order and recover them when damaged. To make all sorts of cyder, mead, metheglin, rum, rack, and many other useful liquors. To gather, order and keep fruit in all seasons. The true art of distilling brandy, strong-waters and cordial-waters. To make all sorts of pickles, and sundry sorts of vinegars. The whole art and mystery of a confectioner. The compleat caterer, or how to know whether flesh, fish or fowl be old or young, new or stale. Rules for frugal, cheap and well living. To destroy all sorts of vermin; with divers other notable things, never before made publick. By D.S. (London, 1690?).

Davenant, Charles, *set forth in a conversation between Mr. Whiglove and Mr. Double, two under-spur-leathers to the late ministry* (London, 1691).

——, *A Report to the Honourable Commissioners for Putting in Execution the Act, Intitled, An Act for the Taking, Examining, and Stating the Publick Accounts of the Kingdom*, 2 vols. (London, 1712).

——, *An Account of the Trade between Great Britain, France, Spain and Portugal, etc.* 2 vols. (London, 1715).

[Defoe, Daniel], *The Trade of Britain Stated: Being the substance of two papers published in London on the occasion of the Importation of Wine and Brandy from North Britain* (London, 1708).

[——], *Mercator, or Commerce Retrieved*, May 26, 1713–July 20, 1714.

[——], *A Brief Case of the Distillers, and of the distilling trade in England, shewing how far it is the interest of England to encourage the said Trade, as it is so considerable an advantage to the landed interest, to the trade and navigation, to the publick revenue, and to the employment of the poor. Humbly recommended to the Lords and Commons of Great Britain, in the present Parliament assembled* (London, 1726).

[——], *Defoe's Review*, ed. Arthur Wellesley Secord, 9 vols. in 22 facsimile books (New York, 1938).

Dickens, Charles, *Sketches of Boz: Illustrative of Every-Day Life and Every-Day People* (London, 1836).

Downing, George, *A Schedule of the Trade as it is at present carry'd on between England and France, in Commodities of the Native Product and Manufacture of each Country, calculated as exactly as possible, in Obediance to the Command of the Right Honourable the Lords Commissioners for the Treaty of Commerce with France, humbly tendered to your Lordships* (London, 1675).

The Economist.

The Edinburgh Review.

Eighteen Reasons why the Duty on Wine Should now be Very Largely Reduced, and Assumed Objections Answered why it should not (London, 1849).

Egan, Pierce, *Life in London, The Day and Night Scenes of Jerry Hawthorn, Esq., and his Elegant Friend Corinthian Tom, Accompanied by Bob Logic, the Oxonian, in there Rambles and Sprees through the Metropolis* (London, 1821–1828).

An Enquiry into the Causes of the Prohibition of Commerce with France, during the present War (London, 1708).

Evelyn, John, *The Diary of John Evelyn*, ed. E. S. de Beer, 6 vols. (Oxford, 1955).

The Examiner (London, 1710–1714).

Facts about Port and Madeira, with Notices of the Wines Vintaged around Lisbon and the Wines of Tenerife (London, 1880).

Farquhar, George, *The Works of George Farquhar*, ed. Shirley S. Kenney, 2 vols. (Oxford, 1988).

Farrington, Joseph, *Memoirs of the Life of Sir Joshua Reynolds* (London, 1819).

Flecknoe, Richard, "In Small Beer," *Miscellania. Or, Poems of all sorts, with Divers other Pieces* (London, 1653).

Fletcher, Andrew, *Political Works*, ed. John Robertson (Cambridge, 1997).

Forrester, Joseph James, *A Word of Truth on Port-wine: Showing how, and why, it is adulterated, and affording some means of detecting its adulteration* (London, 1844).

——, *A Short Treatise on the Unequal and Disproportionate Imposts Levied upon Port-Wine, Shipped from Oporto to Great Britain* (London, 1850).

Fortrey, Samuel, *England's Interest and Improvement; Consider'd in the Increase of Trade in this Kingdom. In which is an account of our commerce with several nations in Europe* (London, 1663).

Foulis, Sir John, *The Account Book of Sir John Foulis of Ravelston, 1671–1707* (Edinburgh, 1884).

Fowler, John, *Recollections of Country Life: Social, Political Sporting and Agricultural* (London, 1894).

Fraser's Magazine for Town and Country, 18 (November 1838).

Frith, William Powell, *My Autobiography and Reminiscences*, 3 vols. (London, 1887).

Gay, John, *John Gay: Poetry and Prose*, ed. Vinton A. Dearing, 2 vols. (Oxford, 1974).

Dr Buchan, by a gentleman of the faculty To which is added, an account of some remarkable cures performed by the Tokay de Espagna (London, 1786).

Gentleman's Magazine (December 1731).

Gillray, James, "'The feast of reason and the flow of soul,'__i.e.__The Wits of the Age setting the Table in a roar" (4 February 1797), *CPBM* no. 8984.

Gladstone, William Ewart, *The Financial Statements of 1853, 1860–1863* (London, 1863).

Grego, Joseph, *Rowlandson the Caricaturist, A selection from his works, with anecdotal descriptions of his famous caricatuires and a sketck of his life, times and contemporaries*, 2 vols. (London, 1880).

Gronow, Rees Howell, *The Reminiscenses and Recollections of Captain Gronow, Being Anecdotes of the Camp, Court, Clubs and Society, 1810–1860* (London, 1892 ed., 2 vols., originally published 1862–1865).

Grosley, Pierre-Jean, *A Tour to London; or, New Observations on England and its Inhabitants*, trans. Thomas Nugent, 2 vols. (London, 1774).

Grove, John, *Wine, Beere, and Ale, together by the Eares* (London, 1629).

Hansard, Thomas C., ed., *The Parliamentary History of England, from the Earliest Period to the year 1803*, vols. 13–36 (London, 1812–1820), continuation of William Cobbett, ed., *Cobbett's Parliamentary History* (vols. 1–12).

Haywood, Eliza, "Effeminacy in the Army Censured," in *The Female Spectator*, (1744–1746), ed. Gabrielle Firmager (London, 1993), 30.

Henderson, Alexander, *The History of Ancient and Modern Wines* (London, 1824).

Henderson, William, Otto, "The Anglo-French Commercial Treaty of 1786," *Economic History Review*, 2nd ser., 10 (August 1957): 104–112.

Hervey, John, *The Diary of John Hervey, first Earl of Bristol. With extracts from his book of expenses, 1688–1742*, ed. Sydenham. H. A. Hervey, (Wells, 1894).

——, *Lord Hervey and His Friends, 1726–1738: Based on Letters from Holland House, Melbury and Ickworth*, ed. Lord Ilchester (London, 1950).

Hickey, William, *Memoirs of William Hickey*, ed. Alfred Spencer, 4 vols. (New York, 1913–1925).

——, *Memoirs of William Hickey*, ed. Peter Quennell (London, 1960).

Home, John, *The Works of John Home, Esq., now first collected. To which is prefixed, an account of his life and writings, by Henry Mackenzie, Esq.*, 3 vols. (Edinburgh, 1822).

Hume, David, *The Letters of David Hume*, ed. John, Young, Thomson. Greig, 2 vols. (Oxford, 1932).

——, *Essays: Moral, Political and Literary*, ed. Eugene F. Miller (Indianapolis, 1987).

In Vino Veritas; or, a conference betwixt Chip the Cooper, and Dash the Drawer, (Being both Boozy), Discovering some secrets of the wine-brewing trade. Useful for all sorts of people to save their money and preserve their health (London, 1698).

The Imports of Great Britain from France: Humbly Address'd to the Laudable Associations of Anti-Gallicans, and the Generous Promoters of the British Arts and Manufactories (n.p.,1757).

James, W. Bosville, *Wine Duties Considered Financially and Socially, being a reply to Sir James Emerson Tennent, on "Wine: Its Taxation and Uses"* (London, 1855).

Janssen, Theodore, *General Maxims of Trade, particularly applied to the Commerce between Great Britain and France* (London, 1713).

Johnson, Samuel, *A Journey to the Western Islands of Scotland*, ed. J. D. Fleeman (Oxford, 1985).

Kehrig, Henri, *Le Privilège des vins à Bordeaux, jusqu'en 1789* (Paris, 1886, facs. ed. Bayonne, 1984).

La Rochefoucauld, François de, *Mélange sur l'Angleterre* (Paris, 1784).

Lecky, William E. H., *A History of England in the Eighteenth Century* (London, 1883, ed.).

A Letter from a Member of the House of Commons to his Friend in the Country, Relating to the Bill of Commerce. With a true copy of the Bill, and an Exact List of all those who voted for and against Engrossing it (London, 1713).

A Letter to the Honourable A——r M—re, Com——ner of Trade and Plantations (London, 1714).

A letter to the Right Honourable Benjamin D'Israeli, MP, Chancellor of the Exchequer, from a Wine Merchant (London, 1852).

Locke, John, *Locke's Travels in France, as related in his journals, correspondence and other papers*, ed. John Lough (Cambridge, 1953)

——, *The Works of John Locke*, 10 vols. (London, 1823).

London Gazette (London), 1702–1711.

Luttrell, Narcissus, *Brief Historical Relation of the State of Affairs, from Sept. 1678 to April 1714*, 6 vols. (Oxford, 1857).

McCulloch, John Ramsay, ed., *Early English Tracts on Commerce* (London, 1856; reprint, Cambridge, 1952).

——, *A Dictionary, Practical, Theoretical and Historical, of Commerce and Commercial Navigation*, 3 vols. (London, 1856 ed.).

Misson, Henri, *M. Misson's Memoirs and Observations on his Travels over England. With some account of Scotland and Ireland*, trans. John Ozell (London, 1719).

Monk, James Henry, *The Life of Richard Bentley, D. D.*, 2 vols. (Cambridge, 1833).

Nimrod (Charles James Apperley), *Memoirs of the Life of the late John Mytton, by Nimrod. With numerous illustrations by Alken. Reprinted from the New Sporting Magazine* (London, 1835).

——, *My Life and Times*, ed. E. D. Cuming (Edinburgh, 1927).

Notes on the Wine Duty Question and Mr. Shaw's Pamphlet [Wine Trade and its History] (London, 1851).

Objections against the Importation of French Wine, Answer'd (London?, 1711?).

Oldham, John, *The Claret Drinker's Song; or, The Good Fellows Design. By a person of Quality* (London, 1680).

Oliveira, Benjamin, ed., *Report of the Meeting of the Wine Duties Reduction Committee and the Anglo-French Free-Trade Association at the Crystal Palace, 9th July 1856; Debate in the House of Commons on Mr. Oliveira's Motion for the Wine Duties Reduction on the 15th July 1856; A list of the general committee; and other particulars connected with the reduction of the import duty on wines* (London, 1856).

——, ed., *Proceedings of the Wine Duties' Reduction Committee, since its formation in 1852, comprising reports, debates in the House of Commons, a list of the general committee, and other particulars connected with the reduction of the import duty upon wines, up to the dissolution of the committee when the measure was carried, through the Anglo-French Treaty, in 1860* (London, 1861).

O raree show; O brave show! Who see my fine pretty show: or the new raree show ballad, to a New Tune, much in Request (London, 1713).

Original Documents Respecting the Injurious Effects and the Impolicy of a Further Continuance of the Portuguese Royal Wine Company of Oporto (London, 1813).

Osborn, Sarah Byng, *The Letters of Sarah Byng Osborn, 1721–1773*, ed. John McClelland (Palo Alto, 1930).

Pepys, Samuel, *The Diary of Samuel Pepys: A New and Complete Transcription*, ed. Robert Latham and William Matthews, 11 vols. (Berkeley, 1970–1983).

[A Physician in the Country], *Vinum Britannicum: or an essay of the properties and effects of malt liquors; wherein it is considered, in what cases, and to what constitutions they are either beneficial or injurious, with a plain mechanical account of how they are serviceable or disserviceable to the human bodies* (London, 1727). Possibly written by James Sedgwick or Thomas Short.

Place, Francis, *The Autobiography of Francis Place, 1771–1854*, ed. Mary Thale (Cambridge, 1972).

Pope, Alexander, *The Correspondence of Alexander Pope*, ed. George Sherburn, 5 vols. (Oxford, 1956).

——, *Poetry and Prose of Alexander Pope*, ed. Aubrey Williams (Boston, 1969).

[A Portuguese], *The Wine Question Considered; or, Observations on the Pamphlets of Mr. James Warre and Mr. Fleetwood Williams, respecting the General Company for the Agriculture of the Vineyards on the Upper Douro, Known in England under the name of the Royal Oporto Wine Company* (London, 1824).

Prior, Matthew, *The Literary Works of Matthew Prior*, ed. H. Bunker Wright and Monroe K. Spears, 2 vols. (Oxford, 1959).

Pückler-Muskau, Herman Ludwig Heinrich von, *A Regency Visitor: The English tour of Prince Pückler-Muskau Described in his Letters, 1826–1828*, trans. Sarah Austin, ed. E. M. Butler (London, 1957).

Queries Relating to the Importation of French Wine (London?, 1713?).

Ramsay, Allan, *The Works of Allan Ramsay*, ed. Burns Martin and John W. Oliver, 2 vols. (Edinburgh, 1944–1945).

Ramsay, Edward Bannerman, *Reminiscences of Scottish Life and Character* (Edinburgh, 1928 ed., first published 1858).

Ramsay, John, of Auchtertyre, *Scotland and Scotsmen in the Eighteenth Century*, 2 vols. (London, 1888).

Reasons Humbly Offer'd against Opening the Trade a Trade with France for Wines (London, 1713?)

Reasons Humbly Offer'd by the Merchants Trading to Italy, Spain and Portugal, against Lowering the Duties on French Wines Equal to those of Italy, Spain and Portugal (London, 1713).

Reasons Humbly Offer'd by the Merchants Trading to Spain and Portugal against the Bill for suspending the Duty of £25 per Tun on French Wines (London, 1713).

Redding, Cyrus, *A History and Description of Modern Wines* (London, 1833, Second edition 1836, Third edition 1851).

——, *Every Man his own Butler* (London, 1839).

——, ed., *Wine Duties Reduction. An abstract of the evidence given before a select committee of the House of Commons upon the import duties on wines, in May and June, 1852, with a draft of the chairman's report* (London, 1852).

Remarques on the Humours and Conversations of the Town. Written in a letter for Sr. T. L. (London, 1673).

The Roaring Bacchanal, a Burlesque on How little do the Landsmen Know (London?, c. 1750–1800).

Rose, George, *A Brief Examination into the Increase of the Revenue, Commerce and Navigation of Great Britain, since the Conclusion of the Peace in 1783* (London, 1794 edition).

Rowntree, Joseph and Arthur Sherwell, *The Temperance Problem and Social Reform* (London: Hodder and Stoughton, 1899, Third edition).

The Royal Entertainment (London, 1660), possibly written by Thomas Jordan.

A Royall Health to the Rising Sun (London, 1649).

Saussure, César de, *A Foreign View of England in the reigns of George I and George II*, ed. Madame Van Muyden (London, 1902).

Shaftesbury, 3rd Earl of, Anthony Ashley Cooper, *Characteristics of Men, Manners, Opinions, Times*, 2 vols., ed. John Robertson (Gloucester, MA, 1963).

Shannon, Robert, M.D., *Practical Treatise on Brewing, Distilling and Rectification, with the genuine process of making brandy, rum, and hollands gin ... With an appendix on the culture and preparation of foreign wine* (London, 1805).

Shaw, Thomas George, *The Wine Trade and its History* (London, 1851).

——, *Wine in Relation to Temperance, Trade and the Revenue* (London, 1854).

Shaw, Peter, *The Juice of the Grape: Or Wine Preferable to Water. A treatise wherein wine is shewn to be the grand preserver of health, and restorer in most diseases. With many instances of cures performed by this noble remedy; and the method of using it, as well for prevention as cure, with a word of advice to the vintners* (London, 1724).

Smith, Adam, *The Wealth of Nations*, ed. Andrew Skinner, 2 vols. (Harmondsworth, 1999— Penguin edition of standard Oxford text).

Somers, John, ed., *A Collection of Scarce and Valuable Tracts*, Second edition, edited by Sir Walter Scott, 13 vols. (London, 1812).

Steele, Richard, *The Englishman*, ed. Rae Blanchard (Oxford, 1955).

Stephens, Frederick George and Mary Dorothy George, *Catalogue of Prints and Drawings in the British Museum: Political and Personal Satires*, 11 vols. (London, 1870–1954).

Steuart, John, *The Letter Book of Baillie John Steuart of Inverness, 1715–1752*, ed. William Mackay (Edinburgh, 1915).

Surtees, Robert Smith, *Mr. Sponge's Sporting Tour* (London, 1853).

Tennent, James Emerson, *Wine, its Use and Taxation. An inquiry into the operation of the wine duties on consumption and revenue* (London, 1855).

Thackeray, William Makepeace, *The Newcomes: Memoirs of a Most Respectable Family*, vol. VII, *The Works of William Makepeace Thackeray*, 30 vols. (Cambridge, MA, 1907).

The Times (London)

A Toast for A--e and Robbin in the French Wine (London, 1711).

Tovey, Charles, *Wine and Wine Countries: A Record and Manual for Wine Merchants and Wine Consumers* (London, 1862).

The Trade with France, Italy, Spain and Portugal, Considered: With Some Observations on the Treaty of Commerce between Great Britain and France (London, 1713).

Trotter, Thomas, MD, *An Essay, Medical, Philosophical and Chemical, on Drunkenness, and its Effects on the Human Body* (London, 1804).

[Tryon, Thomas?], *The Way to Get Wealth: or, A new and easie way to make twenty three sorts of wine, equal to that of France. To which is added, a help to discourse, giving an account of trade of all countries by the author of the way to save wealth; and of one thousand notable things* (London, 1702).

A Vindication of the Conduct of the Ministry, in the Scheme of the Excise on Wine and Tobacco, proposed last sessions of Parliament: With a General Examination of the Reasons which determined the said Ministry to it: The Consequences and Events it would have had (London, 1734).

A Vindication of the Late House of Commons, in rejecting the bill for Confirming the Eighth and Ninth Articles of the Treaty of Navigation and Commerce between England and France (London, 1714).

Vizatelly, Henry, *Facts about Port and Madeira, with Notices of wines vintaged around Lisbon and the wines of Tenerife* (London, 1880).

Walpole, Horace, *Horace Walpole's Correspondence*, ed. Wilmarth Sheldon Lewis, 48 vols. (New Haven, 1937–1983).

[Walpole, Robert?], *A Letter from a Member of Parliament to his Friend in the Country, concerning the Duties on Wine and Tobacco* (London, 1733).

Ward, Edward, *The London Spy* (London, 1698–1700).

——, *Wine and Wisdom: or, the Tipling Philosophers. A Lyrick Poem* (London, 1710).

Warre, James, *The Past, Present and Probably the Future State of the Wine Trade; proving that an increase of duty caused a decrease of revenue; and a decrease of duty, an increase of revenue. Founded on parliamentary and other documents. Most respectfully submitted to the right honourable the President and Members of the Board of Trade* (London, 1823 and 1824). The 1824 edition included "Supplementary Observations."

Wendeborn, Gebhardt, Friedrich, August., *A View of England towards the Close of the Eighteenth Century*, 2 vols. (London, 1791).

Whitmore, William Wolryche, *The Wine Duties* (London, 1853).

Whittaker, Thomas, *A Word of Truth on Port Wine* (London, 1844).

Wilberforce, William, *The Correspondence of William Wilberforce*, ed. Robert I. Wilberforce and Samuel Wilberforce, 2 vols. (London, 1840).

Williams, Fleetwood, *Observations on the State of the Wine Trade. Occasioned by the Perusal of a Pamphlet on the same subject, by Mr. Warre. Most respectfully submitted to his Majesty's Ministers* (London, 1824).

——, *Further Observations on the Wine Trade, and on the Reduction of Duties, etc., in a letter addressed to the Right Honourable, the Chancellor of the Exchequer* (London, 1825).

Wilson, James, "The First Half of the Nineteenth Century: Progress of the Nation and Race," *The Economist*, February 1, 1851: 109–111.

The Wine Cooper's Delight, to the tune of The Delights of the Bottle (London, 1681). Possibly written by James Dean.

Worgan, James, *Port and Sherry, or Britons be wise and merry, A favorite new song, Written and composed by J. Worgan* (London, 1797).

Woodforde, James, *The Diary of a Country Parson, 1758–1802*, ed. John Beresford, 5 vols. (Oxford, 1981).

Wraxall, Sir Nathaniel, *The Historical and Posthumous Memoirs of Sir Nathaniel William Wraxall*, ed. Henry B. Wheatley, 5 vols. (London, 1884).

Wright, John, *An Essay on Wines, especially on Port Wine; intended to instruct every person to distinguish between that which is pure, and to guard against the frauds of adulteration* (London, 1795).

Select secondary works

Adler, Marianna, "From Symbolic Exchange to Commodity Consumption: Anthropological Notes on Drinking as a Symbolic Practice," in Susanna Barrowes and Robin Broom, eds., *Drinking: Behavior and Belief in Modern History* (Berkeley, 1991), 376–398.

Anglo, Sydney, *Spectacle, Pageantry and Early Tudor Policy* (Oxford, 1969).

Antal, Frederick, *Hogarth and His Place in European Art* (London, 1961).

Appleby, Joyce O., *Economic Thought and Ideology in Seventeenth Century England* (Princeton, 1978).

Archer, Jayne Elisabeth, Elizabeth Goldring and Sarah Knights, eds., *The Progresses, Pageants and Entertainments of Queen Elizabeth I* (Oxford, 2007).

Ashton, Robert, *The Second Civil War and its Origins* (New Haven, 1994).

Ashworth, William J., *Customs and Excise: Trade, Production and Consumption in England, 1640–1845* (Oxford, 2003).

Austin, Gregory, ed., *Alcohol in Western Society from Antiquity to 1800* (Santa Barbara, 1985).

Baker, C. H. Collins and Muriel Baker, *The Life and Circumstances of James Brydges, First Duke of Chandos: Patron of the Liberal Arts* (Oxford, 1949).

Barker-Benfield, Graham, John., *The Culture of Sensibility: Sex and Society in Eighteenth-Century Britain* (Chicago, 1992).

Barr, Andrew, *Drink: A Social History* (London, 1998).

Barry, Jonathan, and Christopher Brooks, eds., *The Middling Sort of People: Culture, Society and Politics in England, 1550–1800* (New York, 1994).

Beckett, John, Vincent, *The Aristocracy in England, 1660–1914* (Oxford, 1986).

Bennett, Norman, "The Golden Age of the Port Wine System, 1781–1807," *International History Review*, 12 (1990): 221–248.

——, "The Vignerons of the Douro and the Peninsular War," *Journal of European Economic History*, 21:1 (1992): 7–29.

——, "Port Wine Merchants: Sandeman in Porto, 1813–1831," *Journal of European Economic History*, 24 (1995): 239–269.

Berg, Maxine, *Luxury and Pleasure in Eighteenth-Century Britain* (Oxford, 2005).

Berry, Christopher, *The Idea of Luxury: A Conceptual and Historical Investigation* (Cambridge, 1994).

Black, Jeremy, "The Marquis of Carmarthen and Relations with France, 1784–1787," *Francia* 12 (1984): 283–303.

——, *British Foreign Policy in an Age of Revolutions, 1783–1793* (Cambridge, 1994).

Blaug, Mark, ed., *Pre-Classical Economists*, 3 vols. (Aldershot, 1991).

Boddy, Kasia, *Boxing: A Cultural History* (London, 2008).

Bonnell, Victoria, and Lynn Hunt, eds., *Beyond the Cultural Turn: New Directions in the Study of Society and Culture* (Berkeley, 1999).

Borsay, Peter, *The English Urban Renaissance: Culture and Society in the Provincial Town, 1660–1760* (Oxford, 1989).

Bourdieu, Pierre, *Distinction: A Social Critique of the Judgment of Taste*, trans. Richard Nice (Cambridge, MA, 1984).

Bradford, Sarah, *The Englishman's Wine: The Story of Port* (London, 1969).

Bradshaw, Brendan and Peter Roberts, eds., *British Consciousness and Identity: The Making of Britain, 1533–1707* (Cambridge, 1998).

Brailsford, Dennis, *Bareknuckles: A Social History of Prizefighting* (Cambridge, 1989).

Braure, Maurice, "Quelques Aspects des Relations Commerciales entre la France et l'Angleterre au XVIIIème Siècle," *Annales du Midi* (1953): 67–89.

Brennan, Thomas, *Burgundy to Champagne: The Wine Trade in Early Modern France* (Baltimore, 1997).

Brewer, John, "'The Most Polite Age and the Most Vicious': Attitudes towards Culture as Commodity, 1660–1800," in Anne Bermingham and John Brewer, eds., *The Consumption of Culture* (London, 1995), 341–361.

——, *The Pleasures of the Imagination: English Culture in the Eighteenth Century* (London, 1997).

Briggs, Asa, *The Age of Improvement, 1783–1867* (London, 1959).

——, *A Social History of England* (Harmondsworth, 1983).

——, *Wine for Sale: Victoria Wine and the Liquor Trade, 1860–1984* (London, 1985).

Brindman, David, *Hogarth and his Times: Serious Comedy* (Berkeley, 1997).

Brockliss, Lawrence and David Eastwood, "Introduction," in Lawrence Brockliss and David Eastwood, eds., *A Union of Multiple Identities: The British Isles, c. 1750–c.1850* (Manchester, 1997), 1–8.

Bryson, Anna, *From Courtesy to Civility: Changing Codes of Conduct in Early Modern England* (Oxford, 1998).

Burnett, John, *Liquid Pleasures: A Social History of Drinks in Modern Britain* (London, 1999).

Buruma, Ian, *Anglomania: A European Love Affair* (London, 1998).

Butel, Paul, "Grands Propriétaires et Production des Vins du Médoc au XVIIIe Siècle," *Revue Historique de Bordeaux* (1963): 129–141.

——, "Le traffic européen de Bordeaux, de la guerre d'Amérique à la Révolution," *Annales du Midi* 78 (1966): 37–82.

——, *Les Dynasties Bordelaises: de Colbert à Chaban* (Paris, 1991).

Butler, Robin and Gillian Walkling, *The Book of Wine Antiques* (Woodbridge, 1986).

Cahen, Léon, "Une Nouvelle Interprétation du Traité Franco-Anglais de 1786–1787," *Revue Historique* (July–December, 1939): 226–285.

Campbell, Colin, *The Romantic Ethic and the Spirit of Modern Consumerism* (Oxford, 1987).

——, "Understanding Traditional and Modern Patterns of Consumption in Eighteenth Century England: A Character-Action Approach," in John Brewer and Roy Porter, eds., *Consumption and the World of Goods* (London, 1993), 40–57.

Cannadine, David, "The Context, Performance and Meaning of Ritual: The British Monarchy and the 'Invention of Tradition', c. 1820–1977," in Eric Hobsbawm and Terence Ranger, *The Invention of Tradition* (Cambridge, 1983), 101–164.

——, *The Decline and Fall of the British Aristocracy* (New Haven, 1990).

——, *Aspects of Aristocracy* (Harmondsworth, 1995).

——, *The Rise and Fall of Class in Britain* (New York, 1999). p. 28.

Cannon, John, *Aristocratic Century: The Peerage in Eighteenth-Century England* (Cambridge, 1984).

Carr, Rosalind, "The Gentleman and the Soldier: Patriotic Masculinities in Eighteenth-Century Scotland," *Journal of Scottish Historical Studies*, 28:2 (2008): 102–121.

Carter, Philip, "John Boswell's Manliness," in Tim Hitchcock and Michèle Cohen, eds., *English Masculinities, 1660–1800* (London, 1999), 111–130.

——, *Men and the Emergence of Polite Society, Britain 1660–1800* (Harlow, 2001).

——, "Polite 'Persons': Character, Biography, and the Gentleman," *Transactions of the Royal Historical Society*, 6th ser., 12 (2002), 333–354.

Chrichton-Browne, James, "Claret in Scotland," *National Review* 80 (1922), 397–407.

Clark, Anna, *Women's Silence, Men's Violence: Sexual Assault in England, 1770–1845* (London, 1987).

——, "Manhood, Womanhood, and the Politics of Class in Britain, 1790–1845," in Laura L. Frader and Sonya O. Rose, eds., *Gender and Class in Modern Europe* (Ithaca, 1996), 263–279.

Clark, Jonathan, C. D., *English Society, 1688–1832: Religion, Ideology and Politics during the Ancien Régime* (Cambridge, 1985).

Clark, Peter, *The English Alehouse: A Social History, 1200–1830* (London, 1983).

——, "The Mother Gin Controversy in the Early Eighteenth Century," *Transactions of the Royal Historical Society*, 5th ser., 38 (1988): 63–84.

——, *British Clubs and Societies, 1580–1800: The Origins of an Associational World* (Oxford, 2000).

Coates, Clive, *Grands Vins: The Finest Châteaux of Bordeaux and their Wines* (Berkeley, 1995).

Coffey, T. G., "Beer Street and Gin Lane: Some Views of Eighteenth-Century Drinking," *Quarterly Journal of Studies in Alcohol*, 27 (1966): 669–692.

Cohen, Michèle, *Fashioning Masculinity: National Identity and Language in the Eighteenth Century* (London, 1996).

——, "Manliness, Effeminacy and the French: Gender Construction in Eighteenth Century England," in Tim Hitchcock and Michèle Cohen, eds., *English Masculinities, 1660–1800* (London, 1999), 44–61.

——, "'Manners' Make the Man: Politeness, Chivalry, and the Construction of Masculinity, 1750–1830", *Journal of British Studies*, 44 (April 2005): 312–329.

Coleman, Donald, Cuthbert., "Politics and Economics in the Age of Anne: The Case of the Anglo-French Treaty of 1713," in Frederick Jack Fisher, Donald Cuthbert Coleman, Arthur Henry John, eds., *Trade, Government and Economy in Pre-Industrial England: Essays presented to F. J. Fisher* (London, 1976), 187–211.

Colley, Linda, *Britons: Forging the Nation, 1707–1837* (New Haven, 1992).

Collins, J. Churton, *Voltaire, Montesquieu and Rousseau in England* (London, 1908).

Connell, Raewyn W., *Masculinities* (Cambridge, 1995, Second edition).

Cookson, John E., *The British Armed Nation, 1793–1815* (Oxford, 1997).

Cooper, Anthony Ashley, *Characteristics of Men, Manners, Opinions, Times*, 2 vols., ed. John Robertson (Gloucester, MA, 1963).

Corfield, Penelope, "Class by Name and Number in Eighteenth-Century Britain," *History*, 72:234 (February, 1987), 38–61.

Crouzet, Francois, "Les Importations d'Eaux de Vie et de Vins Francais en Grande Bretagne pendant le Blocus Continental," *Annales du Midi* 65 (1953): 91–106.

——, "Le Commerce de Bordeaux" and "La Conjoncture Bordelaise," in F-G. Pariset, ed., *Bordeaux au XVIIIème Siècle*, vol. V of Charles Higounet, ed., *Histoire de Bordeaux* (Bordeaux, 1968), 221–286, 287–324.

——, *De la Superiorité de 1'Angleterre sur la France: 1'Economique et Imgaginaire, XVIIe–XXe Siècle* (Paris, 1985).

Cullen, Louis M., *Smuggling and the Ayrshire Economic Boom of the 1760s and 1770s*, Ayrshire Monograph no. 14 (Ayrshire, 1994).

Daly, Gavin, "English Smugglers, the Channel, and the Napoleonic Wars, 1800–1814", *Journal of British Studies*, 46 (January 2007): 30–46.

Davidoff, Leonore and Catherine Hall, *Family Fortunes: Men and Women of the English Middle Class, 1780–1850* (London, 1987).

Davis, Derek Cecil, *English Bottles and Decanters, 1650–1900* (New York, 1972).

Davis, Ralph, "The Rise of Protection in England, 1689–1786," *Economic History Review*, 2d ser., 19 (1966): pp. 306–317.

——, "The English Wine Trade in the Eighteenth and Nineteenth Centuries," *Annales Cisalpines d'Histoire Sociale* 3 (1972): 87–106.

De Krey, Gary S., *A Fractured Society: The Politics of London in the First Age of Party, 1688–1715* (Oxford, 1985).

——, *Restoration and Revolution in Britain: A Political History of the Era of Charles II and the Glorious Revolution* (Basingstoke, 2007).

Delaforce, John, *Joseph James Forrester, Baron of Portugal, 1809–61* (London, 1992).

De Macedo, Jorge *A Situacao Economica no Tempo de Pombal* (Lisbon, 1951).

Devine, Thomas M., *The Scottish Nation* (Harmondsworth, 1999).

Dickie, George, *The Century of Taste: The Philosophical Odyssey of Taste in the Eighteenth Century* (Oxford, 1996).

Dietz, Vivien E., "The Politics of Whisky: Scottish Distillers, the Excise, and the Pittite State," *Journal of British Studies* 36 (January 1997): 35–69.

Dion, Roger, *Histoire de la Vigne et du Vin en France des Origines au XIXème Siècle* (Paris, 1959).

Dillon, Patrick, *The Much Lamented Death of Madam Geneva: The Eighteenth-Century Gin Craze* (London, 2002).

D'Oench, Ellen G., *The Conversation Piece: Arthur Devis and His Contemporaries* (New Haven, 1980).

Donaghay, Marie, "The Exchange of the Products of the Soil and Industrial Goods in the Anglo-French Commercial Treaty of 1786," *Journal of European Economic History* 19:2 (1990): 377–402.

Donald, Diana, *The Age of Caricature: Satirical Prints in the Reign of George III* (New Haven, 1996).

Douglas, Mary, ed., *Constructive Drinking: Perspectives on Drink from Anthropology* (Cambridge, 1987).

Douglas, Mary and Baron Isherwood, *The World of Goods: Towards and Anthropology of Consumption* (Harmondsworth, 1980).

Downie, James Alan, "Gay's Politics", in Peter Lewis and Nigel Wood, ed., *John Gay and the Scriblerians* (London, 1988), 44–61.

Duff, David, *Albert and Victoria* (London, 1972).

Duguid, Paul, "The Making of Methuen: The Commercial Treaty in the English Imagination," *História* 3:4 (2003): 9–36.

Dwyer, John, *Virtuous Discourse: Sensibility in Late-Eighteenth Century Scotland* (Edinburgh, 1987).

——, "Introduction—A 'Peculiar Blessing': Social Converse in Scotland from Hutcheson to Burns," in John Dwyer and Richard B. Sher, eds., *Sociability and Society in Eighteenth-Century Scotland* (Edinburgh, 1993), 96–118.

Eagleton, Terry, *The Ideology of the Aesthetic* (Oxford, 1990).

Earle, Peter, *The Making of the English Middle Class: Business, Society and Family Life in London, 1660–1730* (Berkeley, 1989).

Ehrman, John, *The Younger Pitt*, 2 vols. (London, 1969).

Elias, Norbert, *The Civilizing Process: Sociogenetic and Psychogenetic Investigations* (Oxford, 2000).

Enjalbert, Henri, "Comment Naissent les Grands Crus: Bordeaux, Porto, Cognac," *Annales: Economies, Sociétés, Civilisations* 8 (1953): 315–328, 456–474.

——, "L'Origine des Grands Vins," in Charles Higounet, ed., *La Seigneurie et le Vignoble de Château Latour: Histoire d'un grand cru du Médoc (XIVe-XXe siècle)* (Bordeaux, 1974), 3–18.

Fenton, Alexander, "'Wyne Confortative': Wine in Scotland from the Thirteenth till the Eighteenth Centuries," in Christian J. Kay and Margaret A. Mackay, eds., *Perspectives on the Older Scottish Tongue: A Celebration of DOST* (Edinburgh, 2005), 50–51.

Fine, Ben and Ellen Leopold, "Consumerism and the Industrial Revolution," *Social History*, 15:2 (May, 1990), 151–179.

Finlay, Richard J., "Keeping the Covenant: Scottish National Identity," in Thomas M. Devine and John R. Young, eds., *Eighteenth Century Scotland: New Perspectives* (East Linton, 1999), 121–133.

——, "Caledonia or North Britain? Scottish Identity in the Eighteenth Century," in Dauvit Broun, Richard J. Finlay and Michael Lynch, eds., *Image and Identity: The Making and Remaking of Scotland through the Ages* (Edinburgh, 1998), pp. 143–156.

Finn, Margot, "Men's Things: Masculine Possession and the Consumer Revolution," *Social History*, 25:2 (May 2000): 133–155.

Fisher, Harold E. S., *The Portugal Trade: A Study of Anglo-Portuguese Commerce, 1700–1770* (London, 1971).

Flandrin, Jean-Louis, "L'Invention des Grands Vins Français et la Mutation des Valeurs Oenologiques," *Eighteenth Century Life*, 23:2 (1999): 24–33.

Flügel, John Carl, *The Psychology of Clothes* (London, 1930).

Forster, Robert, "The Noble Wine Producers of the Bordelais in the Eighteenth Century," *Economic History Review*, 2d ser., 14 (1961): 18–33.

Foyster, Elizabeth, *Manhood in Early Modern England: Honour, Sex and Marriage* (London, 1999).

——, "Boys will be Boys? Manhood and Aggression, 1660–1800," in Tim Hitchcock and Michèle Cohen, eds., *English Masculinities: 1660–1800* (London, 1999), 151–166.

Francis, Alan David, *Some Reflections on the Methuen Treaties* (Coimbra, 1965).

——, *The Methuens and Portugal, 1691–1708* (Cambridge, 1966).

——, *The Wine Trade* (London, 1972).

Fry, Michael, *Scotland and the Treaty of Union* (Edinburgh, 2006).

Gabler, James M., *Wine into Words: A History and Bibliography of Wine Books in the English Language* (Baltimore, 1985).

Gatrell, Vic, *City of Laughter, Sex and Satire in Eighteenth Century London* (New York, 2006).

Geertz, Clifford, *The Interpretation of Cultures* (New York, 1973).

——, "Centers, Kings and Charisma: Reflections on the Symbolics of Power," in Joseph, Ben-David, and Terry, Nichols, Clark, eds., *Culture and Its Creators: Essays in Honor of Edward Shils* (Chicago, 1977), 150–171.

George, Dorothy, *London Life in the Eighteenth Century* (London, 1925).

Gigante, Denise, *Taste: A Literary History* (New Haven, 2005).

Glatt, Max, Meier, and Gunn, John, Alexander, Wilson. "The English Drink Problem: Its Rise and Decline through the Ages," *British Journal of Addiction* 55 (July, 1958): 51–67.

Godfrey, Richard, ed., *James Gillray: The Art of Caricature* (London, 2001).

Gourvish, Terry R. and Richard G. Wilson, *The British Brewing Industry, 1830–1980* (Cambridge, 1994).

Graham, Henry Gray, *Scottish Men of Letters in the Eighteenth Century* (London, 1908).

Gray, W. Forbes, *Some Old Scots Judges* (London, 1914).

Gunn, J. A. W., *Beyond Liberty and Property: The Process of Self-Recognition in Eighteenth-Century Political Thought* (Kingston, 1983).

——, "Public Opinion", in Terence Ball, James Farr and Russell L. Hanson, eds., *Political Innovation and Conceptual Change* (Cambridge, 1989), 247–265.

Hancock, David, "Commerce and Conversation in the Eighteenth-Century Atlantic: The Invention of Madeira Wine," *Journal of Interdisciplinary History* 24 (1998): 198–219.

Handover, P. M, *A History of the London Gazette, 1665–1965* (London, 1965).

Harkness, Douglas, A. E., "The Opposition to the 8th and 9th Articles of the Commercial Treaty of Utrecht," *Scottish Historical Review* 21 (1924): 219–226.

Harris, Tim, *London Crowds in the Reign of Charles II: Propaganda and Politics from the Restoration until the Exclusion Crisis* (Cambridge, 1987).

——, *Politics under the Later Stuarts: Party Conflict in a Divided Society, 1660–1715* (London, 1993).

——, *Revolution: The Great Crisis of the British Monarchy, 1685–1720* (London, 2006).

Harrison, Brian, *Drink and the Victorians: The Temperance Question in England, 1815–1872* (Keele, 1994, revised edition).

Hart, Katherine and Laura Hacker, *James Gillray: Prints by the Eighteenth-Century Master of Caricature* (Hanover, NH, 1994).

Harvey, Karen, "The History of Masculinity, circa 1650–1800", *Journal of British Studies*, 44 (April 2005): 296–311.

Hastings, Adrian, *The Construction of Nationhood: Ethnicity, Religion and Nationalism* (Cambridge, 1997).

Hay, Douglas and Nicholas Rogers, *Eighteenth Century English Society* (Cambridge, 1997).

Hayes, John, *Rowlandson, Watercolours and Drawings* (London, 1972).

——, *The Art of Thomas Rowlandson* (Alexandria, VA, 1990).

Heath, Dwight B., "Anthropological and Sociocultural Perspectives on Alcohol as a Reinforcer," in W. Miles Cox, ed., *Why People Drink: Parameters of Alcohol as a Reinforcer* (New York, 1990), 263–290.

——, *Drinking Occasions: Comparative Perspectives on Alcohol and Culture* (Ann Arbor, 2000).

Hendrickson, Robert, ed., *Encyclopedia of Word and Phrase Origins* (New York, 1997).

Hibbert, Christopher, *George IV, Regent and King, 1811–1830* (London, 1973).

——, *Charles I: A Life of Religion, War and Treason* (Basingstoke, 2007).

Hill, Christopher, *The English Revolution of 1640* (London, 1940).

——, *The Century of Revolution, 1603–1714* (London, 1961).

Hitchcock, Tim and Michèle Cohen, eds., *English Masculinities, 1660–1800* (London, 1999).

Hobsbawm, Eric, *Industry and Empire: From 1750 to the Present Day* (Harmondsworth, 1969).

——, *The Age of Capital, 1848–1975* (London, 1975).

Holmes, Geoffrey, *Augustan England: Professions, State and Society, 1680–1730* (London, 1982).

——, *British Politics in the Age of Anne* (London, 1987).

Holmes, Geoffrey and Clyve Jones, "Trade, the Scots and the Parliamentary Crisis of 1713," *Parliamentary History*, 1 (1982), 47–77.

Holmes, Geoffrey and Willian Arthur Speck, eds., *The Divided Society: Parties and Politics in England, 1694–1716* (London, 1967).

Holohan, Renagh and Jeremy Williams, *The Irish Chateaux: In Search of Descendants of the Wild Geese* (Dublin, 1999).

Hont, Istvan, "Free Trade and the Economic Limits to National Politics: Neo-Machiavellian Political Economy Reconsidered," in John Dunn, ed., *The Economic Limits to Modern Politics* (Cambridge, 1990), 41–120.

Hoppit, Julian, *A Land of Liberty? England 1689–1727* (Oxford, 2000).

Hori, Motoko, "The Price and Quality of Wine and Conspicuous Consumption in England, 1649–1759," *English Historical Review*, cxxiii, 505 (December 2008): 1457–1469.

Huetz de Lemps, Christian, "Le Commerce Maritime des Vins d'Aquitaine de 1698 à 1716," *Revue Historique de Bordeaux* (1965): 25–43.

——, "L'Entrée de Latour dans le Grand Commerce," in Charles Higounet, ed., *La Seigneurie et le Vignoble de Château Latour* (1974), 199–207.

——, *Géographie du Commerce de Bordeaux à la fin du règne de Louis XIV* (Mouton, 1975).

Hunt, Margaret, *The Middling Sort: Commerce, Gender and the Family in England, 1550–1800* (Berkeley, 1996).

Hunneyball, Paul M., "Cromwellian Style: The Architectural Trappings of the Protectorate Regime," in Patrick Little, ed., *The Cromwellian Protectorate* (Woodbridge, 2007), 53–81.

Jellinek, Elvin M., "The Symbolism of Drinking: A Culture-Historical Approach," *Journal of Studies on Alcohol*, 38 (1977): 852–866.

Jenkins, Susan, *Portrait of a Patron: The Patronage and Collecting of James Brydges, 1st Duke of Chandos, 1644–1744* (Aldershot, 2007).

Johnson, Hugh, *Vintage: The Story of Wine* (New York, 1989).

Johnstone, G. N., "The Growth of the Sugar Trade and Refining Industry," in Derek Oddy and Derek Miller eds., *The Making of the Modern British Diet* (London, 1976), 58–64.

Jones, Clyve, ed., *Britain in the First Age of Party, 1680–1750: Essays Presented to Geoffrey Holmes* (London, 1987).

Jones, James R., *The First Whigs: The Politics of the Exclusion Crisis, 1678–1683* (Oxford, 1961).

Jones, Robert W., *Gender and the Formation of Taste in Eighteenth-Century Britain* (Cambridge, 1998).

Kay, Billy and Cailean Maclean, *Knee Deep in Claret: A Celebration of Wine and Scotland* (Edinburgh, 1983).

Kennedy, Catriona, "John Bull into Battle: Military Masculinity and the British Army, 1793–1815," in Karen, Hagemann, Gisela, Mettele and Jane, Rendall, eds, *Gender, War and Politics: The Wars of Revolution and Liberation–Transatlantic Comparison, 1775–1820* (Basingstoke, 2009), 127–146.

Kenyon, John P., *Revolution Principles: The Politics of Party 1689–1720* (Cambridge, 1977).

Kidd, Alan and David Nicholls, eds., *Gender, Civic Culture and Consumerism: Middle Class Identity in Britain, 1800–1940* (Manchester, 1990).

——, eds., *The Making of the British Middle Class? Studies of Regional and Cultural Diversity since the Eighteenth Century* (London, 1998).

Kidd, Colin, *Subverting Scotland's Past: Scottish Whig Historians and the Creation of an Anglo-British identity, 1993, c. 1689–1830* (Cambridge, 1993).

——, *British Identities Before Nationalism: Ethnicity and Nationhood in the Atlantic World, 1600–1800* (Cambridge, 1999).

——, "North Britishness and the Nature of Eighteenth-Century British Patriotisms," *The Historical Journal*, 39:2 (1996), 361–382.

King, Frank Alfred, *Beer Has a History* (London, 1947).

Kishlansky, Mark, "Charles I: A Case of Mistaken Identity," *Past and Present*, 189:1 (2005), 41–80.

Klein, Lawrence, "Liberty, Manners, and Politeness in Early-Eighteenth-Century England," *Historical Journal* 32 (1989): 583–605.

——, "Courtly *Politesse* and Civic Politeness in France and England," *Halcyon* 14 (1992): 171–181.

——, "Shaftesbury, Politeness and the Politics of Religion," in Nicholas Phillipson and Quentin Skinner, eds., *Political Discourse in Early Modern Britain* (Cambridge, 1993), 283–301.

——, "The Political Significance of 'Politeness' in Early-Eighteenth-Century Britain," in Gordon Schochet, ed., *Politics, Politeness and Patriotism* (Washington, DC, 1993), 73–108.

——, *Shaftesbury and the Culture of Politeness: Moral Discourse and Cultural Politics in Early-Eighteenth-Century England* (Cambridge, 1994).

——, "Politeness for Plebes: Consumption and Social Identity in Early Eighteenth-Century England," in Anne Bermingham and John Brewer, eds., *The Consumption of Culture: Image, Object, Text: 1600–1800* (London, 1995), 362–382.

——, "Politeness and the Interpretation of the British Eighteenth Century", *The Historical Journal*, 45 (2002): 869–898.

Korsmeyer, Carolyn, *Making Sense of Taste: Food and Philosophy* (Ithaca, 1999).

Kuchta, David, *The Three-Piece Suit and Modern Masculinity: England, 1550–1850* (Berkeley, 2002), 91–132.

——, "The Making of the Self-Made Man: Class, Clothing, and English Masculinity, 1688–1832," in Victoria De Grazia and Ellen Furlough, eds., *The Sex of Things: Gender and Consumption in Comparative Perspective* (Berkeley, 1996), 54–77.

Lachiver, Marcel, *Vins, Vignes et Vignerons: Histoire du Vignoble Français* (Paris, 1988).

Langford, Paul, *The Excise Crisis* (Oxford, 1975).

——, *A Polite and Commercial People: England, 1727–1783* (Oxford, 1989).

——, *Public Life and the Propertied Englishman, 1689–1798* (Oxford, 1991).

——, "Politics and Manners from Sir Robert Walpole to Sir Robert Peel," *Proceedings of the British Academy* 94 (1996): 103–125.

——, *Englishness Identified: Manners and Character, 1650–1850* (Oxford, 2000).

Lenman, Bruce, *An Economic History of Modern Scotland, 1660–1976* (London, 1977).

——, *The Jacobite Risings in Britain, 1689–1746* (London, 1980).

Lemire, Beverly, *The Business of Everyday Life* (Manchester, 2005).

Libson, Lowell, ed., *Beauty and the Beast: A Loan Exhibition of Rowlandson's Works from British Private Collections* (London, 2007).

London County Council, *The Conversation Piece in Georgian England* (London, 1965).

Longmate, Norman, *The Waterdrinkers: A History of Temperance* (London, 1968).

Lubbock, Jules, *The Tyranny of Taste: The Politics of Architecture and Design in Britain, 1550–1960* (New Haven, 1995).

Ludington, Charles C. "'Be Sometimes to Your Country True': The Politics of Wine in England, 1660–1714", in Adam Smyth, ed., *A Pleasing Sinne: Drink and Conviviality in 17th-Century England* (Woodbridge, 2004), 89–106.

——, "'To the King o'er the Water': Scotland and Claret, c. 1660–1763," in Mack Holt, ed., *Alcohol: A Social and Cultural History* (Oxford, 2006), 163–184.

——, "Drinking for Approval: Wine and the British Court from George III to Victoria and Albert," in Daniëlle de Vooght, ed., *Royal Taste: Food, Power and Status at the European Courts after 1789* (Farnham, 2011), 57–86.

Lythe, Edgar, S. G. and John Butt, *An Economic History of Scotland, 1100–1939* (Glasgow, 1975).

Macaulay, Rose, *They Went to Portugal* (London, 1946).

Mayson, Richard, *Port and the Douro* (London, 1999).

McLeod, William Reynolds and V. B. McLeod, *Anglo-Scottish Tracts, 1701–1714* (Lawrence, KS, 1979).

McNeill, F. Marian, *The Scots Cellar* (Moffat, 1992).

McCormack, Matthew, *The Independent Man: Citizenship and Gender Politics in Georgian England* (Manchester, 2005).

——, "The New Militia: War, Politics and Gender in 1750s Britain," *Gender and History*, 19:3 (2007): 483–500.

Madden, John, Spencer, "Samuel Johnson's Alcohol Problem," *Medical History* 11 (1967): 141–149.

Malvezin, Théophile, *Histoire du Commerce de Bordeaux depuis les Origines jusqu'à nos jours*, 3 vols. (Bordeaux, 1892).

Mandler, Peter, "The Problem with Cultural History," *Cultural and Social History*, 1 (2004), 94–117.

Marshall, Rosalind K., *The Days of Duchess Anne: Life in the Household of the Duchess of Hamilton, 1656–1716* (London, 1973).

Mathias, Peter and Patrick O'Brian, "Taxation in Britain and France, 1715–1810, *Journal of European Economic History* 5 (1967), 601–640.

McCracken, Grant, *Culture and Consumption: New Approaches to the Symbolic Character of Consumer Goods and Activities* (Bloomington, 1988).

McKendrick, Neil, John Brewer and John Harold Plumb, *The Birth of a Consumer Society: The Commercialization of Eighteenth-Century England* (London, 1982).

McShane, Angela, "The Politicisation of Drink and Drunkenness in Political Broadside Ballads from 1640–1689," in Adam Smyth, ed., *A Pleasing Sinne: Drink and Conviviality in 17th-Century England* (Woodbridge, Suffolk: Boydell and Brewer, 2004), 69–87.

Mendelsohn, Oscar, *Drinking with Pepys* (London, 1963).

Miner, Earl, *The Cavalier Mode from Jonson to Cotton* (Princeton, 1971).

Mintz, Sidney, *Sweetness and Power: The Place of Sugar in Modern History* (New York, 1985).

——, "The Changing Roles of Food in the Study of Consumption," in John Brewer and Roy Porter, eds., *Consumption and the World of Goods* (London, 1993), 261–273.

Mitchell, Brian R. and Phyllis Deane, *Abstract of British Historical Statistics* (Cambridge, 1962).

Mitchell, Leslie, George, *Charles James Fox* (Oxford, 1992).

Mitchison, Rosalind, *A History of Scotland* (London, 2003, Third edition).

Monod, Paul, "Dangerous Merchandise: Smuggling, Jacobitism, and Commercial Culture in Southeast England, 1690–1760," *Journal of British Studies* 30 (April 1991): 150–182.

Morgan, Kenneth, "Mercantilism and the British Empire," in Donald Winch and Patrick K. O'Brien, eds., *The Political Economy of British Historical Experience, 1688–1914* (Oxford, 2002), 165–168.

Multamäki, Kustaa, *Towards Great Britain: Commerce and Conquest in the thought of Algernon Sidney and Charles Davenant* (Helsinki, 1999).

Murdoch, Alexander, "Scotland and the Idea of Britain in the Eighteenth Century," in Thomas M. Devine and John R. Young, eds., *Eighteenth Century Scotland: New Perspectives* (East Linton, 1999), 106–120.

Murphy, Antoine E., *Richard Cantillon: Entrepreneur and Economist* (Oxford, 1986).

Newman, Gerald, *The Rise of English Nationalism* (New York, 1987).

Nokes, David, *John Gay: A Profession of Friendship* (Oxford, 1995).

Nye, John, *War, Wine and Taxes: The Political Economy of Anglo-French Trade, 1689–1900* (Princeton, 2007).

Nye, John, and Pierre-Emmanuel, Dauzat, "Guerre, Commerce, Guerre Commerciale: L'Economie politique des échanges Franco-Anglais reéxminée," *Annales: Economies, Sociétés, Civilisations*, 47 (1992): 613–631.

O'Brien, Patrick K., "The Political Economy of British Taxation, 1660–1815," *Economic History Review*, 2d ser., 41:1 (1988): 1–32.

Orr, Clarissa Campbell, "The Feminization of the Monarchy 1780–1910: Royal Masculinity and Female Empowerment," in Andrzej Olechnowicz, ed., *The Monarchy and the British Nation, 1780 to the Present* (Cambridge, 2007), 76–107.

O'Toole, Fintan, *A Traitor's Kiss: The Life of Richard Brinsley Sheridan* (London, 1997).

Paulson, Ronald, *Hogarth: His Life, Times and Art*, 2 vols. (New Haven, 1971).

Peck, Linda Levy, *Consuming Splendor: Society and Culture in Seventeenth-Century England* (Cambridge, 2005).

Pellicer, Juan Christian, "*Wine* (1708) and the Whigs", *British Journal for Eighteenth-Century Studies*, 27 (2004): 245–255.

Perkin, Harold, *The Origins of Modern English Society, 1780–1880* (London, 1969).

Petrie, Charles, "Politics and Wine," *Quarterly Review*, 93 (1953), 445–456.

Phillips, Rod, "Wine and Adulteration," *History Today* (July 2000): 31–37.

——, *A Short History of Wine* (London, 2000).

Phillipson, Nicholas, "Culture and Society in the Eighteenth-Century Province: The Case of Edinburgh in the Scottish Enlightenment," in Lawrence Stone, ed., *The University in Society*, 2 vols. (Princeton, 1974), II, 407–448.

——, *Hume* (New York, 1989).

——, "Politics and Politeness in the Reigns of Anne and the Early Hanoverians", in John Greville Agard Pocock, ed., *The Varieties of British Political Thought, 1500–1800* (Cambridge, 1993), 211–245.

Pijassou, René, "Le Vignoble Bordelais. La Naissance des Grands Crus," in ed. F-G. Pariset, *Bordeaux au XVIIIe Siècle* (1968), 155–190.

——, "Le Marché de Londres et la Naissance des Grands Crus Médocains (fin 17ème Siècle--debut 18ème Siècle)," *Revue Historique de Bordeaux*, 23 (1974): 139–150.

——, *Un Grand Vignoble de Qualité: Le Médoc*, 2 vols. (Paris, 1980).

Pincus, Steven C. A., "From Butterboxes to Wooden Shoes: The Shift in English Popular Sentiment from Anti-Dutch to Anti-French in the 1670s", *The Historical Journal* 38:2 (June 1995), 333–361.

——, "Nationalism, Universal Monarchy, and the Glorious Revolution," in George Steinmetz, ed., *State/Culture: State Formation after the Cultural Turn* (Ithaca, 1999), 182–210.

——, *1688: The First Modern Revolution* (New Haven, 2009).

Pittock, Murray, *Inventing and Resisting Britain: Cultural Identities in Britain and Ireland, 1685–1789* (New York, 1997).

——, *Jacobitism* (New York, 1998).

——, *Scottish Nationality* (Basingstoke, 2001).

Plumb, John Harold, *England in the Eighteenth Century* (Baltimore, 1950).

——, *Men and Places* (London, 1953).

——, *Sir Robert Walpole*, 2 vols. (London, 1956–1960).

——, *Men and Centuries* (Boston, 1963).

——, *The Growth of Political Stability in England, 1675–1725* (London, 1967).

Pocock, John Greville Agard, *The Machiavellian Moment: Florentine Political Thought and the Atlantic Republican Tradition* (Princeton, 1975).

——, *Virtue, Commerce and History: Essays on Political Thought and History, Chiefly in the Eighteenth Century* (Cambridge, 1985).

——, *The Varieties of British Political Thought, 1500–1800* (Cambridge, 1993).

Poovey, Mary, *Making a Social Body: British Cultural Formation, 1830–1864* (Chicago, 1995).

Porter, Roy, *English Society in the Eighteenth Century* (Harmondsworth, 1982).

——, "The Drinking Man's Disease: The "Pre-History of Alcoholism in Georgian Britain," *British Journal of Addiction* 80 (1985), 385–396.

——, "Georgian Britain: An Ancien Régime?" *British Journal for Eighteenth-Century Studies*, XV:2 (1992), 141–144.

Potter, Lois, *Secret Rites and Secret Writing, Royalist Literature, 1641–1660* (Cambridge, 1989).

Praz, Mario, *Conversation Pieces: A Survey of the Informal Group Portrait in Europe and America* (University Park, PA, 1971).

Prebble, John, *The King's Jaunt: George IV in Scotland, August 1822, "One and Twenty Daft Days"* (London, 1988).

Ribeiro, Aileen, *Fashion and Fiction: Dress in Art and Literature in Stuart England* (New Haven, 2005).

Richardson, Joanna, *Victoria and Albert: A Study of a Marriage* (London, 1977).

Robinson, Jancis, ed., *The Oxford Companion to Wine* (Oxford, 1994).

Rogers, Nicholas, "The Middling Sort in Eighteenth-Century Politics," in Jonathan Barry and Christopher Brooks, eds, *The Middling Sort of People: Culture, Society and Politics in England, 1550–1800* (New York, 1994), pp. 159–180.

Rose, J. Holland, "The Franco-British Commercial Treaty of 1786," *English Historical Review* 23 (October 1908): 709–724.

Saintsbury, George, *Notes on a Cellar-Book* (London, 1920).

Schnakenbourg, Eric, "Les Interactions entre Commerce et Diplomatie au début du XVIIIe siècle: L'Example du Traité de Commerce Franco-Anglais de 1713," *Histoire, Economie et Société*, 23:3 (2004), 349–365.

Schumpeter, Elizabeth Boody, *English Overseas Trade Statistics, 1697–1807* (Oxford, 1960).

Scott, Jonathan, *Algernon Sydney and the Restoration Crisis, 1679–1683* (Cambridge, 1991).

Sekora, John, *Luxury: The Concept in Western Thought, Eden to Smollett* (Baltimore, 1977).

Sellars, Jane, "Frith's Women: William Powell Frith and the Female Model" in Mark Bills and Vivien Knight, eds., *William Powell Frith: Painting the Victorian Age* (New Haven, 2006), pp. 131–144.

Sewell Jr., William H., *Logics of History: Social Theory and Social Transformation* (Chicago, 2005).

Shammas, Carole, *The Pre-industrial Consumer in England and America* (Oxford, 1990).

Shapin, Steven, *A History of Truth: Civility and Science in Seventeenth-Century England* (Chicago, 1994).

Shepard, Alexandra, *Meanings of Manhood in Early Modern England* (Oxford, 2003).

Simon, André L., *History of the Wine Trade in England*, 3 vols. (London, 1906–1909).

———, *Bottlescrew Days: Wine Drinking in England during the Eighteenth Century* (London, 1926).

Sitwell, Sachaverell, *Conversation Pieces: A Survey of English Domestic Portraits and Their Painters* (London, 1936).

Sherwood, Roy, *Oliver Cromwell, King in all but Name* (Stroud, 1997).

Smith, Charles Saumarez, *Eighteenth-Century Decoration: Design and the Domestic Interior in England* (New York, 1993).

Smith, Janet Adam, "Some Eighteenth-Century Ideas of Scotland," in Nicholas Phillipson and Rosalind Mitchison, eds., *Scotland in the Age of Improvement: Essays in Scottish History in the Eighteenth Century* (Edinburgh, 1970), 107–124.

Smith, Woodruff, *Consumption and the Making of Respectability, 1600–1800* (New York, 2002).

Smout, T. Christopher, *Scottish Trade on the Eve of Union, 1660–1707* (Edinburgh, 1963).

Smuts, Malcolm, *Culture and Power in England, 1588–1688* (New York, 1999).

Snodin, Michael, and John Styles, eds., *Design and the Decorative Arts, Britain 1500–1900* (London, 2001).

Stone, Lawrence and Jeanne Fawtier Stone, *An Open Elite? England, 1540–1880* (Oxford, 1984).

Strong, Roy, *The Cult of Elizabeth: Elizabethan Portraiture and Pageantry* (London, 1999).

Stuart, Marie W., *Old Edinburgh Taverns* (London, 1952).

Styles, John, and Amanda Vickery, eds., *Gender Taste and Material Culture in Britain and North America* (New Haven, 2006).

Suny, Ronald Grigor, "Back and Beyond, Reversing the Cultural Turn?" *American Historical Review*, 107:5 (December, 2002), 1476–1499.

Tawney, Richard, Henry, "The Rise of the Gentry, 1558–1640," *Economic History Review*, II (1941), 1–38.

Taylor, Anya, *Bacchus in Romantic England: Writers and Drink, 1780–1830* (London, 1999).

Taylor, Miles, "John Bull and the Iconography of Public Opinion in England, 1712–1929," *Past and Present* 34 (1992): 93–128.

Thomas, Keith, *The Ends of Life: Roads to Fulfilment in Early Modern England* (Oxford, 2009).

Thompson, Edward, Palmer, *The Making of the English Working Class* (Harmondsworth, 1968).

Tosh, John, *A Man's Place: Masculinity and the Middle-Class Home in Victorian England* (New Haven, 1999).

———, *Manliness and Masculinities in Nineteenth-Century Britain: Essays on Gender, Family, and Empire* (Harlow, 2005).

———, "Hegemonic Masculinity and History of Gender," in Stefan Dudink, Karen Hagemann, and John Tosh, eds., *Masculinities in Politics and War: Gendering Modern History* (Manchester, 2004), 41–58.

———, "Gentlemanly Politeness and Manly Simplicity in Victorian England," *Transactions of the Royal Historical Society*, 6th ser., 12 (2002), 455–472.

Trebusek, Marika, "Wine for Comfort: Drinking and the Royalist Exile Experience, 1642–1660," in Adam Smyth, ed., *A Pleasing Sinne: Drink and Conviviality in 17th-Century England* (Woodbridge, Suffolk, 2004), 55–68.

Trevelyan, George MacAulay, *England under Queen Anne*, 3 vols. (London, 1948).

Trevor-Roper, Hugh, "The Invention of Tradition: The Highland Tradition of Scotland," in Eric Hobsbawm and Terence Ranger, *The Invention of Tradition* (Cambridge, 1983).

Trumbach, Randolph, *Sex and the Gender Revolution: Heterosexuality and the Third Gender in Enlightenment London* (Chicago, 1998).

Turner, Jane, ed., *The Dictionary of Art*, 34 vols. (New York, 1996).

Uglow, Jenny, *Hogarth: A Life and a World* (New York, 1997).

——, "Locke's Interest in Wine," *Locke Newsletter* 29 (1998): 119–151.

——, "The Viticultural Geography of France in the Seventeenth Century According to John Locke," *Annales de Géographie*, 614–615 (2000): 395–414.

Veblen, Thorstein, *The Theory of the Leisure Class* (1899; repr. New York, 2001).

Vickery, Amanda, *The Gentleman's Daughter: Women's Lives in Georgian England* (New Haven, 1998).

Wain, John, *Samuel Johnson* (London, 1974).

Wahrman, Dror, *Imagining the Middle Class: the Political Representation of Class in Britain, c. 1780–1840* (Cambridge, 1995).

——, "'Middle Class' Domesticity Goes Public: Gender, Class, and Politics from Queen Caroline to Queen Victoria", *Journal of British Studies*, 32 (October 1993), 396–432.

Warner, Jessica, *Craze: Gin and Debauchery in an Age of Reason* (New York, 2002).

Watney, James, *Mother's Ruin: A History of Gin* (London, 1976).

Weatherill, Lorna, *Consumer Behaviour and Material Culture in Britain, 1660–1760* (London, 2nd ed. 1996).

——, "The meanings of consumer behaviour in late seventeenth- and early eighteenth-century England," in John Brewer and Roy Porter, eds., *Consumption and the World of Goods* (London, 1993), 206–227.

Weinreb, Ben and Christopher Hibbert, eds., *The London Encyclopedia* (London, 1983).

Weintraub, Stanley, *Albert: Uncrowned King* (London, 1997).

Wellington, Donald C., "The Anglo-French Commercial Treaty of 1786," *Journal of European Economic History*, 21:2 (1992): 325–337.

White, Jonathan, "A World of Goods? The 'Consumption Turn' and Eighteenth-Century British History," *Cultural and Social History*, 3 (2006), 93–104.

Williamson, Tom, *Polite Landscapes: Gardens and Society in Eighteenth-Century England* (Stroud, 1995).

Wilson, Ben, *The Making of Victorian Values: Decency and Dissent in Britain, 1789–1837* (New York, 2007).

Wilson, George B., *Alcohol and the Nation* (London, 1940).

Wilson, Kathleen, "Empire of Virtue: The Imperial Project and Hanoverian Culture, c. 1720–1785," in Lawrence Stone, ed., *An Imperial State at War, Britain from 1689 to 1815* (London, 1994), 128–164.

——, "The Good, the Bad, and the Impotent: Imperialism and the Politics of Identity in Georgian England," in Ann Bermingham and John Brewer, eds., *The Consumption of Culture, 1600–1800: Image, Object, Text* (London, 1995), 237–262.

——, *The Sense of the People: Politics, Culture and Imperialism in England, 1715–1785* (Cambridge, 1995).

Winslow, Cal, "Sussex Smugglers," in Douglas Hay, Peter Linebaugh, John G. Rule, E. P. Thompson and Cal Winslow, eds., *Albion's Fatal Tree: Crime and Society in Eighteenth-Century England* (New York, 1975), 119–166.

Wood, Christopher, *William Powell Frith: A Painter and his World* (Stroud, 2006).

Woodforde, James, *The Diary of a Country Parson, 1758–1802*, ed. John Beresford, 5 vols. (Oxford, 1981).

Younger, William, *Gods, Men and Wine* (Cleveland, OH, 1966).

Ziegler, Philip, *King William IV* (London, 1971).

Zook, Melinda, *Radical Whigs and Conspiratorial Politics in Late Stuart England* (University Park, PA, 1999).

Further reading

Cowan, Brian, *The Social Life of Coffee: The Emergence of the British Coffeehouse* (New Haven, 2005).

Hancock, David, *Oceans of Wine: Madeira and the Emergence of American Trade and Taste* (New Haven, 2009).

Mennell, Stephen, *All Manners of Food: Eating and Taste in England and France from the Middle Ages to the Present* (Urbana, 1996).

Unwin, Tim, *Wine and the Vine: An Historical Geography of Viticulture and the Wine Trade* (London, 1991).

Index

Page references in bold refer to illustrations. An individual's position or job is indicated parenthetically where it is necessary for clarity, or to indicate a scholar—but not historical actor—who is cited in the text. Individual wine merchants, whether wholesale or retail, exporters or importers, are listed alphabetically under "vintners" and their primary place of work is given parenthetically.

Oliveira, Benjamin 252
Oporto, Portugal 33–6, 75, 123–4, 130–1,
    133, 136–8, 147–8, 150–1, 175–6,
    179, 241, 243–4
  see also vintners (Oporto)
Osborn, Sarah Byng 124
Oxford 33, 122, 144, 158, 202, 211
Oxford and Mortimer, 1st Earl of,
  see Harley, Robert

Palmerston, Henry John Temple,
    3rd Viscount 252, 255
Panmure, William Ramsay, 1st Baron 202
Parliament 2, 21, 25–7, 29, 33–5, 46,
    50–2, 54, 56, 62–3, 110, 126, 133,
    170, 176, 195, 211
  debates regarding wine 24, 26, 33, 54–5,
      66–7, 70, 73, 80, 146, 167, 230, 240,
      252
  legislation regarding wine 4, 19, 24–5,
      27, 31, 40, 44, 55, 64, 86, 113, 164,
      166, 240, 253
  Scottish (prior to the Union) 2, 46, 49,
      50–2
  see also Wine Act of 1703
Parliamentarians (in mid-seventeenth
    century) 11, 16–22, 27, 44, 47, 76,
    78, 187, 269 fn 9
patriarchy 9
Pedro II, King of Portugal 63
Pepys, Samuel 22, 83–4, 101
Perceval, Spencer 158
Philippe, Duke of Anjou 62, 66
Pitt, William (the Elder) 151
Pitt, William (the Younger), 129, 151, 158,
    165–7, 172–**74**, 226, 247, 251, 259
    graph A.4
  heavy drinking 158, 191, 194, **195**, 196,
      197, 207, 219, 224, 306 fn 42
Place, Francis 188, 221, 224
Plague 25
Plumb, J. H. (historian) 92, 110, 126
politeness 82–103, 139–40, 143, 145, 179,
    184–5, 214, 222, 234
  breakdown of 184–6, 190–1, 214
  of luxury claret 94–103
  middle-ranking critique of 154–55
  in Scotland 114–5
  see also chivalry; masculinity; sensibility
political legitimacy 1, 4, 18, 23, 26, 103,
    184, 186, 219, 224, 229, 253
poll tax (of 1678) 26
Pombal, Sebastião José de Carvalho e Melo,
    1st Marquês de 147, 150–51, **152**

Pontac, Arnaud de 83–6, 89–91, 101
Pontac, Francois-Auguste 84, 284 fn 23
Pontack's Head, Abchurch Lane (tavern in
    London) 84, 86–7
Pope, Alexander 124–5
  The Dunciad 124
Popish Plot 27–8
port (wine) *passim*
  brokers 33, 137–9, 145, 147–9
  complement to sherry 233–7
  crisis (of 1750s) 145–51
  crisis (of 1840s) 246, 314 fn 34
  descriptions of 88, 137–9, 148, 241
  elite taste for 125–6, 153–9
  "Englishman's wine" 145, 153, 162
  growers 147–50
  luxury 161
  merchants *see* vintners (Oporto)
  popularity among middle ranking
      men 68, 121–5
  production 134–7, 148–50
  Scottish taste for 68–71
  strength of 131–4
  symbol of British identity 172–5
  symbol of Whigs/commercial interest/
      middle-ranking men 76–81, 139–43
  vintage 3, 137–9, 149, 159, 161, 173,
      179, 244
  white 90–1, 121–2, 125–6, 129, 136
  see also Douro Company; Pombal, 1st
      Marquês of; vintners (Oporto)
Porter, George Richardson
  Progress of the Nation 248
Porto Bello, Battle of 154
Portugal/Portuguese *passim*
  see also Methuen Treaty; port; wines,
      Portuguese
Presbyterians 27, 104, 117, 176, 204, 226
Preston, Miss 198
Prince of Wales *see* George IV
Prince Regent *see* George IV
Prior, Matthew 125–6
Protestants 19–20, 27, 62, 76
  see also Church of England; Dissenters/
      Non-Conformists; Baptists;
      Methodists; Presbyterians
public houses 105
  see also alehouses; taverns
public opinion 4, 25, 74, 190
Pückler-Muskau, Prince Herman von 209
punch 93, 132, 134, 168, 183, 198–9,
    205–6, 211
  see also spirits/spirituous liquors
Puritans 19–20, 28